ADVANCE PRAISE FOR *SOULS OF MY SISTERS*

"An empowering book with amazing insight . . . A blessing earned from each experience."
—Ilyasah Shabazz

"This book will give black women strength for years to come, but it also is a book for all women. When women talk to women good things happen. This book will teach black women how to survive throughout the ages."
—Congresswoman Sheila Jackson Lee,
U.S. House of Representatives,
18th Congressional District, Texas

"Souls of My Sisters provides an opportunity for us to stop apologizing for what we have no control over and take control of what we can. The Sister Feel Good Section uncovers public health information including a mother living with AIDS. Let's spread accurate knowledge to one another as if our very lives depended on it because, my sisters, it does."
—Debra Fraser-Howze, President/CEO of the
National Black Leadership Commission on AIDS

(continued . . .)

"Souls of My Sisters *acts as a reminder that in life sometimes the joy of our friendships with one another may fade, but the passion for kinship will always continue to burn.*"
—Sheila Foster, Founder of Black Books Galore and President of Kidz First, Inc.

"Souls of My Sisters *provides an honest portrayal of real women telling their stories. The common experience becomes a source of power, which will eventually develop into advocacy for all women of color.*"
—Donna Frisby-Greenwood
Executive Director, Inner-City Games
and Co-Chair, The Black Youth Vote Coalition

"*It is a fact that we will all face many obstacles and challenges in a lifetime. When I put my faith in God, I learned that my barriers become roads to travel and that there is nothing that cannot be faced.* Souls of My Sisters *provides an opportunity for women to face their fears and realize they can triumph against any odds.*"
—Roshumba Williams, Model

"*Like flavorful dishes and spicy stories shared around the dinner table,* Souls of My Sisters *simmers up enlightening experiences which are a tasteful medley that provides nourishment for our souls. . . . Now that's Soulfood!*"
—Tren'ness Woods
Vice President of Communications, Webbe
Granddaughter of Slyvia Woods
(owner of Slyvia's Soul Food Restaurants)

Souls Of My Sisters

Black Women Break Their
Silence, Tell Their Stories,
and Heal Their Spirits

by
Dawn Marie Daniels
and Candace Sandy

Kensington Publishing Corp.
http://www.kensingtonbooks.com

KENSINGTON BOOKS are published by

Kensington Publishing Corp.
850 Third Avenue
New York, NY 10022

Kensington and the K logo Reg. U.S. Pat. & TM Off.
Dafina is a trademark of Kensington Publishing Corp.

ISBN 1-57566-653-7

First Kensington Trade Printing: October, 2000
10 9 8

Printed in the United States of America

VII. Some Good Ol' Fashioned Soul Food   175

VIII. Express Yourself   193

IX. Brothers, Husbands, Fathers, and Sons   211

X. Sister Feel Good   249

XI. "Isms"   271

We dedicate this book to God because through Him <u>all</u> things are possible

In Memory of

Cecelia Hamlet
Kealon Hamlet-Forde
Sandi Hutchins
Yvonne Hutchins
George Jackson
Minnie Judkins
Hon. Mary Johnson Lowe
Emily McClain
Steadlin McLean
Mary McNeil Meeks
Daphne Phillips Bell
Leslie Pitts
Angus Ricketts
Esther Rolle
Dr. Betty Shabazz

Contents

Contents

Foreword
A Word to My Sisters

Ilyasah Shabazz

There is an unbelievable power that emanates from our faith and our love for self. We have insurmountable strength, courage, and depth that are often deeply tucked away until a crisis arises and that challenge needs to be met.

Historically, we have experienced the nobility of educated societies where our forefathers and our foremothers have been the architects of great pyramids, creators of arithmetic, health remedies, perfumes and delicacies, advocaters of religion, rulers of thriving civilizations, giving rise to the world as we know it today. As women, we have experienced the shiver in our spine as we were forced upon a massive slave ship and made to lay in the ship's bow—head to toe with countless other human beings, leaving loved ones behind.

I cannot imagine giving birth to a beautiful child only to wonder when my baby would be torn from my arms and sold off to another plantation. I cannot imagine the heartache and bitterness caused by a slave master who just decides to sell my husband off to the highest bidder. I cannot bear the thought of any child having to lay against his/her will. I cannot bear the feeling of despair when I decide to stand up for my rights and participate in a peaceful demonstration only to be hosed down, to be called "nigger," to be kicked, beaten or lynched by hecklers, bystanders, police officers—simply because I am a human being standing up for my rights and my humanity. Because we have decided to liberate ourselves.

We have witnessed and experienced many atrocities; yet, we have always managed to make a way when life itself seemed hopeless. We have always managed to wear a smile in the face of adversity. What has been our secret? The magic of our faith and our love.

I am a witness to that magic through the tenacity of my father, El Hajj Malik Shabazz, better known as Malcolm X, and my mother, Dr. Betty Shabazz. Mommie was dedicated to her beliefs and was charmed by a charismatic man who had a vision to change the way people of African descent viewed themselves. He was committed to human truth through social advocacy for the benefit of the international community—to remove the psychological scars and racial barriers that inhibited a nation from reaching her full potential. My mother supported her husband's crusade for freedom because his mission was for all oppressed people throughout the world. Through triumphs and tragedies, my mother stood by his side even on that fatal day when he was assassinated in front of her and my sisters.

The love my father had for my mother was unshakable; it gave her the strength to continue his mission while raising my five sisters and me. My mother, who had always lent herself to a progressive cause, participated in The Women's International Conference in Beijing, China, for women's rights.

Despite the many obstacles in her life, she always boasted of the good and praised it. Hers was a life full of faith, perseverance, and triumph. She was determined to create a positive surrounding in which her daughters could be properly nourished with a sense of dignity and pride—to become self-reliant young ladies. We studied African history, French, Arabic, piano and ballet. We traveled to many places and visited many cultures. It was important to both my mother and father that we not limit ourselves to our backyard but that we understand the world at large.

My mother shared a special bond with each of her daughters like none other. She gave flight to our dreams and passed on her lessons in life. Her most important lesson was of loving self. It was respecting self. How can you love anyone else if you do not first love yourself? It was faith, believing in self, and believing in women, our sisters, and the world beyond. It was important to my mother that we loved, supported, and respected one another. Mommie's openness gave us an opportunity to learn from her. Her sister friends would also provide us with numerous stories, some of them quite funny. As my sisters and I grew older, we would share our own stories with one another. This support gave all of us the opportunity to live through our own triumphs and tragedies.

The example my parents set, not only in our household but by the way both Malcolm X and Dr. Betty Shabazz lived their lives, helped me understand that we all have a specific purpose in life—to give back something to others.

I am an educator and a student, dedicated to teaching and learning, and I will strive for improvement in all that I do. I will absorb my surroundings and not become a victim of circumstance. My contribution to humanity is for justice, equality, and self-empowerment. My biggest commitment is to help ensure that children are provided with a sense of self-respect and accomplishment, and are given an opportunity to feel good about themselves.

There is a need to stimulate the learning environment and better equip children to participate in mainstream America as international leaders.

Souls of My Sisters provides an opportunity for black women to claim a collective healing process. This is an opportunity to resume an integral part of our culture—passing on our stories. In these pages, you will find women from all walks of life who will share with you their stories in hopes that they will aid you in the challenges that you face. It is our duty, as women of the twenty-first century, to continue the legacy of the women who have labored, sacrificed, loved, and passed on for us: from the great queens of Africa, to the heroines of the civil rights movements, to the activists, educators, and innovators of the twenty-first century. Let's continue the vision and love one another as sisters.

ILYASAH SHABAZZ has a life dedicated to four passions: 1) the continued growth and understanding of her family legacy; 2) education; 3) government; and, 4) the enrichment and balance that entertainment provides for a full life.

She was the assistant coordinator for the Office of Academic Affairs, City University of New York. She also served as an official member of the United States Delegation, where she accompanied President William Jefferson Clinton on the historic tour of South Africa. In the entertainment field, she has served as vice president for SME Entertainment, as director of operations for KEDAR Entertainment, as coordinator of promotions and marketing for Pendulum Records (a TimeWarner Division), as assistant music agent for William Morris Agency, and as production assistant for 40 acres + a Mule Film Works (a Spike Lee Production).

Currently, she leads a team of individuals to resurrect the Malcolm X & Dr. Betty Shabazz Educational and Cultural Center at The Audubon, New York. She also serves on the Executive Youth Board for The City of Mount Vernon, and is Director of Public Affairs & Special Events for the Honorable Mayor Ernest Davis in the City of Mount Vernon, State of New York. In addition, she is writing a memoir about her life as a daughter of Malcolm X and Dr. Betty Shabazz.

Ms. Shabazz earned a masters of science degree in Education & Human Resource Development; a bachelors of science degree in Biology; and, has graduated from the Hackley Preparatory School in Tarrytown, New York.

Acknowledgments

This work came out of the need for us to fill a void in our own lives that included the need for information, life lessons, and healing. We are inspired by and grateful to the women who believed in us and willingly gave what was most precious to them—their time, energy, life experiences, anguish, hurt, reflections, memories, love, and spiritual journeys that grace the pages of *Souls of My Sisters*.

Firstly, we would like to recognize all women of color who are on their journey to healing and let each one know you are not alone because we are right here with you.

Special thanks to Imar Hutchins for your patience and guidance. Your assistance with the editing of the text and your vision for our Web site are truly appreciated. Melody Guy, thank you for assistance in the editing process and for being the wonderful friend you are.

Special thanks to the Kensington family. Thank you Karen for your undying support and love. Jessica, thank you for keeping us motivated and well fed! Stuart for your true friendship. Thank you Laurie, for seizing the moment and believing in a dream. Special thanks to Janice, Paul, Doug, Gina, Laura, Joan Matthews, and Corinda.

Thanks also to Charlie Stettler, Lynda West, Julia Cabrera and Jennifer Joseph for their endless support. George Jackson, for believing in our vision—may you be dancing with angels.

To the United Negro College Fund for supplying a cause we believe in and truly support.

To Dr. Maya Angelou for her continuous inspiration.

To Ilyasah Shabazz for her unyielding support and love.

To the women who believed in the book from the very beginning and provided the necessary support to make it happen: Allison Moore, Suzanne Cook, Chrisena Coleman, Selena Johnson, Vera Gaskin, Faith Blackburne,

Ursula Miller, Dolly Turner, Maggie Meruczius, and Rhonda Hamilton. Also, Michelle Buckley, Donna Frisby, Lynn Jeter, Victoria Clark, Cheryl Gentry, Barbara Hamilton, Lonai Mosley, and Karyn Swoops for having given wings to this project. Thanks to Deborah Williams, Ph.D. for her great advice and support from her company HERGAME2. To Patti Webster who provided biblical anecdotes and suggested women for the text. To Sheila Foster who provided research for the reading list. To Lorraine Barrett and Angela Foyle for their crunch-time participation. To Micah Morton for her patience, care, and for helping with the women telling their stories. To Gail Parenteau, thank you for your input and support.

Let us not forget the men: Raymond O'Neal, Jr., Glenn Miller, Melvin Taylor, and Marlon Marcelle. Also, Kirk Burroughs who worked very closely with us on compiling interviews. Special thanks to Curtis Taylor, Karu Daniels, and Paul Thomas who were instrumental in landing key essays. To our creative team: Ronnie Wright, photographer extraordinaire, Andrea Fairweather of Fairweather Faces, Inc., and Dana Gibbs, hairstylist. And, Audely Wiggins for his preparation of materials for the contributors.

Many thanks to creative director Janice Rossi Schaus and artist Terrance Cummings for all their work on the lovely cover.

Because of the tremendous undertaking of this text may all of the others who helped to make this book a reality please accept our most humble thanks.

Special thanks from Candace Sandy

To my parents, Patricia and Carlton Samuel, who love with grace and have instilled in me the need to make a difference. To my brother, Sherwin Sandy, his wife, Michelle, and their sons, Marlon and Andre. To my younger brother, Sheldon Samuel, and his daughter, Taylor, who have been a constant source of love. To my aunts for their undying love, belief, guidance, and support. To Aunt Geraldine (Amu), Helen, Jennifer, Henetta, Joanie, Pat, and Joan Braithwaite. To my uncles who are absolutely phenomenal: Uncle Vernell (Vush), Wendell, and Trevor Hamlet. To my cousins, whose love and support sustained me: Jackie, Ann, Paula, Torrie, Jodelle, Donica, Natalie, Kathy, Rori, and Judy. To all of the boys I treasure: Kealon, Terrence, Mark, Trevon, Brent, Roger, Mark, and Martin. To the Fraley family, my Aunt and Uncle Frank, and Lisa Fraley, and to Ollie Gables. To my Godmother Cyrilla LaBorde. To my extended family: Gary and Amy Krakow, Saundra Parks, Yvonne Thomas, and Lorris Sandy.

To Dawn who has provided—for fifteen years—a wealth of lessons learned, hardships fought, visions developed, and shown me what true friendship is all about. With you as a colleague and visionary, the experience of *Souls of My Sisters* has equipped me with an undeniable strength to fulfill my purpose.

To Joseph Fulmore, Jr. who has been my rock.

To Congressman Gregory W. Meeks, his wife, Simone Marie Meeks, the Washington and the New York staffs who have been encouraging and understanding during the development of the book.

To the faculty and staff of New York University and WNYU 89.1 F.M., including Dean Mary Schmidt Campbell, Professor Lynn McVeigh, Barbara Malmet, and Dan Gaydos. To Nadia Suliaman and the Donna Karan family. To the staff of the Brooklyn Children's Museum for their support.

To Al Ragin and Ty Young for your overwhelming thoughts, love, and reality based feedback

To Rachia Hazel and Pa Quita Hazel who provided a view of what tolerance and strength entails. Special thanks to Alithia Alleyne, J.C. Callander, Cristy Colon, Cherise Clarke, Joye Foust, Lisa and George Ghartey, Natasha Gilbert, Jazz Meruczius, Melissa Mann, Andrew Perriott, Kebra Hutton, Noreen Farmer, Marsha and Kasim Steadman-Allah, Michelle Burns, Darren Miller, Desire Ortiz, Gregory C. King, Brenda Bishop, Sheila Thorne, Pierre Orcel (Apple Tours), Carolyn Aikens, Kirk Vanzie, Derrick Johnson, Tanya Holland and family, Tania Tiburcio, Lynn Gonzales, Elizabeth Rodriguez, Steve Grant, Conely Van Reil, Pamala Quinn, Asha Conor, Stacey Cummings, Herb Delancey, Mellicent Dyan, Ruthie Thomas, Patricia Gelman, Elizabeth Jackson, Clifford Lazarre, Chris Latimer, Venus Carroll and Jackie, Michelle, Nick and Patty Williams for lessons learned, barriers crossed, and dreams realized through friendship.

Special thanks from Dawn Marie Daniels

To my very special mirrors, Mark and Martin. You show me my true self everyday. Your love and support, questions and answers, laughter and tears have been the best lessons I have learned in life. You are truly special sons.

Sincere love and undying devotion to my best friend and sister, Candace Sandy. Your unconditional love and support have sustained me for the last fifteen years of my life—you are truly my hero. Your love and compassion inspires me to be the best person I can be everyday.

To my best friend, and partner, Imar Hutchins, you've stood by me and supported my dreams unquestioningly and for that I am truly blessed.

Mom, the love you have shown me and the lessons you have taught me remain with me forever. I love you.

Only a very special dad would drop whatever he was doing on the other side of the country to support his daughter's dream. Daddy, you are that special person and I cannot express in words how much I love you. Thank you.

Grandma, you are truly an angel. You are always there to support anything I do and I am grateful for the love and joy you bring to my life. Alicia and Kim you are always my sweet and quirky inspirations. You give me a fresh breath of air and I couldn't ask for better sisters. Although I don't get to visit with you as often as I like, you are very special to me because you are my brothers: thank you David, Darryl, and Danny for being my brothers.

To Walter and Sharon Hutchins for supporting me and being good friends and great people.

To my special sister friends, Lavonne, Christine, and Melody thanks for the love, patience, and sisterhood. You guys always have my back!

To my publishing mentors, Marilyn Abraham, Sheila Curry, and Becky Cabaza thank you for coming before me and showing me the way.

To my New York University professors, Dr. Harriet Oster, Dr. Sheree Busbee, Dr. Chris Ford, and Dr. Nahama Broner thank you for your many years of philosophical and psychological studies and the ability to pass your vast wisdom on to me.

Lastly, prayers and blessings to my guardian angel, Emily McClain. I know you are in heaven watching over me and have been by my side through everything that I do.

Introduction

Candace and I met in our first year of high school. It felt like we came from different worlds. She lived in Brooklyn, NY and was born and raised in Trinidad, West Indies. I came from Harlem, USA, located in New York City—and I had never even been to Brooklyn although it was right across the bridge. She was very fashionable and I was very conservative. She was a vocal independent thinker. I was quiet and shy and kept my thoughts and feelings tucked away. Even though we had different interests socially, we had an immediate sisterly love for each other. We became fast friends and—even though we seemed to be an odd couple—our relationship was just meant to be.

We've seen a lot and helped each other through some tough times. While we've had each other, we've often wished we had other women to pass their wisdom of experience on to us. A certain brand of wisdom that we weren't lucky enough to get from our mothers or other older women because they didn't have the experience or capacity to help us with our issues. We felt very alone sometimes in our decisions, but we have always been able to go to each other and feel our way through. There has never been a time that I couldn't find Candace by my side to help me cope with life. I have likewise tried to be there for her. It hasn't always been easy, but we've managed. We consider ourselves sisters, soul sisters in fact. In some ways it's a bond more valuable than blood because we were able to *choose* each other as sisters.

Everyone has the possibility for such a relationship given the chance. By being open and accepting, people, especially women, can have meaningful relationships with each other.

To us, black women are like a strong version of a cable television network. The same way cable comes into almost every household broadcasting the same programs for all to see from coast to coast. Black women have many of the same kinds of experiences in their lives no matter who they are. That experience is shared regardless of whether we're rich or poor, from Trinidad or from Kentucky. If we were able to network in some way—spiritually and physically—we would see that we are not very much different from each other. Then we could draw on the shared experience to become stronger.

Knowing other people's stories keeps you from feeling alone. Knowing that we *do* have a shared experience is a source of power. Often we just don't know that the common ground is there. So most of our meetings are left up to chance and fate. With *Souls of My Sisters* we want to even out the odds, so to speak. Our purpose is to give women the opportunity to be able to recognize themselves in other women's stories and gain strength, acceptance, love, and camaraderie through the experience.

We want to be able to share that sense of sisterhood that we cherish so deeply with other women of all ages. We see how lack of communication has torn black women apart. We want to be able to reach out to a network of sisters and bring their souls together in unity. Most of all, we want to make a positive difference in the lives of everyone we meet. At first we thought it to be a naive goal—that was probably inconceivable, but then we listened. We listened to our spirits. We knew that if we were able to give each other so much unconditional love, support, and joy throughout the years, then we would be able to facilitate that energy and help other women come together and do the same.

Success and Opportunity Come out of Chaos

At the time we decided to write this book, we were both on a fast track. Candace had not only begun her own business, but had accepted an opportunity to work with a newly appointed Congressman, Gregory W. Meeks (D-NY), as his press secretary. I, too, had started a new business that was taking off, and I was looking for a new school for my sons. A very hectic time indeed to decide to bring several women together to tell their stories and to promote togetherness among black women. But we were committed. Committed to a mission much greater than ourselves—as we soon found out.

Some women felt our passion and helped out instantly. Others expressed fear. A fear so deep that it left them immobilized. Nonetheless we moved forward. We knew that what we were doing wasn't just about us, but all women. To say that amid all the chaos your issues tend to be brought to the forefront would be an understatement for us. All kinds of issues came up for the both of us. Our greatest fears and our most challenging moments came out of this book. It tore us apart at times and brought us closer as well, and ultimately made us stronger.

The most important thing we learned was, in truth, our blessings are often formed out of our trials and our failures. Sometimes our journeys take different paths, but the evolution of self is what makes our overall mission in life crystal-clear. We learned to recognize that every step we took was a step toward our greater growth together and separately. The writing of this book helped us heal things in ourselves that we didn't realize needed healing. We were numb to a lot of issues in ourselves and our relationship.

Our process helped us to realize that we've suppressed and hidden our pain in order to survive, but now it's time to share and to heal. By collecting and reading other black women's stories, we were able to access communication buried deep within our collective subconscious. We've included these stories in this book to share with you a process you, too, can incorporate in your life. The tools we will provide are simple and will show you new ways to live in the present and change the future without repeating the mistakes of the past.

Souls of My Sisters helped us to put the responsibility for healing in our own hands. Don't get us wrong—psychologists and sociologists have their place, but healing can be even more powerful and effective when it is a communal experience. We want to share with you all that we've learned in the process because we believe, as black women, we are truly the experts of our lives and cultural experience. We must give voice to our own wisdom and tradition.

It is also our responsibility as black women to teach the next generation of women and little girls. They bear the pain of our generations and the scars are evident—teen pregnancy, date rape, and spousal abuse are just a few of the scars which have gotten the attention of the media. But what about wounds that we have internalized? Every time we choose not to face our demons, we hamper not just ourselves, but also those generations to follow.

We must heal ourselves if we want to be of any value to the collective. It's like the flight preparations on an airplane before it takes off. The flight attendant instructs you, in case of an emergency, to get your own oxygen mask on *before* you tend to your children, much less other people. If you're not in a position where you can help yourself, then you're not in a position to take care of anyone else. It's that simple!

How to Use SOULS OF MY SISTERS

Growing up as a young black woman was like the blind leading the blind. We gave each other advice through our teen years about everything from boys to college, but neither of us had the experience or knowledge of many situations. We go into adulthood with the same issues, looking for support from our friends who still have just as much knowledge of what we're going through as we do. There's no handbook to life's little and big problems so we just work it out. Black women are familiar with working it out. When cash is tight, we work it out. When that boyfriend leaves, we work it out. When a family member dies, we know how to step right in and work it out. But sometimes we don't know how to work it out. We do our best, but we still feel insecure or lost when we're in the middle of a crisis. As we've come to find out from our own experiences, crisis waits for no man and especially no black woman. It seems like we're the crisis police. The people in our lives just know we can handle it because we work it out. But do they ever stop to think of the stress and worry we're subject to in our everyday lives?

Souls of My Sisters is a journey to peace and inner harmony through an energy exchange of self-love. We exchange our energy everyday through our thoughts, our words, and our acts. Rarely is the energy we exchange good. In most cases it is contemptuous and hurtful. But that's not the way things are supposed to be. We often project the feelings we have for ourselves onto others, which results in ill feelings and misunderstood messages. We've all witnessed it many times.

You may have been drawn to this book because you are in search of something. You may have recently attained all the things you desired and still feel unfulfilled or unsatisfied. Perhaps you're on the path to attaining your hopes and dreams and need encouragement. Or perhaps you have suffered trauma after trauma and never given yourself time to grieve for the loss of people, possessions, health, jobs, opportunities, or self in your life. The premise behind *Souls of My Sisters* is based on five elements:

- Soul Shock
- The Basic Truth
- Transformation
- Collective Healing
- Celebration

When we speak of *Soul Shock,* we don't mean a physical shock, but an ordeal that is inflicted upon your soul. The shock to the soul is best described as the loss of faith and a total lack of continuity in one's life. A shock to the soul can be so severe that it can cause a complete mental and emotional breakdown of your spirit, often leading to physical discomfort. It's when we lose the sense of having a place to retreat. In some instances alcohol, drugs, shopping, and sex are used to placate the condition, but they never work. Others allow depression to become their best friend, thus inviting suicidal thoughts and a victim mentality to take up residence within their spirits. Often we are left with a skeleton of who we were, which is either damaged or contaminated by the humiliation, pain, and fear that the event has now imposed on our lives. But the soul shock can be a starting point for changing your life.

As women, we are paid in our professional lives to tell, weigh, report, deliver, and enforce the truth. Ironically, we spend most of our personal lives hiding from the *Basic Truth*. The basic truth is that, as black women, we are paralyzed by fear. True fear can be defined as a fear of freedom and being truly responsible for one's destiny. The power we give to our fears robs us from truly being able to fulfill our true mission in life. The lack of truth manifests in every aspect of our lives, but the core being attacked is our souls. We tend to deny ourselves the abundance of love available to us in the universe. We replace it with a self-hatred that is deep rooted in our souls and that tends to make up our identity.

Transformation is the journey in which we as African-American women will have to make to find or create peace in our lives. Transformation is the first step toward healing ourselves. We must change the way we look at ourselves to change the way we are looked at by others.

We sometimes, because of giving so much to others, no longer have anything to sustain ourselves, especially in difficult times. We become weak and sometimes we cling to others, hoping they can give form to our identity.

A *Collective Healing* is what we strive for through the stories in this book. All the women in this book were brave enough to tell their story so they could begin the process of healing and supporting one another. The collective healing will assist us in finding the meaning of life—for ourselves and for those around us.

While some of the stories are heart-wrenching and sad in some cases, they are also a celebration of life. These women are a testimony to the strength and faith that reside in all of us. They have learned or are learning to openly communicate with God and not just reach out to Him in crisis.

Once you have found your healing, it is time for a *Celebration*. We have come together in this book to heal and to celebrate our healing with the world. It's not enough to have gone through a trying time and heal through it; you must celebrate. Through this book we have made new friends that will last a lifetime. Bonds that we will celebrate for the rest of our lives. In these experiences we have brought other women together so that we can heal each other.

We have provided a brief introduction to each part of the book. The introductions should be used as an opportunity to bring your subconscious to the surface, and as you read the stories, they will enable you to ask yourself questions—about how you go about living your life and why. We offer these women's experience to help guide you through the things you may be facing in your life.

If you are looking just for "answers" in the text of this book, you will never find them. Our goal is that this book act as a conduit to your conscience. It will bring up the issues which you've run away from and will force you to look at the wounds you have not healed. All of the answers to your life's questions are inside you. As you utilize the stories of your sisters throughout the book, you will begin your journey to a place of peace and respect for yourself.

Each part concludes with what we call *Your Soul's Sustenance*. Here you will find a biblical quote that speaks to the truths that underlie the part. We also summarize and bring closure to our thoughts from the part's introduction and offer exercises and tips that you can use in your life to expand your spirit and to utilize the stories that your sisters have shared in the part.

Through the process of reading this book, we urge you to grab a spiral notebook or pad that will become, what we call, your *Personal Book of Revelations*. This will house your thoughts and innermost feelings while you experience this book. We will help you review your *Book of Revelations* by giving you questions to ask yourself after each part. The questions will lead you on an introspective journey, ultimately bringing you closer to the communication of the divine truth buried inside you.

You may not want to read this book cover to cover. But keep it with you and read through the book as you feel comfortable, and when you are ready to hear the truth from your soul, your sisters will be waiting.

I

The Woman in the Mirror

Nothing can dim the light which shines from Within.
—Maya Angelou

When you look in the mirror, who do you see? A woman of substance, beauty, and intelligence? Do you see yourself as healthy and able? Do you see the truth, or do you see the lies that you've come to believe?

Why do we believe the lies? Just as easily, we could believe the truth— God made all of us powerful beings. Instead, we allow ourselves to be hypnotized by the daily dose of negative stereotypes and media images. How we perceive ourselves determines the quality of our health—mental, physical, spiritual, and emotional. Whatever we believe about ourselves, good or bad, is what will manifest in our lives. If we are wondering why our lives are unfulfilling or why our bodies feel sick and listless, all we have to do is look at our beliefs and self-perceptions.

We have listened to the opinions and lies of others. We have chosen to believe them, and thus, we perceive ourselves negatively. We believe the lies because we do not know the truth of who we are. Before we blame others for our woes, we must look at the most heinous of lies—the lies we've told ourselves. If you do not care to know the truth of who you are, any lie will do. Sisters may roll their eyes and pay lip service to being self-determined (after all, "we don't take no stuff"), but when it comes right down to it, we are controlled by what we think and say about ourselves. The proof is in the recent discovery that black women have among the highest rates of depression in the country. We already lead the race in obesity, diabetes, hypertension, certain types of breast cancer, and other ailments. At best, our false beliefs and self-perceptions leave us feeling unfulfilled. At worst, they're killing us.

If we can believe a lie, then we can believe the truth. The truth will not be handed to us on a silver platter, however. We're going to have to fight for the knowledge of self. It will be like the salmon's upstream journey. Society tries to move us away from self-knowledge, not toward it. A woman who is in full possession of her mind, is responsible for her thoughts and actions, and is unafraid of bucking the status quo is a dangerous woman. Such a woman is a force of nature. She creates a whirlwind of change in individuals, communities, and systems just by being herself.

But despite all the self-help books and psychobabble, many of us are not happy with our lives. We know that something's not quite right because the activities in our lives do not sustain us. They do not fulfill us. So we get busy, trying to fix things: we go back to school, we launch a "man search," we work harder for longer hours. So what? We make a few more cents, get a little sex, and still we are nagged by self-doubt. Surely this can't be all there is to life!

Until we do the hard soul work that will serve us in the long term, when we look in the mirror, a stranger will continue to stare back at us. We spend more time getting to know our lovers and friends than ourselves. And since we don't really know who we are, we're suckers for all kinds of stories. This is the danger of living an unconscious life: people can define you, label you, and talk about you, and not only will you care, you'll believe them.

Who Am I?

And so it begins, the quest to discover the special beauty and uniqueness that is you. Your journey to self-knowledge might begin with the following sequence of questions:

Who am I?
Is this all there is to life?

"Who am I?" is the greatest question a woman can ask herself. The quest to find an answer is life's most important adventure. Self-discovery is what life is all about. Unfolding within our spiritual activities, our daydreams, our love relationships, our parental responsibilities, our careers, and hobbies is the answer to this all-important question.

For black women, "Who am I?" takes on special significance. For centuries, we have been defined by the dogma, sciences, and opinions of other people. Individual and race survival in the midst of unparalleled odds has been our priority up until now, so our quest for self-knowledge has moved at a snail's pace.

Yet, now there is a spiritual intensification, a mental and emotional awakening that is shaking many sisters loose from their ignorance, self-deceptions, and group divisions. There's an urgent need to break free of the chains that have kept us passive, apathetic, and afraid. We're just so tired of feeling sick, tired, lonely, depressed, and unfulfilled. So we ask ourselves, "Is this all there is to life?" By the simple asking of the question, we begin to get answers.

The answers may prove bitter medicine, but necessary to healing and waking up from our long deceptive sleep. The goals are fulfillment, peace, happiness, knowledge of self, and knowledge of your life purpose. To get there, we'll need to access our reservoir of spiritual strengths.

Courage. We may not like what we find, but the saddest words ever spoken by black women are, "I don't want to know." Fear paralyzes us from moving forward. Fear clouds the beckoning light at the end of the tunnel so that we cannot see the blessing that lies just ahead. Courage, on the other hand, acknowledges the fear, then keeps on stepping. Harriet Tubman, Ida B. Wells, and Rosa Parks had to be afraid, but that didn't stop them from living the truth of their lives and taking their freedom. As we begin to rearrange our lives to suit us and begin to think, speak, and act in more self-supportive ways, we will upset the status quo. It will take courage to continue to move forward. When you feel anxious or afraid, affirm to yourself or aloud, *"I am a courageous woman. The Spirit within calms me and soothes my nerves."*

Patience. Instant gratification is the enemy of patience. We are so used to getting everything in a hurry that we have lost the art and practice of patience. The patient woman understands that, as the old cliché goes, anything in life worth having is worth waiting for. Discouragements and obstacles will come and go but the patient woman endures and calmly waits. Patience is not to be confused with laziness or apathy. While waiting for a manifestation or revelation, the patient woman continues to grow and develop. Everyday affirm to yourself or aloud, *"Time is on my side. I can wait for the good things in life. I'm in no hurry, because I'm a patient woman."*

Faith. Believe in your power to achieve your spiritual goals even when the nighttime comes. When you believe in your blessings despite what circumstances are telling you, your spiritual muscles are being developed. Women who take risks and live life to the fullest always step out on faith. The paradox is, faith cannot be developed without first taking risks. When you're shaky, affirm to yourself or aloud, *"I believe I can accomplish anything I set out to do. God is on my side, and dreamed my dream first. With God on my side, I am invincible!"*

Courage, Patience, and *Faith* work hand in hand in strengthening your resolve to make meaningful changes in your life. Without them, your efforts to discover the real you will be frustrated at every turn. You'll relapse into believing the lies of others. In using these spiritual strengths, however, you will be victorious.

Be encouraged by the sisters you are about to meet. While they may not have practiced the spiritual principles, they exhibited them by telling their stories. As you get deeper within, you'll be amazed at the wonderful new people who will cross your path.

1

Smoke and Mirrors . . .
Perception versus Reality

Terrie Williams

We would all like to say that when we look in the mirror, the reflection is of a woman who is happy with herself and her life. That the woman looking back at us is righteous, caring, and abides by the golden rule: *Do unto others*. We also hope that we're well liked, respected, and personable and that the reflection is a true measure of how others see us. But are we honest? Do we take the time to truthfully reflect on who we are? As African-American women? As human beings?

I have always found that the most important thing to remember in life (and in business) is this: We're all just people! It doesn't matter what kind of face you put before the public. Forget about judging a book by its cover. Deep down we are all fragile human beings, each one a combination of victories and defeats, a mixture of pain and joy, suffering and hopes.

Dealing with people is an everyday occurrence. And while we all need some quiet time to reflect now and then, our interactions with others are probably the most important part of our lives. How we interact with humankind does more to shape our lives, our reputations, and our careers than any other single thing we do.

We need to understand that underneath the image we project—the rehearsed smiles, the perfected lines—we are all identical. We are human beings. And we are here on the planet to hold each other up and to support one another. Sometimes it seems the challenges in life far outweigh the joys—and that's why we need to be there for each other.

As a longtime practitioner of public relations—or as I like to call it, *people* relations—I have always maintained and applied to my work a code of professional etiquette that is based on the fact that we're all simply human beings. In this increasingly unpersonalized world of high technology and communication via machines, the key to success is personal consideration:

treating people with respect, being there for them, and conducting yourself with integrity and compassion.

How do we "appear" to those we interact with and to those we are meeting for the first time? When I look in the mirror, I see a person who has always wanted to help people. Ever since I was a kid, I felt that I was put on the planet for a purpose (as we all are), and that that purpose was to reach out and ease human suffering and pain in any way I could. I've worked hard to be successful, but I always make sure that I make time to give back and pass it on.

Maybe people don't see what you see in the mirror. That's why we should always be aware of how we come across to other people. If you are not sure, find out. It may be a painful lesson, but it's worth enduring. You'll be a better person for it. I'll never forget the lesson I learned about myself almost a decade ago—a deep lesson to be sure, but one that will stick with me for a lifetime. I was a relative newcomer to my public relations career and I thought it would be wise to take a human awareness course called LifeSpring (to strengthen my "people relations"). At one point toward the end of the intense five-day program, we were all asked to pair off with another person. One exercise we did involved having the other person act out what they thought about their partner. So my partner took my pocketbook, flung it across his shoulder, and walked around the room—and the three hundred people in the class witnessed this! His observation was that I was arrogant, aloof, and distant.

I always considered myself a pretty friendly, down-to-earth person so I was really taken aback. Where was this coming from? I asked a few people in the class what they thought about his impression—and they agreed with my partner's assessment. Sometimes "friends" won't be honest with you about yourself, but strangers will. They pointed out that when we took breaks, I would go off by myself and not mingle. The truth of the matter is I'm very shy, and I was afraid to walk up to people and introduce myself. Had it been a business situation, I would have had no qualms about "working" the room. But this wasn't work, and my inhibitions implied to others that I was "distant." *Perception is reality.* If ten people tell you that you look like a horse, it's time to go and buy a saddle, know what I mean?

Sure, my feelings were hurt by the experience. But it was enlightening and important to me to know how people perceived me.

Maybe you've been in similar situations. Or maybe you've perceived something about another person that in reality is way off the mark. Again it's important to remember that we are all human beings. We have all had different lives—lives shaped and perceived together by our childhood and all that we, as human beings, experience growing up.

Those of us blessed enough to have been brought up in a caring, loving environment can certainly be thankful. Sadly, there are too many of us who have faced unimaginable challenges and hardships since the day we were born.

I've worked hard at my career, and I've been blessed with a supportive family, success, and countless good friends, advisors, and mentors. I happened to have worked with a number of well-known people, and I've written a book with the pure intentions of helping other people succeed. Because of this, I often come across people who think the person I see in the mirror is better than they are, that I've accomplished more, that I'm a bit of a celebrity myself.

Nothing could be farther from the truth. I'm no different from anyone else I meet. I have the same personal challenges, doubts, fears, and problems. Once after I gave a speech, a young woman came up to me and said that she really hoped one day people would want to listen to what she had to say. I laughed and thought to myself: "Who in the world would have believed anyone could come and listen to anything I have to say? I'm just Terrie." And I just said, "Girl, I'm no different from you. We're all the same. You can do this, too, and people will want to hear what you have to say."

The truth is you never know what kind of personal baggage someone else is carrying. And just as people may "look up" to me, the fact is that whatever it is you may be admiring or lusting after that someone else has or does, you can count on the fact that there's some part of themselves that they don't like. We may covet some aspect of another person—maybe their success, their mate, hair, looks, and possessions. But we must know that the person we are yearning to be like is probably yearning to be like someone else. Be careful what you ask for.

Remember this about yourself and each other. Nothing is ever what it seems to be. You never really know what is going on in a person's life. People put on facades to mask the pain or cover the suffering. Sometimes people treat other folks with disrespect as a way to hide their own pain and insecurities.

You never know what other people are dealing with. You never know how your actions may affect another person. You never know what driving forces were present during someone's childhood or formative years. You never know what deeper thoughts and intentions lurk in someone's heart and mind.

Perceptions—or misconceptions—can be dangerous and hurtful. And if we all took the time to just stop and think a minute, and remind ourselves that we are all human beings, the world would be a better place. I often think of the story of the grocery store checkout clerk who wrote to advice columnist Ann Landers to complain that she had seen people buying "luxury" food items like birthday cakes or bags of shrimp with their food stamps. She went on to say that she thought all those people on welfare who treated themselves to such nonnecessities were "lazy and wasteful." But who was she to judge? Who was she to perceive what others may be dealing with? A few weeks later Landers' column was devoted entirely to people who had responded to the grocery clerk.

The ultimate life lesson came from a lady who wrote: "I'm the woman who bought the cake and paid with food stamps. I thought the checkout woman in the store would burn a hole through me with her eyes. What she didn't know (and I would never tell her) is that the cake was for my little girl's birthday. It will be her last. She has bone cancer and will probably be gone within six to eight months." Wow, talk about a heartbreaker!

So when we meet someone new, we should always keep in mind that we never know what their background is or what they are personally dealing with at the moment. We should even be aware that those people with whom we've had long relationships are carrying around a lifetime of experiences—good and bad—that have shaped their personas and their outlook on life. Know that there are some basic givens operating underneath the surface.

Sometimes people's defenses are very hard to crack. So think about what might motivate that person. What are their fears, goals, joys, and hardships? Nine times out of ten, they're the same as ours.

I often paraphrase public relations legend Henry Rogers, who once wrote: Understand that your relationship with people has as much to do with your success as all your professional knowledge—maybe even more. The ability to relate well to people may hit you as something intangible, but the results are absolutely tangible. It is a characteristic about your personality that wins love and respect. And it enables others to forgive your oversights, mistakes, and failures—those things that make us human.

As African-American women we've been faced with our own distinctive struggles and challenges through time. We've built on centuries of misperception, intolerance, and prejudice. But if we work on being honest with ourselves and work to become better human beings, the joys outweigh the sorrows, the negative perceptions will fade away, the successes will come our way, our lives (and the lives of others) will be enriched.

And if we commit ourselves to helping each other, to passing it on, and to finding a way to give back, then we'll all be able to smile when we look in the mirror. And we can be proud of the reflection.

Terrie Williams is the president and founder of the Terrie Williams Agency, a public relations and communications firm based in New York City. Terrie's agency has handled some of the biggest names in entertainment, business, and sports. Her clients have included Eddie Murphy, Janet Jackson, Johnnie Cochran, Time Warner Inc., HBO, AT&T, Revlon, Schiefelin Somerset, Essence Communications, Master P, and the National Basketball Association. She is the author of *The Personal Touch: What You Really Need to Succeed in Today's Fast-Paced Business World* (Warner Books) and is currently working on two new books: *The Personal Touch for Kids* and an inspirational book about giving back.

2

When I Was Puerto Rican

Teresa Wiltz

It was the early seventies, and in some circles, notwithstanding the Black Power Movement, we—as in African-Americans—were still known as "Negroes." I was a bookworm of a fifth grader, an integration baby at St. Joseph Hill Academy in Staten Island, New York, a sprawling place where nuns were nuns, moms were housewives, and Martin Luther King, Jr. was, even from the grave, a rabble-rousing Communist.

I hated my uniform and math, but I loved my teacher, Miss A., a former nun who was fond of nose jobs, microminis, and me. So I listened intently one day as she told a story to my class about her best, best, best friend growing up. A best, best, best friend who just happened to be a little black girl. A little black girl who just happened to remind her of me—the only African-American in the room.

(Of course, there was Ernie, the Puerto Rican kid whose skin was several shades darker than mine and who apparently got a kick out of hissing behind my back, "You're Negro! You're Negro!" as if he'd just discovered some dirty little secret. But that is another story . . .)

It was a sweet gesture; it was also an embarrassing one. But my quiet embarrassment at being the center of attention quickly turned into a fervid desire to have my fold-top desk open up and swallow me whole as one of my classmates, a pudgy lass of Irish extraction, stood up and bellowed, "BUT SHE'S NOT BLACK, SHE'S PUERTO RICAN!"

Miss A. corrected her: "She's Negro."

"Puerto Rican."

"Negro."

"Puerto Rican."

Finally, an exasperated Miss A. turned to me and said, "Teresa, would you care to enlighten us?"

My response was a whisper: "I'm black."

It was not shame that made me whisper. My parents made it abundantly clear that being black was something to revel in. I only wish that they'd told me, at that tender age, why I should be proud—and why no one else seemed to be able to figure out what to me was the obvious. (Only my grandmother gave me a clue as she combed out my long black hair, telling me that my locks echoed our Native American ancestry.) Certainly, no one would ever mistake me for "white," as they frequently did my mother—my "tan" (as my mother called it) skin ruled out that possibility. But what did black, or Negro, mean, anyway? In my world, my family was but a few raisins scattered in a sea of oatmeal. And we certainly didn't look like the black folks on TV—"Linc" on the *Mod Squad*, Diahann Carroll on *Julia*, Bill Cosby on *I Spy*, and Sammy Davis, Jr. doing "Here Come De 'Judge'" on *Laugh In*.

So my whisper back in Miss A.'s class came from the humiliation of being constantly singled out, of being questioned again and again about my ethnicity, as if my true identity were some closely guarded secret. It isn't. But the thing is, I've been passing for Puerto Rican/Dominican/Mexican/ Indian/Pakistani/Egyptian/Israeli/Sicilian/Brazilian/Middle Eastern/Jamaican/ Cuban/mulatto/morena/biracial/exotic all my life.

Unwittingly passing. But passing nonetheless.

There is the security guard at work who asks me if I'm "Latin." The aging Dominican in the curios shop who shakes his head like I am betraying *la raza* when I answer his rapid-fire barrage with pidgin Spanish. "*¿Porque no hablas Espanol?*" he asks sorrowfully. The Puerto Rican gas meter man who congratulates me on "holding out against the blancos taking over" my once Hispanic, and now rapidly yuppifying neighborhood. The white woman who asks me condescendingly, drawing out her words slowly in case I don't get it, "Do . . . you . . . speak . . . English?"

My features stamp me as the generic ethnic, the Universal Other. Cab drivers adopt me as their own—no matter what their country of origin.

"You look black to me," a man I was dating told me after he'd witnessed someone mistaking me for a Latina. Well, I look black to me, too. But race and ethnicity are in the eye of the beholder. Context is the key here: In Atlanta, where my family settled after we left New York, race is divided along a strict black/white divide. So back home, I am unquestionably black—albeit a high yella/redbone/moriney/paper bag tan black. Which, of course, brings with it its own special brand of drama.

In New York, where brown frequently comes flavored with a Spanish accent, I am a Latina. In New Orleans, from where my father hails, I fit right in with all the other mixed-race "Creoles." In Singapore, they are convinced that I am Asian Indian and can't understand why I persist in acting like a tourist.

I'm not alone in this we-are-the-world confusion. My mother has been mistaken for everything from Jewish to Mexican, while my dad was once stranded in Egypt because Egyptian officials were convinced that he was a native son with a fake passport.

Even now, on an exceedingly regular basis, someone inevitably looks at my honey brown skin, goofy nose, and curly black hair and asks a series of outrageously impertinent questions: What are you? What are you mixed with? What's your nationality? To answer "African-American" or "black American" is usually met with another quizzical look. "Oh, come on," my interrogator will insist, "you couldn't be all black."

If I'm in the mood, I'll give the inquisitor a history lesson: Thanks to slavery and unscrupulous slave masters who took advantage of their female property, most African-Americans are of mixed race. My family, like many black families, forms an intraracial rainbow coalition that encompasses every shade from ebony to ivory. (And, family legend has it, some of the lighter hue disappeared into the ranks of white folks when it suited them to do so.)

My story is no different from that of many African-Americans; few of us today look exactly the way our African foremothers and forefathers did when they were first forced in chains onto ships that took them far from their homelands. (And as for me being constantly mistaken for a Latina, well, the slaveship express made stops all over the New World.) Because of centuries of miscegenation, most of us are diluted versions of the chocolate original.

This recognition brings with it considerable pain—for who really wants to embrace a legacy of rape? Who wants to claim white relatives who don't want to claim you? But on the other hand, why should we feel shame for being all of who we are?

When he was a kid, my dad would make the occasional trek to his father's hometown of St. Martinville, Louisiana, a tiny burg deep in the bayou where Creole, rather than English, was the language of choice. There, divided by social mores, racism, and a bridge, lived two sets of Wiltzes, one black, the other white, and both undisputedly kin. Occasionally, my dad would cross the bridge, encountering the officially "white" Wiltzes along the way. (Many of the "black" Wiltzes were visually as "white" as the "white" ones.) Heads dipped in acknowledgment, years of family secrets contained in a single nod.

I hear such stories, and am consumed with an urge to know everything about my family—including exactly where Louis Alfred Wiltz, a rumored relative and governor of Louisiana from 1880–81, fits into the multicolored picture.

These days, I'm no longer humiliated by the mistaken identity thing. I laugh, and consider it a compliment that others seek solidarity with me.

But the thing is, I take pride in being a multiracial black woman. Which means that while I recognize that my heritage has many different roots, from African to Indian to European, I am culturally and unapologetically black.

And I like it like that. Or as they say in Puerto Rico, *me gusta asi.*

Teresa Wiltz is on the staff of the *Washington Post.* She has covered everything from fashion to crime to the Los Angeles riots to education to arts and entertainment. Teresa has written for *Essence* and *Business Week* and was a contributor to the book *Body & Soul.* She is working on an upcoming book on debt and her first novel.

3

Discover Me

Sandra St. Victor

I remember being eight years old, doing my chores, dusting the living room. You know we had one of those living rooms that we couldn't really live in, what with the plastic covers and the white carpet and all. The only time I truly spent any time in there were holidays, and when I was dusting or vacuuming. As usual, as I cleaned, I sang. But this time as I was dusting this lamp in a corner, I remember vividly the feeling that arose inside of me. I loved the way I felt as the notes seemed to be born in my belly, then blossom out of my mouth! I felt so comfortable, peaceful, and complete. Of course, at age eight, I didn't really connect those words to the feeling, but I knew it felt good. Right then and there, I felt an innate sense of purpose, I had to sing! I was a singer! That day I "discovered" myself. I was to spend the next umpteen years in search of someone else to "discover" me, or my voice, for the world.

A good childhood and young adulthood are magical. I had that. My parents were, and are, loving, nurturing, supportive, and proud. They were always there for me, at every performance, snapping pictures and taking home movies (which to this day are ruthlessly played for any and everyone who happens to stop by the house, or are even shown to the cashier at the neighborhood Piggly Wiggly . . . gotta love 'em).

And during this magical time, there is no concept of not "making it," or of obstacles that could hinder my success. For a while I seemed to be destined to just float to the top. I went to Arts Magnet High School in Dallas, and was among the best in the music department. I was the lead in the school musical, won a slew of awards and competitions, hey, I even won the crown of Ms. Black Teen Dallas, singing a German aria in the talent segment. While all the other girls wore evening gowns, I sported one of my fathers' sharkskin numbers in the fashion segment (I was always a little different). I went to two different colleges on music scholarships, but I wanted to get out there and work, so I dived headlong into the professional world of music and mayhem. Yep, it was all flowing, I was on a nonstop-direct ascent to the stars!

Obstacles. Hmmmm . . . where could I start? Well, after I left school, I joined a band called Laissez-Faire with Zachary Breaux and some other musicians from a local university. We moved to Port Arthur, Texas, of all places, where Zach was from. We worked in a lean-to shack disguised as a club, called the King of Clubs, for 50 bucks a week. I had begun "paying my dues," as they say, but in my mind I was just happy to be singing and getting paid for it, and I just knew my discoverer would come soon and whisk me off to my destiny. I spent my off time in my little corner of a room in the rented house that I shared with the band writing songs and dreaming. I knew that I wanted to do something positive with my music. I wanted to help people, our people especially. I wanted to touch people, I wanted to be a part of the change, a "message singer." My first Christopher Columbus came in the form of Roy Ayers. He was playing in Louisiana at a club where Laissez-Faire also performed, and invited us to move to New York. New Yawk City! Wow! I was a bit hesitant at first, because he didn't really seem serious to me, and we had absolutely no cash to be going so far away. But off we went to the big city.

Zach left first, and I came a few weeks later. The other guys drove up a few weeks after that. Only two weeks after we arrived that Zach and I got the gig with Roy. Working with Roy was a trip, because he'd been in the game for so long and was a master player. Of course, rehearsing with a world-renowned artist such as Roy was exciting, and with the prospect of all the cities we'd be touring, this whole new world was thrilling to us, so we didn't even think to ask what we'd be getting paid until the day we were standing out in front of Roy's home on the Upper West Side about to pile in a station wagon for our first gig. Zach and I were whispering to each other about how to bring it up, and who was to be the one to ask. I think Zach eventually said sort of casually, "Oh, by the way Roy, how are we being paid?" Roy sort of flippantly informed us that we'd be getting $450 a week. We were trying to be cool, but we gave each other a look that we both understood that said, "Great!" We were used to surviving on $50 a week, so $450 was big time! We didn't know anything about the cost of living in the Big Apple, so this was more than enough to get us eagerly into the car and smile all the way to DC.

I guess the main thing I can say I was made aware of during that time was that the music industry was an old boys' club, and here I was a nice little Southern girl who's mom had instilled a "kill 'em with kindness" attitude in her. I felt like the virgin at the frat party. Zach wasn't totally "in," but being a man, he could sort of belong. I was excluded from the inside jokes, made the butt of quite a few of them, and I certainly couldn't be down on the hang time with the fellas. It was all right, however, because, once again, I was happy to be singing, and the fact that I was the female in the band, singing leads with Roy, and some alone, I got a lot of appreciation from audiences, and that felt awesome.

My next discoverer and discovery was Chaka Khan. She heard me at a club in NYC with Roy, and offered me the coveted position of singing with her, and hiring the other background singers! And me, well, in her I'd discovered a lifelong friend. I can't even begin to tell you how much I learned by working with CK, and just by being around her. Not just about music, singing, and career, but about life period. She showed by example that the most appealing thing about a singer or about a person in general was their lack of fear to be who they are. Their freedom to just live, or sing, or speak. Not callousness, or thoughtlessness, because she is one of the most caring people I know, but simply being true to yourself, whoever that may be. Like I said before, I was always a little different, but now I had a living breathing example of this beautiful, powerful sista who did it every day, and swore by it! She was like "miracle grow" to my thirsty little Southern soul!

Now I need to take a step back for a moment to talk about the most important development in my life. When I moved to New York, and was on the road with Roy for about four months, I found out that I was five and a half months pregnant! Oh boy! I had left my boyfriend in Port Arthur, telling him that it would not be smart for us to keep up a long-distance relationship. Not that he would have been able to do anything for us anyway since he already had a double-digit figure of kids, and had single-handedly populated at least seven small cities. He was a pretty decent guy I thought at the time. He was older, and spoke to me about philosophy and religion in that smooth quasideep kinda way that hooks the young girls. Anyway, the reason I didn't know I was pregnant for so long is that I always had irregular periods, and going for so long without one was no big deal. I didn't start showing 'til six months. So, what was I going to do? Well, of course, I wasn't going to try to raise a child in a city like New York that I wasn't even accustomed to yet. So I decided to pack my things, go home, and get "a real job" to take care of us. My mother said to me, however, and I quote, "Girl, you've come too far to just quit now. You better bring that baby home to your father and I and let us take care of it until you get on your feet."

As difficult as I knew it would be to do that, I also knew how difficult it would be to just stop singing, or to put it off for a few years until my child was old enough to understand. So I continued touring up until a bit into my eighth month, traveling in Switzerland, England, and even Africa with a big ole stomach, rocking back and forth on a stool singing "doo be doo . . . run, run, run!" Until finally, I ran home to have my little girl, Maanami Asha. I recall singing to her in the recovery room, telling her about the plans I had for her life, letting her know the meaning of her name, "beautiful life." This was the most wonderful little package I'd ever received, and she then became my main inspiration.

If you've ever had to just go out of town for a few days and leave your kids behind, then you have experienced the tip of the Titanic iceberg of emotion that a mother feels when leaving a child for an undetermined amount of time. I had breastfed her for a few months, and I loved her so dearly and I knew she loved me. And since I had been an adopted child, for the first time in my life, I could look at something that was literally flesh of my flesh, someone who looked like me! This was the most difficult thing I had to do. Was I making a mistake, or was I doing what was best for us? I wasn't sure. But I gave in to my childhood dreams, my parents' support, and to the many other singing mothers that I knew of over the years, such as Diana Ross, who had to leave her kids with Mom for a while. I'll never forget my daughter's tears each time I left after a visit, or mine.

During the time with Chaka, I was able to do quite a few background sessions. I was taken under the wing of one of the best, Brenda White-King. I was getting pretty well known on the background singer circuit. Lisa Fisher, who I'd hired for Chaka also, put me in touch with V. Jeffrey Smith and Peter Lord. They were forming a group to be put out on Atlantic records, called Evon Jeffries and the Stand. It was a perfect marriage of bumping tracks and meaningful lyrics. I was in heaven! Ghetto Heaven to be exact! That was our hit in 1990, "Ghetto Heaven."

I was really on my way then, right? Well . . .

Unfortunately, in the R & B world in the States, music with a message isn't accepted with open arms. The audiences who heard it loved it, but the industry, for the most part, stood in the way of us really being heard. We were Sly & the Family Stone, Stevie Wonder, and the Beatles all rolled into one. We sold out shows in New York, Amsterdam, Japan, and England. We opened up for Ziggy Marley & The Melody Makers in the States, and the Red Hot Chili Peppers in Europe. But we still could not get label support to take us to the next level. I must have autographed thousands of bootleg cassettes of our music because fans could not find our records in the stores. Go figure. After hitting brick wall after brick wall. The Family Stand, which we were now called, decided to disband. Strike one. No problem. So now I'm really going to be discovered, right, because I'm known and respected within the industry.

I met with a few labels and decided on one label because it was "boutiquey" (an industry term meaning a small eclectic roster). Alas, I encountered the same bullshit there that I had before. When I first signed with them, they had a president and staff that were totally supportive of my different vision. They all got fired. And lo and behold, some of the same staff from my previous label came to this one! AAAAGH!!! What kind of luck is that?! Long story short, first order of business for this staff was to drop me. Strike two. Hmm. What's a girl to do? Find another discoverer again—and I did.

My new label was full of women who had just themselves taken over this department and were hyped about doing things differently. They were my best shot yet to reach my goal. Everything was going well, and I recorded a CD that was truly loved by my label and critically acclaimed: *Mack Diva Saves the World.*

Lofty title, I know. It was a collection of songs to empower sistas in particular, but for my brothas too. I wanted to get my point across that it's possible to be a strong, intelligent, conscious woman, and still be a sensual sexy fem. The plans were laid. I was to be marketed to the ends of the earth! Worked until everyone knew my name! Fame! I'm gonna live forever! Sorry . . .

Okay, so what happened this time? The brotha that was brought in to take charge of promotion didn't like the record. He didn't understand why people liked it so much, and had no intentions of promoting it. So I was buried. Not one promotion gig, not one radio tour, not one anything 'til it was too late. Useless management didn't help either. Strike three! Wait! Wasn't that ball one? Hold up! I'm not out! Not me.

How I've arrived at this point is to me still a quandary. I've had some real high points in my career, such as The Family Stand days, I've written a song that was recorded on The Artist Formerly Known as Prince's CD "Emancipation," I've even done a duet with one of my idols, Curtis Mayfield for his last CD, "New World Order," and I have a song of mine, "I'll Never Be Another Fool," that The Artist produced on Chaka's next CD, "Come to My House." Along with my manager, I've even done a little "discovering" myself. We signed this awesome male group from Shreveport, Louisiana, called "Profyle" to Kedar Entertainment/Universal Records, I wrote a song on their album entitled "Lady." At this moment I don't have a record deal, and I don't know where I'm going next. Still, I'm happy, surviving, and content to be creating and appreciated.

I recently took a trip to Jamaica to decide whether or not to continue trying to "make it" in this game. I went back to that little girl in the corner of my parents' living room, dusting. I recalled that feeling of sweetness that I felt when I sang, how I felt when I wrote a particularly personal song and someone came up to me and sincerely let me know how it touched them. That's why I do what I do. I do it for that feeling of contribution, for the look of pride in my daughter's eyes, and the way my father struts when he has an article on me in his pocket to show to the folks at church. Or just that cute smile my mom has when she hears one of my songs and says, in her high little voice, "That's nice, Sandra!" I do it because it's what I was put here to do. It's my destiny, it's my love, and I can't live without it.

Somewhere out there between Mary J. Blige and Tina Turner is a place on a shooting star for me. Where ya at, Christopher Columbus? I'm over here!

Sandra St. Victor is a singer and songwriter who is working on a new album. She has performed with artists such as Roy Ayers and Chaka Khan and has written songs for singers such as The Artist Formerly Known as Prince.

4

Who Did Your Hair?

Crystal McMillan

There are four beautiful women in my family. My mama would kill me; five. We are not beautiful because we hail from Louisiana, are "high yellow," and have what some call "good" hair. We do not owe our beauty to ancestors who arrived on the Eastern Seaboard with skin as smooth as chocolate and teeth as white as the flesh of a coconut. There is no Native American blood pulsing through our veins responsible for cheekbones like skyscrapers and skin the color of an Arizona sunset. No, we are beautiful, simply because we believe we are.

I read an article a few years ago which talked about the findings of a research project whose purpose was to study self-esteem in young women. The test group was made up of girls between the ages of six and seven years old, equally split between black and white. Each young girl was asked individually if she thought she was pretty. Initially, all of the girls answered yes without hesitation to the question.

Ten years later, when the girls were between the ages of sixteen and seventeen, they were asked the question again, "Do you think you are pretty?" Almost unanimously the white teens answered no. They thought they were fat, that they had bad skin, their hair was too thin, and so on and so forth. At six years old they were the apple of their daddys' eyes and the hope of their mothers' unfulfilled Breck Girl dreams. Understandably, their sense of self was dependent on their parents' reinforcement. At sixteen, however, their world of influence had broadened and they discovered not everyone was as benevolent as Mom and Dad. Their adolescent self-image was very much influenced by external forces.

The sixteen-year-old black girls, on the other hand, had quite a different point of view. Aesthetically, both racial groups ran the gamut from what is traditionally thought to be pretty to what is considered plain, or to be honest, down right homely. The black teens in the test group, ten years later, all responded as adamantly as they had the first time, "Yes, I most certainly am pretty." Irrespective of what you and I saw, regardless of what society had deemed as the standard for pretty, it did not matter. These girls were so sure of themselves, no one could have convinced them otherwise.

I could give a long rhetorical opinion on why I think the study proved out the way it did, but I am neither psychologist or sociologist. My take on the subject is from the vantage point of a black woman who is also less than perfect (to the untrained eye, that is). And just like the girls in the study, I am quite happy with what my mama, my daddy, and the good Lord gave me. The results of the study made perfect sense to me, at least from the perspective of the black teens. The cross-cultural phenomenon I will leave for the psychologists to explain (which I think was really the point of the study). It is quite obvious to me that black women are quite comfortable with the skin they're in. This study proved it and my personal experience has also validated the results. For *us*, *"fine"* is neither a state of health or a point of debate.

I cannot recall the periodical or the exact month and year I ran across this report, so if I am ever asked to document this, y'all are just going to have to take my word for it. I know that I read it in a reputable journal. I want to say *Newsweek* or *Time*, but don't make me lie (because I will). I realize this was not the most significant study of the decade. But for whatever reason, the results have stayed with me, and from time to time, they enter my thoughts. I think because it begs a question I have often thought about: *Is it healthy to have an opinion of yourself that the rest of the "world" might not hold?* In the final analysis, I believe it is. I guess my true question is, *How deep does the self-assurance go?* Is it enough to encourage us to apply for admission to a top ten university even after we discover they are only accepting 10% of the applicants for admission? Is it enough to convince us to send in that résumé, knowing full well they require a four-year degree and all we have is a two-year Associate of Arts degree? If not, then maybe not. We have got to create our own opportunities. There are no more sliding scales. Proposition 209 took care of that.

It occurred to me that a shortcoming of this study was the decision to end the research in adolescence. Had the researchers followed those same black women to age twenty five, forty, or even sixty, they would have gotten the same message each time. One much like that of my fifty-nine-year-old mother, when I commented on her growing waistline. "This ain't nothing but bloat," she said, grabbing the excess inches in both hands. "Nothin' that a citric of magnesia and a good panty girdle can't fix." I couldn't help but chuckle (to myself, of course). My mother's waistline would have required major surgery to bring it in line with her imagination. Yet even with a forty-three-inch waist, she still thought she was *"fine."* You gotta love it. And if you're like me, you gotta feel it too; like in those private moments when you try on a new outfit and do a Naomi Campbell catwalk "thing" in your bedroom mirror, because you know you look good. And then again sometimes the feeling hits you boldly, like when you walk into a crowded room and claim it; because every now and then you gotta test your skills.

There is an unmistakable aura of self-confidence that surrounds black women. It emanates from that intangible place we know as soul. This soulfulness gives us the self-assurance to be the first one on the dance floor knowing full well we have not danced in years. It gives us the confidence to volunteer for a church fashion show even though we are no longer our prechild size 10. It also allows us to pick up the sword to right a wrong, to state our peace or defend our home and hearts. Yet it does not give us the courage to admit that we can't read. It does not give us the sense of purpose needed to finish adult school when we're twenty-nine because we dropped out of high school at sixteen because motherhood was calling. There are so many of us in places we don't want to be in and in awe of careers and positions we are afraid to aim for. We need to find a way to use that soul, spirit, spunk, whatever you choose to call it, to help get what we want and so desperately need to fulfill our life's potential.

We have developed a great sense of self when it comes to our outward appearance. We don't miss a beat when it comes to looking the part. But we sometimes fall short when it's time to *"walk the walk* and *talk the talk."*

I love to see a sister put together from head to toe, standing tall in a sea of people. But I feel a greater sense of pride when she speaks and her words are eloquent and wise. Most of us can probably remember a seventies R & B hit entitled "What You See Is What You Get." If I could, I would rewrite that song and call it, "What You Get Is More Than You See." Because if all that mattered was the superficial, what value would soul and depth have?

What you see when it comes to our black women will almost always delight your senses, but it shouldn't stop there. It goes without saying that we make more than a minor commitment of time and money to our appearance. We can throw an outfit together in a heartbeat. No doubt because we have hit every sale between President's Day and Christmas (gotta make those dollars do the most). Wardrobe we got covered. Give us an occasion and we are there with bells on—just as soon as we get our hair done, that is.

God did good by us, we are not complaining. We come in all shapes, sizes, and shades, each as enticing as the next. Whether we are a compact Size 6 or a full-bodied 16, it's all good. He did real good in fact. But He didn't make it easy when it comes to our hair. I swear somewhere in the Bible it should read, "And on the Eighth Day, God created beauticians." They say prostitution is the oldest profession in the world. Not in our neighborhoods.

It ain't easy making that weekly, or if you're lucky, every-other-week appointment to the beauty salon. So when we make the effort, not to mention drop the cash, we go the limit and then some. We might start with finger waves on one side, and blend them into an asymmetrical cut on the other, with a Cinnamon Jazzin' curl falling over one eye. And if the stylist can work it, a few twists somewhere in the back. Black women don't have hair stylists, we have magicians. But we look good.

To be honest, when you see our sisters during rush hour on the busy streets of Chicago, D.C., or Philly, they will be dressed to the nines and they will have some bouncing and behaving hair. It might not be all their hair and I ain't mad, just as long as it's doing what they paid it to do. So for the stragglers or up-and-coming young sisters who haven't learned yet that less in more, I'm feeling you. I know that thirty-five dollars is not easy to come by and it's even harder to let go of. After you've waited an hour or two or three in a wobbly chair with a ripped vinyl seat that pinches your thigh every time you move, and you've thumbed through every magazine on the coffee table—twice, (though none of them were published in the current year)—you want your money's worth when it's your turn on the hydraulic throne. And when it finally arrives, you take your time getting bumped, twisted, braided, glued, sewn, or whatever it takes to get "glam." The sisters waiting on the sidelines who minutes ago were comrades in arms, complaining right along with you about the wait, are no longer a consideration—you served your time.

Our flair is sometimes overstated—a little outrageous even—but I know what it's like to have issues in your life that seem insurmountable. For a brief reprieve, we don't mind waiting all day in a beauty salon, listening to the latest gossip, knowing full well when we get out of the chair ours is the next story to be told. We are not insulted to patronize a place of business staffed by a cluster of little women who chatter through surgical masks (and right through you) in an unfamiliar tongue while little fat naked statues smile at you from an incensed shrine. We need a fill. As our petite friend applies the final topcoat, we are torn whether or not to tip her the full $2.00 or use $1.00 of it to pay for the quick-dry machine. Because as much as we would like to sit and "chat," we are always running behind schedule.

I've learned to not be so judgmental of my sisters who make it their business to look like a million on a $5.15-an-hour job. (Thanks, Bill, we ain't mad at you.) If it's doable; go for it. And if at some point they have to get flossy on what's left over from their unemployment check because their baby's daddy didn't drop off his; I understand that too. And while it may not be my personal preference, if long, curved, burgundy nails and fuchsia lips lined with black eyebrow pencil make you feel like a diva; more power to you. Because when you look up and it's the first of the month and you're $150 short on the rent and during your commute home from work your favorite color, red, lights up on your dashboard and reads CHECK ENGINE and as you scan the mail sitting on the kitchen table you notice the phone bill has arrived in a pink envelope . . . again. I've stolen from Peter to pay Paul too.

There are times when we seem to be spinning our wheels, dealing with the same issues, the same problems day after day and week after week with no apparent relief or reward. In the midst of the chaos we are expected to hold things together, to be strong, to answer our children's questions when they ask, "When's my daddy coming home?" And we reply, "I don't know, baby . . . soon." And the truth is he's in prison doing five to ten. And the real truth is absence does not make the heart grow fonder. And when that well-meaning but nosy neighbor asks how our son is doing and we say, "Oh, baby he's fine," and deep down inside we know he's doing drugs in a den of thieves. I've swallowed that pill too.

Every day greets us with at least one new challenge; sometimes it's just getting through the day. We may never win the battle, but then again we might. We could win if we sisters, we women, take that same verve, that same uncontainable spirit and turn it inward and allow our souls to ignite an eternal flame. The energy from that flame could create an abundant source of power. Power like the energy created from water rushing through dams and wind whipping through the arms of windmills. We can create a new energy within ourselves. Nature has proven if a force can be contained and directed, it can create power. Our spirit, our sense of self, is powerful. We have not yet discovered its full potential. We may not change the world, but we may not need to. Our challenges are much more immediate, much closer to home. Small victories are still successes.

Wouldn't it be wonderful if, when our daughters asked, "Where's my daddy?" we could honestly reply, "He's working overtime, sweetheart, trying to save for a new house for us." And when our pastor asks when he's going to see our teenage son again, we could proudly tell him, "Reverend, he told me to tell you he'd be sure to attend service when he comes home from college for winter break."

There is no doubt that we have soul. It is the foundation on which we build our faith. It is the source from which we get our strength to protect our children, honor our elders, express our love. But in and of itself soul is not enough. We need it as our anchor, absolutely. But from that base we need to develop some other stuff. The stuff that enables us to fight this new fight. The battle is no longer being waged in the streets of Montgomery, Alabama. It is being carried on in corporate boardrooms and congressional committees. It's a new day, sisters.

I've learned in my few short years that soul does not have to be dark and heavy like the gravy on your grandmother's smothered pork chops. It can be as light and sweet as the toasted marshmallows on her candied yams. I am inspired by the soul of my sisters that manages to be luminous and steadfast even with the weight of life's circumstances looming over-head. It is this mastery of spirit and keen sense of self that sets us apart and, if directed, can make all the difference in our lives and the lives of those we love.

It is no small task to be the trailblazer. When it is your job to raise the bar for your family, your community, your people, the burden is real and it's heavy. There are too few of us with engineers, doctors, and attorneys dangling from our family tree. We cannot turn to Uncle Dr. Neurologist for guidance and encouragement as we struggle through medical school. We cannot call on Brother Circuit Court Judge to help us write our briefs for the Law Review during our final year of law school. We've got to go it alone and it is not easy. Not in 2000. We had a break for a good ten or fifteen years. Those of us coming through in the seventies and early eighties got the benefit of the labors of those before us. The clock has been turned back, so to speak—no affirmative action, no apparent conscience. I don't care where you went to school—10 does not equal 100. You cannot deny us the right to learn to read and write, deny the power of the vote and representation, and expect that a few benevolent years can make up for lifetimes. It does not add up, not on pen and paper and not even on an Excel spread-sheet. We have to start demanding change again, creating change again, and inspiring our youth in the process. Otherwise, we are going to lose this bat-tle, not only for ourselves, but for our children as well.

I have faith in us as a people, as a gender. And while the weight of the world shouldn't rest on our feminine shoulders, it so often finds its home there. We women made from Adam's rib, who crossed oceans in the belly of vessels crowded with sick and hopeless, survived. We women who gave birth in cotton fields and nursed our children and continued with our labor flourished. We same women need to know as those sixteen- and seventeen-year-old young women knew, that even in our humblest moment—when we are overdue for a trip to the beauty salon, and it's been three weeks since our last fill and that bad-ass Donna Karan suit we wanted to wear to the job interview is not in the closet but at the cleaner's—even still we are a formi-dable force. Only then will we understand the depth and source of our power. And with that knowledge begin to test our limits and, hopefully, discover there are none.

All I have left to say is, when I stop you on a street in D.C., L.A., Chicago, New York, or Philly and ask, "Who did your hair?," don't tell me your play sister's mama's cousin's neighbor did it. Ain't we sisters?

Crystal McMillan is a writer and is currently working on her first novel.

Your Soul's Sustenance

I sought the Lord and He heard me and delivered me from all of my fears.

We have been in many situations where we have been forced to look at the truth of who we are and had to learn to love ourselves all the same. Our friendship has helped us take a better look at ourselves through each other. We can see things in each other that we see in ourselves. These can be qualities that we love about each other and want to improve in ourselves, or qualities that we don't quite embrace, even though we love each other all the same. Having a network of women in your life helps you to heal the illusions in your mirror.

Our natural instinct as humans is to seek happiness, satisfaction, or love to fulfill our need for security, joy, and belonging. But as women, we try to live up to what we believe *others* perceive as beauty and what we perceive as belonging. We cut, dye, and weave our hair; wear color contacts and paint our faces and dress our way into an image that we believe is better than we are now.

We hide facts about our lives, hoping that no one believes that we are a fraud and don't deserve to be where we are in life. Often we try to avoid our colleagues at cocktail parties because questions outside the workplace are too probing. We often wear a mask in order to appease others and satisfy the void that is within our souls. Unfortunately, that void cannot be filled with the material things we purchase or the sleepless nights spent worrying about what's going to happen next or the constant cravings for the love we know we deserve.

Knowing Ourselves Through Each Other

You attract people who are parts of you. Different parts of you. Some people may reflect your overall personality. Others may represent one or

two minor parts of what make up the beautiful being that is you. And sometimes the mirror images of yourself are distorted like mirrors in a funhouse.
The distorted images create funny, grotesque reflections of the truth.
Often, this is fine with us, because we don't want to see what's really there
anyway. But you can see anything in a mirror if you look hard enough. Most
times what we *do* see is exactly what we *want* to see. The problem is what
we see is often filtered through other people's perceptions and the little lies
we tell ourselves. The truth is we are all beautiful, but we must be able to
look past the distortions to see the truth. Not many of us can look directly at
the truth. It's almost like the sun—it's blinding.

Every day we try to adopt some of the better parts of each other in our
lives. It may show up in different ways. To be able to really look at another
person and see yourself is magical. If you can look at that person with unconditional love and still be objective, that means you can have the qualities
that you want for yourself.

Taking the Good with the Bad

When you embrace a person fully, you have to take the good with the
bad. And sometimes the bad isn't our own. Sometimes the bad is something
we need to be able to see and recognize to understand other people and to
be able to better understand ourselves.

We've been told so many lies about ourselves that sometimes we don't
know what to believe. As black women we all need to take a look in the mirror and be honest about what we see. We may not always appear to others
or ourselves as we wish, but there is beauty in the truth of what we see. The
dictionary defines *truth* as "sincerity in action, character and utterance, the
body of real things, events and facts, transcendent, fundamental or spiritual." As black women we spend a great deal of time hiding from "the body
of real things"—the truth about us as a people and as a sisterhood. We lie to
ourselves about who we are, what our contributions are to the world, and
who is in control.

We tend to take care of everything and everybody, but we don't take care
of the most important thing in our lives: our inner selves. A girlfriend of ours
told us, "I barely have a chance to eat one decent meal a day, much less sit
down and write in a journal or meditate." Think about it; if you barely have
time to nourish your body, what's happening to your soul? If you think of your
soul as a power source for daily living, like most people think about fueling
their bodies and minds by eating nutritious food, is your soul starving?

Growing up we were told breakfast is the most important meal of the day. And we're sure you've heard the "eat-three-square-meals-a-day" speech. And what about the four basic food groups? Don't you think that your soul should be taken as seriously as the Surgeon General would tell you to take care of your body?

Get with the Program

We would like to share with you some simple ways we've found to nourish and care for your soul. We've kept in mind our hectic friend and her busy schedule when devising these small ways to build up your soul. Think of them as your daily soul "supplements" just as you would take a multivitamin.

Keeping a journal is the best way to look at yourself in the past, present, and future. Both of us have created for ourselves a journal that we call our *Personal Book of Revelations*. We refer to it this way because every time we write in it, we reveal pieces of ourselves that we sometimes don't reveal to others. We learn from our book about how we've handled situations in the past and how we can improve upon our coping skills today and in the future.

We understand that it's hard sometimes to start a journal, but you will soon find that it is always worth it when you look back on it. We've provided some simple questions to get you started. We will include questions throughout the book, so there are no excuses. These questions will help you begin the process of healing and enable you to embark on a journey of self-revelations.

Your Personal Book of Revelations

When we say "The Woman in the Mirror," it is a way of us stopping and looking at who we truly are. Beauty is an internal acquisition and it comes from being at peace with your mission in life and through the love of a higher power.

- Do you encompass these virtues in your own life?
- Are you comfortable with who you are? Or do you float through life dealing with problems without taking one moment to nurture yourself?

- Can you honestly look in your own mirror and truly say you like what you see?

As black women we withdraw on a daily basis from the bank of self, which has been left with insufficient funds for some time. It's time we stop and invest in our spirits.

II

Spirit Moves Us

*I have reached a point in my life where I understand the
pain and the challenges; and my attitude is one of standing
up with open arms to meet them all.*
—Myrlie Evers

As the only woman in the meeting, Yaa wondered how all of these sup-
posedly strong and powerful men could be such cowards. What was
happening to her country? How could these so-called leaders have just allowed the greatest of disgraces to occur—and stand idly by watching the
whole thing? She knew that it wasn't her place to speak out, but the *spirit
moved her* and she just had to speak her mind:

> *Now I have seen that some of you are afraid to go forward and
> fight for our king. If it were the brave days of old, chiefs would not sit
> down and see their king taken away from them without firing a shot.
> No white man could have dared speak to the Chief of the Ashanti in
> the way the Governor spoke to you chiefs this morning. Is it true that
> the bravery of the Ashanti is no more? I cannot believe it. It cannot
> be! I must say this, if you the men of Ashanti will not go forward,
> then we will. We the women will. I shall call upon my fellow women.
> We will fight the white men! We will fight till the last of us falls in the
> battlefields!*

Spirit moves us at any given time. The spirit that we talk about is not the
spirit that we do things in, it's the spirit of God that moves us forward as a
people. We don't just mean black people, but people period. While all of us
may not have come up in the church, we have all been touched by the spirit

that emanates from our beings. That spirit has moved so many of us through hard and sometimes trying times.

Ever since the beginning of time, societies have been dominated by men. We women have always had a "place" that was defined by men. It is only now that society in general is *starting* to recognize our collective and individual value. But even in the midst of male hegemony, sisters have always let the spirit move them to action, even when it meant taking those in power to task. That's exactly what Yaa Ansantewa did. And she wasn't just talk either. She was action. She followed through on her promise to lead the nation into battle by bravely leading the fight of the Ashanti people against the British colonizers in Ghana. Hers was the last major war in Africa led by a woman.

Your actions are examples of what happens when you allow the spirit to lead you. When you get yourself out of the way, you can finally let *God* work *through* you!

After meeting with and interviewing hundreds of women, we discovered that one common ground all of the women had was the belief and trust in a power higher than themselves. An old saying, which has been passed down from generation to generation, is: *God, will not give you more than you can handle.* Our spirit has always been able to sustain us as women. Spirit has paved ways for many, opened doors for others, and even allowed some to cling to life when it seemed impossible.

Spirit Will Carry Us Through

Spirit is our foundation as we move forward. It's our rock. Since the beginning of time it has been and it will always be. Spirit moves us to do things that sometimes we don't plan to do—like stepping out and knowing that spirit is right there working with us.

Black women have always had that kind of spirit. We've always had that unseen tether that kept us connected. Spirit is moving us whether we go to church, the mosque, or elsewhere for spiritual guidance. We all have that fundamental spirit because women before us had it. It's something that runs through us. It's a spirit that never dies. So when spirit moves us, there's simply no getting around it. As long as we exist, spirit will move us to step out and do what needs to be done.

Spirit moved us to do this book. People thought we were crazy. Obstacles have come our way that seemed insurmountable. But we pressed on in the spirit of knowing that what we were doing was in God's name. That's what we mean when we say "Spirit moves us."

Spirit moving you is about combining openness, devotion and divine inspiration to manifest the greatest potential that God has placed inside you.

The key to our belief is our devotion to a higher power. The realization that there is something beyond us that determines the course of our lives. We must recognize that we play a large roll in our decisions, but if we are devoted to living to honor our higher power, we will be free of worry and stress and allow ourselves to be divinely inspired. Being devoted means putting God first in our lives. Yaa Asantewa gave God first consideration in her decision to speak up. God led Yaa Asantewa to do what was best for her people, not necessarily for her personally.

Why does it sometimes seem that others are moved by spirit and you're not? What are you lacking that they have and why are they so special? They're open! Open to the greatness that God has to offer. Openness is one of the fundamental principles for progress. If you are open to the blessings that God has to offer you, you will be able to accept those blessings and appreciate every last one. When we close ourselves off to what the Universe has to offer us, we won't receive anything. If your door is permanently shut, how will people come in and how will you get out? It's the same with your blessings. You won't be able to receive them or pass them on to others.

Even though it wasn't Yaa Asantewa's "place" to speak out in a meeting of chiefs and elders, she felt divinely inspired to speak the truth of her conviction. Her truth was not spoken out of disrespect or condemnation, but out of a conviction to save her people from certain death. When we are divinely inspired, all we can do is speak the truth. The truth is not our truth, but God's truth. Once we recognize that within us spirit is moved by God, we can always speak God's truth.

We all have the power to stand up to whatever circumstances or problems face us, our families, or our communities. Spirit is trying all the time to lead us. Sometimes we're just not listening. Sometimes we're just not allowing ourselves to be led. *Spirit moving you* means tapping into the legacy of sister Yaa and letting your thoughts and actions be guided along your own spiritual path.

5

I'm Alive

Tara Jaye Centeio

A couple of weeks ago, I found myself face to face with death. Not the physical kind—as far as I know, I am a very healthy twenty-three-year-old Cape-Verdean/African-American woman. And no, I hadn't lost someone close to me. Each member of my immediate family and everyone I love is still living and breathing and doing. But still, crouched in a small window seat of a Boeing 727 on the way back from my hometown of New Bedford, Massachusetts, I was confronted by death.

At that moment, it occurred to me that this was not unfamiliar territory. I'd been facing death for as long as I could remember, and its image had been nothing less than terrifying. It held the kind of fear that takes one's breath away, causes the heart to beat irregularly, and changes an entire lifestyle to one of supposed "risk-free" living. So yes, I had been facing the fear of death, and because this fear was so strong, I was experiencing something even more debilitating—a slow, torturous, spiritual death.

I had always been aware of how different I was. On a hot and sunny August afternoon, the kind where the wind blows just enough to curb perspiration, my preteen counterparts resolved to sneak into the woods to smoke cigarettes. These were not "deep" woods. Actually, the tall, full evergreen trees formed a small cluster that lined the side of a neighbor's house. And this was not just any neighbor—this was a neighbor who knew all of us, and worse, who knew our parents. But I followed because, although I felt uneasy about the idea, I didn't want to be left out. My contemporaries stood in a semicircle and carefully passed the cigarette from one set of eager fingertips to another, each one completely convinced of his enviable smoking skills. They were intrigued by the rebelliousness of this brief, but significant ceremony. They were proud of their daring trip to the edge. But me, I simply stood there motionless, while my mind raced with thoughts of all the potential reprimand waiting at home. I quickly puffed on the cigarette, which by that time had been reduced to a thin rim of tobacco, and practically tossed it to the girl standing to my right. Then I left, with an intrusive heaviness upon me.

Most of my younger years were like that. At the time, my fear played antagonist to the spirit of youthful (and sometimes stupid) experimentation. The other kids smoked marijuana. I made myself unavailable. My girlfriends began their journey into the realm of sexuality. I ran and hid beneath the wisdom and comfort of my mother's advice. They got acquainted with speed and other chemical "highs." I had absolutely no interest. And so then, during those extremely influential days, my fear worked well for me. It was a fear of getting into trouble, of finding myself in danger, of falling victim to the evils of the world.

Time brought me from an awkward twelve-year-old to a blossoming sixteen-year-old, and new adventures set themselves before me. Interestingly, the same hovering fear that had kept me out of compromising situations as a young girl was slowly becoming a hindrance to my growth. My friends got their driver's licenses, but I had reservations. *What if I drive off a cliff? Hit somebody?* Fear of accidental death. Fear of hurting people. The girls went out late at night and made new friends, but I stayed home. *What if the other people don't like me? What if they all get drunk and leave me there?* Fear of judgment. Fear of abandonment. The days—the years— went by, and each new opportunity that presented itself was clouded by the spirit of fear. I doubted everything around me, including myself and my potential. I doubted my relationships with my friends. When one of them was in a bad mood, I just knew it had to be something I did. They would often laugh and call me "paranoid," and being in the process of learning myself, I never contested.

Upon graduating from college, things started happening for me. Good things. I landed a job I loved. I finally got my license at twenty-two, bought a house and a new car (but still didn't drive on the highway). I was interviewed by *Black Enterprise* magazine.

It seemed that I was on the fast track to success. Strangely, the fear didn't go away in light of these accomplishments—instead it grew stronger and developed a grip on me more powerful than I had ever known. *This is too good to be true. Something's going to happen. I'm going to die before I get to do really miraculous things.* Desperate to finish everything in time, I began living my life as a checklist. House—check. Car—check. Pledge Delta Sigma Theta—check. I acquired many things at a fairly young age, and though this meant a great deal to me, I still wasn't happy. I wasn't fulfilled. I smiled during the day and cried at night, constantly wondering when my time would be up. I was spiritually dead.

I realized, as every dawn awakened me to anxiety, and consequently pain, that I couldn't live like that any longer. I needed something bigger . . .

stronger. People had attempted to introduce God to me before, and I said I knew Him. I said I believed, and I did believe in Him. But I didn't trust in Him. I didn't have faith in what He could do for me and through me. So I ran. It seemed like too big a commitment, and again the spirit of fear came against me. *What if I go to Him and fail? What if I give my life, then mess up and annoy Him to the point where He's just through with me?* Though it may be a point of contention for many "on-the move" twenty-three-year-olds, it wasn't the sex I didn't want to give up. It wasn't the cursing and the gossiping, or the occasional social drinking. It wasn't even the Sunday morning sleep (though I do love my sleep). No, my addiction was bigger than any of those things. It was the control. All my life, I had been trying to control the uncontrollable. It was as if I didn't trust God to direct my path correctly. After many attempts to create my own fate and just as many failures, I surrendered. I "let go and let God," as the old folks say. I decided to practice trusting Him, to practice my faith and believe that it could, that it would, grow into a powerful source of peace and happiness for me. It was hard, because fear knew me all too well. That demon had been living with me for so many years that it knew just what to say to me, how to say it, and when to say it in order to make me doubt myself and others . . . in order to make me doubt God.

And now, as I confront the reality of what my life has been about, I finally see that I have a choice. I am choosing faith over fear. This is the road I'm on. As I sit here typing this piece of my life, I want you to know that I don't presume to have all the answers, but what I'm beginning to understand is that I don't have to. I don't have to know everything that's going to happen and when it's going to happen and how it's going to happen, because He knows ALL of that. I haven't been on this road to freedom for very long, but I know I don't want to turn back. To me (and I believe God feels the same way), it doesn't matter how long I've been on it or how quickly I'm walking. It only matters that I'm willing. And no, I don't know exactly where I'm headed, but learning to give up control is making this walk a lot less tiresome. Sharing this burden is lightening my steps, and trusting God's compass is taking the fear out of it all.

I read somewhere that fear and faith have the same power, they just yield different results. When it comes down to it, they both translate into believing something's going to happen before it ever happens—really believing. And then expecting it to come about. If we can practice fear so well, which only produces pain and suffering, then we can surely practice the faith that can liberate us. Pray on what you want for your life, and believe it will happen. Close your eyes, breathe deeply, and believe . . . it's working for me . . . and I'm alive.

Tara Jaye Centeio is a writer for Hallmark cards and is working on her first novel.

6

Today My Soul Will Fly

Pamm Malveaux

As women we are not taught how to listen to our intuition. We are not taught how to delight in ourselves let alone how to celebrate the life force we are. Instead, we are taught that everything we need is outside of us. In truth, life is a journey *inward*. A painful lesson I learned the day I laid on the terrace of my rented home in Los Angeles completely covered in a blanket of glass.

A few minutes before, I was fighting with my then boyfriend. He was having another one of his explosive fits. As I was backing away from him, I stepped through a floor-to-ceiling window and suddenly I couldn't move. Kenny came running up to me breathless. I could see he was scared. I must have looked a mess. How did I get myself into this? I was rushed to the hospital, and all I could think about was the television shoot I had to begin in three days. One of the largest television companies had trusted me with doing one of their specials and here I was lying on my back in a tremendous amount of pain with Kenny at my side crying. His sniveling really pissed me off! He was a well-known music executive, and this incident would ruin his career. In fact, as I blinked away the tears and wondered if I would walk again, my intuition reminded me that his anger that night came from the fact my career was going well and his wasn't.

Lying in the hospital room I sought freedom. This was a choice I definitely had to take responsibility for making. That night waiting for my medication to kick in, I had a long talk with God. I told Him I felt like I had a recurrent starring role in a bad TV rerun! For many years my career had taken off. I had been one of the pioneering African-American music video directors of the early nineties. I was a single mom making a lot of money. In essence, my bicoastal life was all about work, money, more work, and more money. Yet on the inside I was lonely—confused about who I really was on the inside vs. this public perception on the outside. I not only wrestled with trusting people, I wrestled with trusting myself. After all, I didn't know me . . . had no idea what my voice really sounded like. I had never taken the

time to ask God why and how He'd created me in His image. Even my previous marriage had been fast paced. My ex-husband and I met on a morning
express train into Manhattan and three weeks later eloped. Five years and
one child later, he announced he was leaving to marry a local politician's
daughter. (He was such a gold-digger!) Okay . . . my world was slowly crum-
pling but I refused to let it get the best of me! I realized that for me to be a
successful filmmaker, I had to become a spiritual person in a big way. I had
to believe so much in what I was doing . . . believe that what I was doing
was important in a spiritual way.

Kenny had a limo pick me up from the hospital. I had the maid pack his
things! One day later, I walked on to the set and began shooting the special.
Even the doctors said I shouldn't, but I knew I couldn't let this opportunity
pass! Forty-two stitches later, God propped me up and the shoot was a success.

Yet on the flight home, I still felt like my life was shutting down. The
codependent side of me really needs to get a grip! I had internalized the
pain and anger to get the job done. But now I needed to heal. I had to get
away. But I couldn't leave my kids and just wander off to some mountaintop
for a few months. My daughter was starting preschool and my son high
school. They needed a mom who was healthy and whole. God, You really
need to walk with me now!

My mom met me at the airport and I could tell she was excited about
something. I wasn't going to spoil her happiness with what happened to me
in L.A. As we put my luggage in the trunk of the car, my mom turned to me
and said I was joining her on a cruise to the Mayan ruins in Mexico. My dad
would watch the kids. Wow! All I could do was break down and cry. God really heard my plea for help. Two weeks later we set sail.

Now I believe there are no coincidences . . . There was a reason God
wanted me in Mexico. Immediately upon arrival in the small town on Playa
del Carmen, with its quaint little houses and roadside markets, I felt a sense
of peace. This place was amazing! As I walked through the ruins, I remember hearing God tell me to "go to the farthest corner of the ruins." I was
obedient. No sooner did I find the farthest corner than a swarm of butterflies surrounded me. It seems like hundreds of pink, orange, and fuchsia
butterflies circled me for a brief moment before flying away. Again I heard
God's voice say, "The pain you've experienced is no different than what a
caterpillar feels as it's turning into a butterfly. You must always remember
that when life seems mundane, take the time to seek the 'inner pocket'—
that gap so called by some *to listen in wonder at the oneness available*. I will
always give you the answer with the question. Your path will be lit with the
first step. Your way will always be cleared with the looking." A warmth came
over me, and suddenly I knew inside everything was going to be okay. All

the limitless power of creation was mine to draw upon whenever I needed it!

I could have stayed there all day. As I was about to leave, I looked down and by my right foot was a heart-shaped rock. I did a double take! I picked it up and I knew . . . the angels knew . . . God took me all the way to Mexico, away from the madding crowd, to show me how much He loved me. He and I were truly one! I was crossing the bridge into a new energy and together with Him as my lover and my partner the possibilities were endless! I could face the unexpected as well as the future with faith and hope and love.

Today, my career is still hectic at times, but my children are ever more wonderful! There's even a new man in my life, a man of valor and integrity. My lesson in self-love taught me how to reach out with unconditional love and compassion. I've learned not to worry so much about outcomes. I'm not trying to end my life before it's time through pity parties and thoughts of unworthiness. I know a higher wisdom deals with outcomes and knows a time for all things. More importantly, I learned you can't measure healing by just physical results. Healing occurs at many levels. Real healing occurs at the heart level. Loving one another. Timeless wisdom easily grasped but practiced by few. I tell you my story in love. I walk with you along my journey, your journey so that today, your soul will fly!

Pamm Malveaux is a film director. Her new company, Urban Bayou, is currently in preproduction on several film projects.

7

Ascendance

Ivy Simmons

I have found that when we hear the word *ascend*, we think of the Creator's ascendance to higher spiritual planes. Rarely do we reflect upon our own status and work toward our ascendance to higher spiritual elevation. Do we feel we are not worthy enough to attain the highest level of development on earth? Is it necessary for us to expire from this life and pass on to other dimensions in order to have ever-present joy and light?

When this came to me, I looked up the meaning of *ascend* in the dictionary. Funk & Wagnall's Standard Dictionary stated that, *ascend* means to rise by degrees, move upward. Ascendancy is the quality, fact, or state of being in the ascendant; domination. Ascendant-rising; superior, dominant; position of supreme power, preeminence; domination (1). Ascension, to me, is about taking ourselves higher—morally, ethically, psychologically, physically, and spiritually. The higher the elevation, the better vantage point from which to gain perspective. A bird's eye view allows us to understand how things move and flow. We can see the floor plan, cityscape, and an entire region! Through elevation we can have supreme power over ourselves! That could mean so much for the quality of our existence and those that surround us.

Most of us think of this elevation as being nearer to God. However, most of the major religious texts instruct us to fear God and be beholden to His rules. Most of the "Good Books" demonstrate that we are children of God. As children, isn't it a natural consequence that we should want to be like Him and grow to His level of understanding? We fail to remember that, as a child of God, we at our essence are Godlike. We find it hard to remember that we will be like Him if we rise to the fullness of our development. Now you know that the parent that tempered rules and guidance with openness, kindness, and love always proved more approachable, admirable, and attainable than the one we feared. We can't connect and see ourselves in an entity we fear. We fear it. We want to run and hide from it. Fear blinds us to the truth and incapacitates us to movement. We cannot see clearly with fear clouding our vision. Our right mind is not free to guide us when fear abounds. With fear, we are afraid to take even the briefest look at ourselves. Without fear we have the ability to see that, as God's children, we are God, just as you are your parents. How can we be our whole selves if we fear ourselves?

Is there an inherent self-denial in recognizing our Godlike nature while simultaneously being taught to fear God and His wrath? Why would we ever fear the same quality that is our inner nature? Once we look at ourselves as part and parcel of God with love, knowing that we are learning and teaching always, we can reach our highest plane of existence here on this earth.

Reaching the pinnacle of our being is not a long and arduous road. It is a road of steady application to oneself, tapping in and upgrading objectively on a weekly, daily, and hourly basis. I have been on this road myself on and off again for many years. Every step I take in this life adds perspective and fodder for growth. It is good. Also know that everything I am sharing with you is projection. I am still learning the lessons. I *know* it in my right mind, yet putting it into action and living it moment to moment is a different yet tangential affair. I am not yet at my highest. I can't quite imagine it fully, but I know it when I have those moments and times of moving in spirit and truth. It feels so wonderful. Words cannot describe. A lot of times it represents itself as synchronicity. Coincidences are not random. They are instances of spirit arranging things for us to see, take notice, and gain some insight. Whether we take the time to pause, give thanks, and learn is completely up to us.

Often, as women we speak of our coincidences, intuition, déjà vu, seeing something in a dream, and hours, days, weeks, years later we see the physical expression of what we have already borne witness to. These are all expressions of our Godliness. When answers to the hardest questions seem to come from nowhere (since we know we have never read a book on neural linguistics), and it could not have been "common sense" to the rescue since that is based on having had a smidgen of prior knowledge, we know it is our divine inner nature, our beyond all, extending itself to us.

When we are living as grace-filled, whole, and balanced beings, we understand that there is nothing we lack and that there is plenty of everything in this world. There is no need for competition. Who cares what that sister is doing in her cubicle? No need for attachment. No need to wonder about receiving if we give. No need for worry. Why? For we create everything in our life. Example—if you think you will be broke . . . you will be. If you second that with speaking it, you definitely will be broke. Lastly, if then you are scraping away and holding on to things—you will remain in that state. Living modestly, knowing that everything you need will come to you once you create it within yourself and believing in the never-ending bounty of this universe, is the way of abundance.

When we know that everything is accessible to us, it is so not necessary to hold on to things. Allow things and people and experiences to move freely in our lives. Attachment to an idea, what we think should happen, a person, an object, anything, leads to blockages. We hold on, and if we are so busy trying to hold on to one thing, we do not have the freedom to touch another experience. Our friend determines she wants to move on, so give thanks for the experience, the lessons we learned, the teaching we were able to give, and let go. We get released from our job. Well, give thanks for the experience. Once again there were lessons we gave and received in that space.

We are always where we need to be right now to give and receive those lessons. Next week we will be in a different place yet it is still perfect for us. Every space is a good space as long as you see the lesson and learn it. Ever wonder why you keep getting in certain types of situations over and over again? The first time you didn't learn the lesson! Spirit had to put you right back there so hopefully this time you will get it. Each lesson prepares us for the next stage of our lives. It may be a better job, an opportunity for our own business, or time to pursue a hobby that turns into the best thing to ever happen to us! But if we are attached to that job, we become bitter because it did not pan out as we wanted, even though somewhere within us we knew it was best for us to leave. If we do not do what we are supposed to do of our own volition, the Creator moves things around to force us to do what we should be doing. He wants us to elevate and expand ourselves so He inspires us or those around us to make it happen. Now, back to this bitterness we feel when we don't stay on "our program." That bitterness is a fear of new things, which leads to willfulness. No, I did not say willpower. Willfulness. We want something because we want it or because it makes us feel secure (which is why we want it) regardless of what it really means for our lives or how it will affect others. This is not the positive manifestation of will.

All of that is rooted in fear. Hmph. FEAR. That is a whole 'nother letter. But know this: Never let fear be the motivator or deciding factor in ANYTHING you do be it big or small because it all impacts your life. Fear is a noose that will tighten slowly and suck the life out of you . . . if you let it.

Excuse me—that was a tangent, but a necessary walk I had to take with you. Now on to a more positive, light-filled subject—abundance.

The positive manifestation of anything begins with knowing and believing that there is an abundance of everything in this universe. That knowledge alone transforms us and allows us to give freely and absolutely. When we feel empowered to tap into the universal energy source and not just our own personal reservoir, which can be depleted by poor eating habits, improper mental attitude, lack of rest, and physical activity, we can do anything. We live on higher ground with more room for an expanded heart, perception, perspective, experiences, and life. When abundance is understood, we are not motivated by the theory of reciprocity. The true spirit of giving is not looking for what we will receive in return. Wondering what we receive for this favor or that gift is, quite honestly, bartering. We will give this much of ourselves because we think we will get this in return. Enjoy giving. Give something each day—a smile, a laugh, a good word or deed. Understand we are really giving to ourselves, and don't we deserve such goodness?

When we give to ourselves, we always receive an endless flow of gifts. We may not be able to draw a direct line from one gift given to one received, but . . . who cares! Aren't surprises the best anyway? Guess what, we also need to learn how to receive. When we feel we are not worthy, we cannot receive, and when we cannot receive graciously, our gifts stop coming because we do not allow them to enter our life. Then we have the nerve to wonder why life is not what we want it to be. Isn't this a demonstration of self-hatred?

On the road to self-actualization, we let go of those habits of hate because we are moving toward a complete life. When striving to live fully, we are enabled to look objectively at our thoughts, actions, and intention. Assessment of where we are without ego coloring our honesty is a true ability. We can say I was wrong to yourself and to other individuals in our lives. At this time, we are not fearful of their thoughts about us because truth motivates our actions. Ego is acknowledged yet not given the controlling power it desires to keep us in good face. This good face ego has us strive toward, leads us to lie, cheat, and remain immobile when opportunities are presented—what if we fail, what if they don't like us or our work, what if we do this and we get more work yet, then we cannot handle it so we are only good for a little bit, what if it is a joke, they don't really want us . . . Yes, ego is a master trickster and manipulator. It has worked on "protecting" us for as long as we have been living. It does its job well. Here is some good news about ego. It does not feel the need to be a guard dog to our existence when we have no fear of our true power as beacons of light and love because we love ourselves completely. With the absence of fear there is freedom to love.

Thank you for taking this journey with me, and I pray you accept these words and grow from them as I have during this writing. In writing this, I hoped that you would feel me, but mostly I want you to feel yourself. All the answers to life lie within you. We are so externally based for our validation when half the time we say, "I knew that," or "That's what I thought!" Yeah, you did so go with that. Time alone is so great. Every historical and New Age guru says it, and there is totally something to that. Being with God is great for internal development—sitting in the grass among some trees. And if you can't get that close—a picture or some plants, running water, anything will do. Just do it. The work of being a bigger, brighter, bolder being is ceaseless—ceaseless in the amazing joy it brings.

LOVE + LIGHT + LIFT + LAUGHTER = LIFE

MOVING IN LOVE, LETTING LIGHT SHINE, LIFTING ALL AND LAUGHING = A
LIFE OF ASCENSION

Ivy Simmons is a twenty-six-year-old graduate of Spelman College. A former professional dancer, she is a principal in two concerns in which she is co-creator and partner. Maatrix Internationale is a corporate finance and management consultant firm, while Gloss Media is a firm specializing in publicity, public relations, event marketing, and the structuring of foundations.

8

Whose I Am

Patti S. Webster

It's interesting. I was in the church. My great-grandmother (Ruth Anna Brown) started our church in 1929. After her passing, my grandfather (Denvil Harley), grandmother (Adeline Harley), and now my mother (Pat Webster) continue the legacy of being servants to Jesus Christ. My father (Sid Webster) is associate pastor. So if you wanted to talk about a Preacher's Kid (PK), I was a PK all the way around.

I was taught at a young age to fear God, trust God, consult God, and hear God. We reverenced God in everything. Sabbath keepers and Pentecostal praisers, we were brought up not to wear jewelry, makeup, or listen to secular music. Women couldn't wear pants, we couldn't go to movies, we couldn't watch cartoons, we couldn't go to the prom, we couldn't dance. We couldn't, we couldn't, we couldn't. Luckily I was raised in a large family where there was a lot of love and a lot of games. But I had a worldly yearning to see more, to experience life, to test the "other side." And that's what I did.

When I went to college, I totally denied any association with God, my church, and my family. I tried and did everything I could think of that went against what I was taught. Why? I guess it's because at a young age I felt "forced" to be part of the body of Christ. I felt forced to be in church every Friday, Saturday, Sunday, Monday, etc. I felt forced to have to obey the rules of the church, some of which I never understood. I felt betrayed that I couldn't hang out with my friends and do the things they were doing. So, rebellion set in—desires took control—a new life began.

Well, let me say this. When God has His hand on your life, He has His hand on your life. No matter what you try to do or where you try to run, He'll let you know He's there. For example, after college, I stayed in D.C. and began working at a small health benefits firm. Every day I would go to a small deli near the office to get breakfast. This particular morning, the cashier asked me what church I belonged to. I told her vehemently, "I don't belong to any church." She said, "You may not belong to any church but the spirit of God is all over you." In retrospect, I guess I should've heeded her words. But being stubborn and the rebellious fool that I was, I didn't.

So, after working various entertainment-related jobs in D.C., I moved to New York. It was there my life started to unravel and God started dealing with me and only me. I took one job, it didn't work out. Took another job, it didn't work out. Was robbed twice of EVERYTHING! Ended up working for a major public relations firm, gained a plethora of experience, but the job didn't work out. During the time I was at the major PR firm, I had moved back to New Jersey. I knew God was working on me . . . but I didn't know yet how to yield to His voice.

I can't tell where the road turned. I can't tell you the exact day I heard God's voice for myself. But I know I started to seek Him for myself. Everything in my life seemed to go wrong. I had nowhere else to turn. I started my own PR firm, things seemed to be going well, then I would hit a bump on the road. But God's love and grace were always surrounding me even though I didn't know it. You see, when I was growing up, living a life for Christ was something I was supposed to do, had to do, it was required because of my life history and lineage. I had no choice in the matter. When I came to know God for myself, all of that changed.

The strictness of my early years, I understand now, was to teach me obedience, an obedience I now treasure as I continue to grow and develop a closer relationship with Jesus Christ. But I had to make a choice for myself. When I was younger, the choice was made for me. As I now yield to God and fall deeper and deeper in love with Him everyday, I know God chose me. He had chosen before the foundation of the world. And guess what? He loves me so much, He let it appear as though I chose Him.

I know without a shadow of a doubt, that I was meant to be a member of the body of Christ. I, too, know that it was the prayers of my grandparents and parents which stayed the hand of God's mercy and grace upon my life. So says the word, "Train up a child in the way he should go, and when he is old, he will not flee from it." I'm a witness to that.

I'm glad I'm a PK. I'm glad to have the roots in Christ that have been a part of my family from generation to generation. I'm glad to know that I am in Christ and Christ is in me. It's great to see the change He has made in my life. I have a long way to go, but God continues to work on me and I pray daily that I will have the hunger and thirst for Him all the rest of my days.

I'm happy to know that I'm home, yet when I leave this earthly place, I will reign eternally with my Father who is in heaven. But the best thing is that God doesn't look at me as Ruth's great-granddaughter, Denvil and Adeline's granddaughter, or Pat and Jack's daughter. My family lineage means nothing to Him. To Him, I'm just his little Patti.

Patti S. Webster is the president and CEO of W & W Public Relations, Inc., a full service public relations/special events firm based in New Jersey. Representing more than 40 clients in film, television, music and sports. W & W will open offices in Atlanta and Los Angeles in late 2000.

9

The Spirit Train

Leslie Harris

I scrambled around in my pocket looking for my metro card. A train was approaching the platform, and with things going the way they had since my alarm jolted me out of my sleep at 5:37 A.M., I knew that the number 4 train was on its way into the 42nd street station. I decided to give up my useless search for the card and took out my faithful token that I kept stashed away for just such an occasion—which usually occurs on a Thursday or Friday of any given week .

When I finally made it through the turnstile, I hauled ass down the steps, taking them two at a time. I may only visit the gym once a month, but step class has nothing on the New York City Transit obstacle course. On an average sprint to the jawlike doors of an awaiting train, you must hurtle over two homeless people and the occasional stroller; dodge in between individuals who are standing on the platform waiting for the next train, but refuse to move an inch in either direction so as to block your entrance to your train; not to mention the football dummies that come tumbling out of the open doors for the full four seconds that are allotted for passenger exits and entrances, leaving you no choice but to block and tackle your way into the uninviting cars.

Needless to say that this exercise usually ends with the metal doors slamming shut mere inches from my face. Today was no different. I took one step back as the train pulled away, glaring at the passengers jammed into the steel cars like sardines.

I peered down the platform. Another train was on its way. This time I teetered on the edge of the platform, in line with the perceived train door entrance. I was determined to get a seat. As the train slowed to a stop, I congratulated myself for correctly assessing exactly where the train doors will open with slide-ruler precision. When I saw a clearing, I dashed to my favorite seat. You know the one that only seats two, but if you spread out your belongings just right, no one else will bother to sit next to you. Just before the smile could set on my face, my eyes zoned in on a loud-talking, generous-sized woman making her way toward my haven. Today of all days I did not want to hear any noise. No undiscovered comedian telling stale jokes for the amusement of tourists; no unknown harmonica player, tuning his instrument; least of all, not the ramblings of this woman who has just tripped over my outstretched legs to get to the seat next to me.

As she apologized profusely, I contemptuously uttered "Don't worry about it" and kept my eyes averted. I glanced sideways and gave her the once-over. I wasn't sure if she was homeless or just dressed in old, raggedy clothes. She wasn't dirty so I figured that she may be poor and crass, but not homeless. Before the train was completely out of the station, the woman started talking again, as loud as ever. I looked around for the band of people who'd entered the train with her, thinking, no hoping, that she was talking to one of them. I desperately searched the faces of the passengers in our corner of the metal box hoping to see an inkling of acknowledgment for my ignoble seat mate. Then with startling realization—as each one of them dropped their eyes, glanced back at their paper, or just openly looked on at this loud, uncultured woman in disgust—I deduced that she was not conversing with any one of them, she was talking to me!

I thought quickly to myself. *What did she say?!?* Oh, she was rambling on about some tickets to the circus that she either got, or didn't get, for her children. I was laconic in my consolation. The last thing I wanted to do was to encourage this woman. I was not surprised to see that she did not need too much feedback to sustain a conversation. Now she was talking about how upset her kids were going to be because they had their hearts set on seeing the circus. I just nodded and kept staring at an advertisement overhead—the things they do with print media nowadays! I figured that if she asked for money, I would give her the spare change in my purse. Why not? She seemed harmless, even if she was speaking loud enough to blow out my left eardrum.

Surprise of all surprises, she was not asking for money. So I relaxed a little and started to really listen to her. I expanded on my one-word answers. The woman was trying to figure out what excuse she should tell her children for not getting the circus tickets. After all, she could not tell them the truth, which was that she had waited on line for five hours then refused to accept the only tickets that were remaining. The tickets were for seats in the last row in the tent, which would make it impossible for her children to interact with the entertainers. She wanted to get her "money's worth." As she saw it, countless other children would have good seats, giving them a better view of the show, so her children should have the same opportunity. Why should her children have to settle? She went on to say that she had to settle too much in life and she refused to let her children start settling this early in life.

As she preached her sermon on settling, I continued with my condescending manner, "Good for you, that is an important lesson for you to teach your children." Who would have thought that a twenty-six-year-old could be so ridiculously pompous when talking to a woman that is past her in age and experience . . . twofold. As I turned to get a better look at my neighbor, I was halted by the soft golden brown eyes of a loving mother. She could have been anyone's mother, mine or yours, but instead she was mother to a couple of very lucky children. A mother who will teach her children that you only hurt yourself when you settle. In the end, anything is not always better than nothing.

Being the self-centered egotist that I was, I thought about how her words related to my life. I drudged through my days bearing my fangs at the world. Okay, I was not completely happy with my life, but then who is? At least I had a job. Many of my friends were still looking for work. At least I was in a relationship. Many of my friends were still waiting for Mr. Right. As I listed my accomplishments mentally, I realized that too many of them were prefixed with the phrase *at least*. I began to wonder exactly when I had let go of my dreams and decided to take on the role as a settler. Was it when I was turned down for the job of my dreams when I first graduated from college? Or was it when I found out that the black football player that I liked only dated white girls? I can't put my finger on it now, but this transformation must have happened unbeknownst to me, and it took a total stranger, a loving mother, to make me take a hard look at my life.

As a black woman in corporate America, I am given the opportunity to make more money than I had hoped. I have an impressive title for my age and experience, giving me the opportunity to manage many high-profile projects. However, I have to ask myself if I have achieved my original dreams or have my salary expectations and management goals been downsized due to the harsh realities of life—which usually hits you somewhere within the first six months after graduating from school.

When I left the green campus grounds of my alma mater on graduation day, I was on top of the world. I expected nothing less than what I had achieved thus far. Now I am looking at my accomplishments, meager as they are, with a feeling of relief for having made it to where I am today. I never expected the climb to the top to be easy, not by any means. But my goodness, I did not expect it to draw blood every step of the way. It's okay to stop and recuperate, maybe even get a transfusion if needed, but it is not okay to stop somewhere between your personal heaven and a private hell. It is not okay to settle for less than what you want.

As the train approached 14th Street, my friend got herself together to make her exit, from the train and out of my life. She had reached her destination and turned to thank me for talking to her. Can you beat that? She thanked me for talking to her. All I did was begrudgingly lend her a haughty ear; what she did for me was to rekindle the light at the end of my tunnel. I glanced around at the people who had looked away earlier. They were still reading their papers and inspecting the insides of their eyelids. I wondered how many of them, if any, had experienced a similar epiphany as myself. No, it seemed that I was the only one listening to my friend's words of wisdom. Lucky me . . . unlucky them.

Leslie Harris is an aspiring writer.

10

Mama, Are You Scared?

Darnelle Taylor McCullough

I remember Ma as a strong, classy, beautiful, single parent, five children deep, poor, not a pot to piss in, nor a window to throw it out, respectful, funny, charming, and always a lady.

Me, being the youngest child, at age three, took on the sleeping quarters that were once occupied by the infamous man known as Daddy. My comfort level with Mom was so great that, even in my teens, a fearful night would cause me to scurry into her bed for that ultimate kind of comfort. The essence of her being there was her spirituality. The warmth of her body was like the wings of an angel that would immediately absorb my fears.

Even at the age of seventeen I would sneak into her bed, though mind you, there was very little space in her bed for a grown me. But in a low voice, I would nudge her and she would awake to this familiar question: "Mommy, I can't sleep, can I get in?" Sometimes she would sigh at the request, but never ever turned me down. She would say while moving over, "Oh, come on in," like the comforting wings of an angel and I would close my eyes and find sleep.

I was too proud to let anyone know that my restless nights would lead me to a comfort zone, the angel, my mom. We had a strong, spiritual thing going on. I was so tapped into Mother that the mere expression on her face, or her body language, would let me know her inner thoughts. She never had to say a word. She trained all of her children to deal with her on a spiritual level. THE CONNECTION. Deac, Carolyn, Doreen, Tommy and me. We were all "Liz's Kids."

At the age of thirty-six, I would again ask my mother for the last time to move over and let me in. It was time for me to give her what she had given me on many occasions, the comfort of wings. I had to become her angel, now that death was moving upon her quickly. She was in the last stages of AIDS, and within a short time she would be dead. I remember asking myself, "What could I do to make these last days of her life meaningful, for her and myself? What could impact on our spiritual selves, so that both could come away happy, loving, and complete?" But I was scared. I wanted all of this to go away. Reality had set in, and with the strength of GOD and a prayer, I walked into my mother's bedroom. There she lay helpless and very sick.

Promising myself to stay calm, I said to my mom in a quiet voice, "Move over, I'm getting in." Without a sigh, she moved over, knowing that my wings were now ready for her. We would bring each other to that very special comfort zone. I remembered my first words to her: "Are you scared?" She replied:

> *No, I am ready and I am okay with this.*
> *It is important that you are too.*
> *Don't worry, for I will be fine, and I will be with you always.*
> *Not in the shape that you now see, but in other ways*
> *And you will know my presence.*
> *You go on and live your life to the fullest,*
> *and always keep your head up.*

I looked at my mother and realized that we had both just wrapped our wings around each other. The relief was so rewarding that I almost couldn't wait for her to get to the other side. It has been ten years now and my mom is keeping her word. She is just busy and I am listening.

Darnelle Taylor McCullough is the president of Djohn & Co. which specializes in consulting and marketing for the fashion industry. As a liaison for manufacturer and retailer, her company is responsible for breaking deals well over the million dollar point. Married to Norman J. McCullough for twenty-one years Darnelle is also the proud mother to Cadet John McCullough. Darnelle is in the process of completing her first novel.

11

I Stretch My Hands to Thee

Shirley Childress Sexton

Included in my prayer at the beginning of each interpreting assignment is a giving thanks for the opportunity to be of service, to be productive, and earn an honorable living. My work as a sign language interpreter, facilitating communication between the deaf and hearing people, satisfies my soul.

My deaf parents, Herbert and Thomasina Childress, always worked diligently. "Do it now" was my mother's motto. She sewed clothes for us and others—with precision and finesse exemplified in every garment. And I remember my shoemaker/repairman dad proudly wearing a pair of leather sandals he had made as his trademark. Customers came specifically to his shop, looking only for his proud expert handicraft. Their strong work ethic influenced my two sisters and I to always think in terms of productive careers.

In the beginning, my employment focus was narrowed to typist and secretarial work, even studying secretarial science in junior college. But my spirit and that last supervisor who told me to go to lunch and take my name plate with me helped guide me to my present path of striving toward excellence in developing my gifts and works in deaf and hearing communication.

I was chosen to do this work. Having deaf parents taught me American Sign Language. The ability to study deafness at the University of Massachusetts was definitely God's way of putting me at the right time . . . All praises due, being invited to sign interpret for Sweet Honey in the Rock was the ultimate truth that God has shown me. We really "are the ones we have been waiting for."

Dr. Bernice Johnson Reagon, I think, showed such wisdom, insight, and foresight when she invited Dr. Usaye Barnwell to a Sweet Honey audition/workshop. Bernice set the stage, in my opinion, for Sweet Honey's world to include deaf people, which broadens the perspective of both artist and audience.

The deaf culture and the African-American culture have so much in common that it makes this sign interpreter's job of cultural mediation that much easier. "Father, I Stretch My Hands to Thee"—that hymn from which the title of this essay is taken connotes a face-to-face conversation—an essential ingredient in deaf communication.

Also, Sweet Honey's repertoire largely includes songs of a narrative or storytelling nature, another strong aspect of deaf culture. Just ask my mother how her day was or what happened at the store, and you will get in great detail a gleeful account that included more information than you would have thought to ask, for she's a storyteller par excellence!

My deaf heritage; my skills, talents, and knowledge of sign language interpretation; and my sense of rhythm and music have combined to enable me to be an interpreter, teacher, and consultant specializing in interpreting performing arts and music. I can truthfully say I've waded through the waters of the Sweet Honey in the Rock experience . . . yes, they will take you there with pride and glory.

To be sure, the challenges continue: Imagine five African-American women singers alternately leading songs of spirituals, gospels, and blues with a passion. It truly and gracefully energizes the spirit. I think of my work as still a growing and developing process. One struggle, for example, is conveying a visual rendition of the call and response style of singing, which is a didactic exchange requiring my body shifting to indicate dual components—as when interpreting two people in conversation. Such songs as "In the Morning When I Rise" or "Sometimes I Feel Like a Motherless Child," or more contemporaneously, Nitanju's "Run."

To sum my sharing, our work is, as Dr. Barnwell intones, "More than a paycheck." In so doing, we are blessed to be in an environment of health and healing, conducive to an expression of our God-given talents, and encouraging learning and positive growth. I am giving thanks for the opportunity to be of service and stretching my hands to thee!

Shirley Childress Saxton works as a sign language interpreter, teacher, and consultant. She holds a Bachelor of Arts degree from the University of Massachusetts at Amherst. She was born to deaf parents, Herbert and Thomasina Childress. Her two sisters, Maxine Childress Brown and Dr. Khaula Murtadha Watts, and her two sons, Reginald and Deon, all Sign. She is newly married to long-time friend, Pablo Saxton.

12

I Am Enough

Felicia Middlebrooks

I used to think a wedding ring was the ultimate symbol of acceptance. It meant that you were a member of some sort of exclusive club of valued beings. And in my twenties, virtually every post-college-degreed woman I knew who didn't have that coveted ring, one spoke of herself in terms of lack, as though she was somehow defective. We all had impressive careers, beautiful clothing, good looks, and perfect health. Yet we weren't counted among the *"accepted."* Societal standards offered no refuge. Every magazine cover and talk show focused on romance and relationships, drawing a clear differentiation between the haves and the have-nots.

Single status wasn't supposed to be viewed as anything more than a temporary place. It was analogous to having a learner's permit. It was assumed you were going to drive *eventually*. I, like many other unmarried women, were stuck in *neutral* and didn't like it one bit. Well, in my late thirties I got that wedding ring, and made a startling discovery: That wasn't "it." I soon realized that in my desire to put an end to my single life and obtain the ultimate symbol of acceptance, I'd neglected to honor myself in allowing adequate time in making my decision. There is great value in waiting. It always reveals the true motives of the heart. Not waiting leaves one open to deception. That's what happened to me.

Regrettably, after a whirlwind romance over a few months, I consented to marry someone who hid his true self from me. I woke up and discovered I was with a man whose values and character were diametrically opposed to mine. He didn't want a wife, he wanted a trophy. Fidelity and sanctity were foreign concepts to him. I'd once heard someone say, "Water always seeks its own level." I didn't understand that analogy, until now. Like begets like.

I've come to understand that you usually end up with the person you thought you deserved. If you see yourself as single in the sense that you're incomplete, then you will draw unto yourself another fragmented person. My marriage, one I'd prayed and hoped for after spending many years building my career, was brief and ended in divorce. A devout Christian, I never dreamed my life would take such an horrific turn, but it marked the beginning of a very necessary spiritual journey . . . a journey for which I praise God for now because now I understand that the true meaning of being single is to be whole. The ultimate acceptance is not derived from a degree with honors, clear skin, a decent financial portfolio, a well-appointed home, a marriage, an accolade-filled career or an effervescent personality. The ultimate acceptance is knowing God loves you. You are already enough. This journey has taught me that truth. When the student is ready, the teacher will come.

By the time I was twenty-seven, I was at the top of my field in broadcast journalism. At thirty, I was already earning a six-figure salary. It wasn't easy getting there. It took seven years to obtain my bachelors degree in communications from Purdue University. I worked my way through school, slaving at a number of radio and TV stations reporting and anchoring. At the same time, I worked in the steel mills, covered in oil from the tips of my steel-toed boots to the top of my yellow safety helmet. I was tethered to a dream of success.

I grew up in a middle-class family of four daughters in Gary, Indiana, in the sixties and seventies. My dad was a steelworker and my mom a teacher. It was an exciting era. We had our first black mayor, and the Jackson 5 had hit the big time. We even had our first black Miss Indiana. The steel industry was booming then, the economy was solid, and neighborhoods still had whole families intact, complete with block clubs and dances heralding the Motown sound under the streetlights on weekends. There was choir rehearsal on Saturdays, church on Sundays, piano lessons on Tuesdays, and great family outings a couple of times each month. This was the good life. There was no street violence back then, and people still said please and thank you.

I was a sensitive little girl. Timid. Afraid of my own opinion. In fact, back then I didn't even realize I had an opinion . . . not one that mattered anyway. The awkwardness of adolescence made high school scary. I was tall and lanky, like a black Gumby. Acne and reading glasses did little to boost my confidence. And when the orthodontist suggested braces, I tried to have a fit. It worked. I managed to convince my parents to delay the procedure until I was mature enough to handle it. I got them at twenty-four.

College days were wonderful. I started growing up. I dated a lot, pledged a sorority, and got a firm place in the black choir on campus, solos to boot. I didn't understand why at the time, but even then with my flurry of activities and achievements I still didn't feel as if I fit in . . . there was a hole in my soul. I was the epitome of the so-called birth order chaos: the middle child, in a tug of war with her siblings . . . wanting to be the oldest, jealous of the youngest, trying to figure out where my place was. I dangled like a participle. The more emptiness I felt, the more I tried to fill up with *things* and people and the approval of people.

I became an overachiever. I lived my life on a performance treadmill. You might say I hungered to belong and I looked to relationships to complete me. I feared being rejected. Rejection comes in many forms: a shattering experience of betrayal by someone we love and trust, a put-down by a teacher, being passed over at work, being dumped in a friendship. No matter what form it takes, the consequences are the same—leaving you disillusioned and abandoned.

I was a perfectionist, and my longing for acceptance magnified the importance of other people's affirmations. I wanted to be the best daughter, the best friend anyone could ever hope to have, the best student, the most loyal girlfriend, the best employee, etc. I wanted to be enough. And when it came to serving God, I wanted to give Him a flawless performance. That, of course, was impossible, me being human. I knew scripture well, but only in my head, not in my heart. I knew all the verses that said Jesus loved me, yet it was quite a revelation to discover that God actually wanted me to be *transformed* by the *experience* of His love.

Now, after much prayer and daily times set aside to be alone with Him, I can relate to God as a loving Father from whom I draw a deep sense of secure belonging. I am no longer inadequate. None of this happened until I came to understand that when you're in Christ, pain is a process with a purpose. Father always has a reason for allowing things in our lives. Sometimes we don't understand it. That's where trust comes in, because trust requires unanswered questions. Pain gets our attention. It's God's megaphone. And as you mature spiritually, you begin to understand that the lesson you don't get this time you're doomed to repeat until you learn what it is God is trying to teach you. This place of pain for me was not a vacation spot I'd ever hope to return to. So I was all ears.

When I decided to face my internal struggles head-on—my grieving over a broken marriage, and that gnawing sense of feeling less than whole— I bore my soul before God naked and needy. I finally had to hold myself accountable for my own behavior and examine how I contributed to my undoing. I made a quality decision to spend time alone with God, and as I sought answers, He began to reveal Himself to me. It was the greatest, most powerful spiritual transformation I've known to date.

Through a great journey of pain, I came to understand that God never required me to *perform* to win His approval. I didn't have to "do" things for God's love. I learned that God was more interested in my "believing" than in my "doing." His son Jesus took care of all the work on Calvary when He died for my sins, so there was nothing I had to "do" to complete myself. I had become dependent on the opinions of others to shape my identity, and I wrongly trusted that human relationships would fill a void that only God Himself can fill. By God's grace, I learned that the Cross is the ultimate symbol of acceptance. There is no greater love than that.

This transformation didn't happen overnight. It took place over a period of a few years, during which time I was hit with a number of calamities outside my broken marriage. I was in the midst of a consumer fraud lawsuit. I'd purchased a dream house, then after three inspections I discovered the builders were crooks. My home had no insulation, though it looked like it could have appeared in *Architectural Digest*. Chicago winters were fierce with no heat. My home inspector died, depriving my lawyers of a testimony during trial for my lawsuit. Then my father was stricken with colon cancer. There was one thing after another, but guess what? I survived. So did my dad.

I'm not grateful for those troubles, but I praise God for what I've become because of them. I won the lawsuit and my father is completely healed. It took some harrowing experiences and some tough introspection before I understood the real truth . . . and that is, I'm enough. You are enough. We're enough because God Himself created each of us complete in Him. And His love has no caveats, no contingencies.

Most of us were groomed as little girls to believe that someday the right guy would come along and sweep us off our feet and grant us significance. What I've learned is that you were *born* with that significance, and no amount of ill treatment or disrespect—no matter what the source—will ever change that. And if you choose to believe otherwise, then you risk allowing yourself to be caught in a state of perpetual inconsequence. For me, wisdom has come with age.

If you've heard that life *begins* at forty, believe it. It is an era in a woman's life that broadens her perspective. It is a time of self-discovery and self-acceptance. A termination of the mystical. You trade cloudiness for clarity. You begin not to care so much what people think of you. You don't necessarily devalue their opinions—you just begin to understand that those voices don't determine your worth, nor do they dictate your role in humanity. Those voices need not be your external conscience. It's a stripping away of all your surfaces, like removing old wax from the linoleum flooring of your existence. You can finally face yourself. You can embrace your qualities and strengths and acknowledge your foibles.

Now that I know what I know in my state of wholeness in Christ . . . I'm open to a new beginning. A discerning eye is drawn to the extraordinary. Therefore I fully expect to be united with an emotionally and spiritually healthy man who shares my values and can share my dreams in God's timing. But whether that happens or not, I'm completely fulfilled as I revel in an eternal love that will never leave me. At this juncture, a Christian mate would simply be an asset to a life already well lived.

I can laugh at myself and be grateful for all that I am. I can finally experience what's been true all the time. God created me and you, and predestined us before the very foundation of the world. Our lives have purpose. We are already enough in Him.

Felicia Middlebrooks is a morning anchor for WBBM Chicago, a CBS station. In addition to providing voiceovers for national commercials, Felicia is also the president of Salt Shaker Productions, an entertainment company.

Your Soul's Sustenance

*Even though I walk through the valley of the shadow of
death, I will fear no evil because thou art with me.*
—Psalm 23:4

Faith is something that is intangible. We've witnessed through the stories that these women experienced their faith in different ways. As an inspiration, an epiphany, a sudden bolt of clarity, a feeling, or a small voice that guided them to do what they needed to do. Most of all, they found a way to tap into that source deep inside themselves when they needed it the most, but always knew and praised God even in the quiet peaceful times as well as in the darkness of their struggles.

Prayer helps us to build our faith the way exercise helps us to build physical strength and endurance. Even though you may not see or feel the results instantly, prayer works as a faith builder and will always be there when we need to have the stamina to get through a rough time or rejoice for the joyful times in our lives.

We have learned to strive for *prayer-fection*—instead of striving for perfection and constantly falling short with disappointment and endless frustration. Prayer-fection is the closest any of us can get to perfection. In our prayers we can quiet our souls and find the inner peace we need to achieve peace with ourselves and God.

Prayer-fection is a technique that is more focused on inner peace and gratitude than asking for material things or situations you wish to happen. Find a quiet time that you can make your own. Solitude is best in this time so you can focus on your prayers. Inner peace is what we seek in this exercise so we must quiet our minds and expel the commotion of our everyday activities. It is important for these moments to be free of the chaos that we all have in our lives. We must allow our spirits to be free and able to explore the inner peace and solitude that we all need to move through our day with ease. You may surround yourself with comforting items that soothe your soul: a picture of a loved one, flowers, candles, incense, water, etc. Take five minutes and let yourself unwind. Even if you just woke up, this five minutes is important because you must release your dreams from your conscious-ness as well. You don't need to stick strictly to five minutes, but you will know when you are ready to proceed. Allow yourself to slowly relax and close your eyes. Breathe in through your nose and out through your mouth in calm rhythmic breaths. Allow yourself to communicate with God. Release your spirit and let it communicate your goals with God. Don't ask, but have a conversation with God and reveal what your goals are to Him. The purpose of this exercise is to fortify your relationship with God and in-corporate quiet time for peaceful reflection and praise. This time in your day will help you to fortify your soul and constantly renew your faith.

Your Personal Book of Revelations

It's not God's fault! We've become a society so focused on blame that we don't know where to start or end when it comes to all the accusations flying around. It has come to a point where some people have taken it too far. They blame God for their problems, and that's where we have to say no more to the blame game. That's exactly what it is—a game. No one wants to take responsibility for their actions so they play an adult game of tag in search of making the next man It. Well, God is the only one who can master this game because He can never be responsible for the blame of anyone's problems or woes.

God has a plan for each and every one of us. We have all been in a point in our lives when we believe there is no relief and God must have forgotten about us. Quite the contrary, each heartbreak, disappoint, loss, and illness bestowed upon us is a gift God has given us to put us closer to our destiny. It is natural to feel a sense of fear and doubt, each prayer is a spiritual jour-ney, which will bring us closer to the answers that we are looking for and the challenges we need to grow. Embrace your challenges; use the power of prayer and the spiritual messages presented in your life as empowerment and fulfillment for the spirit of completeness.

- Do you pray?
- If so, to whom do you pray, meditate, or praise a higher power?
- Do you only call on God when you are troubled, or do you praise Him when things are going well?
- Do you blame God for a horrible life, or do you see it as a lesson you are forced to live through time and time again until the lesson is heeded?

- Do you look for the signs which are indications of your destination, or do you ignore them because of fear?
- Is your faith easily wavered, or has it increased over time?

It's time to take responsibility for your soul's well-being now. Let your spirit guide you through this and every journey in life.

III

Count the Ways

Love is or it ain't. Thin love ain't love at all.
—Toni Morrison

I will live this day as if it is my last.
This day is all I have and these hours are now my eternity. I
greet this sunrise with cries of joy as a prisoner who is
reprieved from death. I lift mine arms with thanks for this
priceless gift of a new day. So too, I will beat upon my heart
with gratitude as I consider all who greeted yesterday's sun-
rise who are no longer with the living today . . . Why have I
been allowed to live this extra day when others, far better
than I, have departed? . . . I will live this day as if it is my last.
And if it is not, I shall fall to my knees and give thanks.
—From Og Mandino, *The Greatest Salesman in the World,* pp. 74–77

How often do we love today as if it is our last? How often do we wake up thanking God for eyes that work and the very breath of life itself? How often do we say everything that needs to be said to everybody that needs to hear it? How often do we treasure every infinitesimal moment of the day—putting all of our heart and mind into actions that actually mean something in the whole scheme of things?

We never seem to be able to truly count our blessings until we lose them (or at least come close to losing them). Counting the ways means instead of listing everything that is wrong in your life, honoring and taking an inventory of everything that's *right.* It means, when confronted with a new challenge or so-called problem, *counting the ways* that it can work—why you *can* succeed. Instead of thinking yourself out of your blessing, when you approach life with the unconditional love that's the very basis of life, you realize that everything around you is for your good.

We Have What We Need

Counting the Ways that love is in our lives and celebrating them is how we bear witness to the fact that we always have just what we need. We are always looking for that special someone who will finally love us, but in the process, we overlook the love that is right under our noses. It's sad, but, women often associate the word "love" with the romantic stuff that we think dreams are made of. But there's more to love than roses, chocolates, money, and good sex. Sorry, ladies! This section of the book isn't about loving our mates, it's about loving ourselves. The men will have to wait.

Some of us never associate the love of self with the same importance we stress on the love of another. It's truly a simple concept: How can you love someone else if you don't love yourself? Ask yourself who is the most important person to you? If the answer isn't you, then we have a problem.

What Is Love Anyway?

When asked to define it, we all have very different interpretations of love. Some of us associate love with what we were raised to believe on television, and when it falls short of that—as it always does—we are lost and feel cheated. Some may utilize and or confuse love for lust, passion, and sexual desire. Some women love others until it hurts them mentally, physically, emotionally, and financially.

You have to know that love isn't just about sex, physical passion, or ultimately a union written on flammable paper. It's about a giving of yourself to *yourself* that can't be matched by a one-night stand or a dead-end relationship.

Black women are the group that society as a whole has always looked to to raise their children, provide them their fundamental needs, cook their food, provide their clothes, and do basically everything. We've done it throughout the ages and have never really been celebrated. We all know that we are the caretakers of the world, but whom do we go to when *we* need support?

We've always been a giving group of women, and we've been called upon more out of history's circumstances to do things that a lot of other women weren't forced to do. So, we felt like it was our duty not only to help bring black women together but to celebrate their many facets at the same time.

Unconditional love of others has been our motivation. We've sacrificed so much for others that we rarely sacrifice for ourselves. We need to take that unconditional love and lavish it on ourselves.

It's hard to break patterns that have been engraved in our psyches for hundreds of thousands of years. We must learn to take all the love we put out in the universe and give back to ourselves. We can't lie in wait for someone else to come along and give it to us. We've suffered in abusive relationships waiting for love. We've had babies we weren't ready for, knowing they would give us love. We've stayed in dead-end jobs because we think our bosses love us. It needs to stop! These women are about to let us know about the love they've found in their lives.

13

All in Due Time

Kimberly S. Varner

"What are you saying?" I said, with a hint of disbelief and hurt in my voice. "Nana, I think I know what you're saying and I don't like it! I LOVE MEN! I LOVE BLACK MEN!" That's what I remember telling my ninety-seven-year-old grandmother who, two years ago, insinuated that I was a lesbian because I hadn't dated in a few years. She said, "Do you like women? You're always going out with women. I don't like it. Where are the men?" I cannot tell you how absolutely shocked I was by what she was trying to say. Although she never came out and said the word "lesbian," her words were as clear as a bell.

Was it a crime not to date for a while? To take a break from unfulfilling and stagnant relationships? I refused to let my grandmother, whom I adore with all of my heart, or anyone else, force me into a relationship to ease THEIR fears of who or what they thought I was or what I should or should not have been doing in my life. Phew!

From June of 1994 to January of 1998, I had not been in any type of re-lationship; partly by circumstance and partly by choice. That's a long time for a sister in her midtwenties living five minutes from Washington, D.C. (aka "Chocolate City"). I went out on a few dates, but nothing panned out romantically. When I think about it now, I honestly didn't want any of them to develop further. Truthfully—I was tired, scared, and empty.

I was tired of being in the dating game and ending up in situations that turned out to be extremely unhealthy. Being a soft-hearted person at times, who's always tried to make everyone happy, I found myself in predicaments that often made me mad at myself and unable to look myself in the mirror. On and off for a number of years, I had a "thang" with a man who seemed to mesmerize me and who knew me better than I knew me. That's pretty sad. I finally ended it in tears when I realized that I loved him more than I loved myself. In another case, I found myself involved with an army man who was a functional alcoholic. After we dated for a few months and I was hooked, I found out by chance that he was married! Clearly unhealthy and drama-filled madness. Lord knows my parents didn't raise me to be like this!

I was scared after quickly reading every single word of every E. Lynn Harris novel from cover to cover, realizing that there were a lot of brothas out here going across the net. As if in a game of tennis, from woman to man to woman to man, on occasion lying to their partner and passing on the HIV virus. Fault! I prayed, "Lord, *pleeeeze* don't send one of those brothas my way." I know sisters who found out their husbands were leading double lives and were certainly not who they appeared to be. I felt devastated and betrayed for these women.

After a couple of months of being by myself, I kind of got used to it. I realized that things would happen for me in due time. My motto was just be patient and live my life. I hung out with my coworkers, the GNO (Girl's Night Out) crew, my dear Sorors of Alpha Kappa Alpha, and when I went home to the Bronx, my high school crew. It wasn't that bad being single. Really it wasn't! Well, sometimes it was, but that was no reason to jump into another fire without looking.

My friends from college were marrying off quickly and felt the need to ask me what in the world was I waiting for. Others asked what was wrong with me. "Nothing!" I would say. "I'm just chilling for now." I wasn't in a frenzy to get married, because I saw some of the drama my married friends were going through. I am not a *Drama Mama*, so I intended to take my time and get myself together. I decided the first step toward pulling myself together would be to get myself together spiritually.

I always believed in God and went to church while growing up, but I finally decided to really develop a personal relationship with God. After living in Maryland since 1990, I finally found a church that I loved in 1996. I joined Dayspring Community Church in Greenbelt, Maryland, which is Bible-based, spirit-filled, and just keeps it real! I converted from Catholic to Baptist and felt myself absorbing all that I could about the Lord. After a few months, I didn't have that empty unhappy feeling anymore. I learned the importance of reading the Bible, praying in faith, fellowshipping with other believers, and witnessing to those who didn't know God. I began to understand that once I built up my relationship with Him, everything else would fall into place—love life, career, finances, everything.

My friends Don and Foluke told me about a book for single Christian women called *Knight in Shining Armor*, by P.B. (Bunny) Wilson. From the sound of the title, I wasn't too excited about hearing about a fairy tale concept, but I decided to read it anyway. It turned out to be a great book! This sister breaks stuff D-O-W-N about putting Christ at the absolute top of your list of priorities. This means allowing Him to lead you in all areas of your life, including leading you toward finding the right mate—a mate who also believes in and serves the Lord. The book also suggests a six-month spiritual reconstruction, in which you don't date anyone, you remain prayerful in Christ, keep a journal, complete the assignments in the book, and read some other suggested readings. It's a major commitment, but it's worth it.

I read the book two times before I decided to do the six-month plan. I wasn't dating anyone, so it wouldn't be difficult, right? Wrong? I signed my contract in the book on July 4, 1997, but on the very next day, at my line sister's wedding, I met a man who made me think twice about that contract. He was nice, mannerable, athletic (I saw him the day before playing basketball!), and absolutely handsome in his tuxedo. "Lord, why are You doing this to me?" is all I could say to myself as we exchanged numbers.

We called each other off and on for a month and I still had not told him about my six-month commitment. I really liked him! My prayer partner Raina, who had already gone through her six months, told me not to delay any further. I kept on saying, "He's going to think that I've lost my mind!" What if he just says, "Thanks, but no thanks?" Well, I realized that if he couldn't handle it, then we wouldn't go any further than a friendship.

When I called him, I found myself babbling. "Uh Ron-I-uh-I'm doing this thing right-and-uh—it's a spiritual reconstruction—and-uh-I can't date for six months." Silence is all I heard, not a peep. I finally asked him did he think I was crazy. He said, "No. I've never heard of this before, but if this is what I need to do to be with you, I'll wait."

"Really?" is all I remember saying with the largest smile on my face. "Are you sure, because that means that I won't see you until January?"

"Yep, I'll wait," he said. "But can I still talk to you on the phone?" I told him, "Yes," knowing this probably wasn't what P.B. had in mind, but I didn't think one or two calls weekly would hurt.

Ron came to town in September with his cousin and my line sister for a Hampton-Howard football game. Before he came, he actually asked me if he could come to the event first. How considerate. He truly respected me and what I was trying to achieve. I said, "Why not? I can't stop you from coming to a paid event." It was great seeing and spending a few hours with the man that I loved speaking to so often.

When January rolled around, I felt good. I had not only reconstructed my relationship with God and reconstructed the Kim who had gone down the drain, but I was now going to see the man that I knew God had sent into my life.

Almost three years have past since Ron and I met and we are still together—trying to remain grounded in the word and be obedient to Christ.

Our friendship has flourished and our hearts joined by God's own hand. Our biggest challenge is remaining celibate, which is difficult, but it's a challenge worth facing.

As for Nana, she's just as happy as she can be since I have Ron in my life. Now, she wants to know if I can give her some great-grandchildren before she dies. I told her, "If you can hold on until you're 100 or 102, I might be able to help you out."

Kimberly S. Varner is a technical writer and trainer for an IT company in the Washington, DC area and a staff writer for *Sister2Sister* magazine.

14

Let Love Abound

Reverend Patricia Webster

I am one of the most blessed among all black women. As mother of five children, I am most grateful to my parents for the upbringing and training that I received. In our society today, it is almost a rarity that children are raised with both parents.

In our home, small in size yet big in love, there were ten children. Our parents taught us the importance and value of loving each other as they demonstrated their love, first to God, then to each other, third to us, and finally to our neighbors.

To me, First Corinthians 13 is one of the most beautiful chapters in the Bible. It is also one of the most famous in world literature. Here you read about the greatest of all realities. What is the greatest reality? Love! For me, the "God" kind of love—an unselfish and beautiful love which I experienced through my parents as I grew up.

I didn't know what it was really like to lack food and clothing. I didn't know the sacrifices our parents made so that I, as a child, could be happy. I never realized until I was older that my father would put cardboard in his shoes so that I could wear "Buster Brown's." They were popular in my day. I had no idea that my mother had only one good dress that she would wear to church and have to wash and wear again each week, yet I never heard either of them complain.

I now know that when you love truly, it is unselfish. I found out that, then, there is no end in what you will do for someone else. My parents not only demonstrated this love to their children, but also to everyone else. Love is the greatest gift in the world. My parents instilled in us that God is love, and His love must flow from Him to us to others.

By the time I became a teenager, I had the love of God deep inside of me. This immeasurable love was now placed in a young girl who, at times, would give her last dollar to someone in need.

My parents left us a legacy that will never be forgotten, and I pray that my children will, through the love of my husband and me, continue to have the love of God demonstrated throughout their lives and their children's.

Sometimes we may think: Where is the love that should be spread throughout the world? It seems as though things should be getting better. The Bible is very clear to us when it speaks to us about love. Luke 10:27 says, "Thou shalt love the Lord thy God with all thy heart, and with all thy strength and with all thy mind; and thy neighbor as thyself."

If we think about how we *should* love God, it should be with all of our powers—a sincere, fervent, intelligent, and energetic love. Then He tells us to love one another as He has loved us. There is nothing, absolutely nothing, that is more important than learning how to love, first God, and then one another. Often, we think that we automatically love, but we must teach our children to love God and their neighbor. This love must extend beyond our blood brothers and beyond our Christian friends, to all people.

Real love requires concentration and effort. It means helping others become better people. It demands our time, often our money, and most importantly, our energy.

God's love for us is complete, and He wants us to love as He loves us: unconditionally. Love never fails. Nothing works without it, and there can be no failure with it. When we live by love, we cannot fail.

If we could fully comprehend or understand the great return from living God's love, we would probably be competing with each other, each of us trying to love the other more.

If we build our families on love, we can win back those who have strayed. We can win them back to Jesus with the "love of God." If we begin to build our businesses in love, we will prosper beyond our wildest dreams.

When love rules, prosperity can flow and friendships will grow. We are "love creatures." God made us out of love. Jesus died and rose again out of love and He sent His spirit to live in us to teach us how to love as He loves. Love is absolutely essential for each of us. Let's teach our children and let us show our neighbors how to LOVE God first, and then everyone we meet. LET LOVE ABOUND—it's the greatest gift of all times!

Reverend Patricia Webster is senior pastor of the Shiloh Pentecostal Church, Inc. "Christian Love Center," 139 Davenport Street, Pastors Brown-Harley Blvd., in Somerville, NJ 08876. She is married to Sidney J. Webster and has five children and five grandchildren. Pastor Pat, as she is called, is a life-long resident of Somerville, New Jersey.

15

I'm Just Mary

Mary J. Blige

I can't pinpoint what it was that made me decide that I'd had enough of what was happening in my life. I remember reviewing some photos and seeing myself looking pretty bad. That may have been the beginning, but who really knows?

At the time I didn't understand that I was about to embark on a spiritual journey. I just knew that I didn't like some of the things that were happening in my life, and most of all some of the people involved. I had the support of my mother, Cora, my sister, LaTonya, who was like a second mom to me, and most of all, God. But at the time I felt like no one person could protect me from the pain I had inside. This journey I had to take on my own and I was really, really scared.

I grew up in Schlobohm, a low-income housing project located in Yonkers, New York. My mom raised me along with my two siblings. My dad left for a while when I was younger, but later returned. Most people are familiar with how my career began. First, I made a tape recording Karaoke-style at one of those booths in the malls. The tape was passed along to my friends and family. Finally it landed in Andre Harrell's office at Uptown Records and he signed me to a deal.

I really had no intentions on being a singer, I just enjoyed doing it. I sang in the junior choir at church and sang all around the house sometimes waking up my family. But I never felt that I would actually become a singer. It all happened so quickly. At seventeen, I was just beginning to understand who I was and what I was supposed to be. I went from being an "around-the-way girl" who was battling with low self-esteem to the title folks bestowed on me as the "Queen of Hip-Hop Soul." How did I become the Queen of Hip-Hop Soul after one album?

I didn't know how to act, what to say, or what was expected of me. That was a big mistake, because if you don't know what you want in the music business, there are a hundred people who will make it up for you. My opinion was *out* and the opinions of the agents, publicist, managers, and record label executives were *in*. I had to hire everyone to do everything for me. Or so I was told. I even hired a couple of fashion stylists and I still ended up on *People* magazine's worst-dressed list! Did that make any sense?

Listening to these people didn't work, so I did what most teenagers do, I retreated and rebelled. It seemed glamorous but deep inside I was hurting. I would be so hard on myself. I didn't understand why people loved it so much when I released my first and second album—it just came naturally to me. When I would look into the audience and see women singing along to my songs and crying, I'd wonder, "Does my music touch them that much?" People I would encounter would tell me that this was my calling, my purpose, my destiny. But I wasn't sure if it really was.

On stage I felt naked, unprepared, and definitely unaccustomed to the scrutiny and criticism I was getting. It came from all over. This was no walk in the park—being a performer meant I had to "perform" twenty-four hours a day. There were the photo and video shoots, radio promotions, public appearances, and tours around the world with chart-topping acts like Boys II Men, Bobby Brown, TLC, and Jodeci.

There was a lot of miscommunication in my camp. I was selling millions of albums and still certain things weren't getting done. So I was blamed for the lack of organization. I was in chaos and I literally felt I was falling apart. My temper was uncontrollable at times and I would curse people out if they upset me, especially the reporters. I would be interviewed and some of the reporters would walk away saying I had a bad attitude. I was just straight up with them. They would ask some of the dumbest questions and I would give them dumb answers. To some reporters I even had to say, "Get out of my face." I would hide my face with a hat and wear sunglasses at all times—it didn't matter if I was inside or out. Some of my fans would start picking up on this as a fashion statement. But in reality I was putting up a shield. I wanted to hide myself because I was self-conscious, scared . . . even timid. But what people got out of it was that I was being distant and difficult. So many people asking questions about my personal life really got to me. Put yourself in my shoes for a minute. Just because your job is public, would you want your personal life to be public as well? How would you like to read about your personal life in the newspapers every week? Believe me, you don't, and it was not easy on me.

My friends started changing. Or maybe it was me. I was so eager to please them because I needed people who would love me just for me. But I started trusting people less and less. I had to survive in a world where my opinion did not matter. Someone always knew better and I was constantly criticized. Things started shutting down for me, not professionally but personally.

Just like most black women, I made the mistake of believing that a man should and would complete me. I craved a loving and supportive relationship with a man, but the partners I chose were going through their own internal battles. Some tried to utilize me as a stepping-stone. Now that I think about it, they really didn't have the patience to supply me with the love and support I needed then. Some of them were simply concerned with just themselves.

I didn't like myself and I sure didn't care what happened. I could not understand why people in entertainment were so cruel to each other. I found myself doing things to fit in and understand the business. I would do things and not care about the consequences. I drank and took lots of hard drugs just to dull the pain. It was rough; I would drink myself to sleep or frequent all-night parties, hoping they would comfort me and make it all right that I missed a performance or interview. I had not even finished high school, so whenever someone would say something I didn't understand, I would feel stupid.

My finances were a mess. I let people and circumstances come in the way of my financial success. I wasn't on top of things, and because of my unpredictability, I wasn't making as much money as I could have. Missing appointments, interviews, and performances was finally hurting my bottom line. I began to realize that it was myself I was hurting and not everybody else. I would spend recklessly on clothes, shoes, jewelry, and whatever caught my attention. Those things gave me another type of high. I didn't slow myself down enough to look at the business side of things. The old Mary just wanted to party and have a good time.

I was caught up and I had to get out. I gave away my power and I had to regain it back. Where do I go and how do I rescue me from me? God has always been a part of my life, but when you are caught up, you can't hear or see Him. I dropped to my knees and started reading the Bible. It became my inspiration, my words of wisdom, and my teacher. As I relearned how to incorporate God into my life, I realized I had forgotten how to even talk to Him. But once I started talking to Him, I couldn't stop. I forgave myself for not caring about Mary. During this time I learned to accept who I was—the shy, funny, sensitive, loving, and sometimes irrational Mary.

It wasn't easy at first and sometimes I would cry myself to sleep. I was so hurt by the pain of certain relationships. Eliminating bad relationships from your life can be difficult because you become dependent on a bad situation and you use it as a crutch—an excuse for not living up to your potential. I realized that I might love someone who is not good for me. There were days when I was so depressed, I just wanted to crawl and hide somewhere. I was looking for a comfort zone and at times my family provided it. With their help I started tapping into the energies around me—writing music and taking examples from situations around me.

I tried to hide behind my music but I couldn't. I had to be accountable for a lot of things. People and fans wanted so much from me but I felt like I had no more of me left to give. My family showed me that I had other roles to play besides being a singer, performer, and lyricist. I am a sister, friend, aunt, daughter, and most of all a child of God. What I did for a living did not define who Mary was. I learned that I was the one who had to set the definition and parameters of my life. I was crossing the line and it was taking a toll on me physically and mentally.

Was I living up to my full potential? Was I creating a positive situation for myself? God created my gift to sing but I created the chaos in my life. I had to take responsibility for it, name it, and claim it. It was a heavy burden, but I had to decide who was going to survive: the self-destructive Mary, or the Mary I knew that was waiting to blossom. The only person who could change anything and put my life on track was Mary.

Things were happening to me, because I was permitting them to happen. Finding peace within myself allowed me to choose the reactions I gave to things, enabling me to control the situation. Even my responses to reporters have changed. They are just as nervous as I am and they may ask a stupid question, but they have a job to do. If I feel that I am being disrespected, I just calmly say so. You can't even imagine how many people appreciate it when you let them know they have crossed the line. I walked away from the drugs and alcohol and started surrounding myself with people who really cared about me. Most people don't give a damn about you and your problems. All they see is the money and the perception of fame. It's natural—we are trained to worship things perceived as unattainable. Some of these people didn't care about themselves, so what made me think they cared about me? They were attracted to what "Mary" does for a living and some of the men were jealous of my job. Realizing all this took a lot of weight off my shoulders. I hadn't even realized how much energy I was giving these folks.

I came from the ghetto but I had to learn to leave it behind when it was time for me to work. Now I am much more focused on the business side of things. You don't need a degree to manage your finances, just a basic knowledge and the power and ability to ask questions—lots of them. I took back the power I had given away. It was my business to decide on how I should dress and wear my hair. What I also realized is that insecurity, self-doubt, and not loving yourself are adversaries that everyone fights on a daily basis. We all just handle the battle differently. My fight was public and so was my recovery.

I also began to understand what my purpose is in life. We each have a purpose and some people go their whole lives without finding theirs. My purpose is to bring people's emotions to the top through my music. We all spend too much time tucking away the feelings and the hurt and pain. Through my music I give people the opportunity to see through my eyes, feel through my music, and experience the spectrum of their own emotions. My music makes people happy or sad, laugh or cry, pray or celebrate.

In reflection I've realized that in this business sometimes your critics' opinions become public opinion. I internalized their opinions and started believing what they were saying. But the new Mary has a renewed faith in God and is still struggling to love herself and working on her education. The new Mary is planning one day to own a home filled with children and a dog. The new Mary is also hoping to have a man by her side who respects her for who she is and who she will become. The new Mary looks back and asks herself, "Would I do it all over again?" Her answer: "I wouldn't change one single thing."

Mary J. Blige crowned the Queen of Hip-Hop Soul by her peers has changed the face of music since her chart topping album "What's the 411" just six years ago. Since then Mary has added actress and spokes model to her list of accomplishments. Still in the process of healing Mary looks forward to still more spiritual growth.

16

Love's Story

Gloria Bromell-Tinubu, Ph.D.

Three summers ago, I decided that I would not continue to live a half existence; that the suffering had to stop; and that the wounds needed to be healed. I decided that it was time for me to soar. The real me. Not the wife, the mom, the professor, or the public servant. It was time for me, the spiritual being, the mature woman, the lover, the giver, the doer, the thinker, and more, to blossom. It was time for transformation . . . time for coming into the knowledge of love's story.

So I embarked upon the journey of healing, learning, and becoming. A journey which resulted in multiple crescendos. It began with a period of fasting and praying, which happened to last forty days. It peaked when I came into a full knowledge of what it means to love oneself, to love unconditionally, and to be loved. It's a kind of knowledge and knowing that occurs at the subatomic level of existence. A kind of knowing that transcends time and space.

For far too many of us, we trap ourselves in beliefs, relationships, and situations that, as Roberta sings, kill us softly and deny us the opportunity to experience unconditional love of self and others. They quietly rob us, almost microscopically, until we are a lattice-like shadow of our True Selves. We wonder why we feel so incomplete. We wonder why the loneliness feels inescapable. We've lost bits and pieces of ourselves and we can't quite figure out exactly when or how it happened. But sure enough, it happened. We find ourselves withered, undernourished, and underdeveloped.

So, we must begin the task of transformation, of becoming. The transformation occurs as we examine and change our beliefs about our True Selves and our love relationships. So, I share with you my understanding of love's story by telling the story of our belief systems, our True Selves, and our love relationships. Love's story is a rite of passage, and as I see it, a requirement for the quantum leap in our level of awareness, that is, our transformation.

Our Belief System

Our belief system (which is culturally determined) is the total of all we believe about life, ourselves, and our relationship to the universe. It is not the "truth" of what we are. If it were, it would remain constant and would be the same for everyone. It is what we've created and come to believe is true about us. Because we created it, we tend to defend it at all costs. Most of our dissatisfaction in life comes from the difference between what is true and what we believe to be true.

These deep-seated beliefs are held in our subconscious and are responsible for our life experiences. Everything that *seems* to happen is simply a mirror image or reflection of what's going on in our subconscious. Our life is governed by what *is* true. However, our experience of life is governed by what we *believe* to be true.

A few deeply rooted beliefs tend to serve as a guide or even control our lives and love relationships: (1) There is something inherently wrong with us, which allows us to accept abusive treatment from others and ourselves (known as the guilt complex); (2) we are a physical body; (3) because we think we are a body, we appear to be separate; therefore we think that all our good comes from a power which is outside and separate from us; and (4) because we believe we are a body, it has certain needs; therefore, we are not whole or complete.

If you are wondering whether or not these deep-seated beliefs are at the core of your belief system, just take a look at how you experience life. Not what happens to you, but how you experience it.

Even when we hold these deep-seated beliefs, all is not lost. The good news is, while we may never transcend our belief systems, we can transform them. We can begin the transformation with "love's story." Love's story is: you are Love (Innocence), Spirit, One, and Whole.

Our True Selves

We are Love (Innocence). We are Spirit. We are One. We are Whole. We are complete spiritual beings "having a human experience." Spirit is free, giving, forgiving, loving, and does not possess. Spirit is the essence of our reality. It is truth. It simply employs our bodies and minds to express itself. Therefore, our minds and bodies must be in harmony with Spirit as recognized by the ancient Kemetic value system, MAAT, and the foundation of MAAT is love.

Furthermore, we can't get love from "out there" because love is who we are. And love's nature is giving. As you give love, it increases. It is only by expressing or giving love, which is what we really are, that we come to a greater awareness of who we really are. High self-esteem comes only from a greater awareness of our True Selves.

With our subconscious *mind* yelling and screaming and holding on to our deep-seated beliefs, how can we express and experience our True Selves? It is through guidance from our inner vision, our Spirit. Being guided by the Spirit is *right-mind*edness. It is righteous thinking. Our Spirit knows our reality is love and that we are whole. It is the voice of love; therefore, it tells love's story.

Guidance from the Spirit is transformational: it operates lovingly, gently, harmoniously, peacefully, and instantaneously. However, the Spirit is not obtrusive; it must be invited to offer guidance to our True Selves. So how do we invite the Spirit? We start with purpose. We affirm our daily purpose, which is a greater awareness of Love/Self. Then, we ask: "Spirit, what would you have me see differently today?" Hence, you begin the process of displacing *wrong-mind*edness with *right-mind*edness. Then, we must let our purpose guide our choices and relationships.

Our Love Relationships

Successful love relationships are founded on right-mindedness, while unsuccessful ones are founded on wrong-mindedness. The former seeks to "give," while the latter seeks to "give to get." The story of wrong-minded love relationships (known as "romantic" love) goes like this: "I'm in love with your ability to keep me feeling good about myself. I've got a guilt complex and a physical body with all these needs. I can't handle it by myself because I'm incomplete. I need you to make me whole. So, you are responsible for my happiness and I depend upon you for it. So if I'm not happy, it must be your fault." Sound familiar?

But love's story, which is founded on right-mindedness and transformed relationships, goes like this: "I am Love. I am Spirit. I am Connected. I am Whole. I know who I am, and I love who I am. I feel good about myself. My happiness depends on me. The purpose of my relationship is to share my wholeness and support my individual purpose of greater awareness of Love/Self. My partner and I are committed to ourselves, to one another, and to the relationship."

Most people have untransformed relationships that are based on possessiveness, guilt, domination, and control. Because of its predominance, we accept it as a natural way of life. It's important to note, however, that a transformed relationship cannot come from persons who have not been transformed as individuals. As complete, actualized, and transformed individuals, we have no limit to the amount of wholeness we can "give" to a relationship. On the other hand, the amount of wholeness you can "get" from a relationship is very limited. As we begin to examine our love relationships, we will see what the relationships tell us about what we think and believe about ourselves.

As we strive to give wholeness to a relationship, there are bound to be some behaviors on the part of our partners that are acceptable and some that are not. We must think, feel, and express gratitude for the things that we like or admire and forgiveness for the things we dislike. We ask Spirit, our inner vision, to help us see it differently, which is the first step in the process of forgiveness.

When making a decision about ending a love relationship, ask yourself: Is this relationship nurturing to me? Am I alive in it or am I dying softly? The decision to end a love relationship because, by doing so, it allows you to experience your purpose, which is a greater awareness of Love/Self, is rightminded. Considerations such as the need for approval and the fear of "hurting" others need not cloud your thinking.

We all share the need to feel loved, understood, and appreciated. However, we must first love, understand, and appreciate ourselves. Our "True Selves" are created in the image of the "True Spirit." As Spirit, we are Love (Innocence), we are One, we are Whole. This is the essence or truth of our reality. Therefore, love relationships are places where we express and experience the love that we are. This is love's story.

But there are other stories that are imbedded in our subconscious mind and are a part of our belief system. These stories influence how we think of ourselves and others and, therefore, determine our expressions and experiences in love relationships. They are stories of guilt, definition of True Self as body, separateness, and incompleteness.

We have the power to transform our faulty or wrong-minded belief systems. In doing so, we are transformed and so are our love relationships. The choice and responsibility are ours and no one else's. We all have images of our "ideal" partner. The question becomes: "Are we the kind of person they would be attracted to?" We must be the "ideal" partner before we can *find* the ideal partner in someone else.

We are the only ones who can transform ourselves, and it begins with the knowledge and acceptance of who we are. It is entirely up to us. No one else is coming along to save us. We choose. Peace be with you.

Gloria Bromell-Tinubu, Ph.D. is an associate professor of economics at Spelman College, Atlanta. A former member of the Atlanta City Council and candidate for mayor, she is married and the mother of four children.

17

To a Son of a Dear Friend

Jean Cooper Buchanan

During much of your life you witnessed a unique relationship between your mother and me. You probably wondered first why we spent so much time retelling stories of our growing up. After all, since it was a mutual experience we were re-creating, why couldn't we just leave it up to our individual memories of the occasion? No, my dear, that would assign a trivial meaning to our shared remembrances. Making them as inconsequential as the weather or traffic conditions of a particular day. For your mother and I, the act of sharing *was* what was of significance here.

What you were observing as you grew up to be the wonderful young adult you are today was true friendship. It is still a mystery to me how two people can share the same experiences and *not* have the bonds of friendship emerge. Every day I am so grateful for the blessing of friendship.

Perhaps it is common personality traits that caused us to become friends. Ours was not the usual adolescent friendship which was socially supportive. On the contrary, both of us were adamantly individualistic. And this very independent trait then made neither of us the servant of peer approval.

Our friendship began in junior high school. We were in the same homeroom class from seventh grade through our graduation from high school. We were also members of the same Girl Scout troop for those same years. Thus we had plenty of contact during our adolescent years.

I found your mother to be a very easy friend to have. Beyond her individuality, what I really admired about her was her ability to have views without being judgmental. As a teenager, I wondered why so much time was wasted talking about other people's behavior or appearance—especially when the time spent would not result in changing either. I guess we both understood—even at that early age—that LIFE is an individual journey. It is shaped by observers and critics only if you believe that they possess more understanding of you than you have of yourself.

As a member of the Scout troop, your mom was one of the most skilled campers, but always one of the volunteers for anything that had to be done. She didn't brag about her accomplishments as others did, but quietly moved on to improve her own skills. All in all, one of the most important things I learned from her was how to be a quiet leader.

My best friend also taught me one of the most important outgrowths of quiet leadership: If you are a good and dependable follower, you will almost certainly be asked to serve in some role of leadership. As an adolescent I often wondered why some people would fight, sometimes viciously, to become the head of some organization. She demonstrated throughout her life that a job well done was its own reward.

Your mother taught me the value of positive competitiveness. She was self-assured but not jealous or competitive toward others. Long before the current expression "personal best" was in the daily vernacular, we were practicing it. Think how much valuable time we were able to save in order to spend time with each other!

So many memories. Your mother as one of my bridesmaids. Your mother as my mirror. Even your mother as my "football buddy." She went to Ohio State and I went to Michigan—two of the biggest rivals in all of college football. One year the annual game was played in Ann Arbor and we went together. I've always thought of that day as symbolic. The whole world cared so much who won the game, but we could have cared less. All we wanted to do was to be together. That was a bigger victory than any football team could ever win.

After college we both left our native Louisville, Kentucky. I settled in New York City and she went to Philadelphia. After she met and married your father, we remained in touch with each other. Our visits were usually quiet weekends at home. Again the main feature of these weekends was the chance to spend time together. You and your father were often the captive audience for our "war stories," as we came to call them. We shared newspaper articles with each other and talked about everything under the sun. And of course, no visit was complete without a knock-down-drag-out game of Scrabble!

After you had grown up, you asked me why every time I came to Philadelphia to visit your family, I "never wanted to do anything but sit around." I guess you have figured out by now that simply being with my dear friend, your mother, was the single solitary purpose of the visit.

I guess we were all so happy and comfortable that we couldn't imagine anything tragic happening to such a good and vibrant person. Unfortunately, this wonderful friend, and anchor in my life and yours, left us too early. Far too early.

The only way I was able to cope with the pain of losing your mother was to be thankful for having been being blessed with the experience of being her friend in the first place. I am still amazed at all the wonderful experiences we shared as we grew from one phase of our lives to the next.

Whenever I think of her, I hope in some way I contributed to her happiness as she did to mine. Words—even superlatives—are inadequate to describe how I felt and still feel about her.

There is a song, though, that always reminds me how much she meant to me:

> *Did you ever know that you're my hero?*
> *I can fly higher than an eagle,*
> *You are the wind beneath my wings.*

Jean Cooper Buchanan is a retired teacher of music from the High School of Music and Art in New York City. A native of Louisville, Kentucky, she currently resides in Queens, New York.

18

Friendship

Kia N. Skrine

Loving you is a work in progress. We've been so close and experienced so much, yet I've discovered that a majority of the time that I've known you has been spent in torment, grief, frustration, and pain. This roller coaster of a friendship—this lifestyle of risking devastation for the hope of a thrill with you—has been intoxicating. But I don't blame you. My loneliness and depression were not your fault. My feelings of inadequacy were not my gift from you. The fact that I hid behind the masks of comedy and tragedy while my own countenance was fallen, while my spirit grieved and while my soul wore mourning clothes, was not by your design. What I can attribute to you, however, is provoking me to change—for provoking me to such a point of self-examination that I had to remove you from the formula that would ultimately yield my happiness.

My focus was all wrong. My joy, my peace, my everything centered around you. I had no other close friends at the time, and I was so off by thinking that having you as my "best friend" was enough. This essay, this letter to my sisters, is not meant to offend you. Actually, it has nothing to do with you at all. I've got to share how my insecurities, how my fears produced within me jealousy, bitterness, rage, suicidal thoughts, controlling behavior, and desperation. I've got to share it—with or without your consent. It's all part of the process in loving you and all of the friends to come.

I describe my time in this particular friendship as a roller coaster. I was allowing myself to be yanked from turn to turn, whipped around unexpected corners and miscalculated ups and downs. I was going through loop after loop, holding on for dear life because I was afraid that the harness that held our "friendship" together would break, and the friendship that I hoped for would cease to exist. I was a willing passenger on the ride of my life. Why? Because although I liked things about me—i.e., my ambition, my focus, my drive—I had not yet discovered what loving me was all about.

To give you a little information about me: I am passionate about maximizing the gifts and talents within me. I am fervent about pursuing what brings me joy in life, and I do it without apology or explanation to those who disapprove or fail to believe that it's possible. Over and over again throughout my life, God has used this ideology that I've embraced to move me closer to the woman that He's created me to be. It's interesting that "love" would temporarily get in the way of this.

The friendship started off pretty cool. We had our disagreements, but we were able to seemingly resolve them and move on. We were so much alike. We shared the same interests and had taken similar paths in getting to the point of our meeting. Because we clicked so well, we vowed to have each other's back no matter what. Having my friend's back to me meant giving of what I had, refusing to violate our friendship in ways in which I had in ones prior, as well as being supportive and encouraging. Being my friend's friend meant that I felt safe—trusting that I could reveal the mystery of who I was without chastisement or rejection. I made myself vulnerable. But I also confused that vulnerability with being a weaker vessel.

A few months into our friendship, I created a breach—I was not completely honest about an incident, and it took several conversations for the entire truth to come out. I was afraid of losing my friend. I felt awful and knew I was wrong. The worst part of it all is that the lie was more devastating to the friendship than the actual incident. I apologized to my friend, repented before God, and forgave myself for being so fearful and stupid—I thought so anyway. But my friend lost trust in me and I spent the next two years trying to prove that I was trustworthy. I allowed the guilt of my deceit to alter my own sense of self-worth. I allowed the way my friend dealt with the hurt of what I'd done to affect my self-image. My friend couldn't trust me, and reminded me often. It seemed that whenever we'd have a disagreement about pretty much anything, I'd get that reminder of how ending our friendship was an ongoing consideration. My friend was being honest, which I truly appreciated. However, the threat of losing the bond we shared continued to linger over my head. Nevertheless, we agreed that we were going to continue in our friendship, and try to move on from this situation.

I began walking on eggshells—wanting to do and say everything right, trying to restore the breach in our covenant. This, I perceived, was the best friend I had ever had and I didn't want the friendship to dissolve. My focus was on pleasing my friend and I neglected the still, small voice that told me to take a step back and begin again. Instead, I allowed my mood to be regulated by whether or not things were going well between us, and I gave value to my own self-worth by what my friend thought of my character. As time progressed, I not only deferred my will, I embraced false notions of myself as a result of my friend's distorted perceptions of me. I despised who I was becoming.

Obviously, the dynamic of our friendship changed. I was insecure about where I stood in our friendship. "Was I your best friend as you were mine?" I thought. "Was I the only one unveiling my soul and inner thoughts?" I felt like I was suspended in air and became afraid of hitting rock bottom without the safety of a net. I feared rejection, being friendless, and the threat of other people being more acceptable than me. So I did everything in my power to keep my friend needing me. That way, I rationalized, our friendship would have to continue. I gave out of what I had and what I didn't. Oftentimes, I'd become resentful once my supply was dried up. My giving was perverted because it became a control mechanism. I also tried to monopolize all of my friend's free time so that no one else could enter the picture. I'd rearrange and plan my schedule around my friend's activities so that I would be available to make my presence known among any new people that came into the equation. I was mean, disapproving, and offensive. As sickening as it is to remember, I have to admit how desperate I had become.

The time finally came when enough was enough. Our friendship ended and I went through a serious depression. Thoughts of suicide and other destructive behavior vacillated within the fibers of my mind. All the while, I was praying—asking God to remove the yoke that was suffocating the life out of me. I know scripture—not just by head knowledge, but by revelation. I knew that what I was experiencing in this friendship was not God's best for me. But I didn't realize that my opposition to letting go of this toxic friendship hindered God's movement in the situation. Because I was not looking at myself through the eyes of God's grace and mercy, I basked in condemnation and guilt, and became motivated by "friend-pleasing."

I continued to pray and work through the pain and devastation of the broken person I saw in the mirror. I didn't understand how I could descend into a pit of hating who I had become, while knowing the potential of who I could be. That was so frustrating. My hope and trust in God are what glued the pieces of my brokenness back together. I returned to my "first love"—Him—and I learned to love me.

As a result of this experience, I've taken a lot of inventory of the unfruitful weeds that have spoiled the vine of my self-image and pruned them one by one. It's been a journey of trimming the fat that has covered the beauty of who I am within. I've had to remove the distorted glasses that caused my eyes to process inaccurate illusions of me. I've had to realize that whatever someone else says about me is either confirmation or inaccurate—it neither defines nor diminishes the masterpiece that God has created of me. I understand that I am not perfect, and that everyone isn't going to accept me or view me as I truly am. However, I can't stop walking in forgiveness and repentance when I or anyone else falls short. I can't stop growing and abiding in God's grace for the sake of pleasing someone else. When I walk in that kind of commitment to me, I can walk in a true commitment with my friends. I can love, celebrate, support, and be encouraging knowing that my arsenal is full with that same love, celebration, support, and encouragement for myself.

Again, my love for my friend is a work in progress. Our communication lines have recently reopened. As I continue on this path of self-acceptance and love, we've got to become reacquainted. This time, I'm using new eyes of understanding. As I get a more expanded vision of myself, I am able to see others more clearly. I'm also more at peace with me and what I have to offer to my friends.

Kia N. Skrine is an actress who has been seen on film, on television, and in theaters throughout the United States. She has written a variety of material ranging from articles to scripts—all of which have been published and produced for the stage, print, and broadcast media. Ms. Skrine currently resides in Los Angeles.

Your Soul's Sustenance

Love Ye One Another

There are so many people less fortunate than us. When we count the ways that we are blessed, we wake up in the morning saying:

But for the grace of God there go I. . . .

Then and only then will we realize that the fullness of the blessings and love is in our lives and be able to truly honor them.

Celebrate Good Love. Come on! Let's celebrate good love! Now that we've seen how we count the ways that love appears in our lives, let's celebrate. Celebrating good love has to do with making a conscious effort to give back the love we receive. Surround yourself with positive people and like minded sisters. Fellow contributor Chrisena Coleman, author of *Just Between Girlfriends,* is a good example of a woman who celebrates love of her fellow sisters. Each year during Columbus Day weekend she invites women from all across the country to gather for a sisters' weekend without the husband and kids. Everyone comes back rejuvenated and refreshed. Start your own sisters' day, weekend, or retreat.

We have learned to take those moments and pass them on to others. It's like a huge chain letter. You do loving things for people knowing that the chain will continue. It really does take just one person to start and that person is you!

Your Personal Book of Revelations

Love comes in many different ways. Here are some questions to help you ponder the ways in which you receive and give love in your life.

- Have you experienced love in the true sense of the word?
- What is love to you?
- Do you have love in your life?
- Describe the loving relationships that you have in your life.
- Do you crave love?
- Do you have a supportive network of friends and family?
- Are you a loving person?
- What can you do to improve receiving and giving love?

Remember that love is the glue that keeps us together.

IV

All in the Family

In search of my mother's garden, I found my own.
—Alice Walker

Did your parents ever tell you that you were beautiful? Were you ever told that you were smart and unstoppable? Did they listen to your stories and foster your dreams? If you did not have your father in the picture, did you ever feel that your mother chose her boyfriend or stepfather over you? What was your relationship with your mother like? Did your parents turn a blind eye to things happening in your own home? Were your parents supportive of your education?

Some of you may find these questions odd, but in the average black family there is a breakdown. You may not have experienced this breakdown personally, or admit it happened to you, but we're sure you have witnessed it firsthand. Whether it was with an elementary school classmate who had emotional problems when you were a child or a coworker in your life today struggling to raise her own children alone. Our black families are in crisis. We've been degraded and dehumanized for hundreds of years and we are still suffering from the effects. We'd like to share a story of family with you before you begin reading this section so we can all try to better understand the bond of family.

The family is the foundation of any individual, the core of our being. It's where our first memories are made as well as where our loving relationships are developed. We learn our communication skills and survival techniques in the context of our family. Our first lessons in life come from the successes and failures of the members of our family and extended family structures that include our schools, churches, and social organizations. Our family instills our fears and courage as well as our values and beliefs, which become the fiber of our being. It's where our insecurities are developed. Our ethics, morals, views, and perceptions of the world and the people in it are developed from our family.

Our views of men are developed in our families. We hear things like, "Men are no good they leave you when you need them the most just look at your daddy. Get more out of life than just a husband. Go to school and meet a *good* husband. Be independent and never take no stuff from a man." The list goes on and on.

Our family is a loose mix of some of the most intelligent and illogical people we know. They want to be accepted despite their quirks and shortcomings just like anyone else. Any unsolved incidents that have occurred within our families usually manifest themselves as acute challenges in our own lives such as mental, physical, and sexual abuse. If the wounds are left untreated, they can turn into a pain that you will languish in for the rest of your life. The pain from the wound will eventually give you the permission to self-destruct and sabotage everything from your career to your relationship with your own children.

There are very few traditional black families left. Cliff and Claire Huxtable or the ideal television family isn't the predominant family structure in the black community. The white paradox of family and motherhood is not a model readily adopted by the African-American community. You know the *Leave It to Beaver* model: The white picket fence and the stay-at-home mother with the 2.5 children and the husband who supports and maintains the household. Today in the black community you have a mix of unmarried mothers and fathers, stepparents, lesbian or gay couples with children. Grandparents are rearing over 60 percent of the black children being raised today. Our children yearn for the kinship and security of family just as adults yearn for the need to feel accepted and loved.

We need to be aware of the times in which our parents were raised. The dehumanization that our parents and grandparents experienced was passed on to their children consciously and subconsciously. If you were told—and the culture supported the message—that you were nothing, you would begin to believe it too. It wasn't that long ago that schools, restaurants, and even bathrooms were segregated.

Spiritually and emotionally America has not been supportive of black people. Some black men just could not take the pressure and left. We are not making excuses for these men, nor are we blaming them. What we want to focus on is the hurt and chaos they left behind. Mothers were left behind often to raise more than one child in poverty—not to mention loneliness—without an effective support system. It's no wonder why we see so many celebrities and athletes giving praise to the mother who raised them alone.

On the other hand, if your father was the dad on the block that stayed, chances are you shared him with the other children on the block. He and the men like him helped raise the neighborhood's children. He was known as "Pop" to all of the children. He was shared by all who needed that male role model, and his own child was forced to share him too.

There are a lot of people raising children who aren't prepared. They are not fully developed emotionally or possess a keen sense of self, which leads to their children not possessing the same qualities. With all of this said, you have to look at yourself and ask yourself what is your accountability and contribution to the issues within your family. Sometimes we fuel the fire for situations and circumstances, because of petty jealousies and envy. Other times, because of hurt bestowed upon us, we are comfortable with the title of victim instead of taking control of the healing process and getting our life back.

One of the biggest issues among black women is the relationship we have with our mother. Most women we have spoken with have had issues with their mothers—some of them irreversible. Why? For many reasons black women have struggled with motherhood. Some mothers we met chose to sacrifice a close loving relationship with their daughters. These mothers chose to be strict and distant because they did not want their daughters to make the same mistakes that they made. A few women kept a family secret instead of dealing with it, and they let it take over their lives and the lives of their families. Some of them made a decision, a bad one, and still stuck with it hoping it would work out when all the while it was affecting their children. Imagine carrying that type of burden for the rest of your life.

Each case is unique, but these women did the best they could with or without resources. We need to forgive them. Remember you are a child of God, and regardless of how you got here, you still have to rise to your highest potential to fulfill your destiny and purpose.

Think about it—despite our history, we've managed to stick together. We've worked on rebuilding our family structure to fit our needs in a modern-day society—when our history tore our families apart. We've adopted friends as surrogate parents for our children. For us, blood has always been more a kinship of spirit than just of body.

We all haven't had the best experiences with our family, but the flexibility that we have come to rely on in the African-American community allows us to be able to get the love and support we all need. We are not unfamiliar with the stories of black children who were left parentless and were taken in by relatives or neighbors and raised as their own. We've always had the tradition of picking up the pieces and taking in a child or a person in crisis. That's our strength as a community, which is just a larger version of a family. Our tradition is important, and it is so deeply embedded, it's truly too hard to take away from us.

19

Grandma Dolly

Dolly C. Turner

To say it takes a village to raise a child is just grazing the surface. I was raised in a segregated environment with all black teachers, both men and women. You were reprimanded, scolded, and even spanked. A call from school to your parents was a message that you were going to be spanked again. As a child, the preacher, Sunday school teacher, custodian, and the neighbors on the route home were all a part of your parental community. I raised my two daughters the same way. I made it clear to the teachers at school that "all you have to do is make a phone call home and I'll be there in a moment's notice." Those principles that my mother raised me by were the same values I used to raise my own children, but they do not hold true today. Accusations of child abuse, neglect, and aggression are issues raised when parents today attempt to follow these antiquated principles. With the absence of a parental community, grandparents today must become the neighbors, teachers, custodians, and preachers that once were. The wisdom I have will allow me to incorporate my values and principles with the new generation's method in a silent but effective manner.

All too often you hear white society talk about our single parents. When I divorced in 1974 with two young daughters, divorce and single parent homes hadn't reached the epidemic level that they have today. People (both black and white) feel as though black women can't accomplish much because there is no father in the home. What American society fails to realize is that black women have led single households since slavery. Our families have been torn apart since our arrival here, but it hasn't stopped us from producing senators, congressmen, presidential candidates, secretaries of state, doctors, lawyers, accountants, engineers, authors, internationally renowned artists, presidents of major American companies, and strong black women and men. Oftentimes, I've seen that even when there are fathers in the home it was still the mothers and grandmothers that attended PTA meetings, recitals, etc. Unfortunately some of our black men don't participate fully in the rearing of their children when they are present in the home or absent. This is a separate issue. The difference between yesterday and today is that the migration of family members to various parts of the country or even opposite ends of a city has led to a breakdown in the immediate community and support system that is the foundation of a "village."

Being raised by a black mother, grandmother, or aunt has gone a long way in my life. My mother was the backbone of my family. Although my father was at home and very instrumental in our upbringing, he let Mamma take the reigns. Though she never knew it, he taught us about the birds and the bees, a lesson that has followed me and been passed on through my children to grandson. He taught my sister and me about our monthly cycles and hygiene. It was he who picked up what we needed from the drugstore. My mother and aunt (we all lived together) taught us social graces, how to speak correctly and distinctly and to always talk with your head up (talking with your head bowed was something indicative of slavery and cowardliness). They told us that if you think the white person you are addressing doesn't like blacks, shake their hand, look them in the eye and don't turn their hand loose, so you can see the blood run to their face and see the veins in their nose widen.

My mother and aunt were both teachers. My aunt was the first black school superintendent of education but couldn't even have an office in the Board of Education because she was black, but she commanded respect. And I did the same for my children and grandson. To this day, I remember and I quoted to my grandson often, "I may be dead and gone but you'll remember what I taught you, it may have little meaning now but way down the road, you'll see what I said was right." The importance that black mothers and grandmothers have played is always evident when I'm watching a sporting event on television. All the black athletes are quick to say, "Hi, Mom," or they say, "If it weren't for my grandmother, I wouldn't be where I am today."

At seventy-one years old, I made a decision to join my youngest daughter in Washington, D.C. to help her raise my twelve-year-old grandson. I wanted to bring my "village" to her. It was a tough decision because I was born in Oklahoma, and my roots were there. Although I left for twenty years to attend college and graduate school and pursue a career, I returned home to raise my children when they were in preschool. I'd been in Oklahoma City for the past thirty years until this past November. It was my home, where my friends resided, and my family had died. My daughters had been encouraging me to move for years but after awhile their coaxing stopped. I firmly told them that my home was in Oklahoma—I was happy to visit, even for extended periods, but a permanent move was out of the question.

My reconsideration of the move all started when my daughter wanted my grandson to visit me 1,100 miles away each summer beginning when he was four years old. My daughter called it bonding. I didn't understand it at the time, but all the pieces are falling into place now. My daughter thought it would be a good idea to send my grandson to me because we were so far apart, and she wanted him to be able to relate to her experiences of growing up in Oklahoma. I was pleased about that, but I kept thinking that when I see him the next time during Christmas he won't remember anything we may do or say. But I began to make plans for things we could do together that would be memorable. Both his mother and my other daughter helped me with planning. They would say, "Momma, you know what to do with children. That comes easy for you; just raise him like you raised us and do all the fun things you used to do with us." We took long walks, and I told him that grandmothers don't walk as fast as mommies so he could take his time. We went to the zoo and had picnics at the lake. We also collected one rock, put our names on it and the year that he visited. To this day he still says, "Can we collect a rock like we used to do or sit under a tree and just whittle, can we go to Stroud, Oklahoma, [the country] and watch them fry fish in the big black kettle or dig a hole and cook a turtle? Can we fly a kite and go on a picnic?" He's twelve years old now, and he remembers all these beautiful memories that my daughter called bonding. He even, at some point, told his mom that he'd like to live in Oklahoma. I believe all these experiences were something special that we shared. These were experiences that sometimes in the midst of hustling and bustling large cities with hectic schedules and only one parent, who is trying to be all things, that only a grandmother, who is in no hurry can provide her grandchildren. God always has a plan, and He laid the foundation for the relationship my grandson and I have had during these summer visits.

When I lived apart from my daughter, I worried about her work schedule. She and my grandson arrived home around 6:30 P.M. daily. She had to organize dinner, homework, and his bath. I wanted to make life easier for them. My grandson needed her youth and vitality, which she must sustain in this fast paced "new generation" world she actively participates in. But he also needs my slower pace, wisdom, and older values that together provide the means for a healthier, happier child.

I realized that my grandson needed even more wisdom than his mother could provide him. I have lived longer than my daughter and gained so much wisdom. My good and bad experiences can be shared as a teaching tool. I could answer questions like, "Grandma in your day did people. . . ?"

He wouldn't have to refer to an encyclopedia to seek the answers; he could sit next to a living encyclopedia to listen and learn.

Another reason why I decided to move was based upon my feelings and beliefs of the meaning of "family." What is it all about? I was taught that a family that prays together stays together. I still believe that today, and this had the strongest impact on my decision to move. I felt that I was making the supreme sacrifice by moving. I was comfortable, I didn't get up until I was ready, or go to bed until I was ready. If I wanted to cook I did, and if not, I'd go out to eat. Most of all, I knew I'd miss my church and its members who became my extended family. I sang in my choir, one of the soloists in fact. I worked with the food pantry, the Wednesday night mission, taught summer Bible school, adopted two god-children who I selected so I could be a grandparent to them, and attended Bible study. I ate with my pastor and his wife and their family each Sunday along with other misplaced young people and their families. I was happier than I had been in years. I pondered over my move for about four months. I always told my daughters when they had a decision to make, fold a piece of paper in half and put down all the reasons "why" on one side and all the reasons "why not" on the other. I did this and there were no reasons why I should not move that I could come up with. And there were countless reasons why I should move. It was at this point, that all of my indecisiveness left. I gained a whole new lease on life when I moved, and I've never looked back.

Now that six months have passed, we are even closer than before. My grandson needed to see what a truly extended family was all about. His father's side of the family is very large, but thus far, the only indication I've had that a sense of family unit exists, or a spirit of togetherness was present, was when someone needed a partner for a card game of spades or dirty hearts. My grandson becomes the extra player. Or they need him when the clothes need washing, or the lawn needs cutting, or the fence needs mending. There are big family dinners on Sundays where each person gets a TV tray and goes to the TV to watch the game or whatever, but there is no real conversation. His father's family seems to put a lot of attention on their own adult recreation, but not on the needs of the child, or the importance of making a child a part of the family. With my daughter's father's family, we get together on holidays, we have food, fun, and intellectual conversation, but we don't see them at any other time. The odd thing is that I watched and participated in the development of all these cousins, and they had the benefit of an extended family, but for some reason, they haven't continued that tradition. In both of these family experiences, I believed my grandson was missing something. The most important things I felt were absent were intimate conversation or an opportunity for him to give input about his perspective, and to share his life experiences, and for someone else who was older and wiser to share theirs. These are things that help shape our character.

He's had the opportunity of seeing my hair turn silver right before his very eyes, the slower pace that I walk, and the laugh lines around my eyes. Though I had all the toys a child could want growing up, my father taught me how to put a string through pop-cans and walk on them. These games and others, like how to make stilts, play marbles, mumbly peg, to whittle, and to ride a bike without any hands I also passed along to my grandson. I made sure I taught my grandson about natural fun (fun without video games, etc.). It gives us more time to laugh, share, and to interact. My grandson was shocked that I knew more about yo-yo's than he did. I taught him how to "go around the world" and "walk the dog." All of these things he found to be more fun than all of the expensive toys he has now because there was a sense of togetherness and bonding. My grandson loves to hear my stories about how my father took my sister and me to the fair, and all the cotton candy and candied apples we'd eat, and about our long walks home afterward. My dad would take all the neighborhood children on Halloween to the ice-cream store. Because of segregation, we couldn't go inside to eat so my father would go in by himself and tell them that he was buying ice cream for all the children sitting outside on the curb. Eventually the store owners would agree to let my dad bring out two cones at a time. My grandson always comments on how much fun it seemed to be. With these stories it gives him a sense of connection to his elders and what their lives were like. I think grandmothers are important because they help maintain a sense of history, and they hold on to and share the basic fundamentals of life's experiences without all the glitz and glitter of today.

Since I've been with my daughter and grandson, I've been blessed to see the change in their lives. My daughter seems much less stressed out, and she's now able to create more of a personal life for herself. I'm so happy that she can go on dates and to travel for business when she needs to. My grandson has also improved his grades in school, and I can now help with his extracurricular activities like soccer and basketball. I scream the loudest at the games. He seems to be happier as well. I'm not sure what I might have to do with it, but even the communication between my daughter and her ex-husband seems to be better. Sometimes people tend to straighten their acts up when they know someone who cares is standing watch. Although I do feel lonely sometimes and I miss my friends, my life is very fulfilling. I'm glad I had an opportunity to be here for my daughter when she needed me and before my grandson became a teenager and started to feel he might be too grown to talk or spend time with Grandma. And, by the way, my grandson loves my silver hair!

Dolly C. Turner is originally from Oklahoma City and recently relocated to Washington, D.C. to live with her daughter and grandson. Dolly is a multi-talented woman; she is an educator having taught dance and physical education and had presided over departments at various colleges and universities, high schools, and elementary schools in various parts of the United States. Dolly produced her own children's television show "Dolly's Treasure Chest" that aired on PBS and achieved such success that she was asked to consult on *Sesame Street*. She is currently working on a novel.

20

Retwisting the Ties That Bind

Lisa C. Moore

I do not trust my mother.
But then, she never trusted hers.

Let me be clear: I love my mother. I love who my mother is finally becoming, a more whole person than she was when I was growing up. Someone who is learning to love herself, who is finally growing up herself.

I love my mother's mind, how quick and agile and curious and cunning it can be. I love my mother's tongue, how she turns perfectly innocuous English language into sharp, cutting words aimed at those who do her wrong. I can only wish I was that smart, had such great timing. I'm working on it.

I love how my mother loves to play games—whether they be board games or the big boys' games—learning the ins and outs of them and becoming masterful. I'm in training to run with the big boys myself, and she takes great delight in that.

I love the elegance of my mother, how she holds her hands, the way she angles her long neck, the way she holds her head high. I admire the fullness of her lips. I think I've inherited some of these things.

But what I also seem to have inherited is a mistrust of people. Starting with my mother.

I have just finished a fantastic novel about mother-daughter-mother reincarnation. It made me cry at the end, at the daughter with the grandmother's memories, coming back to comfort the mother. I wonder at the act of taking a child in one's arms to comfort. So many women I know talk of their mothers as if their mothers are their best friends. But I can't recall any instance of being comforted in my mother's arms. Caged is more the feeling.

What am I missing?
Did she ever feel comforted in her mother's arms?
Trust comes from unconditional love.

I've heard stories about my grandmother. Of how she would yank elbows off the wooden edge during mealtime to teach that rule of the dinner table. She is a witty and elegant woman, and a stickler for manners, rules. I don't remember ever seeing her take my mother in her arms; physical contact was rare, save for the hello and good-bye hug. I don't remember her saying anything comforting to my mother at all, actually. When we'd visit, I remember her usual tone as more of a "you deserve what you get." I always thought it was for marrying beneath her "station in life."

My mother was not taught to love herself. She was born out of wedlock in a time when such things were a sin, a stain on the child as well as the parents. And when her sister came along later, born within the safety of a marriage, the inevitable comparisons began. This much my mother has told me.

Feeling not quite "as good as," not "enough," and certainly never "better than," how can a little girl learn to love herself? I know these things are passed on.

Trust comes from feeling comfort and stability and reliability. I never turned to my mother for those things. After too much disappointment, I stopped asking early on for rides to school, from school, to anywhere. I learned how to catch the bus, and learned the inherent freedom from asking and not getting. When my mother offered to take me anywhere, I refused. I preferred the bus driver's schedule—I knew he'd be at the corner at 7:46 A.M. I asked my father for things, because sometimes things promised by my mother—money, clothes, shoes—didn't come through, and the not coming through was always at the last minute.

Did her mother not follow through on promises? Did her mother promise her anything?

Because my mother had to work to make ends meet, I cleaned house, cooked, braided my sisters' hair, washed clothes, fed children. My mother tells a story of her father requiring that the bathroom sink be cleaned and *dried* after *every* use. She tells me this as if to say, "You don't have it that bad."

This story never comforted me.

Did she ever feel comforted? What about her mother, my grandmother? Who comforted her, told her she was loved, taught her to love herself? Who showed her, through consistent behavior, that she could rely on her mother's words and actions? Who taught her to pass it on—or not? Did she ever learn?

During my years of mothering my sisters, I've learned you can't give love if you don't love yourself first, but my mother was ill equipped for the rigors of parenting. You have to give and give and give, and have enough left over to give to yourself. She didn't have that. I was lucky; I learned about consistency and reliability from my father.

A respect for boundaries yields trust.

When I was in fifth and sixth grades, I kept a diary. Once some kids in class stole it from my purse and read it aloud to the class, snickering at my attempts at describing my body's newfound changes. I was devastated, and subsequently kept to myself in school. A few years later, in ninth grade at a new school, I took up a journal again, only to discover my mother was reading it regularly and asking me about certain passages. I gave it up for good then—at least until I was in my late twenties. She said it was the only way she would know what was going on in my head, since I didn't volunteer information. My mother's quest for knowledge about her excessively quiet daughter made me dig in my heels, learn to be secretive about private thoughts, phone calls, writing, desires.

Now I've learned to relax a little—not be on one extreme or the other. But little things still trigger the mistrust, such as my sister looking through my mail and asking who the sender is, borrowing something without asking, or even just asking. Any semblance of what I consider too much curiosity is cause for alarm.

Did her mother respect her boundaries? Were any set?

Lack of trust yields an incomplete sense of self.

A memory: of talking to my younger teenage sister, who still lived at home, while she detailed the latest hurt from my mother. But my sister reacted, talked back, something I never dared do. I kept repeating, "You said that to her?" And she kept saying, "Yeah! Who does she think she is? I wouldn't do that to her!" I sat there amazed at my sixteen-year-old sister's womanish audacity, defying authority.

After I hung up, I had a sudden memory of me being awakened in the middle of the night by my mother. I may have been about ten. She shook me awake, told me to get my ass up, why didn't I finish cleaning the kitchen, "You left dishes in the sink." She was tired, and yelling; I was stunned at the vehemence of her words. "I work all day for you, and I come home and can't even get y'all to keep the house clean! What good are you? HUH?" And I slowly began to walk to the kitchen to wash the offending dishes. I don't remember crying. I do remember feeling wooden.

But some twenty years later, I have burst into tears, crying at the fact that I never remember feeling angry. And I feel incredibly angry now, angry like my sister did. Questioning, like my sister had. Sad. And thinking, what other parts of my childhood did I lose? How many memories have I blocked because I wasn't allowed to feel, to express my feelings?

I'm sure my mother has a different memory, if she has one at all.

But my mother has told me her memories of me learning to read at age three. Me crawling out onto the roof of the house as a baby, how scared she had been to come upstairs to check on me in my crib and find that I had crawled out of the window next to the crib and onto the roof.

I try to imagine the terror of a new mother finding her child sitting with a view of New Orleans, with the protective crib sides down. I can't do it.

There are some good things. Because lack of trust produces an almost paralyzing fear of the unknown—having no control over what's going to happen—I've had to force myself to take great leaps of faith, like publishing a book, starting grad school, moving to new cities where I don't know a soul, traveling by myself, being comfortable with being alone. Having to depend on me, myself, and I. Learning to love myself. I am learning to trust my intuition.

My mother admires this about me, says she is proud of me, wishes she could do the same.

When will she learn?

I do not trust my mother.

But I am working on building an adult relationship with her, which is what I'm hoping for. It's a slow process. My instincts run counter to it. The childhood I'm rebuilding for myself doesn't include her. I am rediscovering emotions I never thought I'd own, like playfulness, anger. But we have learned to dance around my childhood and hers, and are coming to grips with being adult black women who are irrevocably tied to one another.

Lisa C. Moore, a native of New Orleans, is descended from a long line of teachers and musicians. She is the author of *Does Your Mama Know?* and the founder and publisher of Red Bone Press, the nation's only press devoted solely to black feminist issues.

21

Pass It On

Vivian Scott Chew

First Baptist Church, Far Rockaway, New York—my mother was the secretary, my uncle the chairman of the Trustee Board, my brother the organist, and my godmother the resident "call and response queen." Not going to church was not an option for me from conception to age eighteen. I've always had a connection with God, primarily through gospel music of the church. It wasn't until I was faced with the toughest four months of my life that I began to truly understand the concept of faith.

On Saturday, May 21, 1994, I visited my mother, who was suffering from a disease called polymyocytsis—a form of muscular dystrophy. Weekly Saturday visits had become a custom ever since she had become bedridden by this dreadful disease. She no longer was able to greet me at the front door, cook me a meal, or even call me up at 11:30 P.M. after the news as she had done for many years. It had been about four years since she could walk, and she was wheelchair bound. Saturdays were the days that she looked forward to and that I dreaded. For as much as I truly loved my mother, I also missed the mother I grew up with. The mother who, as a single parent (my father picked my birth date as the day of his departure), raised my brother and me in a healthy middle-class environment. The mother who put me through private school and supported my brother through college. The mother who took me and my then two-and-a-half-year-old daughter in after my soon-to-be ex-husband kicked my ass for the first and last time.

The woman who always held her head high in the midst of adversity could no longer be the pillar of strength that I had become accustomed to. I was now a mother to my mother. She depended on me emotionally, mentally, financially, and physically. On that particular Saturday, my mother told me that she was tired and wanted to cut our visit short. But before I left, she told me something that I had heard only a few times before from her. She told me that she loved me. She passed away at 7:00 A.M. the next day.

The week to follow was, needless to say, one of the hardest weeks of my life. My brother, who was always in charge of the family business, ran the show as expected. But it was not until we had to spend the night and day together making funeral arrangements that I noticed the blotches on his neck. He explained that they were "nothing, just shingles." I also noticed how much weight he had lost. It was then that I realized my brother had AIDS.

My brother, Lawrence, and I were not close as children primarily due to our difference in age (eleven years), but we grew close after the birth of my daughter, Loren. As a gay man, I knew my brother might never have children, so I gave him the honor of having a child named after him. Through the years, we learned to truly love and respect each other's similarities but, more so, each other's differences. He never openly discussed his sexual preference. I guess he always just assumed that I knew. Whom he slept with never mattered to me. He was my big brother, my hero, the smartest man I knew, and now during the same week of burying my mother I also had to face the reality that my brother was going to prematurely leave me.

It all happened so fast. On July 10, just one week after I gave Lawrence a surprise party for his forty-seventh birthday, I received a call from his companion, John, that he was missing. He never showed up to work that day, and his assistant was quite alarmed that she had not heard from him all day. Finally at about 10:00 P.M. that evening, my brother drove up in a cab in front of his home where both John and I had been waiting. He was shoeless, completely disoriented, and obviously suffering from dementia. We got him to the hospital, where he was admitted. Due to patient confidentiality, the doctors would not tell us what was wrong with him other than he had a temperature of 105 degrees and was battling an infection. I asked if they could tell me what his T-cell count was. It was 35. My brother was in the last stages of his battle with AIDS.

The next month and a half was grueling. I had to accept my brother's destiny and mourn the loss of my mother at the same time. I had two major recording artists with hit records both demanding my time and a teenage daughter who did not want to talk about any of this. It was then that I had to sit down and have a little talk with God. Why was He punishing me like this? Why was He putting such a heavy burden on me? I was tired. Tired of talking to doctors, tired of going to the hospital, just tired of being tired. But it was my grandmother's words that came to me at a time when I was ready to fall apart. She used to say, "God will not give you more than you can handle." In my eyes, my grandmother should have been given honorary sainthood. She always knew the right thing to say and do. It was her words, fifteen years later, that would get me through this storm I was weathering. Every time I would receive a call that yet another infection had invaded my brother's body or when I was asked to donate my blood to him every other day to help keep him alive, it was her faith in God's promise that kept me going. It was also her spirit entering my soul that told me what I had to do next. I had to prepare my brother to die.

So it was on Tuesday, September 18, that I walked into my brother's room and announced that I had the cure for his illness. He didn't have to be hooked up to a ventilator anymore. The doctors could now unhook all the tubes that had been keeping him alive. I told him that I had read his will, which had made provisions for his namesake, my daughter, to attend any college of her choice without financial consideration. I told him it was time to go to heaven and be with our mother. It was time to let go of his earthly body and receive his reward.

In typical stubborn Lawrence Murphy tradition, he continued to hold on, but there were no more twitching movements from his body. He no longer shed tears which the doctors insisted were involuntary (I knew better). There was a peacefulness that was in his room when I entered. He was ready to go home but he needed my help during this final leg of his journey. So on Thursday, September 20, 1994, I donned a gown, mask, and gloves; got in the bed with my brother; and had the doctors unplug all of the apparatus that was keeping him alive. I was fortunate to have gotten him to sign a living will giving me that authority. I said a prayer, held him close, told him that I loved him, and within minutes he took his last breath. I could feel his soul soar around the room, finally released from bondage.

I have been told that faith is the belief in things unseen. Faith has become my middle name. Faith is what gets me through the day. Faith is what made me understand why at the age of thirty-six I had become a motherless/fatherless/brotherless child. I learned through faith that my mother, father, and brother had to die so that the traits that they possessed, that I admired the most, would be passed on to me. I received patience from my mother, a carefree spirit from my father, and tenacity from my brother. I thank them often for these gifts. I have truly come this far by faith.

Vivian Scott Chew is the founder of TimeZone International, an urban marketing company that focuses on the marketing/promotion of artists outside of the U.S. The company incorporates street marketing, artist development and production/album projects. Vivian and her husband, Ray Chew—Musical Director of "It's Showtime At The Apollo" co-own an events creation company—Chew Entertainment. They reside in Teaneck, NJ and are parents to two daughters, Loren and Bianca.

22

About Healing

Nefatiti Brooks-Rochester

It was a beautiful wedding. The peaceful Caribbean setting combined with the truly felt warm wishes of my new husband's family was everything I had hoped it would be. The ceremony, performed by my husband's father, took place at sunset. Gentle ocean waves lapped at our bare feet and provided background music as we recited our matrimonial vows. All in attendance agreed that it was a blessed occasion. My wedding day was for me one of the happiest days I have experienced yet. It marked my entrance into two new roles. I was now a wife and very soon to be a mother. The day was also very significant for me because I had finally made a decision to come to terms with my relationship with my mother. For twelve years my mother and I had an on-again-off-again relationship. We would communicate fine for several months then something would happen and a year would go by without contact. Usually the something was so trivial it was silly, but the actions taken and the things said after were often harsh and painful.

Each time there was a break between the two of us, I would go over the events in my head, trying to understand exactly what happened. I never could figure out why my mother was so angry or why the anger was so lasting. There was never an incident that, in my judgment, warranted being unforgivable. Yet the cycle continued. When I was in my late teens and early twenties, the distance between us did not phase me. College life was fun, and my friends and I spent our time doing the things that young people do. I was focused on exploring life and pursuing my goals. I was learning to be an adult. Although I felt the weight of being on my own with no support, it was the first time in my life that I felt I could breathe freely. The fact that my mother did not call or visit and was unresponsive when I did disturbed me but was quickly pushed aside. I believed that in time things would get better. In the meantime I was branching out, leaving behind an overprotective shield that could not accompany me on my journey. I did not realize that what I considered growing up and becoming independent my mother saw as rejection. A steadfast wall of confusion, lack of communication, and hurt slowly erected itself between the two of us.

Time passed and the friends that were constant companions in earlier years began to follow their own paths. Time spent alone helped me to address familiar feelings that had been tucked away in my heart since the day I left my mother's house. I believed that the void I felt in my life was my missing mother, and I thought that a good relationship with her would bring wholeness. I wanted to know of her life and experiences, to see if she had any of the same difficulties or triumphs that I had. I wanted to know her and I needed her to know me.

With a renewed sense of purpose, I began again to pursue a relationship with my mother. At times it did seem as if progress was being made though we continued to have problems. We were talking on a regular basis and that was an improvement. This time even if I was hurt or insulted by her attacks, I continued to keep the paths of interaction open. I made the concessions, I took responsibility for any misunderstanding, but it was not working. We were not getting to know each other because we were not really communicating. Expressing how I genuinely felt about things usually resulted in an argument. To be safe when together, we busied ourselves with tasks rather than talk. On the phone our conversations were limited and often uncomfortable. The relationship that I had fantasized about having with my mother had not materialized despite my efforts. What was accomplished served only to further undermine my own personal security and self-esteem. The spiritual strength that I strove for was constantly compromised by the pressure I inflicted upon myself to have the woman who gave me breath in my life.

For years I lived with obvious disregard for my mother. I cannot claim to understand her even a little, but because I am no longer a child, I can accept that maybe the reasons for her behavior have nothing to do with me. She wasn't acting the way she was just because I didn't clean my room or listen to a teacher during recess. Just as I am responsible for my actions, so was she, even when the actions were directed toward me. There were times when I made excuses for her and times when I outright hated her. Convincing myself to believe that she cared and was concerned about my life was a necessary illusion that helped me to survive many hard times. . . . But it was time to move on.

I could handle the lack of emotional support and I had learned how to provide roots for myself to grow from. I believed that happiness was possible even though my mother did not love or could not show love to me. But I could no longer handle, accept, or believe that the surface and vindictive relationship that we had was healthy or uplifting. My mother did not come to my wedding. It was not the first time that she had chosen not to participate in a major event in my life. But unlike college graduation, the wedding experience was not one of devastation, taking months to recover from, but instead it was a fulfilling and joyous occasion. I allowed my happiness and the happiness of those in my life to be enough for me. Finally, I accepted that I would not have a mother-daughter relationship that was loving, supportive, and strengthening. Finally, I was able to put the guilt and confusion behind me and know that I was not less of a person or less likely to be loved. My decision that day was to heal and allow my spirit freedom from the ideals of what a mother or a daughter should be.

The mother-daughter relationship has been characterized as "the greatest love affair" and one of the most difficult. From time to time we hear of or read about stories where the mother has murdered her children or did great physical or emotional damage to them. More often the stories told are ones that elevate our beliefs in human nature. These are the stories of extreme love and sacrifice. Regardless of the stories, we all know that it is a relationship that has much importance in our lives. Your mother can make you doubt even your strongest convictions by showing a slight disinterest. And the smallest hint of acceptance means the world to you. The many women who have strong relationships with their mothers, grandmothers, or even a mother figure treasure those relationships dearly. I don't believe that there is a relationship that can teach as much or bring you as much strength.

For women whose story may resemble my own, my advice is to ask God for help and, with the most effort you can gather, try to work through the difficulties. But do not sacrifice your own happiness or mental well-being to do so. If the two of you cannot repair the relationship, it does not mean that you are invalid or unworthy of love. Strengthen your love of self and embrace the love of those present in your life.

I did not learn to be a loving woman from my mother but through a curriculum of trial and error. It was an experience that my soul required in this lifetime. My mother is also experiencing the lessons of her lifetime, and when she is ready, we will try again.

Nefatiti Brooks-Rochester is the coowner and cofounder of the Postcard Factory. She is also a new mother to her beautiful son, Max.

23

Mother Love

Kathy Starks Dow

When I got married twenty years ago, I acquired a new name, a new mate, and a new power. As two young, educated black professionals, my husband and I were a power team. Not only was I respected for my accomplishments, but I was now being respected for his accomplishments too.

With the dual power of marriage, I was given another instant power: motherhood. I became an instant custodial mother of his ten-year-old daughter, Joelle.

While there is no course on how to be a mother, there is a natural instinct on how to love, protect, and guide a young life. I call it "Mother Power." For me it was like a second chance to have my own life, but with the wisdom of my mistakes and an outlook that was not quite as innocent or naive. I took to it like a duck to water.

This little girl, my new daughter, entitled me to rights to determine when she ate, what she wore, and when she changed her clothes. I woke her up in the morning and told her when to go to bed at night.

I had the power to determine where she went to school, whom she played with, who came to our house, and whose home she went to. I also determined who babysat her, I chose her doctor, and I began to choose every little thing that would affect her life.

I told her when she could stay after school, what activities she could join, and what classes she should take. If she wanted to participate in something, she had to get my permission. This was an easy and natural power.

I supervised her involvement in church; I encouraged her friendships and discouraged her male entanglements. I took this power for granted and expected compliance.

In this little girl I had more power than I could imagine. Every day I became more and more important to her. I was there whenever she needed me. I told her what medicine to take if she felt sick; I told her what excuses to use when she needed excuses.

I didn't misuse the power. It wasn't an abusive power; it was just a natural, "somebody's gotta be in charge" power. An "I'm the mother and do as I say" power. An "I know what's right for you power, 'cause I've been there, done that," power.

I told her what I thought, impressing upon her what to think. I taught her my morals. I made decisions for her when necessary and used my power of persuasion to help her make her own decisions. I influenced her. I molded her, and in so many ways I created her. This was a personal power, which had nothing to do with the outside world. I wasn't interested in ruling outside my home.

I challenged her, I punished her, I guided her. I was the conductor and the director. If she breathed, I knew about it. I listened when she thought I wasn't, and I heard when she thought I didn't.

I decided when boys could call her, determined to save her from the catastrophe of early, neighborhood sex education. I set an arbitrary age at which she could date. I decided which movies she could watch. I gave her rules and guidelines that she was expected to follow. I had the power of a drill sergeant in the army, and I expected her to jump when I said jump.

As she grew up, I began to encourage her to make decisions for herself. But to some degree I still kept my finger in the pie. I had spent many years in her face and I could tell she valued my opinion. What else could a mother ask for? I had succeeded. She came to me with her questions and even with her secrets. If there were things on her mind, I knew she would come to me.

When she became college age, she asked me where she should apply, and when she was accepted, she asked me if she should go and I saw to it that she went wherever she wanted to go. It was to be the start of her independent life. I was excited and I'm sure she was breathing a sigh of relief.

As a young adult, she continued to seek my opinion, questioning what I would do in certain situations. I was proud that we had developed this type of relationship. This was my daughter in every sense of the word. We were a team. I was her secret weapon in the relationship with her father, and I was her weapon against any outside force that threatened. I had her back.

As she got older, we talked about how to handle coworkers and bosses. If she needed to make a career decision, she consulted me. When she dressed for interviews, she modeled for me.

We discussed friendships, whom to trust and whom not to trust. I told her about "girlfriends" and that she had to choose them carefully. I explained that there would only be one or two true, honest-to-goodness women that she should trust with all her secrets. (I, of course, thought I would be one of them.)

We discussed men. I knew about her boyfriends and I even knew a little

more than she thought I did about what they were doing in their relationships. (A mother's gotta know these things.)

I figured if she needed to confide in anyone, it would be me. I had suc-
cessfully completed Mothering 101. I had taken her into adulthood. I was
proud of her, I loved her, and I was looking forward to sharing the rest of
her life and accomplishments with her.

With one phone call the power structure that I had created for seventeen years came undone. It is a moment that I will never forget.

My husband travels quite often and it is not unusual for him to call me
late at night. Many times we are in different time zones and I am awakened
from deep sleep by his phone calls. Often I don't even remember what we
talked about the next day. But this time, it was different. While it was 3 A.M.,
it was the tone in his voice that startled me.

"Wake up," he told me. "I need to talk to you." As I reached for the light,
I sat up in bed and my heart began to pound. I had no reason to think anything bad was about to happen . . . we had a solid marriage, but for an instant I wondered, "Is he getting ready to tell me he's not coming home?"
Good Lord, I wasn't ready for that.

In three seconds the crushing truth took my breath and power away. My
power structure crashed and burned. He told me that our daughter was in a
relationship that we didn't know about (though my husband will forever say
he knew, that he attributed it to a father's instinct), and that she was pregnant and was going to have the baby.

Secrets, betrayal, and lies, these were the first things to deal with. How
could she be in a relationship that I didn't know about and hadn't controlled? Second, how could she be pregnant and not come to me first? I was
devastated. For the first time in seventeen years my child had made a decision totally without me, without my input, and it was a decision that would
change her life, my life, and our relationship forever.

For me this was to be a lesson about mothers losing control over their
daughters as they become women. Mothers not being involved in the decisions that are being made. Daughters giving control to the men they love.
Nowhere had anyone told me how to deal with this. I was on a new frontier.

I had been the "boss" for so long, that now to be downsized was blowing
me away. None of this is what I would have chosen for her. This isn't the
way I wanted her to do it. We were much too successful to have an unplanned pregnancy. This thing had spiraled out of my control but I continued to try and hold the reins of power. How could I change this situation?
How could I correct this?

My mother power hat was on and I was trying everything I knew to
make this not happen. It was, however, beyond my control. She was a grown

woman, twenty-six years of age, a college graduate with nursing school in her future.

The time had come for me to step back. Abdicate my throne. I was no longer the "know-all, be-all mom." I had created a human being who was now thinking on her own and making her own choices. I needed a crash course on surviving the demotion of motherhood.

I spent weeks going over how this could have happened. She and I had two major talks in which she told me that she carried on this secret relationship because she knew I wouldn't approve. She informed me that this was her decision and that it was final. I was not a part of it nor would I be directing any of it. She had confided in other people and that had given her the strength to move forward with what her heart wanted. It was a done deal.

I will always admit that I would not have chosen this particular man for her. Nor would I have wanted an unplanned, unmarried pregnancy. Through the confusion and hurt I never considered losing my daughter. There was no ultimatum: "Him and the baby or me." I was just going to have to find the place in my head that would allow my heart to do what I knew was the right thing. Accept it and move on.

It was the beginning of a new relationship: a woman/mother to woman/daughter relationship. While she will always be my daughter, she taught me that being a mother has a beginning and an end. That, eventually mothers have to relinquish control.

Some mothers do this without much trouble. Others of us have to learn the hard way. God gave me my life, and while He entrusted hers to me, it was not mine. I learned that all other lives that we touch, guide, or direct are just moments in time. Every person has the right to control his or her own destiny, and that's what we, as mothers, ultimately wish for. Independent, strong, confident, decision-making children.

My daughter and I have come out of this as strong as ever, maybe even stronger. She has propelled me to a higher level and given me yet another gift: two beautiful granddaughters, Jordyn and Madison, and a loving, kind, and dependable son-in-law. (He, by the way, is a great father and he loves my daughter very much.)

I also learned that it was because of her love and respect for me that she was unable to confide in me. I had made my desires and dreams for her so vivid, that she felt failure when they collided with what she wanted for herself. In reality, I had failed her by not giving her the confidence to know that I would stand by her side no matter what.

She knows, without a doubt, that I will never abandon her. That while we may disagree, I give her the right to make her own decisions, I love her, and it's never "my way or the highway." She is my child, always and forever. And while there were others who supported her decision before I did, it is I who has stood by without a moment's hesitation.

She is happy, and in the end that is all I could ever have wished for. So now as I watch her own "mommy power" grow, I know the same day will come for her when her little girls exert their own personal power and take control of their lives whether it is what she wants or not.

I'll be there when she calls.

Kathy Starks Dow is a former newspaper reporter for a Rockland County, New York daily and the recipient of the Golden Apple Award for excellence in reporting. She is a former high school journalism teacher, and a published poet. Kathy is currently working on a book about her teenage daughter's life.

24

Mommy Dearest

Melody Guy

My mother's mother—my grandmother—left my mom when she was an infant. No one has really ever told me the story. Today, I guess you'd say she was suffering from postpartum depression, but back then, all anyone knew was that she deserted her child. They found her in a park, crying, with my mother beside her. And then she was gone.

My mother was raised by her grandmother and her father, my Pop-Pop. At some point, Pop-Pop's sister moved into the house with her daughter and that was my mom's family.

My mom doesn't like to talk about her mother. Over the years little things would slip out. When I was younger, I would inquire, not realizing I was treading on potentially dangerous ground. "Why don't you like your mother?" I once asked her. I must have been ten or so at the time. "If someone treated you like a dog, you wouldn't like them either." I was a little confused because my grandmother wasn't around to treat my mother like anything, so I didn't understand what she meant.

How must it have been for her? To feel rejected by your very own mother. And then to be a mother yourself. To four girls. My mother was an only child.

My relationship with my mother has—evolved. I'm the oldest. My mother and her people are rather fair skinned—light caramel. My dad and I are the same complexion—milk chocolate. When I was little, my mother didn't know how to do my hair at first. She had never dealt with hair my texture before and would send me across the street to a neighbor to get my hair done. My younger sisters were lighter in complexion and had wavier hair. Sometimes neighborhood kids would say to me, "What happened to you?" because I was darker and had "nappy" hair. It bothered me a lot, but it was never anything I ever heard inside my house. In fact, if I had told my mother about it, she would have dismissed it as nonsense. I don't think I ever did.

When I was younger, I dreaded Sunday nights—especially during the school year. On Sunday nights I was convinced my mother hated me. That was when she pressed my hair for the week and we would fight, argue, and it would always be a tense time. I'd sit by the hot stove as my mother heated up the pressing comb on the burner. I was constantly flinching because I was afraid of being burned, especially on my forehead and my ears—and somehow felt—and I'm ashamed to admit this now—that she was going to burn me on purpose. Sometimes the arguing got so bad that my father would come up from the basement—he was usually tinkering on something down there—and just stand there for a while. I had enough sense to be ashamed of my behavior, and while he was there, I calmed down a bit. Plus I felt his being there meant she would be extra careful and not burn me. I can probably count on one hand the times she actually did burn me (and she never did burn my forehead), but one particular time, she burned my ear, and when I complained she said, "Well, you shouldn't have had an ear then." I can laugh about it now, but at the time I took it as an indication that I had to protect myself from her. Now, I'm grateful that she cared enough about me to put up with my behavior week after week.

A couple of years ago my sisters and I decided to take my mother on a vacation. Just us girls. We really hadn't gone on a vacation as a family that wasn't to visit relatives. We stayed at an inn in Cape Cod and had a ball. My mother was so happy and relaxed, and she really opened up to us on that trip and told us things about her life we had never known like how she met Daddy, what attracted her to him, and what it was like for her growing up. Recently she said that was one of the best times of her life.

This past Christmas, she gave me a kiss. Now that may not seem like a big deal but it was. Affection is kind of awkward for her. Not so much when we were younger, but as we got older, it was kind of hard to get close to her. She would always act like she didn't want to be bothered. But my sister asked for a kiss on the cheek, and then said, "Now, give Melody one." She gave me a kiss, and we both acted like it was a chore, but it was so endearing and meant a lot to us both. Even now my mother is evolving, changing. Whoever said there are no second acts definitely doesn't know her. She is more willing to put her feelings on the line with us now. She lets it be known that we are important to her and that it is important that we feel the same.

My sisters and I are so protective of my mother. We treat her like she's fragile sometimes to the point of exasperating her. But even though I am in my late twenties, she can still turn me to mush with a look. I definitely know when I'm in trouble. Her lips get real thin and she squints her eyes. But there is no real meanness there. Just a little fleeting displeasure that we will joke about later. This happened a few years ago when I convinced her to go on a day hike which she had never done before and we got lost. It was starting to get dark and we were going around in circles. Since it was my idea, she looked at me and said, "You get us out of here right now!" I did.

I never doubted that my mother loved me. I knew that. She took care of me, washed my butt, pressed my hair, made sure I had clean clothes, and supported me in my endeavors. But now it is a treat realizing that my mother likes me as well. Likes me as a person. That it wasn't all about duty and not doing what her mother never did for her. I've come to realize that she showed her affection by making clothes for me when I was little, or making her fried chicken (my favorite) when I was home from college. Or that she would at least listen to my newfangled, cockamamie ideas out of respect to me—even if she had to do the prerequisite rolling of the eyes first.

Mommy, I am very sorry your mother never got the chance to know you. But maybe she did the best thing she could at the time by leaving you. Just maybe she did. If she was incapable of being a mother to you, who knows what damage she could have done. So don't be angry with her. I'm not. I just feel sorry for her. I'm sorry that she didn't have you in her life, and that she hasn't had an opportunity to see the woman, the mother, you've become.

Melody Guy is the proud daughter of Carolyn Guy. She is an assistant publishing manager and editor for Villard Books. While she currently resides in Brooklyn, she is originally from Boston.

Your Soul's Sustenance

I am my brother's keeper.

Family is important. Whether you haven't spoken to your sister for years, you can't stand your mother, or you don't know where to begin to look for your father. You are a mere composite of your family: their personalities, their physical makeup, their morals and ideals.

Since family is part of the core of our being, they become a source of great pain. Since most of us received our foundation from our families, we also often suffered trauma to our souls from family experiences.

Most of our families are in crisis. We are often pitted against one another, and most people would rather spend a holiday alone than deal with their families.

First, trace the core of the issue. Look within yourself and seek to understand your contribution to the situation. Understand why you feel the way you do, and use your book of revelations. Sometimes simple conversations turn into shouting matches, and favoritism among parents, petty jealousies, a parent's will, and even skin color and hair texture can fuel the smoldering fire.

Find out why you have hostile feelings, and ask yourself are they worth it? Choose your battles carefully because your energies are the most precious resource you own. Do not waste them on people who will never change.

Your Personal Book of Revelations

Family comes in many different forms, as we've witnessed in these essays. Have you thought about who you consider to be your family lately?

- Describe what family means to you.
- Describe your family and your relationship with each individual member.
- How do you fit in the composition of your family?
- Does everyone communicate in your family?
- Can your family become disruptive and even embarrassing?
- Do you accept family members for exactly who they are and what they do in life?
- Examine your insecurities. Do you see similar traits in your mother or the person who raised you?
- Is your family supportive or loving or both?
- What situation occurred in your family that still has a tremendous amount of pain for you?
- Do you still harbor negative feelings which stemmed from your family?
- Can you forgive your family members?
- Do you put parameters on your life as far as your family is concerned?
- If you could change an attribute of your family, what would it be?
- Do you look to your friends and others as a surrogate family?

Remember, we are all fortunate enough to find our family wherever we look.

V

The Color of Money

Possession of material riches without inner peace
is like dying of thirst while bathing in the river.
—Paramhansa Yogananda

What is your perception of money? Have you always thought that the person with the most money has the most power, or were you raised to believe that money is the root of all evil? Do you feel that if you had more money, all or most of your problems would disappear? Or are you just interested in building a safety net by socking away money for a rainy day? We work for money instead of money working for us. Money is just a tool. It's not meant to be hoarded or wasted, revered or shunned. It's meant to be utilized—and used correctly.

However, it is not the amount of money that we make; it is the money management skills that we lack that often lead to our financial woes. African-American women are one of the largest consumer groups in America, spending well into the billions. Just in hair products alone we spend millions. Most times we indulge in impulse buying—instant gratification, but the feeling is often fleeting.

James Baldwin put it eloquently: "Money, it turned out, was exactly like sex, you thought of nothing else if you didn't have it and thought of other things if you did." Oddly enough, chances are very few of us were privy to money management lessons from our parents. Money has been a mystery, and our parents may have had limited disposable incomes. They may have lived paycheck to paycheck or had a passbook savings account. But today there are so many options to diversify your savings, and it can be extremely confusing. Between CDs, IRAs, Mutual Funds, and the highs and lows of the stock market, it's hard to keep up.

Somehow our parents and society led us to believe that we would marry a doctor, a lawyer, or Prince Charming, and he would take care of all our financial needs. With divorce, separate living arrangements, and shared responsibilities of childrearing, only the financially fit can keep their head above water. A woman can no longer depend on a man for her financial needs.

What's scary is now there is such a focus on getting money by any means necessary from the media and our environment that men are scamming women for whatever they can. Some women will do anything to be in the company of a wealthy man, including experiencing abuse and dehumanizing and sexually comprising situations. We have sat with a lot of women, some of them extremely powerful and rich, and although they enjoy the pomp and circumstance of their lifestyle, they are usually unhappy. Only because, just like you, they thought that attaining money or marrying the right husband would make them happy. You begin to realize that you missed the precious moments in your life. Some of those moments and relationships can never be replaced. There is a definite breakdown of morals and ethics, making us plain and simple "crabs in a barrel."

But our ancestors knew the power of money and used it to try to make the world better. When Booker T. Washington was trying to build Tuskegee, it was an unprecedented mission. Back then black people pulled together because education was more valuable than gold to them. People gave literally everything they had so that the young people would be able to have an education. In *Up from Slavery*, Booker writes about when he was calling on everyone to try to help raise the money to build Tuskegee from people, many of whom "had spent their best days in slavery":

> *Sometimes they would give five cents, sometimes twenty-five cents. Sometimes the contribution was a quilt, or a quantity of sugarcane. I recall one old colored woman, who was about seventy years of age, who came to see me. . . . She hobbled into the room where I was, leaning on a cane. She was clad in rags; but they were clean. She said: "Mr Washington, God knows I spent de best days of my life in slavery. God knows I's ignorant an' poor; but," she added, "I knows what you an' Miss Davidson is tryin' to do. I knows you is tryin' to make better men an' better women for de coloured race. I ain't got no money, but I wants you to take dese six eggs, what I's been savin' up, an' I wants you to put dese six eggs into de dedication of dese boys an' gals."*
>
> *Since the work at Tuskegee started, it has been my privilege to receive many gifts for the benefit of the institution, but never any, I think, that touched me so deeply as this one.*

That sister was willing to give all she had to try to make things better for her people. She had been saving to come up with six eggs! To even think about this today is mind-boggling. Even though to us—and even to people in that day—it doesn't seem like a lot, to her it was everything. And that's why, to Booker, it was such an important gift. A million dollars wouldn't have equaled those six eggs from that sister.

Today we have so much, but truly give so little. We don't even give to ourselves for things that will make us better people. Instead we go through life with a lack mentality.

If you don't own something in your mind, you'll never be able to own it physically. Sometimes people say, you seek your "mental equivalent." This just means that, no matter how much money you happen into, if you're not a person with a wealth mentality, then you'll never be rich.

You see it all the time where people hit the lottery and end up broke and pitiful a year later. Or with athletes or entertainers who suddenly strike it rich, and before you know it, they're going bankrupt. And these our role models? We're so caught up on trying to own things, that the things we own end up owning us. Our quest for instant gratification through material possessions only leaves us ungratified, broke, and without the power to change our situation.

We've Got "Issues"

Everyone has issues with money . . . EVERYONE! Don't hide it and deny it. If we all pulled credit reports, they probably wouldn't come back as clean as we would like. You can snicker if yours does, but nine out of ten of ours don't. We can't all claim to have great credit, great education, nice clothes, food on the table, or any of the other things we need and use in life without a little struggle. Take comfort, you're not the only one. A good friend of ours told us—while we were whining about being behind on a few student loan payments, no less—if we took a look at Donald Trump's credit report, it wouldn't come back so pristine: he's a multimillionaire but a few years ago he went bankrupt! Don't worry. The richest people in the world started off in debt and were able to turn things around. So can you, so can we.

It Makes the World Go Round

Money is a big deal to a lot of people. It has a certain kind of romantic power over people, not just black women, over people period. A perfect example of this concept is the show *Who Wants to Marry a Millionaire*. We all know how that turned out! At night the airways are littered with how to get rich quick. The truth is that with more money comes responsibility. The basic idea is that you have to plan and work hard to bring balance to your life—not just money but love as well. As the old saying goes—money can't buy you love.

In this chapter, sisters will face different sides of our issues about money. We all want prosperity and abundance in our lives, but learning from our sisters can help us figure out exactly what we have to do to attain it.

25

Misconceptions of the Truth About Self and Money

LisaRaye

People have these automatic misconceptions when they meet me. Often I hear them say, "you have such a strong opinion about things." Some say I come across as I know everything, that I am strong, that I have no problems, and that I'm a woman with a lot of power. Those statements may be true, not just for me but for every black woman. That does not mean that there isn't a flip side to me or to us—a vulnerable side. Black women have many sides and facets to their lives and personalities. Don't get me wrong, black women have problems. Sometimes we just have to lay in bed at night and figure out how to conquer them all. What direction do you want to take? What options will this situation give you? And, what are you going to learn?

Dealing with people's misconceptions of me is something that I have had to deal with everyday. To protect my sensitive side I choose my friends carefully. Being an actress only complicates the situation because it makes it harder for people to separate LisaRaye from the characters LisaRaye portrays on screen. Just because I take a role doesn't mean I have the same personality, values, or lifestyle of the character in the film.

Things change when people see you in a movie. They think, "Damn girl, you are really doing it, you're really getting paid now." Just because they've seen a couple of movies that I have done they think I'm rolling. The movie *Players Club* was my first film and what makes people think that I got paid a hell of a lot of money for a small black production? Money isn't everything, because I couldn't have paid for the recognition or publicity that the *Players Club* gave me. It wasn't an Arnold Schwarzenegger or Bruce Willis film where the studio gave us a huge budget like $80 million. Black movies are $5 million or $8 million at the most, but that is going to change very soon. You think about how many levels of work it takes to produce a movie and wonder how they get to the big screen at all.

The value of money and business has been instilled in me from a young age—my family manages a chain of hotels/motels. Growing up I never told them that I didn't want to continue with the family business. If you grew up in a family business you automatically knew what you were going to do when you got older. One thing I knew was that since I was around the business since grammar school, I was sick of it. I could not find the words to tell them that I did not want to do this anymore. How do you tell your family that something that they have invested all of their time and energy—physically, emotionally, mentally, and financially makes you sick? The business supported all of us for so many years, but I didn't want any part of it.

When I was growing up I knew we weren't a poor family; the family business provided a financial cushion. We were a little bit more than middle class. I never had to experience the word no when it came to money. I was the only child, and my parents wanted me to have everything. On vacations I was always allowed to bring a friend along so I would have company. As I got older I started noticing that I was never invited back on their family trips. I watched as my family always willingly gave friends, family, and other businesses loans. Some of those loans were never paid back. My parents always took it in their stride.

So, with those things firmly implanted in my psyche I went to college and majored in hotel/motel management. When I got out of college I started doing some modeling as a hobby. At that time it was just a hobby so I never had a steady job, and I still worked at my family's business. I was sick of it, and I let it be known that this was not where I wanted to be career-wise. I would go to work, but I wouldn't stay there very long—my heart and spirit weren't in it and it showed.

When I started modeling it gave me a competitive side that I wasn't aware I possessed. It was definitely something I needed to succeed in that business, but of course modeling wasn't paying enough. My mother was concerned about me not having a steady income, and she was looking out for my best interest but I didn't know that at the time. So when I came out to Hollywood my mother said, "LisaRaye, is this one of your get rich quick schemes?" I was like, "No, Mom!" Her skepticism gave me the determination that made me say to myself I gotta make this work, show them and me that I can make it happen. I had that "Chicago East Coast Hustle" about me. I used that competitiveness from my modeling and pageant years to get up and make something happen.

When I landed in Hollywood I learned a couple of things. I knew when I came out here I wasn't going to wait on any tables. It was an awakening. "You have to believe in what you have and use what you've got to get what you want." That quote came from *Players Club,* and actually it is so true, but not just for the world depicted in the movie, but for life in general.

What you possess spiritually is the only thing you truly have, and my spirit was telling me that I was going to make it.

I did videos and guest-starring roles, so I never had to take a 9 to 5 to survive. I had enough of that with working in the hotel business. I made sure that I saved every extra penny and eliminated any sign of struggling mentality. Looking back on it now, it wasn't as easy as it sounds. It was really a shock to my system since I never had to budget myself before because of my parents' support. Knowing what I ultimately wanted helped me fall into line with my spending habits. I became thrifty and did the best I could with cutting corners. When the rent and utilities were due and I thought I wouldn't be able to cover it, a video, small part, or commercial would come along to tell me that this is where I was supposed to be.

I always had a style about me that regardless of what was going on at the time, I never became desperate. If you act desperate, you will be treated like you're desperate. Even though there is a blackout in Hollywood, and black actors and actresses aren't getting the work that they deserve, I have always accepted a part because I either identify sometimes, or even sympathize with the character, or the role presents a unique challenge to me as an actress.

What I have been able to do is to diversify myself and not limit my capabilities. That includes acting, voiceovers, spokesperson, public appearances, and I will gladly do a music video if I agree with the lyrics and/or message. I look at money differently knowing that Hollywood is fickle, and it is a blessing that I am working. I psyche myself up to believe that I am doing the work for the exposure and not the money. When the check does come it is a surprise, and gratitude comes with that. I do get lump sums, but you have to factor in 10 percent management, 7 percent to your entertainment lawyer, 15 percent to your agent, 33 percent to Uncle Sam, and when it is all over you are almost working for free. You become the Chief Financial Officer of your own enterprise both personal and professional.

It's not easy to keep your spirit strong in Hollywood. People criticize and attack you verbally every chance they get. I allowed one of my very first acting teachers and coaches to express his opinion on what my accent sounded like to him. In the middle of a class and in the middle of a scene he said, "I sounded very uneducated." I stopped the whole class, not only did he bruise my ego, but he hurt my damn feelings. I came out like a lion with the typical black girl, "What the hell do you mean because I have a Southern drawl I can't be a doctor, lawyer, or your mother?" I broke it down to him. When I was finished not only was he apologizing, but he also offered me free classes. Needless to say I walked out of the classroom and never returned until *Players Club* came out, and I had the lead. I plopped down the tape on his desk and I said, "Here, this is my movie, the lead—with my uneducated ass," and walked out.

I was searching for my spirituality and some type of peace. I needed clarity, because there was so much going on around me it was beginning to affect me spiritually. People and their negativity, managing money, a commuter relationship, a full-time career, motherhood, and success. You have to use those life experiences to elevate you and challenge yourself. But I wasn't looking for another challenge; I was looking for peace. I had tried everything; my daughter went to a Catholic school and took Mass lessons. I was raised as a Baptist, but I even looked into becoming a Jehovah's Witness. One of my girlfriends said, "Why don't you try chanting?" I said, "Yeah right. What does that mean?" But at that point in my life I was willing to try anything to find the inner peace I desperately needed in my life. My friend introduced me to Buddhism, and I started chanting like it was a magic genie.

At first I was leery, *I am going to try this and if it doesn't work then forget it.* What Buddhism brought to my life was a sense of calm and peacefulness. I meditate in the morning for an hour and during that hour I was amazed at how at peace with myself I became. It was incredible. I was so calm throughout the day. I always felt like I had a chip on my shoulder, but after meditating it felt like it was a happy and appreciative chip. I felt much more stable and focused enough to know what that day meant to me and what I had to accomplish by the end of the day.

I've always had goals, and I write down everything. My life consisted of lists, like I have to go to the grocery so I can get apples, oranges, and peaches but there was no format about it. I would just go to the store, and if they didn't have any peaches, I would be mad. Buddhism taught me to do this in an orderly fashion, and if the grocer didn't have any peaches, it was okay, I could just go to another store. You have time, and that is all you have, and time is on your side. So I wouldn't be upset if one store didn't have peaches. In the past I would have wanted to make them have peaches, now I just go to the next store. If they didn't have peaches there, then it wasn't meant for me to have peaches that day.

It was the way I looked at everything as opposed to the glass being half empty, I would say it was half full. That was what Buddhism has done for me. I also believe in karma, what goes around comes around—cause and effect. You can sit up and pray all day long, but if you don't take any action, ain't nothing gonna happen. What happens with me is I do believe in a higher superior being, I just don't choose to call it God, Lord, Allah, or Buddha. It's not that we chant to this fat Japanese man called Buddha, that's not what it is about. I just consider the superior being the universe and being in rhythm with the universe.

Being in rhythm with the universe has given me the ability to seek my goals; they do change yearly but my main goal stays the same. When I first came to Los Angeles all I wanted to be was an actress. A couple of months after that I realized that acting was just a hobby, and I wanted to use it as a stepping stone for another goal. My goal became to utilize my new found fame and fortune to develop nursing centers and homeless shelters.

The idea actually came from my mother and father who always shared what they had. During the holidays we fed homeless people, and it was a profound experience for me as a young girl. I actually saw the appreciation on the faces of the people we helped. The same people would come back year after year looking forward to those meals. It was so rewarding, and I started being aware of the blight of the homeless. I am looking into establishing shelters and foundations in Chicago and Los Angeles. I want them to be places where people will be welcome and they would have to work within the facility to help others like themselves.

I look forward to being married, and becoming a wonderful wife, and having more children. The career thing—I love it, but it is still a hobby to me and when it isn't fun anymore I want to sit my ass down and say this does not run me, I run it.

LisaRaye has starred in such movies as the *Players Club*, *The Wood*, and *Rhapsody*. She was able to do all that she has done with a tremendous amount of love and support from her fiancée, Tony Martin, who plays for the Miami Dolphins, her daughter, Kai, and her mom, Katie, who still gives her advice on money.

26

The Color of Money

Deborah A. Williams, Ph.D.

What is the true color of money? I have often asked myself this question. On a daily basis, I observe men and women, young to old, who are willing to do anything—beg, scam, steal, lie, and even kill—in the quest for "the almighty dollar." For eleven years I have been the wife of a professional NBA athlete and have met, spoken with, sipped tea, and cried with some of the richest, most successful, and accomplished sisters in the world. My assessment: Puff Daddy was right . . . "Mo Money, Mo Problems."

Although it is difficult for those yet to reach that level of success to understand it, those who have know this to be true. What *is* the true color of money? Perhaps *it is blue.* Money can bring a tremendous amount of sadness, loneliness, and isolation to those who have it. So many of us assume that once we have obtained a certain amount of money in the bank, that we will be happy and our lives will be perfect. How soon we realize that it is merely a fantasy, an aberration. In truth, unless you have fed your spirit, no amount of money, celebrity status, or power will help you escape feelings of emptiness and aloneness. Someone who has been a part of the professional baseball lifestyle for many years once said, "There's nothing worse than feeling sad and alone in a stadium with 20,000 people." She was right.

The public sadness of my beautiful and talented sisters, Phyllis Hyman and Halle Berry, is a perfect example. To the world, they are gorgeous and gifted, successful and rich, seeming to have everything, including all the trappings of success. Yet inside, their souls screamed to be attended to and nurtured. The sadness can threaten, and in some cases succeed, in tearing down the very fiber of a person's being. Certainly, if peace of mind and contentment were something to be bought, I would have stocked all my closets, drawers, cabinets, and cupboards to save for a rainy day.

Perhaps the color of money is *yellow.* With money and success also come fears that are sometimes overwhelming. Fear of failure, of not being able to live up to the high expectations that have been set for you, and fear of being loved for *all* the wrong reasons.

Or could the color be *red,* filled with anger and resentment toward agents and managers who treat you as if you were stupid and naive. Or anger about being used, even by some family members and close friends . . . Betrayed and lied to "for the love of money."

Green is the actual color of money, but also the symbol of envy and jealousy that success breeds. How many times have you heard echoes of the phrase "you've changed?" Have you? Or have others' perceptions and expectations of you changed? What happened to the days when your friends would buy you a hamburger? Now, you must eat steak and lobster, and your friends don't even attempt to reach for their wallet . . . even for the tip.

Being rich is a state of mind. Some of the most magnificent and full experiences are available at relatively no expense at all. Some of us have money, but our spirits are poverty-stricken. To be truly *rich* requires an emotional investment in faith, in caring, in peace, family, health, and self. If you can keep your soul revitalized through the faith that God will guide you, soothe you, and be your loyal friend . . . the only color that matters will be in the heavens, and we all know that those streets are lined with *GOLD.*

Deborah A. Williams, Ph.D., is the president and CEO of HerGame2, a sportswear company for the active professional woman. She is a mother and loving wife to Herb Williams, center for the New York Knicks.

27

True Lies

Victoria Clark

True confession time—I record every penny I spend. Whether I buy nail polish, furniture, books, gifts, or a drink after work—it all goes into my Quicken computer program. I itemize my ATM withdrawals as well. Three years ago, I began dutifully recording how I spent my money on a daily basis. Now, I set aside an hour each week for the Victoria financial update. At a glance, I know if I've had a week of spending under budget or an overwhelming case of the *I wants*, giving a fierce butt-kicking to the *I needs*.

Currently, I have one credit card, Visa, and a charge card, American Express. (Okay, I have a Barney's card but I use it once a year at their warehouse sale.) I even called Visa to get my annual percentage rate lowered from 17.9 percent to 14.9 percent. I put money away every month into a mutual fund and make a plan to sock away money right before April 15 into my IRA. And I'm always searching for ways to keep more of my pocket money for me. My rationale for this somewhat rigorous attention to my cash flow is that I never want to wake up one day and discover I'm broke—fear can be a motivating force! I want to wake up one day and say I'm ready to purchase my own private sanctuary with my cash. My rationale is also inspired by the money lessons I learned from my mother.

I have my mother to thank for creating my need to be financially diligent. When I was ready to go to college, my mother wasn't prepared for me to go. For eighteen years, the plan was college, college, college. Yet my mother, as a single parent, hadn't prepared herself or me for the financial reality of paying for college. I had to do that myself. I became fluent in the language of student loans, interest rates, repayment plans, TAP awards, and grants—*fast*. It was an eye-opener.

That lack of planning made me very frustrated and pissed at my mother. Wasn't my mother supposed to teach me about saving money, paying bills, and all that other stuff they blab about on CNBC so I could be an independent woman who could take care of herself? My frustration changed, slowly, to the realization that no one taught *her* about money and how to manage it.

It definitely wasn't a subject in school. And my grandparents didn't pass on any information to her about how to manage and save money—so how could she pass on this information to me?

My family experience taught me the valuable life lessons of *never* relying on others for financial security and to educate myself about money. I researched every possible opportunity to get the funds to pay for my education and expenses. Work-study, loans, summer jobs—I became incredibly anal when it came to figuring out how to pay for college. I don't have stories of wild Spring Break trips or nights spent out dancing and drinking during my college years. The necessity about having to work to pay for college made it very clear to me why I was there: to get a degree and, then, get a job.

When I got my first "real" job at twenty-three, I couldn't wait to find an IRA for retirement. I asked everyone for advice and read every financial magazine about ways to save money. I made a vow that there was no way I was going to have a lack of planning be my reason for not having the kind of life I wanted. That was the legacy of my mother's financial bewilderment. But there have been detours. . . .

My jones for tracking and saving my money does not mean I follow a frugal lifestyle. I am proud to say that I am materialistic. It's my money! I worked for it so I should do what I want with it. If I want to have a maid come in to clean my apartment, I'm going to do it. (I tried to explain this logic to the man I was living with at the time and he was completely lost. We broke up shortly thereafter.) If I want to invest in a company, I do.

If I want to try a more expensive hairdresser, I try it. Money is supposed to help improve my quality of life, not be a straitjacket holding me back from living the life I want.

Yet, for some time in my twenties, money had me confused and a little loopy. Whenever I was depressed and unhappy, I went shopping. A bad day at work, I had to buy something. A fight with a boyfriend meant a pair of shoes just for the hell of it. I bought a lot of worthless stuff in a quest to make myself feel better. I didn't understand the difference between "I want" and "I need." The words "I need" prefaced everything. *I need these shoes. I need that dress. I need this bag.* Reflecting on that time, I needed everything. And although I didn't run up any spectacular credit card debt (thank God, the voice of mother Victoria warned me to be careful), I was still out of control. The situation was made easier by my decision to move into a boyfriend's co-op rent-free. (Yeah, I still can't believe it, either.) So I had a major portion of my income going to shoes, meals, dresses, jewelry, makeup, and anything else that was in a department store.

Two things happened to change that devil-may-care attitude. I left my job in public relations to start a toy company with my then-boyfriend. I was twenty-six years old and made the leap of faith to live on my savings for the years it took to start up the business. I had to change my wild-spending ways. The belief that I needed everything was replaced by a simple question: Do I need it? When I started asking myself that, I started walking away from a lot of stuff. And although my initial financial wake-up call at eighteen was necessary for me to get comfortable with money, the second one made me examine how having money and not having it made me feel.

I had to face up to the fact that I used money and the things I bought with it to boost my self-esteem. I held on to the faulty belief that if I was able to buy a thousand-dollar dress, I must have been a great person. It was much easier for me to believe that something expensive could make me a great person. Being forced to live on a limited income made me rethink why I felt the way I did. Today, I feel stupid for having believed that and then I remember—stupid is temporary, awareness is forever.

The second thing that happened is I became the financial person for the company we created, One World Toys. Because it is an entrepreneurial company, I had to learn how to make sure we didn't spend money recklessly. I scrutinized every expense for its value to the One World bottom line. I became emotionally detached from the company's financial decisions. There was a simplicity to the decision-making process of possibly purchasing computer equipment or investing money for the research and development of new toys—would it help the One World Toys bottom line? This experience was LIBERATING! It didn't' matter how I felt about the money; what mattered is if it would help One World Toys grow and thrive. In applying that same approach to my personal checkbook, I learned that money didn't have to rule how I felt about myself. I could rule it and even work with it.

This is not to say that all my money hang-ups have been completely eliminated—that would make me a sane, single black woman in New York and who wants that? But I have stopped using what I buy as the means to feel worthy and good about myself. And even though I am conscious of where my money goes, I do know that my net worth isn't determined by the fluctuations in the stock market or the balance in my checking account. Instead, it's determined by how I feel about myself, whether I've got five bucks or five hundred in my bank account. At the end of the day, I'm still a good, thoughtful, funny, kooky black woman who can still be a little anal at times.

Victoria Clark is the president of One World Toys, Inc., a multi-ethnic toy company. One World Toys customers include FAO Schwarz, Target, and Kaybee Toys. Ms. Clark is currently developing an animated children's television show.

28

Wants, Needs . . . and Self

Cheryl Procter

Money has always been a clouded mystery to me. Only recently while sitting in my finance class for my MBA did I realize how money and your ability to understand, manage, and control it is so important.

I am a twenty-one-year veteran of the public relations arena and am currently a regional public relations manager for Home Box Office (HBO). Prior to joining HBO, I was a consultant to Fortune 500 companies in the Chicago area. Earlier in my career I owned my own company and implemented publicity and marketing strategies for companies such as Anheuser Busch, Nissan North America, and Eastman Kodak Company. In my twenty-odd years, I have counseled CEOs, middle managers, and hundreds of young aspiring communications moguls. I have been elected chapter president to the Black Public Relations Society and Public Relations Society of America. I've got enough honors and awards to fill a small room. In passing, I have heard accolades such as "You are absolutely brilliant," "team player," "great marketing or PR plan," and "wonderful job." My comment in jest was always, "If I'm so good, why aren't I rich?"

Come to think of it, I really wasn't kidding. If I was so good, where was the money to show for it? Isn't life based on the reward system? I took stock of my life and I wondered, what does it mean to be rich? I realized that being wealthy isn't just about having material possessions, but also—and more importantly—being wealthy of spirit. Looking at my life, I have to say I am extremely wealthy. I have two wonderful healthy children, a cozy comfortable home, a great career, and I recently became engaged to my soul mate, Terry.

We all wonder what happened to the money that passed through our hands throughout the years. Why did I not know how to keep it? Money is the one thing that rules our lives—if we let it. It can translate into how we will raise our children, where they will be educated, what type of vehicle we will drive, what type of home we will live in, and establishes, in certain circles, status. I wondered how come so many of us have not learned how to manage money when it plays such a big part in our lives?

While having lunch with a new acquaintance, I started talking openly about the issue of money. In our lunch meeting my acquaintance mentioned a book she'd just read, 9 *Steps to Financial Freedom,* by Suze Orman. In the book, Orman encourages the reader to take a step back in time to the earliest moments that you can recall when money meant something to you, when you truly understood what it could do. I started thinking about the effects of money and my feelings toward it. Did I fear it? Or did I enjoy it? Or did I use it to bury an incident in my subconscious, which I may have forgotten?

I was always the little girl who had an entrepreneurial spirit beyond that of the ordinary lemonade stand. At age seven, I learned how to sew from my grandmother and I hemmed pants and skirts for extra money. When I was a few years older, I learned to make jewelry and created wonderful designs for sale to neighbors and family. As a teenager I taught dance lessons and even typed for extra cash. Growing up, my dad constantly reassured me that "I will always provide what you need and you must work for what you want." When I was a kid, it was the best deal ever. Whenever I needed something, he gave it to me, and if I wanted something, I just worked for it. My dad was responsible, generous, loving, and always gave his children the best. My mom, a teacher's aide, then certified special education teacher, left the responsibility of paying the household bills to my father.

On the other hand, my father had an uncle who everyone in the family whispered was rich. He was sometimes grouchy, and as kids, we would make jokes that his gifts of money were so small. Somehow we equated being rich with being grouchy. In school and in church, we would often hear the saying, "Money is the root of all evil," and I guess I always associated my uncle with that saying. I guess on some level I felt that too much money was evil.

When I went away to college, I continued to teach dance for extra money, worked at Sears, and met my first husband, Michael. He belonged to a singing group that was a hit on campus and in the small town where our school was located. I was asked to choreograph for the group, and before I knew it, we were dating. I was thrilled. I returned home one weekend to attend a wedding with Michael and most of all to introduce him to my mom and dad. I had traveled home on Greyhound, while he drove his own car with friends. For my dad, this was an indication that he cared more for himself than for me. Of course, I didn't see it that way, and nine years later we were married.

In the beginning, we had a great relationship; we would talk until the wee hours of the morning and shared many happy times together. He bought me jewelry and provided everything I ever wanted. But when it came to money, we clashed constantly. When it came to my needs and that of the household and family, we were not in sync. I was brought up to take care of my needs first. I had watched my grandmothers do it, my father do it, and now it was my turn to do it! When our marriage ended, the money issues were at the center of our disputes.

I used to beg for the answer to the question, "CAN SOMEONE TELL ME WHY I AM ABLE TO DO MORE WITH SO MUCH LESS MONEY AND ONLY ONE LESS DEPENDENT?" The basic need items hadn't changed, the mortgage, gas, lights—OK I spent a little less on food, but my child-care bills soared. I now know what my Aunt Minnie meant when I was bragging as a young girl about how much I made from selling jewelry. "The magic isn't in making the money, honey, it's in managing it! How much will you have the next time I see you?"

Today I'm in a healthy relationship where my wants and my needs are a priority. I'm changing my focus from making the money to managing the money I have. I'm no longer concerned with the deposits being made to my savings or checking accounts, but the deposits of time and love being made to my family, friends, and young public relations professionals looking to carve out a niche in this world of work.

Cheryl Procter is a corporate affairs manager for HBO. She currently is completing her MBA and is on her way to being wealthy.

Your Soul's Sustenance

But this I say, he which soweth sparingly shall reap also
sparingly, and he which soweth bountifully shall reap
also bountifully.
—II Corin. 9:6

We have great news for you. You are already wealthy. In the course of your lifetime 1 million dollars will have gone through your hands. It is what you have done with it that counts. Did you use it to improve your education or expand on a skill? Knowledge is a commodity that only increases in value as time goes on. Did you save it for the ability to say, "I quit because I am being disrespected," and it held you over until you were able to find another job? Did you use it to improve your living conditions, giving both you and your family a place to build memories and where you felt comfortable to send your children to the store? Did you give it to your church, the place where you worshipped maybe as a child, where you were married and or the place you seek solitude when things got rough? Did you use it to build bonds and memories with friends and family—nothing too expensive, just a picnic lunch, picking up Grandma's prescription, or baking a cake for someone's birthday? Did you use your money by giving it to a charity of your choice or purchasing something for someone to eat because you knew they were hungry? Did you use it to invest in your child's education so that he or she could have a successful life? Or did you have the best car, thirty pairs of shoes, four designer handbags, and the latest makeup, perfume, and clothes? Some of which you have used only once.

We often use money as replacement for the love that we really need and want. A lot of us have used money to fix things emotionally that just couldn't be fixed.

Money has been used to comfort us when a man has left. Money has been used to soothe us when we've been disappointed by not getting that promotion on the job. We have been bought with money: CHEAPLY! You know we are talking to you.

A lot of people are in debt. Being in debt when it comes to money is the equivalent to being in debt when it comes to your self-worth. If we can't heal our relationship with ourselves, we are going to have issues with money. A number of black women are beginning to recognize this phenomena and are working on healing, and when they do, they begin to see the changes in the way they treat money.

It is never too late to begin thinking smart about your money. Begin early in your career and establish a retirement account and focus on a goal. If investments are your best strategy, make sure that you diversify and research funds and programs before jumping in. Here are a few more tips to help you get started:

- Review how and what you spend your money on.
- Figure out your total debt. (We know it's hard, but it's worth it!)
- Commit to paying off your debt.
- Seek assistance by attending local Debtors Anonymous meetings or seeking counsel from a local budget and credit counseling office.
- Build an emergency savings and have it deducted directly from your paycheck whenever possible.
- Think about buying real estate and building equity and credit.
- Develop a financial filing system to keep track of your finances.

If you are a parent, one of the fundamental lessons you can teach your child is the value of money. Children watch your behavior, so when you borrow to get your hair done and the light bill isn't paid, they are likely to repeat the same pattern. Give your children an allowance and insist that they save. Check with your financial institutions and on the Internet for savings programs for children. Better yet, encourage your child to get a summer or after-school job. It will give them a greater sense of responsibility.

Your Personal Book of Revelations

What better topic to write about and get answers than your relationship with money? Draw on your feelings about money and the way it makes you feel to have it and the way it makes you feel when you think you don't have enough.

- How did your family handle money?
- Were you ever bought anything when you behaved?
- Do you gravitate toward men who buy you expensive gifts?
- Do you live beyond your means?

VI

Show Me the Way

The moment you move out of the way, you make room for the miracle to take place.
—Dr. Barbara King

You wouldn't be the person you are today if it weren't for people who helped to show you the way in the past. Someone kept you from running out in the street when you were three years old. Someone made sure you were fed. Someone was there to answer your questions when you were confused. If this weren't the case, you wouldn't be here today. It may have been your parents, a teacher, relative, employer, or well-meaning stranger.

Whether you would like to dispute the level of time and care given the fact is, you may not be able to repay the people who helped to show you the way when you needed guidance, but the way you show the universe that you are grateful for the blessing of having had someone there is to do the same thing for someone else.

Being shown the way and showing other people the way are just two sides of the same coin. You have to be humble to be a follower. And you must be able to be a good follower if you ever want to be a leader. It takes a big person to be humble because really being humble means having your ego in check. It means not having to take the credit for everything good that happens. It means being able to follow the direction that someone has laid out for you.

Helping someone only serves to help ourselves. It's called reciprocity. Reciprocity is the way the universe pays us back for every thought, deed, and word we put out in the ethos. Reciprocity is a checks-and-balances system designed to give us exactly what we deserve.

If you don't have the humility, respect, and foreknowledge of the universe's law of reciprocity, then you'll never be able to get yourself or your ego out of the way long enough to be in a place where anybody can help you. And if you can't follow the example that someone else has set, then you'll never be able to be a role model to anyone else.

Showing each other the way is how women who have come before us give us the advice that we need to get through the things that confront us in our lives—whether it's relationships, work, or anything you can think of. We all want someone to be that sort of spiritual mentor—someone who can impart some wisdom or a word of advice because she's gone through it and she's able to pave the way for any other person to see and learn from her experience.

From the trials and triumphs that some of this book's contributors recount, for example, on starting a business from scratch, you can get the feeling of someone mentoring you for a minute or even for a lifetime.

There are a lot of different kinds of mentors in our lives. We've had mentors in our careers that showed us all they knew and they did it freely. They just wanted to help us. And they were great examples of how to deal in business as a businesswoman. We still consider these women as mentors. Now, we've moved on to a different phase of our lives and maybe there will be new mentors who will come along to help us in this phase. We all go through phases and changes, and mentors come to us just when we need them.

Learning from Each Other

There are certain things we need in our lives, and we all have something to learn from each other. We can all show each other the way. A mentor is not necessarily a friend; you can learn from a stranger without having known her personally. Even a homeless person on the street can show you something if you're open to learning the lesson. That's the beauty of having people come into your life like that. They can be a mentor for a lifetime or a mentor for a minute. A person who shows you something usually does it by example. You can learn from many examples in many people's lives. You can learn from a child. You can learn from a ninety-two-year-old woman. You can learn from anyone if you're open to learning something about yourself.

We're Standing on Lots of Backs

We stand on the shoulders of all that came before us. In the oral traditions of our ancestors, stories would be passed down from generation to generation. Some of the stories are "old wives' tales" that teach us a lesson. We often tend to discount this kind of old-fashioned thinking, but today women need the old wives' tales and more to face the plethora of situations both in our personal lives and business.

We have to remember that love, support, and lessons in life come from a rainbow of places.

29

Shape Shifting

Karen Taylor

I have had as many career changes as I have had hairstyles. I have been a fund-raiser, promoter, special events coordinator, marketing specialist, entrepreneur, and publicist. And yet, I am still trying to achieve my ultimate dream.

At the age of seven, my cousin told me I was "anointed with success." I have been consumed with "makin' it" all my life. This feeling can possess you like a demon. It makes you cry, laugh, and feel hopeless when nothing seems right. I am now going through growing pains in the process of becoming what I believe will be my job of life—producing for television and film.

I have been on the success path all my life. I spent six years working at the premier entertainment companies (Double XXposure, EMI, Elektra, and Sony), holding national positions in publicity. I thought I had found my niche. After the fifth year, I began to question my goals. I was motivated, but the passion was gone. Getting up in the morning and going to work were becoming a chore—I was dying a slow death. Being a publicist was no longer challenging. I wanted more. But what? Freedom. Freedom to take a chance. Freedom to grow, make mistakes, fail, and ultimately get back up and try again.

At thirty-one years of age, I am taking a chance on myself and life. I am allowing myself to be vulnerable. Sometimes, I think you do your best when there is no feeling of security. I have managed to shape other folks' careers—now, it's time to shape mine.

There are many events, people, and places that have impacted my life. During my sophomore year in college, the movie *She's Gotta Have It* and the filmmaker Spike Lee made me fall in love with cinema. One year later, I met Spike Lee at an ATM in Brooklyn. He was in preproduction for *School Daze*. I approached him. Seizing the moment is the epitome of opportunity, luck, fate, and balls. I asked Spike if there was a role for me in

School Daze. Flatly, he said, "No." Then, I asked him if he had any intern-
ships and would he speak at my school? He said yes to both.

Working on *Do the Right Thing* was a once-in-a-lifetime experience—it
changed my outlook on life. I witnessed black people call the shots on a
movie. It was a great experience. I was mesmerized by the talent on the set:
Robin Harris, Ernest Dickerson, Samuel Jackson, Rosie Perez, Martin
Lawrence, Giancarlo Esposito, Ruth E. Carter, Robi Reed-Humes were all
unknown then—all looking for their big break. Just like me now.

It was 1987, I was a junior at St. John's University, and just runnin' shit. I
was the quintessential student: politically active, in the honor society, a
news reporter, chairperson of the Black Women's Committee, activist, and
in my mind, on my way to becoming the next Oprah Winfrey. My first ambition was to be a news reporter. Well, that changed when I visited a television station and realized that vibe wasn't me. That was the first *real*
indication that I would go through many careers—before I discovered my
true calling.

I started working at the United Negro College Fund. I got a job by simply following my instincts and dropping off my résumé with the reception-
ist. Within days I got a call from them offering me a fund-raising position. I
worked with them for a year, then I went to the United Way to take an account executive position. I was at the United Way for almost two years when
I got sick—sick of begging for money! However, I realized I was getting
closer to something because I enjoyed pitching and making the sale.

When I was at the United Way, I met a brother named Wendell Haskins.
He was friends with Puff Daddy (in his pre–Rap star days), and we would
go to these dope ass parties called Daddy's House. This was my first taste of
the music industry and I loved it.

One day, I was at Wendell's cubicle and we were talking about life and
dreams—you know that talk. While I was sitting there, I saw a *Rolling Stone*
magazine and he told me his friend was a publicist for EMI Records and his
group was in the magazine. Wendell explained to me that a publicist is the
person who makes the pitch to have the artist in magazines and on television. The lightbulb went on in my mind—my next career?!? Well, it was
soon after that that I resigned from the United Way. Did I have a job? No,
but I had a vision. I mailed my résumé to all the record labels I could think
of and ended up at Capitol Records.

While there and working in a paid internship at Blue Note/Capitol
Records, I got caught up in some gossip and was dismissed. I learned a
priceless lesson—even when you are innocent, you are guilty by association.

My next job came to me via an advertisement in a brochure. I was looking at a media brochure and there was something special about the ad for
Double XXposure—a black-owned public relations firm on Seventh

Avenue. I knew I had to work there. I called Double XXposure and sched-uled an interview. I impressed them with my charm and was hired as a paid intern. Well, in no time the lady that hired me quit—timing is everything. It was up to me to show and prove—hard work, late nights, networking, and being relentless were paying off. The owner of the company, Angelo Ellerbee, took me under his wing and nurtured me into becoming a "real" publicist.

At Double XXposure, we didn't have the greatest clientele. Most of our artists were unknown except for Carl Payne (Cockroach) from the *Cosby* and *Martin* shows. What we didn't have in clientele we made up for in co-ordinating fabulous special events. Angelo had promoted me to Director of Media Relations, after I had secured some key television and print place-ments for Jade, Patra, and Shabba Ranks' dancehall tour. During my tenure at Double X, I really enjoyed the industry—the parties, concerts, free CDs, and the chance of living a dream. My hard work was paying off and my rep-utation was growing.

Remember my friend Wendell Haskins? His friend was leaving his job at EMI Records and guess who got the job? Me, the ex-fund-raiser. Leaving Double X was difficult—it had become my second home. EMI offered me an incredible opportunity—it was time to grow.

I loved working at EMI. I really discovered my talent as a public rela-tions executive. I was blessed to have worked with some talented vision-aries—Digable Planets (the year they won the Grammy), Dianne Reeves, Najee, Shara Nelson (Massive Attack), Guru's Jazzmatazz, Speech (Arrested Development), The Spinners, Joi (pre-Baduizm). My biggest accomplish-ment was designing and implementing the press campaign for D'Angelo, with his critically acclaimed debut album, *Brown Sugar.*

When you are on a roll, you are also wondering what else can happen? Well, the most powerful woman in the music industry, Sylvia Rhone (chair-person of Elektra Entertainment), recruited me for a marketing position. I had arrived. This was one of the most difficult career decisions I had to make—I literally wrestled with the opportunity. I wanted to work and learn from Sylvia, but I didn't want to leave EMI. D'Angelo was just percolating and I had more to do on the project. I was confused. I decided not to take the job, until Sylvia called me and convinced me otherwise. I went to Elektra—I hated it!!

I resigned from Elektra, and my fiancé at the time encouraged me to start my own business. I gave birth to my company, TaylorMade. I was an entrepreneur—I used all my connections with the label executives to se-cure accounts. I did it for seventeen months and I represented some good record labels: Virgin, Hollywood, A&M, Arista, Perspective, and Hola, Jellybean Benitez's Latin label.

I was on my way to freedom—until greed came knocking. I was made an offer to work for Mariah Carey's label—Sony/Crave. It sounded like a chance of a lifetime—would I risk my freedom for a routine job? Yes. I wanted to work for Sony Records and this was a new company with a lot of potential.

My job at Crave was in the capacity of publicity and artist development. I worked there for one year until the doors closed. I was enjoying my job at Crave—finally I was integrating publicity with artist development. When Crave was being absorbed, there was a media position available on the West Coast. I interviewed for the post, but I realized I was wasting my time. The love for press was gone. I was beginning to question my motives—money or passion? I tried to convince myself that it was passion, but that wasn't true. I only enjoyed the creative aspect of my job. At Crave, the talent was good, but not exceptional. I wasn't working with the likes of D'Angelo, Maxwell, or Badu—simply producer-driven projects. I didn't love the music. I had to reevaluate myself and wonder where did the love go? How could I feel that hungry, burning sensation again? I had to move forward.

Currently, I am pitching original programming to television and cable and coauthoring a book on sports. The passion is back. However, there are days when I scream, cry, and wallow in self-pity. I know it will be okay—I'm a survivor. I'm right back where I started. A friend told me—you have to constantly reinvent yourself until you get it right. I am trying to get it right this time.

I pray that the Lord continues to show me the way. Please.

Karen Taylor is the president of TaylorMade, which provides publicity and book projects for the entertainment industry.

30

Married to the Civil Rights Movement

Frances Darcy Hooks

It has been a seesaw thrill. It has been interesting. Good, bad, scary, pleasant, all of the adjectives you can name. And it has been an interesting journey. I don't think I would trade it for anything. But I don't think I would have asked for it either. Growing up in the South I probably would have not been exposed to the kind of political and social-activist lifestyle I have lived these past forty years if I had not met my husband, Benjamin Hooks. I would have followed the traditional route of getting a job, teaching, or following in my mom's footsteps of settling down to a normal life. That was how I started out working as a teacher and guidance counselor. But it didn't last. After I married him, things changed, and so did I.

My husband was very active in the community. He was then appointed to the bench and became the first black to serve in criminal court in the South. Once he became a judge in Memphis, there were a lot of the activities he'd participated in in the past that could no longer do. He had to be careful and set an example so that there would be opportunities for other blacks that followed him. It was important that we made a way for other blacks to participate in the political and judicial process. I was taking on a role that my husband couldn't do that allowed me to expand my horizons. As women, we must be mindful to utilize every opportunity we get to expand our skills and horizons.

We would go to rallies and open meetings. I would go with him but I wasn't the vocal personality he was. Slowly I started doing some of the things he had done in the past that his new job restricted him from doing. I started speaking and having a very vocal presence in the community, and it changed my life forever.

It was interesting and somewhat challenging. But other times it got on my nerves. I wanted to be like any other typical woman back then. I wanted to go shopping or find something refreshing to do such as a peaceful lunch with friends. But instead of being able to go home, fix dinner, and go to the shopping center, I would go to a meeting. With a certain amount of knowledge comes responsibility; with a progressive husband and hostile environment you find yourself rising to the occasion.

But that was the times. I had to rise. It was the position. If I wanted him to have more opportunities as a breadwinner, then I would have to perform my role. I got busy. And I grew into the job. And you must understand that I loved my husband and I loved serving in my role as wife. But that didn't mean I was not my own person. We worked together as a team. And it was he who had the best opportunity at the time, so I supported him. He was the breadwinner.

During the time my husband was working with the Southern Christian Leadership Conference (SCLC), the group came to Memphis and I would entertain them. And when he went to Alabama or other places, I would stay home. There was a time and place for everything.

When I was on the road traveling with my husband or at some important meeting, people would call me "the shadow of the super police department." I had a shadow over my husband and the activities he was involved in, because I knew when things were right or when they weren't. I had an active role in his life, and wherever I had to say something, I would say it. That is very important. When you are married, you have to know what your role is, and that doesn't mean staying in your place. It means understanding what is important and what needs to get done. So I would make speeches for him in his absence, and because of how I carried myself, the people would accept me although they wanted my husband.

But I didn't let any of this bother me. It was like a seesaw. We went up and down. But I have always been a person who likes the back row. I have never liked being up front. He was a minister but he wasn't preaching. I would go in with him but sit some other place where you would not expect the speaker's wife to be sitting. Now I have been a preacher's wife for forty-three years. And I never sit down front. It allowed me to see things from a different point of view. It also allowed me to help my husband. And that is important to remember. You have to be a step away from the center of the action to see what is really going on.

But all the while, running around with my husband didn't stop me from being myself. I was selected as one of the first black guidance counselors in the late 1950s. There was a group of us black women sent to the State University to be certified as counselors. And I taught for twenty-eight years. And the contributions we made were important. I am extremely proud of my young black kids before the days of desegregation. Back then the college recruiters came into the high schools. Often most of the discrimination came from among black teachers just as it would in an all-white school. They had their own special children they wanted to see succeed. So we started a program where college administrators came in and every student in the school could see the recruiter. I am really proud that the program and it has lasted for more than thirty years.

I enjoyed being with my husband and being involved in his activities but I never let the activities or the marriage affect who I am. You must always keep a strong sense of self. My husband always supported what I was doing. And by the same token, whenever he needed me, I was there. And while every program we were involved in was important to me just like teaching, so was my marriage. Balancing many things is the role we are born into as black women. And if I might say so, we do a great job.

It was our ability to balance work, family, and community activism that allowed us black women to make a significant contribution to the Civil Rights Movement. There were so many women who did lots of hard work during the Civil Rights struggle. The men were up front and we made sure that signs were made. The children were cared for. Whatever snacks or food they needed, we made sure things ran smoothly. And we also filled in on occasion for our husbands.

During the protest marches around the South and in the city of Memphis, we would make signs and talk with the people. And when the men were on the verge of giving up hope, it was us black women who kept insisting that there were to be brighter days ahead. We just did what we knew had to be done like our forefathers and mothers had done. We kept our faith, we kept a prayer on our lips, that message in our hearts . . . that there were no big "I's" just little "you's."

We had to keep our eyes open and watch for everything. When you stop and think about the things we wanted to say and do but couldn't because of the tenor of the climate, you see that we surpressed a lot. It just wasn't kosher. We waited *on* and waited *for* our men—but sometimes they didn't want to hear from a woman. That's when we had to let the world know that, yes, we do have a voice. Our voice was strong as the trumpet. But it was *how* and *when* we used it that made it strong. A black woman has to know when to speak and when not to. When to act and when to move on. It is hard at times but you learn. You learn.

Today, most young women don't really focus on the group movement. They have been told that you are armed with what it takes to make it. But when you face the realities of the situation, what do we own? I have a daughter who has two sons. I have four children. I tell my daughter, once you are armed with a basic education, good manners, good speech, and the ability to think, don't let anybody stop you from achieving your goals. Somebody might put a stumbling block in your way. But if you can't get it out of the way, move it or find another place. The man is supposed to be the leader. And if we think he is going down the wrong street, we are supposed to stop him. But some men are like trains that are out of control and can't be stopped. So get out of the way and move on. Remember we are black women. And we are the center of the marriage, the community, and the movement. Use your power. And balance it with your skills.

Frances Darcy Hooks is a former teacher and guidance counselor. She has been married to Benjamin Hooks, executive director of the NAACP, for forty-nine years. Her life has been devoted to working with pride and dignity for the betterment of African-American people.

31

A Life in Full Bloom

Saundra Parks

Today, The Daily Blossom's eclectic, provocative, and alluring arrangements can be found executive suites, corporate offices, private homes, and at numerous special events and charity events. From the beginning, I had a feeling that I wanted to open a business that would allow me to express myself. I have realized a dream that many thought was impossible. In all ways, I have come full circle. And The Daily Blossom is a constant reminder of two of the greatest joys in my life: family and flowers.

Growing up, I was exposed to both flowers and the entrepreneurial spirit. My lovely childhood was filled with fresh, green lawns; and neat rows of tulips, that were created by my dad, an urban landscaper. I spent many worthwhile hours with him, watching him, and learning about soiling and seeding, and replenishing the earth. Having role models was extremely important to me. I truly believe that they were the foundation of my success as an entrepreneur. My parents instilled within me the courage, faith, and instincts to start and grow my own successful and sustaining enterprise. In addition to the cherished time that I spent with my father, I was in awe of my dear mother, who was the third African-American woman hired by Metropolitan Life Insurance. My mother was blessed with many talents, including an eye for decorating and color, as well as style and exquisite taste. My Aunt Sarah, who was a restauranteur, combined tenacity with a vibrant spirit to produce the best soul food ever.

One Christmas, my father asked me if I would like to help him to sell poinsettias wholesale to gain a feeling for the horticulture business. I remember driving up to Harlem with my girlfriends, and selling over three hundred pointsettias in restaurants and on the street. I knew something monumental was happening in my life.

I knew that in business, flowers were abundant, whether corporate offices or banks. I immediately called everyone in corporate America that I knew and didn't know. And so The Daily Blossom began in the kitchen of my one bedroom, Upper West Side apartment.

I had a sense of gardening sprawling rose bushes and flowing ivy—but not cut flowers, so I took courses to learn this craft. Creating the business took a great deal of courage and vision. The challenges were daunting. Building a business from scratch—building a brand name for my company in New York, one of the most competitive markets in the world—without financial resources was a tremendous undertaking. But working with nature was something that gave me a sense of joy. For me, shaping flowers and exotic plants into floral masterpieces that touch people, brings me unbridled joy. At The Daily Blossom, our work is expressionistic. We use the most beautiful flowers from around the world and mix unusual textures, contrasting interesting colors with traditional monochromatic hues.

As our business, The Daily Blossom, flourished so too did our clientele: American Express, Earl Graves, LTD, Essence Communications, MTV-VH1, Pepsi-Cola, Phillip Morris, The Equitable Companies, Inc., Time Warner, Sony Music, and luminaries such as poet Maya Angelou, Ed Bradley, Andre Harrell, Whitney Houston, Toni Braxton, Jon Bon Jovi, Johnnie Cochran, Lauryn Hill, Mariah Carey, Star Jones, and Russell Simmons.

Communication and relationships are important to me. I was fortunate enough to be chosen to be a spokesperson for American Express for national television and print ads. In addition, I was featured in *Black Enterprise*, *Essence*, and was on the cover of *The Executive Female*.

My education, vision, tenacity, and courage; and a strong belief in what I need to do, ultimately provided me with the skills to build a strong client base. Part of my success is that I am able to go into a space and communicate with a client, and together we can meet their needs for their space through floral arrangements. For me, creating an environment of style with flowers that govern people's lives, is more than a job, it is a mission that provides me with a sense of pride, passion, and purpose.

Saundra Parks is the president and CEO of The Daily Blossom store and studio. She is currently working on *The Daily Blossom Book of Flowers,* a coffee table book.

32

No Excuses

Sherma Wise

I remember it as if it were yesterday. It was almost dark outside and my playmate's mom called me into the house and told me my dad had phoned and told me to come home. Happily, I skipped down the street, my pigtails flying in the air with every step I took. I ran up the curved sidewalk between the two huge evergreen trees which stood on our front lawn. I walked in the front door, and there sat my dad and my grandmother and our next-door neighbors. I asked, "Where's Mommy?" I was always a very small and thin child for my age. My father picked me up and pulled out this gray steel lock box that he kept very important documents in. He sat me on top of this cold box and told me, "Mommy was killed in a car accident today."

At seven years old, I certainly understood the finality of death, but I still could not believe I would never see my mommy again. Her death is a very deep and profound pain I carry with me today. It is still as vivid and real to me as if it happened yesterday. Even as I am writing this, I had to get a box of Kleenex to wipe the tears streaming down my face. At the very moment my father told me she was gone, I knew my life would never be the same. I knew she would never again sew beautiful clothing for me for special occasions, often from scratch and from memory without a pattern to guide her. I knew she would never make the matching mother-daughter outfits she used to make for us or put my hair in "Shirley Temple Curls" for church. I knew she would never come into my room and help me say my prayers and kiss me good night. I knew from that point on, it was Daddy and I alone.

I started my story with this tragedy early in my life because it truly shaped me into what I am today. It's why I think the way I think, do the things I do, and why I have the drive and determination to "press on" during adversity and uncertain times. Because I was dealt this hand early in life, I could have felt sorry for myself all through my childhood because I did not have a mom, *or* I could draw strength and courage from the things I remember about her. Life is all about choices, and I chose the latter. I have a very special father. He taught me early on that it would be a dishonor to her memory to use her death as an excuse not to excel and not to realize my full potential.

My father and I set out to build a life without my mother. My grandmother (my dad's mom) at age sixty-four moved in to help my dad with me. She played the traditional role, cooking, cleaning, and providing moral and Christian ideals to our household. My grandmother was an example of quiet strength. She was able to share firsthand information with my father about single parenting. She had raised two sons (my father and his brother) alone after moving to Chicago. Her husband died at an early age of pneumonia.

As I continued to grow, my father was constantly challenged. He never stepped down from a challenge. A man raising a girl child in the late sixties and early seventies was still looked upon as unthinkable. Daddy never wanted to remarry. He told me he never wanted another woman to have undue influence over me. He was very clear about how I was raised. In many ways he sacrificed his own happiness for me. Of course, he had lady friends and I knew them all. They were nice respectable women, but as soon as the "M" word came up, Dad would head for the hills.

In many ways my father raised me the way a man would raise his son, with an unyielding sense of self-confidence; never allowing me to doubt my self or my abilities. My father insisted on many things from me, and he really did not leave much room for compromise. Getting a good education, good behavior, and perfect diction were preached constantly in our house.

I was bused to predominately white schools starting with the fifth grade and continuing through high school. I remember having a heated discussion with my father about my speech pattern. At one point he said, "As long as you are in my house, you will do as I say, and I say you will speak the 'King's English' and you will speak it properly." At which point he promptly hopped into his car and went downtown to Sears and purchased a reel-to-reel tape recorder. I was required to read passages from books and record my delivery. I guess I was about eleven or twelve years old. I had to do this until my diction was flawless. I felt like Eliza Doolittle in *My Fair Lady*. I told him I was tired of my friends telling me I "talked white." Eventually I got over it. Little did I know he was preparing me for a career choice I would make later in my life.

He was definitely involved in who and what my outside influences were growing up. He made sure I was surrounded by children whose parents had similar goals and values as his and that my friends wanted to succeed in life. Many of my friends from high school (although they are spread to the four corners of the world) are still close to me today.

Our family is very musical. By training, my father is a professional musician. Many of my cousins are professional musical performers. So, he also made sure I not only took the obligatory years of piano lessons but also had an appreciation and understanding for all kinds of music. From jazz to James Brown; Bach to Italian arias.

His influence and guidance helped me select a career path that would allow me to influence and effect change: "The Media." My first job out of college was as a radio news anchor. After two years, I moved into television news as a reporter, then an anchor. I worked at various stations. The things my father taught me helped me deal with the professional and personal challenges that I would be confronted with in the highly competitive world of broadcast journalism as an African-American female. He also prepared me for my current challenges.

While working as a reporter full-time at a television station, I landed a part-time position as a half-time reporter for an NBA basketball team. The experience opened an entire new world for me. Now, people who know me know that I'm a great networker. Well, I would arrive at the arena on game nights and would view it as a huge room "to work." I saw it as an opportunity to meet people and develop relationships with those on the business side of sports to really learn how the system worked. While everyone else was cheering on their team and trying to get interviews with the players, I was trying to learn as much as I could from the presidents and general managers of the teams. I felt the world was indeed my oyster and I learned to seize the moment and create my own opportunities. I started to develop this unshakable desire to "do my own thing," whatever that was. My father told me I came from a long line of entrepreneurs (my mom, her father, my uncle, and my mom's twin sister all had their own very successful businesses).

After learning that, I began an all-out assault to achieve my goals. I had gotten to know a number of the players on the team. I was able to talk one of the NBA's biggest stars into cohosting a talk show with me. It was an instant hit. It was that move that gave me the courage to quit my job and start my own television production company. Don't misunderstand, we did not make a dime, but this experience provided me with the confidence I needed to know that I could create, produce, and cohost a TV project on my own terms.

Many people are immediately faced with the challenge of overcoming fear. It is one of the strongest forces in the world. After years of observing me, my husband has told me on more than one occasion, "You don't have enough sense to be afraid." I think that's a good thing. But for those of you who do, "Get over it." You need to make a decision: Are you going to *watch* life? Or *live* life? It is that simple. You have to get out there. Now, I am not advocating throwing caution to the wind. Don't forget my father did raise a practical woman. But you absolutely must, must, must take some risks. It is impossible to achieve success without it. Even if you fail, you must continue to try.

Overcome self-doubt and don't allow anyone to tell you, "You can't." Dare to be different and don't apologize for it. See things that are not there in almost everything you do; set about to find the void and fill it.

Many people talk about passion. When you find it, believe me, you'll know it. Your passion will be your lifesaver when you feel as if you are drowning; it will be your best friend when you are all alone. Your passion will be contagious and infect others if you are using it right. I once was working with an executive at Walt Disney on a project who had told me, after the project was over, that I had the tenacity of a "junkyard dog" because of my determination to finish the project.

You must surround yourself with people with positive energy. These people will be your cheerleaders when you are just too tired to take one more step. And believe me, you will get tired. I am blessed with a husband who allows me the latitude to live my dreams. It has not been without a lot of sacrifice, but he understands the "Big Picture" and our goals. He just wishes I would hurry up and get here. I have a group of friends, some of whom are working with me on my latest project and who, in many instances, have been my lifeline. They have urged me to keep pushing. They have opened doors—to their homes, their Rolodexes, and anything else to support me in every way humanly possible. So hold on to your friends; they are the most valuable commodity there is.

There are times when pursuing your dream is extremely difficult. There are those dark moments late at night when you just can't sleep and you ask yourself, "Am I crazy? Why am I doing this? I could have a great job and probably a six-figure salary in no time." Then I stop and think about how I measure my success, and right now it's by creating my own happiness and blazing my own trails on my terms!

Don't be afraid to dream. Fear is a paralyzing emotion that we all need to get rid of. Don't forget to do your homework, and seek as much information as you can from whomever you can. Exploit every opportunity presented to you, and learn to create opportunities of your own. Develop a game plan and surround yourself with positive people who share your passion.

Remember, things don't just happen—you do truly control your destiny! We'll see each other at the top!

Sherma Wise is the CEO of Media Wise Productions, responsible for productions such as "Her Sports Live with Sherma Wise," "Teen Talk with

Reggie Miller," and "Basketball Hall of Fame" for the Indiana Basketball Hall of Fame. Sherma currently resides in Indianapolis, Indiana with her husband Gregory Thomas who is an attorney and is the chief counsel in the office of the Indiana Attorney General.

33

The Girl in the Gang

Yashema Blake

I grew up in a rough section of New York City. My mother sent me to a school outside my neighborhood because she thought I would get a better education. As I got older, out of convenience she began sending me to the neighborhood public school and that is when all of the problems began.

I was always a leader but for some reason I became a follower in school. I wanted to just fit in. I was one of those girls that you should never dare, because I would always do it. I wanted to prove my strength. I was about thirteen and the Judge Judy of the neighborhood. If someone had a problem everyone would come and get me. I would set the person straight, but for some reason I always felt like I had to carry everyone's burden.

I am the middle child and my mother's only daughter. I had two brothers. I remember the day clearly when my oldest brother was missing for three days and his baby's mother was calling every hour on the hour. There were six detectives who came to our door and asked to speak to my mother. They told her that her first born was dead. My oldest brother was only nineteen. They found his body wrapped in a carpet, hog tied, with the back of his head blown away. I was devastated. I can still hear the blood-curdling scream of my mother that night.

I was fifteen and automatically the oldest child in my family by default. I felt like I had something to prove. I blamed myself for my brother's death. I thought if I were a boy, maybe we would have been a team and things wouldn't have gone as bad as it did. What made it worse was that it was his so-called friends that killed him. These people sat in our house, ate our food, and called my mother Ma. My brother always thought these guys were his boys but I knew they weren't.

Looking back at it now, the turning point of all of our lives was when my father left. I was around ten and we had everything in our home, cable television, clothing, food, and money—we were living well. We were raised as Jehovah's Witnesses with a strict religious background. My mother met my father when she was finishing her college education. She was from a family of twelve who really didn't have much, and she was mesmerized by my father's street-slick ways. Dad was a drug addict in recovery, and she thought that if she was the perfect wife and made a perfect life that Dad would be perfectly happy. Ma built her whole life around this man and he loved it. He worked in the street and she took care of the kids. The reality was that my father was a pimp and a hustler. Not to mention the drug addict who slipped in and out of recovery, but in her eyes he was the ideal husband and man. When my father left he moved only a few doors down to live with an eighteen-year-old girl who had her own kid. Ma became an alcoholic to numb her pain. The picture that she drew of her husband slowly but surely faded, and she was loosing her mind. She no longer had time for her kids. Although she had a degree, she chose to flip burgers at White Castle at night. Eventually she had to look to welfare because she had three children she could not take care of.

Dad was taking care of the eighteen-year-old and her child like it was his, knowing down the block he had kids starving. I mean we were eating rice and oodles of noodles and were poverty-stricken. My brother got tired of worrying about where our next meal was going to come from and began selling drugs. That was the beginning of the end for him.

For a long time I hated my mother. I used to tell her that I wasn't going to listen to her because it was her fault that Dad left. Her boyfriend propositioned me and I told her, but she still kept him around. I was so angry with her that we would both get into it. I knew my mother was jealous of me because I never took shit from a man, and I always had the finest things. We would physically fight, and I almost killed her one day because I hit her in the head with a lead crystal lamp. She has twenty stitches inside and outside of her head. After that my mother was so scared of me that one day without warning she packed up her stuff and left.

I got into the gang because I always felt cheated. I had no one to turn to, and I never trusted anyone to hold any money for me, so basically I was on my own with no education and three kids to raise who I had at ages fourteen, sixteen, and twenty-two. I was selling drugs in a certain part of New York that was really lucrative. Some guys warned me not to even think about selling on the block anymore unless I became a Blood gang member. One of the guys that I used to talk to all the time vouched for me and said that I was cool and knew how to make a lot of money. Well, they didn't give a fuck because I wasn't a Blood. With my hard head I kept selling. By this time they were pissed and said, "Who the fuck do you think you are? Do you think because you are a female nothing will happen to you?" The money was good so if this is what it was going to take to feed my family then I would do it. Welfare wasn't making it; after paying rent, buying clothes, and putting food on the table there was barely anything left. I had three mouths to feed and I just couldn't survive on welfare. I did what I felt I had to do. Where else was a black uneducated mother of three children going to make any money?

My family came first so I joined the gang. The Bloods broke down what it meant to be a Blood. I didn't agree with their beliefs at all, but I figured I could use these guys for protection from other dealers as well as from the cops. I was told what I had to do to join. In the initiation you either kill an enemy, fight thirty-one seconds with the entire gang, or pull a juks (that is, robbing someone). I couldn't see myself taking a life, I never believed in taking what wasn't mine, so I went for the thirty-one seconds. I went through with it and I was a member for life.

From the very beginning they thought I was an informant. They were extremely skeptical of me because I didn't wear the flag or beads. They would always tell me, "If we catch you without those things we are going to beat the shit out of you." It was hard because we had meetings at least once a week, and if you missed them, you would have to go another thirty-one seconds or pay a fee for not showing up. The fee varied from $10 for a late fee, $20 for not coming, and it would go up and up. If you continued not to make the meetings, they put you on probation. Of course I tried to make all of the meetings.

One of their beliefs is that all Bloods should carry the burden of all Bloods. I was told to hide out fugitives in my home. I had to provide things for people I didn't even know—perfect strangers. I often asked myself, "Why do I have to carry their burdens because I initiated myself into the organization for protection from the streets?" If anything, you need protection from them! They are the same people who are threatening you all of the time. They are really the enemies. I saw so many people call each other brother and that same brother killed the next brother. I have seen girls call each other sisters, and then cut each other the next day. It is a no win situation; the only way out is death or jail. They try to tell people that it is an organization to help the community. Blood means Brotherly Love Overrides Depression. I don't see it, I don't see any brotherly love at all. All I ever saw was them hurt and lie to each other.

I think I was looking for my older brother in this gang, someone to teach me. I miss being the little girl. These people just seek and destroy everything around them, and they don't even love themselves. Every time I see Bloods on the street, I have to go up to them and peace them. You can't walk past them; you have to let it be known who you are.

I am so ashamed of it. It is pure nonsense, and the gang is for losers. I am not a loser. I have potential, and I want more out of life than to be involved in this. I want to leave the gang but they already told me that if I left, they would kill me. I am risking my life because I was exposed to their meetings, secret hiding places, and arsenal locations. I am a moving target because they have a lot to lose with me alive. I am practically a dead woman. I have so much to lose, and I am rolling with people who have nothing to lose.

I don't know what I was thinking when I joined. Gangs are filled with ignorant people who are looking for love. They do things to impress people. A lot of the members have no parents, either they're dead, in jail, or on drugs. I was exposed to them because I had no place to go, but I am not from the streets. If I had my way, I would have had my parents stay together and maybe all of this would not have happened.

I hate my life. I have slept with men that I was not even attracted to. I felt like dirt and I felt I had no options if I wanted to feed my family. You are probably saying that you had options like soup kitchens. Take a walk in my shoes and you will run right back to your own. It's easier said than done.

I am hoping that someone hears my story and realizes that there is nothing in the streets. If you are a young girl looking for a thrill, take your education seriously and believe in yourself because the street is only filled with lies. I may have had the furs, cars, a beautifully decorated apartment, and the finest clothing, but I have never, never had a day when I was happy in this gang. I don't know what it is like to let my hair down and feel free. I thought money would make me happy, but I found out the hard way that it really means nothing. Some days I pray for death.

I am a mess and I am trying to patch things up inside of me. I feel as if I have scars that can't be mended. I almost feel like this had to happen to me because if I had lived a storybook life, I wouldn't be as strong as I am today. I am afraid for my children so I am willing to take this chance with my life. I only pray that their lives are better for it.

Yashema Blake is a pseudonym to hide her real identity. She escaped the gang two days after this piece was written and hopefully is starting a new life for herself and her children.

Your Soul's Sustenance

*In returning and rest shall ye be saved; in quietness and in
confidence shall be your strength.*
—Isaiah 30:15

Shortly after the Civil Rights Movement it seems that a great many black
folks worked really hard, accomplished extraordinary things, and closed the
door behind them. Clearly that is evident in Supreme Court Justice
Clarence Thomas, someone who benefited from affirmative action and who
now claims that America does not need it. Because of men and women like
this there is an entire generation of people who are fast approaching their
thirties who have lacked any mentorship or career advice

Plain and simple we have been miseducated about our ability, creativity,
and originality since slavery. In *Miseducation of A Negro,* written in 1933,
Carter Godwin Woodson said it best, "When you control a man's thinking
you do not have to worry about his actions. You do not have to tell him not
to stand here or go yonder. He will find his proper place and will stay in it.
You do not have to send him to the back door. He will go without being told.
In fact, if there is no back door, he will cut one for his special benefit."

How do we begin as women to reclaim our creativity, originality and
have healthy mentorships and share without fear of being hurt or disappointed? Realize that business is the art of strategy. Choose who you mentor carefully but share your knowledge with everyone you meet. Be
available for lectures in schools, take a child to lunch, or give opportunities
to the mailroom clerk who you know has a tremendous amount of potential.
Or if you see someone doing a good job, tell them. Your acknowledgment
will make their day and possibly inspire them.

To achieve true immortality just simply teach others. If you have become established in your field of interest, hobby, or sport, you should
choose another person, be it an adult or a child, and share your knowledge
with her. You can take her to the office with you, or if she works with you,
show her something new that she might not have already learned about the

business. You'll find that it opens people up to asking questions and that they are truly interested in what you do.

If you don't feel like you've quite arrived at what you are doing, ask someone for help. You'll find that people are very open to talking about what it is they do and answer your questions. It may be related to a career change or a problem with the office computer; don't be afraid to ask. The only thing holding you back is you. Go for it!

Here are a few tips to help you focus on your career and share with others:

- Have regular meetings with your manager—this keeps the lines of communication open and available.
- Join professional groups, organizations, and associations.
- Life is based on relationships, and helping one another can be one of your most vital assets.
- Everything you need to achieve your purpose you have readily available to you right now.
- We always have time to give and receive guidance.
- Keep your personal life personal. Giving your colleagues and coworkers blow-by-blow information—on things like your sex life—can be a death sentence.

Your Personal Book of Revelations

We can always lend ourselves to others to help bring someone up in the ranks. Likewise, there is always someone who can answer any questions you may have.

- What career path have you chosen?
- How have you gotten there?
- Was there anyone to mentor you, and how did he or she do it?
- Do you leave anyone out at work?
- Have you been left out?
- Do you have new career goals?
- What are your greatest dreams?

Do research and then follow through. What are you waiting for?

VII

Some Good Ol' Fashioned Soul Food

Back then food meant security and comfort. Food meant love. It didn't matter what you ate, just that you had enough.
—Oprah Winfrey

Girl, Mrs. Williams knew how to cook some good food. She spent her whole life feeding people. The white people she worked for. Her fellow church members. People who would just "happen" to stop by around dinnertime. And of course her large extended family of relatives and friends.

She spent her whole life cooking. The only thing was that she spent her life cooking for everybody else—never really for herself. She and countless other black women have been responsible for feeding America since day one. The tradition is echoed in so many black families. To this day, getting together for big dinners is the most important thing that many black families do as a group. Mrs. Williams is just one of a million sisters who have used food as the tool for being the family matriarch.

So, why is food so important? Quite simply: Because eating food isn't really about nourishment of the body, it's about nourishment of the soul. It's about the good times and that warm feeling that we get when we are gathered together with loved ones and are all partaking of a common meal. Breaking bread with those who mean the most to you nourishes the soul. That's why we call it *soul* food.

Food has also been a crutch for us. It has been a way of comforting ourselves when nothing else works. It has been a form of expression for black women. Our emotional dependence on food is one of the reasons that so many of us are overweight. Food isn't just about breakfast, lunch, and dinner for us. It's about love. It's about happiness. It's about sharing and giving and loving. When we prepare food with love, it's "soul food." Whether it's a breakfast of ham and eggs and grits or a bowl of oatmeal, even scraps from the master's table, food—because we were slaves—was made and served with love. It didn't matter if we had a bowl of greens or a piece of fat pork. Whatever we had, we cooked with love because that's what we had to give.

Today some sisters are vegetarian and some aren't, some are macrobiotic and some are junk-food junkies. But no matter what, it's not what we eat that's important, but the fact that for most of us food is still an emotional experience that it has everything to do with loving ourselves and those around us.

What Is Your "Watermelon"?

Soul food is not necessarily the best for us from a health perspective because it is descended down to us from slavery. Slaves had to eat the worst parts of the meat—the parts no one else wanted. Thus, hamhocks and chitlins and all the foods that were cast away as unwanted by white people became the staples of the slave diet. Believe it or not, watermelon is one of the only things that kept slaves alive, which is why black people are so identified with it today. Here's why:

Watermelon grows very easily in the sandy soil that exists in much of the American South. In North Carolina, for example, you can just spit some seeds on the ground and come back in a couple of months and have big healthy watermelon growing and ready to eat. The reason we say watermelon kept us alive is that it is so high in fiber that it was able to cleanse the digestive systems and intestines of slaves whose diets were otherwise so bad that they would have had all kinds of health problems. One's body naturally craves high-fiber foods when it's overworked trying to break down foods that aren't really the best for it. So slaves were naturally attracted to watermelon. For this reason, many people say that watermelon was God's gift to the slaves.

But just as food is as much about nourishing the spirit as it is about nourishing the body, we have to ask ourselves what are we eating metaphysically? What kinds of thoughts and feelings are we allowing to become one with us? Chances are, if you're like most people, you've been "eating" a lot of negativity, self-doubt, and other thoughts that are not helping you get where you want to go in life.

But remember, God always gives you just what you need. Just as God gave the slaves the watermelon to keep their systems functioning in a time of crisis, God is giving you what you need as spiritual food for the crisis you're facing in your life right now. You only have to ask yourself, what is your *spiritual watermelon?*

Food, for us, has always been there through the good times and the bad. We know that personally we have used food to fill voids in our lives at times when food wasn't necessarily a good way of filling the void, but it was *there.* We think now we've learned to fill the voids with other things and not just food. Things like *love* for ourselves, like *friendship,* like *peace.* Those are a part of our spiritual watermelon. But it's more specific than that and it's particular to each individual person. You can't read this book and get the answer, but you can read this book and ask the question! There is a gift from God growing right in your midst—right under your nose—that, if you allow it to nourish you, will help to counteract all the negative people, situations, and thoughts that you have been making part of yourself for so long. Let these sisters help you to find that gift and claim it as your own.

34

The Healing Table

Jessica B. Harris

Let's face it, most of the folks cooking in our world are women. From mother's milk to funeral meats, we feed the family and make sure that there's a meal on the table. Cooking has always been one of our ways of nurturing each other and healing ourselves. We may giggle quietly when we see the stereotypical women on the television sitting down to drown their sorrows with a quart of Baskin-Robbins, but when we think about it, for generations we have spoken to each other over platters of fried chicken and bowls of potato salad. Crisis-torn families are knit back together while savoring slow-cooked string beans and munching savory cornbread. Dishes are passed, conversation begins, and healing takes place. Whether it's a single mom taking time out of an already hectic schedule to bake cookies with a child or a stood-up sister trying to soothe the my-man-done-left-me-I'm-stuck-home-on-Saturday-Night-and-I'm-evil blues with the latest recipe from *Essence,* or a grandmother making the family's favorite tea cakes for the last time with gnarled hands too arthritic to hold the spoon. Food is how we affirm our survival and how we show we care. It's no accident that black films from *The Nutty Professor* to *Eve's Bayou* to *Soul Food* all have scenes with a family gathered around the table.

The table, be it kitchen, dining room, or picnic, has always been our preferred location for communion. We come by our love of the table rightfully; for four hundred years we have labored at the tables of others in this hemisphere. Now that we're able to sit at our own tables, we delight in the communion that they provide. We pass the pickled beets while joking about Aunt Lalage's boyfriend who got away. We pick at the turkey carcass while remembering how Grandma so loved the gizzard that no one ever got a taste of it. Plus we dawdle over Sunday morning biscuits recalling with a smile how the hoecake never got beyond Poppa's hands. Somehow all of our fond memories just seem to be filled with our own version of visions of sugarplums.

I know just how important our culinary traditions are to our individual survival, and how representative they are of people's survival in this country. In this hemisphere, it's always startling, then, to find out just how many of us have retreated into the "I don't make anything other than reservations" mode of thought. There is a growing group of women who pride themselves on not being able to boil water and feel that the ability to cook somehow diminishes their effectiveness in the realm of business. To them I want to holler, "Wake up, girlfriends! Don't throw out the cast-iron skillet! Hang on to those recipes that Grandma handwrote and be sure to get your mama's written down too. Cooking is a part of our history, and losing recipes or ignoring culinary traditions is about as big a crime as throwing out family photographs or burning the family Bible.

The fact that we've kept ourselves together throughout our history around the table and that we've survived makes our food a potent symbol for us all. Whether we revel in pig at least once a year, because it enabled our ancestors to survive, or we eschew swine for all of the past that it recalls, we are marked by our food, and the communion of the table at which it is served. Make a point of having one meal with your family at least once a week. And that means even if you are only a "guest," cook your favorite dish, set the table, sit down, take time out, and make it a special occasion for communion. If you're by yourself, play your favorite music and treat yourself to the healing powers of the table. Live with your sweetie? Make the meal the occasion to discuss the week and its happenings, to heal all rifts and begin anew. Pamper yourself and your companion with a meal that lets you both show your love. In this rush-rush world of emails and faxes, multi-screen televisions, and keeping up with the guy in the next cubicle at work, we have allowed ourselves to be reduced to quick bites grabbed on the sly and hurried nibbles of unhealthy food. Take time out, sit down at the table, and let the power of the healing table soothe you.

Let the healing table work its power across generations as well. Sit down with your children and allow them to help in the kitchen, at least one day. Time spent peeling carrots is punctuated by conversations that might not otherwise take place. Parents will find that it's easier to teach manners and demeanor if all come together at the table and the reasons behind "Sit up straight" and "Don't pick your teeth with your fork" become clear. They'll also find that the ability to cook and to set the table is empowering for girls and boys alike.

Bring the grandparents into the fold. The tales that they tell and events that they recall around the table create memories, remind us of family history, and connect us with one of our most potent weapons in the battle for survival. Ask a neighbor over and create an "aunt" or "uncle" if your relatives are too far away. The important thing is to sit down at the table and talk. Some things are just easier to say across the remains of a shared meal. Things like "I'm sorry" and "I love you" and "I care" seem to be easier to articulate when they have been preceded by a warm casserole, a simple stew, or even the latest fusion food creation from the *chef du jour.*

It's no wonder that we feel a twinge of nostalgia and a surreptitious tear falls when we watch films from the fifties and hear tales of growing up in quieter times Down South or even in the urban North when the mean streets weren't quite so fierce. In those days we knew that the cry from the window meant there was food on the table. Whether or not it was a lavish spread of ham with biscuits, greens, and all the trimmings, the simple sharing of it helped us to center ourselves and to know our place in the universe. We all understand the potent power of food; we just need to remember to take time out, sit down, and let the healing table work its magic.

Jessica B. Harris is a cookbook author, food historian and consultant. Her most recent book is *The African Cookbook: Tastes of a Continent* (Simon & Schuster, 1998).

35

Soul Food

Monica Jackson

Double chocolate ice cream soothed my pains and let me know that everything would be all right. Frozen pound cake wrapped its arms around me and gave me comfort. Oreos made love to me, and take-out lasagna sated my passions.

Food has always been center stage in the lives of humans. Like air and water, it's a building block of our survival. We celebrate food. Feasts mark our passages through life and food can give us a pleasure as special and keen as any solitary sexual pleasure. Food pleases and eases our souls.

We are a gregarious species, we humans. We need to gather together. We need support, nurturance, and intimacy from others. We need to talk and touch. We need a lot and sometimes we don't get all we need. Especially we black women.

Our cooking never lets us down. Like singing, dancing, and athletics, cooking is a place where we are allowed, even expected, to shine. Our kitchens are the hearts of our homes. We cook and feed and nurture the masses. We comfort and give and at the end of the day we sit at our table and we comfort ourselves, too. Good food is like good lovin'. There's no such thing as too much.

Good food had taken us through the fire and we've survived. I remember when a big woman was a strong woman and Lord knows we needed all the strength we could get. We had to be the strong ones, strong for our families, for our communities, for ourselves. Strong for our men, too, because that was one thing they weren't allowed to be. A strong black man is a threatening black man. So whom do we lean on when the world is heavy on our shoulders and our backs are bowed?

We cry out to the Lord and moan in church. We fan our faces and lift our heads, gathering strength from the Lord. And we reach for another slice of cornbread. If the food was there and it tasted good, we'd be fools not to eat it. Being slim was the least of our concerns.

It's only in the latest generations that we have come into competition with white women. In our grandmother's time it was unheard of for a black woman to be judged on a white woman's terms. No, we are not on equal terms with them yet, but with every generation that passes we come closer. Now, we go head to head with them for promotions. We might audition for the same Hollywood roles. We possibly draw the glance of the occasional white man who is not above considering color when he looks for his potential mate. And if we are thin enough, we may even make the cover of *Vogue* magazine. To compete on their playing field, we've accepted their rules.

We know how important being slim is to them. When we step outside of our own world, fat is no longer strong, proud, and fine. In the main, white America perceives fat people as uncontrolled, uncaring, sloppy, dirty, low-class. If we judge ourselves by their terms, fat is bad and food becomes the enemy.

Food was my lover and my enemy, my closest friend and fiercest foe. I did food wrong and it stabbed me in the gut. It took me a long journey to see that food was simply . . . food—a good thing, and a deserved pleasure, but food is no lover and not even a dear friend. Food couldn't plug the holes within me that needed to be filled with love.

You know that empty feeling? Not hunger, but more like a gaping, endless hole somewhere around my solar plexus that extended to my heart. For years, the only way I could think to fill it was with food. Food was cheap, available, and ostensibly non-addictive. Food was my mama, my friend, and lover. Always reliable, it never hurt me or caused me pain.

I loved creamy sweet stuff that slipped down my throat and lingered in my gut; the rhythmic movement of my tongue and jaws and the heavy, calm feeling I got. What else did I have that would make me feel as good? I was an only child, raised to entertain myself, to soothe myself. I read books continually, scribbled in endless notebooks and I ate. I ate a lot.

If my destiny were to be a cook in the big house or a hardworking field or domestic servant or merely a Big Mama for my family, getting fat would have been fine. But my mother, a woman who grew up in the sixties, a woman riding the crest of the baby boom, knew the world had more to offer me.

My mother pictured me raising my wings and competing with whites at their level. She knew a fat child wouldn't cut it, much less a fat woman. My mother put me on my first Weight Watchers diet at seven. Dry canned tuna, hardboiled eggs, and salads with vinegar only are foods of my childhood, interspersed with penny candy, cream sodas, Charleston Chews, and thick roastbeef sandwiches on white from Mama Joy's deli on the corner of West 113th and Broadway.

I attended a different school every year, often living with a different family. I was a black child thrust into a white world with no support. I didn't understand the ramifications of this; I only understood my difference, my wrongness. So I ate.

Always the new girl in a white school, being fat and black was a big deal. I was smart, too, and this didn't make it any better. My white teachers would curl their lips and turn up their noses along with my peers. My extended family was middle-class blacks, scuffling to make it in a white world. They judged me by white folks' standards and that is how I judged myself. What I wanted most was simply to disappear. Food eased my pain, but the pain never stopped coming. A vicious cycle. I was a strong child and I did what I had to do to survive. I escaped to the fantasy world that books provided. I created my own fantasies through words and stories, and I ate.

My body lengthened and elongated with puberty. I only spent a few months in any one place, but still boys discovered me and I discovered them. I was on my own, out of control, and I couldn't handle it. My sexuality terrified me.

At thirteen, I reverted back to isolation and food with the plentitude of my father's stocked refrigerator and the sexual safety of the nearby all-white suburban school. I gained a lot of weight.

It lasted a year. At fourteen, I was in Atlanta with my mother's bare cupboards and the occasional meals she cooked of baked chicken or fish, a salad and a vegetable. She won her own weight battles by subsisting only on such food. So by the time I was fifteen I could fit into size nine jeans. But the lessons I learned about my sexuality, body, and the use of it continued to scare me.

I was sent to my mother's sister at sixteen. Her sister was only twenty-three years old and had a husband and two children. Her husband couldn't resist my charms, and in my loneliness, youth and confusion, I couldn't resist his. I gained about five pounds every week.

In a few months I left their home. I ended up attending three schools in my senior year, too naive to realize that I was allowed to drop out. By the end of my senior year I weighed well over 200 pounds.

In the years that followed I simply added layers. My obesity was constructed out of traditional self-comfort and founded in fear. I wrapped myself in blankets of flesh and anesthetized my pain with food. I became unnoticed, a discounted person. I waddled through the world with my bulk as if I were swaddled in blankets. I no longer had to hide in my room. I carried my isolation around with me.

Somehow, even though I still think Freud was full of crap with his sexual explanations for everything and notions of penis envy and Oedipal complexes, using food as a universal salve and protector does go back to sex and the fundamental need for love. Sex became synonymous with fear and shame, and the fat allowed me to avoid the issue completely. Food filled up the holes the lack of love left within me.

In my mid-twenties I joined a severely restrictive, isolating, and loveless religion. I was untouched by any man for the next ten years. I was safe and satiated and insulated and I grew massively obese.

But at thirty-five years old and 325 pounds, my misery turned to anger. I hated my life and I hated myself. I had to make a change or I was going to die because there was no point in living. I tried to change; how I tried. I went on every diet imaginable and even paid for a personal trainer, à la Oprah. Eventually, I sunk to my knees in defeat with tears streaming down my face. I couldn't do it. Everything I had I put into it, and I couldn't. I was a worthless slab of fat. I looked death in the face and knew that I had reached the end of my rope and was ready to fall off.

I decided to have surgery first instead. A stomach staple would mean certain pain, possibly death, but probably change. I went under the knife at the end of 1994. Complications followed and a feeding tube had to be put in. I couldn't swallow my own saliva. I moved across the country to my mother who dutifully put formula and water down my tube.

I never left the house. Television has always bored me so I read stacks of books and filled another stack of notebooks with stories, bad poetry, and musings. After a little while, I decided to write a book. I'd heard of a line of African-American romances. I hadn't read romance since adolescence because I'd become thoroughly disgusted with the omnipresent lily-white heroines and the predictable storylines, but romance was the only sort of book I thought I had a chance of selling. I finished the book by spring and sent it off with little hope of acceptance. It was a little different for a romance, but I was happy that at least I tried.

I met a man in early summer at the bookstore. There and the library were the only places I ventured out of the house. My book sold by late summer, and I married that man in the fall. He became my protector, my isolator, and my tormentor. I left him when my child was seven months old. Love had always hurt, and in his case it hurt physically, too. It wasn't for myself that I left. My protective instincts were even stronger when it came down to the ones I love. It wasn't that he choked and beat me, it was that he dropped my baby on the floor when he went after me. Then when my small cocker spaniel attacked him in my defense, he stabbed her with a pen.

I ended up back with my mother. I continued to write and sell romance novels in between filling angst-filled journals. I ate. I gained weight. I isolated myself in my apartment for three years, protected and safe from all but my own misery. I also thought a lot and somewhere between thinking, reading and writing, I found answers.

There was a book I wanted to write with a fat heroine. I wanted to break away from fantasy and write a portion of my experience. I didn't want my heroine to lose weight at her happily-ever-after ending even though I wanted her to find self-acceptance and love. I needed to write about a woman's reality, which is often painful. I had to get inside her head and give her flesh meaning. I wanted to show her frailties, her imperfections, her mistakes and her tears. I had no idea how I was going to do it within the confines of the romance genre. But somehow I knew I would, and I did. My wonderful editor took a chance on a different sort of heroine in a different sort of story and it worked.

The catalyst for my fat heroine's self-realization was her love for her daughter. My character stopped dulling her emotions with food and allowed herself to feel her own pain. It didn't kill her. She dedicated herself to health and let go of her obsession with body size. She asked her daughter if she would allow others to make her feel bad for the color of her skin or the texture of her hair. "If you're eating healthy and exercising, your body is what it is."

We are what we are. My heroine found love, but she also found herself and that was ever so much more important. She went back and reintegrated the part of herself that she'd ignored in her haste to compete sexually on the white world's terms. She took back the part of her heritage that said being big meant she could be sexy, fine, and strong. She reclaimed the fact that she could be large and still be healthy and good.

Those are the steps we need to take to find ourselves. The key to self-acceptance is self-definition. I define myself. I define myself not as fat, sloppy, and uncontrolled because I'm not a size six. My body is strong, healthy, and exercised. My body is exactly as it should be. I exercise to build my body, and I exercise my heart to build the courage for intimacy.

The key to self-acceptance is courage. It's courageous to reach out to replace the comfort that food so easily holds out with the far more satisfying but dangerous comfort of opening yourself to other people. It takes courage to step up to the majority's world but refuse to accept its standards as your own.

The key to self-acceptance is love. Loving yourself, loving God, loving the creation. Love within can't help but spill out and over to others. Fear and love cannot coexist, and with love within and without, I am free. I can be me and it's more than enough because I have so much more to give than the size of my rear.

Food is no longer the balm for my soul. There is a still, quiet place within me that satisfies me more than hot cheesy pizza can. The laughter of my child, the love I have for myself, my friends and family soothes my pains and fills my heart better than sizzling barbecued pork ribs with a side of potato salad. Now don't get me wrong, Sara Lee still tastes good and Oreos with a cold glass of milk can't be beat. They have their place, but it's in my stomach, not in my heart.

Monica Jackson is a multipublished author. Her latest book is *Never Too Late For Love* (BET, June 2000). She lives in Kansas with her family.

36

Soul Food Diva

Patti LaBelle

Most people would refer to me as an extremely outrageous diva who is known to lose her good sense on stage from time to time. But, when the music hits me it's almost like being in church. I roll around stage, and kick off my shoes, and the music just flows through me the way only God can permit it to.

But just as music has always been a passion of mine, so has food and a love of cooking. Being in the kitchen has always been a soothing ritual for my soul. I was one of those children who never liked to go outside. Partially because I loved my mother so much and partly because I was extremely shy. I would literally be right under my mother's apron.

My mother had her best friend who always lived with us. We called her Aunt Naomi. Now when she and my momma would get together, the aroma from that kitchen would get your head to spinning. The kitchen was like a girl's club. Besides getting some good food, you were sure to get some of the latest gossip and some juicy news about one neighbor or another. All harmless and a lot of fun. It got so bad that my momma would bribe me to go outside, and I would flatly refuse. How could I miss the girl talk and the smell of some serious down-home Southern country cooking? How could I miss the fresh smells of fried chicken, fried corn, barbecue sauce, hot ribs, rolls, greens, grits, and gravy cooking in that kitchen? Everything was seasoned just right. It could and would make a grown man cry.

Now my father knew his way around the kitchen, too. It was pure magic the way Daddy made those eggs and grits. Let's not forget that he made some serious hot sauce that could make you think that you died and went to heaven. Daddy was also pretty famous in Philly for his roast pig. He had a ritual with roasting a pig. In the summer he would buy a whole pig and dig a hole in the middle of the backyard. He would then roast it to golden brown perfection. That pig would be so good, people would line up just to buy a piece of the skin. It would be sizzling in the pit and the smell was enough to send your stomach into jumping jacks. Now I know in Hawaii they do the same thing for what they call a "Luau," but for me nothing comes close to the way Daddy did it. I've never smelled anything like it before or since.

One August afternoon, I was about ten, my father was frying some fatback and corn and I just couldn't wait to taste it. I wanted it so bad that I took a fork and stuck it in a big piece. As I was trying to pick it up, the pan fell over and the hot sizzling grease flew all over me. My skin peeled—literally peeled. The pain was unbelievable. I thought I was dying. But, thank God my clothes protected me from most of the spilled grease. The grease still managed to burn my neck so badly I still have scars and discoloration to this day.

Anyone would think that being burned would be enough to keep me out of the kitchen. Absolutely not! The kitchen has always been my refuge from the outside world. Whenever my mother managed to shoo me out of the kitchen I went to the shed in the backyard which was a "kitchen" of my own. I used a bucket as my sink and one of those aluminum sterno cans was my stove. I would spend hours cooking anything and everything. I would even take some of my momma's roast pork and other meats and make my own barbecue sauce for it. It was as hot as a firecracker but, it was good. Even Momma and Aunt Naomi had to admit that my cooking was simply delicious.

As my career took off we were on the road a great deal. I was well known for cooking on the road. It all began in 1965 with the bad boys of rock, the Rolling Stones. The Bluebells and I were flying for six straight weeks. I just could not handle the dull, tasteless airplane food. Everything was so bland. It's gotten better over time, but back then it was sad. So I began carrying hot sauce in my bag—it would jazz up the taste of any food. I used to get laughed at by many musicians, but after a while they took up my cue. Now, when I'm out on tour, there's no telling what you might find in my suitcase—spices, electric pans, and everything I need to whip something up—all right next to my clothes and shoes. Most of the time I will fix food for the entire band. Right after a show I will go back to the hotel and cook. It relaxes me and it gives me a chance to unwind. I guess my seasonings appealed to Mick and the boys because when they came to Philly they asked me to cook for them—sixteen years later!

With my mom and sisters gone I still feel warmth from being home. My home is the center and a must-do of many of my friends in the entertainment industry when they pass through the city of brotherly love. I have cooked for Luther Vandross, Debbie Allen, Donna Karan, Bill Cosby, Oprah Winfrey, Vivica Fox, Duane Martin, my babies and countless more. I still find fond memories in food and you can give me some ol' fashioned soul food any day.

Patti LaBelle is known as the diva of R & B. She is the author of two best-selling books *Don't Block Your Blessings: Revelations of a Lifetime* and *LaBelle Cuisine: Recipes to Sing About*. She is currently working on a new album and book.

Your Soul's Sustenance

*Ye shall eat in plenty, and be satisfied, and praise the name of
the Lord your God, that hath dealt wondrously with you;
and my people shall never be ashamed.*
—Joel 2:26

Remember the saying you are what you eat? It's true. We live such fast-paced lives that we sometimes forget to eat or we have a diet based on junk and fast food. How can we maintain a healthy soul if we can't even take care of its physical casing?

Food is the fuel that allows us to perform the tasks that make us great. We can put premium gasoline in our cars, but rarely do we put premium food in our bodies. Too many black people die prematurely from hypertension and complications from diabetes and obesity. We need to make time to incorporate better foods into our diets. We need to be more careful about what we eat. We need to really examine the foods we eat. Read the labels of the foods you purchase.

Food can be our source of comfort, but we need to change the foods in our diets that we choose to comfort us. Instead of reaching for a candy bar as a quick fix, how about satisfying your craving with a piece of fruit.

Your Personal Book of Revelations

- What are your meal patterns like?
- Do you eat three square meals a day?
- Do you snack excessively?
- Do you eat when you are depressed, angry, or happy?
- What are your goals when it comes to food?
- Are you more interested in eating healthy or just losing weight?

Write down everything you eat and drink and the times in a diary for a week and examine your diary at the end of the week. Are you surprised by the foods you eat? Did you forget to write some things down?

VIII

Express Yourself

Most of us love from our need to love, not because we find someone deserving.
—Nikki Giovanni

Since the first settlers landed in what's now America, black women have been objects of sexual desire. During slavery, business as usual was for the slave master to have his way with whatever female slave he wanted. Whether or not she had a black husband was irrelevant. This not only emasculated black men but also created plantation politics that are still with us in some ways to this day. And of course, babies born to raping slave masters were slaves themselves, or as the laws were written: children "followed the condition of the mother."

Today some of us are inhibited by our early sexual experiences, some of them dating back to our childhood and including sexual, mental, and physical abuse. As adults we may still be nursing wounds from a past relationship or an incident with a person you thought you could trust intimately.

Society plays a large part. There are more sexually explicit lyrics, movies, and online programming than ever before. Within our own community sisters are looked at and treated as sex objects. Fashion models or video girls are either very light with long straight hair and mimic the white standard of beauty or, on the other extreme, are very dark with short naturals and are considered "exotic"—whatever that means. Brothers are caught up too. They don't want you to straighten your hair because they want to be with a "natural" sister, but when the next sister walks by with bone-straight hair, they're chasing behind her like dogs in heat.

If It Isn't Love . . . ?

With all of this historical baggage, it's plain to see that we've got issues when it comes to sex. First of all, sex is a form of expression. But how we express ourselves sexually is *supposed* to be about love. A lot of times we misconstrue this and think of "sex" as equal to "love."

Sex isn't something that is about physical pleasure, it's about expressing your love for someone else. And through that expression you can let yourself go. There are so many different possibilities. But again, the key thing about sex is love. If you're not in love with someone and haven't truly thought about where you are with that person, then things can get very cloudy. It's not what it's supposed to be, and instead becomes something else.

A lot of women use sex as a device, almost like a game. Instead of expressing love, they're expressing anger; they're expressing revenge; they're expressing entrapment. We need to get back to expressing the love of ourselves before we step out and express our love sexually with someone else.

There are a lot of men who are having sex with multiple partners. A lot of women are willing to put themselves in that position because they don't love themselves. They're willing to sleep with a man who may be sleeping with two or three women. When you do that, every time you're with that person, you're losing a piece of yourself because with the sex goes your sense of self-worth. You're wondering if he likes you better or not. All this puts you as a woman in a very competitive position. Once you allow this, you're giving of yourself things that you might not be able to get back. So sex, as an expression of love, is something we have to take very seriously.

Even talking about sex has been taboo for a lot of black people for whatever reason. But we do have to talk about it so that we understand what we're doing, who we're doing it with, and why we're doing it. A lot of times women feel like they have to have sex to keep a man. If they say "No," they're afraid he'll leave and go to someone else. Why are we really doing it? Why are we subjecting ourselves to this? Expressing yourself also means being able to express your desire *not* to have sex.

In this part, sisters will share with us about a subject that many of us are afraid to talk about. By their open and honest sharing, we can all learn priceless lessons about ourselves. By not being afraid to talk about sex, we can help each other reconcile our hearts, our minds, our bodies, and our actions when it comes to sex. Then and only then can sex be the loving form of expression that it's supposed to be.

37

The Power of a Decision

Donna Marie Williams

Since my divorce in my mid-twenties, I've had my share of roller coaster relationships filled with sexual thrills and emotional dangers galore. I'd get high on the romance and plunge into depression when it all fell apart. Each collapse inevitably led to longer and longer periods of aloneness and celibacy and lots of grief, loneliness, and despair. Not once in all those years did I willingly choose to become celibate. I, like so many women, felt that celibacy had been forced upon me, so I fought its presence in my life with every ounce of my being.

The way I entered into those periods greatly undermined the potential inherent within, not only the celibacy experience itself, but the love relationships that could have followed. Because I was so desperate to be with a man, any employed man, I was constantly on the lookout for men to rescue me from my "imprisonment," and I often settled for men who were not right for me.

In addition to the loneliness, I was extremely sensitive to society's harsh judgment of women who find themselves alone. We are "spinsters," "old maids," and "dikes." Since we are perceived as not being able to get a man, we are not "woman enough," attractive, or lovable.

In the African-American community, we women may pretend that the opinions of others don't count, but they do. We may tell ourselves that the purpose of our high spending on acrylic wraps and tall hair is to make ourselves feel good, but honestly, we're trying to compete for what we believe is a limited supply of men. We black women are so busy trying to outdo each other in looks and material goods that we've forgotten what's important in life. The quest for meaning and purpose has been replaced by the acquisition of gold jewelry and the man hunt. Some of us will even go so far as to knowingly have sex with involved men. What have we come to?

Black religious institutions are notorious for determining a woman's worth based on the presence or lack of a man in her life. In our churches, mosques, and temples, an elitist hierarchical system shapes our interactions and determines our social status. At the top, of course, are the wives of the pastors, ministers, and deacons. Close behind are all married women, followed by celibate single women. Last and certainly least are the "backsliding" single women. Heaven help the single woman who is suspected of sexual activity. She is gossiped about, "prayed" for, and "ministered" to with an air of self-righteousness and subtle condemnation. These single women are often plagued by feelings of low self-worth and many eventually end up leaving the church.

I often wonder how many women are in prison because of their association with men. Prostitution, drug addiction, domestic violence, petty theft, grand larceny. How many female inmates have stolen or sold their bodies for love? We will sell our souls to be with a man.

Believe it or not, I'm not criticizing men (although they have a long way to go in healing their enraged souls). I'm against women's automatic acceptance of and participation in a system that requires the male presence to validate our self-worth. I know this sounds like feminist talk, but I'm not a feminist. I really do love men and deeply desire a soul mate relationship with one. But time alone has caused me to think about male-female relationships. I question the things we women take for granted, like "One day my prince will come and we will go riding off into the sunset in his Cadillac and live happily ever after." Or the single mother version: "One day my prince will marry me and adopt my children." As if I'm not enough. My love of men and my healthy sense of self-worth independent of men—do these two dynamics have to be mutually exclusive?

Whether we like to admit it or not, our identities and experiences as women are shaped by our interactions with men—the presence or lack of a man, how big a ring he's bought, how much money he's spent, and how well he displays in public. We are so desperate to measure up socially that we have settled for man-sharing relationships, "polygamous" relationships, uncommitted, unfulfilling relationships, and abusive relationships. We stay in relationships way past their natural death. There are many good men, but our girlhood conditioning, desperation, unhealthy involvements, and soul scars prevent us from recognizing them when they cross our paths.

Our poverty and scarcity mentality regarding men is born in girlhood and grows like a weed under the hypnotic spell of endlessly repeated statistics: twelve black women to one black man; black men outnumber white men in U.S. prisons; homicide is the leading cause of death among young black men. In our *Waiting to Exhale* discussions, we hypnotize each other: The few eligible black men available only want white women, or they're gay, unemployed, or on drugs. This has become our mantra and, thus, our self-fulfilling prophecy. We women of power have surrendered our faith and common sense to the facts but not the truth.

The truth is this: If we truly want a man, we can have that soul mate–marriage relationship, but only if we are willing to wait, heal, and grow into the fullness of womanhood. If we continue to have hit-or-miss relationships, hoping against hope that the man will marry or commit to us, then we will continue to remain unhappy and at war with black men. Likewise, if we engage in a celibacy practice that is judgmental, self-righteous, or fear-based (i.e., scared to death of men), our chances for meeting Mr. Right are equally slim.

Fear is the emotion that underlies all of our irrational behaviors—married women are afraid of losing their husbands, single women are afraid of never finding one. The saddest phrase spoken by many a humiliated single woman on TV talk shows is "I got a man," as if having a man validates her humanity or her womanhood and redeems her social status. Our fear of being caught without a man drives us to lie, cheat, and accept poor treatment from men.

I, too, have moments of fear. In my darkest nights alone I have seen my future as one long stretch of desert—dry, lifeless, manless. Nothing but fear. It was fear that kept me in bad relationships that led to emotional and physical abandonments. It was fear that kept me in relationships way beyond their natural death. Finally, however, I was forced to face my fears and grow up into mature, responsible, liberated womanhood.

A couple of years ago I made a decision that completely changed my life. I decided to practice celibacy. I wish I could say that I made my decision because God told me to or because of a lofty moral revelation, but I can't. Lackluster romance and an inner emptiness turned me off to sex. I had been dating this man for about a year. I felt a fondness for him, but no deep, passionate love. I had been badly burned by the fathers of my two children (they both walked out on me during my pregnancies), and I didn't want to love too much.

On the morning of my great decision, I vowed to never let another man into my life who did not love and treat me as I deserved. I was jumping off a cliff with no safety net below. There were no male prospects in sight, and my role models were few. I only knew church women in fear of hellfire who had made such a decision, but I decided to jump anyway. I trusted God to see me through this wilderness experience. I decided that I would learn to love my own company and that I would use this time alone to heal emotional wounds and obliterate self-defeating relationship patterns. With no romantic emotional distractions, I wholeheartedly pursued my life mission goals, which included being a better mother. My decision to practice celibacy was as much for my children as for me. They deserved a mother who was emotionally calm and there for them.

In effect, I was withdrawing my participation from an increasingly brutal marketplace of souls. In my younger days, I was able to cope with the emotional roller coaster well enough to risk love time and again, but I now get motion sickness from the ride. My last experience landed me at the doctor's office. After my two years of celibacy I entered into a serious relationship with someone I had known for many years. We planned to marry and even set a tentative date. Turns out, he was not as serious (i.e., monogamous) about me as he professed. I regret that I got involved with that man, but because I had made such strides during my time alone, I was able to cut the relationship quickly. I paid a price, however. Not only did my blood pressure rise forty points, my weight fluctuated, and my menstrual cycle virtually disappeared for two months.

I got busy. Following doctor's orders, I went through a battery of tests, started exercising again, and calmed myself down. Most importantly, I reconnected to my healing, sensual practice of celibacy. The brief relationship showed me that I was not infallible and that I still had plenty of work to do on myself.

Today, I am happy to say that I am finally beginning to discover what an incredibly magnificent woman I am. I did not know that while I was in those destructive relationships. I needed celibacy to discover, accept, and love my strengths, idiosyncrasies, and frailties. Recently, my sister and I were talking about my decision to hold out for my soul mate. I told her that when you really begin to love yourself, you are no longer able to tolerate emotional or physical abuse. My sister replied, "You'd better be prepared for a very long wait."

I am prepared to wait for my soul mate for as long as it takes. If I didn't have a life full of the love of good friends and family, meaningful work, and play (dolls, dancing, and other stuff I'm still exploring), I would have been crushed by my sister's pessimism. Although my ideal will always be that special soul mate relationship, my joyful practice of celibacy is not a bad second.

The way of celibacy can be difficult, but so can being involved with someone who does not treat you like a queen. Some women say that celibacy is not for them and that they are capable of having sex with no strings. How can that be? The very mechanics of the sex act creates strings, also known as soul ties. During sex, a woman receives and then retains a man's essence, and thus can be connected to him years after the one-night stand. We women can do a lot of things, but I question the wisdom of having casual sex or sex with a man whose commitment, fidelity, and even sexual orientation are in question—especially during this age of AIDS and other sexually transmitted diseases. Better to wait for that special soul mate–marriage relationship than infusing your spirit with the unknown.

Liberated womanhood is not about burning bras or sleeping with any

Jamal, Tyrone, or Harry who begs. The invention of the pill doesn't give us the right to throw away our common sense. Liberated women maturely interact with men (no attitudes necessary) and care for their bodies responsibly. Liberated women have learned to love men as human beings, not penis machines or redeemers from social shame. For those of us who want that special relationship with a man and who can trust in the process of a healthy, sensuous, spirit-filled celibacy, liberation means owning responsibility for your body and, when the time is right (and you'll know when it is), sharing your body with the one who is worthy.

Donna Marie Williams is the author of *Sensual Celibacy, Black-Eyed Peas for the Soul* and *Sister Feelgood*. She conducts workshops on teen abstinence, publishing and writing. Upcoming books include *Black-Eyed Peas for the Millionaire's Soul* and *Love Smart! The Heart You Save May Be Your Own*.

38

A "One-derful" Night

Tamara "Taj" Johnson

Who knew, that out of all the men in the world to have a one-night stand with, I would pick someone who would become one of my best and most supportive friends.

I grew up in Brooklyn, New York. My best friends were Khouri and Renee. We were so different—but this was an advantage because we had lots to learn from each other. Khouri was older, more talented, and more "well off" than Renee and me. Renee was the youngest and the femme fatale of our trio, and I . . . I was the sedate one, the one afraid to try anything. I guess I didn't want to take a chance on losing anything else. I had lost both my parents by the time I was fourteen years old. I ended up being raised by an older cousin who also lived in the city, spending summers in Cleveland with my grandma. Back then I was looking for stability and what was, and still is, my definition of that handsome husband, a big house with a fenced-in yard, where my 1.5 children and dog can play.

Even then it was Khouri's vision and gift of voice that was leading the way. We formed into an increasingly popular girl group. We started singing around the city, and entered tons of talent shows, some we won and some we didn't. Within four years we became so well known we started to get requests for session work. As our popularity grew in the music world so did the attention we received from men.

Khouri and Renee were like kids in a candy store. Truly, "enough" wasn't to be found in their vocabulary. I had my dream of the ideal man that would give me the dream house and family and I wasn't going to be shaken from that. I had fallen in love with Demitrius and quickly moved in with him. Over time, my dream turned into a nightmare of emotional and physical abuse. I was hesitant to enjoy the group's newfound popularity. But Khouri and Renee thought I was acting like a "goody-goody" and started calling me an "undercover ho."

Soon Khouri and Renee started slowly excluding me from their activities, eventually completely separating themselves from me. I was in real danger of losing my best friends, and I was feeling extremely depressed and alone. I couldn't believe this misunderstanding was going to split us up, and I desperately wanted to fit in again.

My chance came when we were to perform at Jones Beach for a Greek Festival. We were booked to sing background vocals for one of the local acts. None of us had a car so we planned to stay overnight in a hotel and then catch the train back in the morning. On the day of the show, as Khouri, Renee, and I walked over to the venue for sound check, it was impossible not to notice the handsome black men that seemed to be everywhere. Khouri, Renee, and I somehow ended up with our eyes on the same man. With an arm full of T-shirts that he was selling, he walked up to the car that we were sitting on. His name was Raymond. He was tall, dark, and handsome with a well-toned body. He wore his hair in a low-cut fade and had the sexiest lips I had ever seen.

The three of us were held in his trance. Raymond spoke in a deep, soft, seductive voice, like a true "intelligent thug" full of verse and knowledge. I remember thinking that if anyone was ever going to embody my definition of the dream man, it had to be Raymond. Almost instantly I felt myself reaching for Raymond's arm and cuddling it into my chest. Getting little objection from him after making that bold move, I started half-jokingly calling him "my man" aloud. Khouri and Renee clearly got the message, quickly made excuses, and left us alone.

I found out that Raymond worked with the show as a promoter. I was impressed and we continued to talk right up until it was time for us to take the stage. So quickly Raymond had engaged my heart and mind! I believed without a doubt that he was the one for me, and I invited him back to my room after the show. He did not accept my invitation right away, explaining that he was putting on an after-party which would last late into the night. He would call later to let me know. I didn't care if I had to wait up all night to see him again, just as long as I did get to see him again before we left.

After the show I went back to my room and waited. Around a quarter to one Raymond called and asked if he could stop by. "Of course," I said. I needed some time to freshen up, so I asked him to drive to McDonald's and pick up a shake and some fries before he came over.

It was moving all too fast, but not enough to drown out the one or two moralizing thoughts about how out of character this was for me. I'm the "goody-goody," remember! There I was all too willing to justify what I had planned as a gesture of solidarity to my girlfriends. I had to admit it was all conscious planning that had me primping and posing my most seductive moves in the bathroom mirror, preparing to seduce the man of my dreams. A man I had known less than a day!

Finally, when Raymond's knock came on the door, I was nervous. I nearly had to gasp for breath. I invited him in and we quickly went over and snuggled up on the couch. As we talked for what seemed hours, I found out that he ran his own promotion company and he was definitely marriage material. All this seemed too good to be true, and of course it was, since there was one "minor" detail . . . a live-in girlfriend!

Keeping in mind the girlfriend information, I invited him to stay since it had been a long day and we were both very tired. In the bathroom I undressed and put on my sheerest Victoria's Secret nightgown. I thought, "Hey! What's it going to hurt to let him see what he'll be missing?" When I came out of the bathroom, I found that Raymond had already undressed down to his T-shirt and boxer shorts, which showed off his perfect body tone even more.

I turned down the covers of one of the twin beds and we climbed in. We slowly started to cuddle and the cuddling turned into kissing. I quickly cast off the feeling that I was going to be punished for acting so hastily, and, worst of all, dealing with someone else's man, but that feeling was curbed when Raymond's mouth moved from my neck and was now sucking and tonguing my breasts.

I surprised myself with how easy it was for me to let myself go with the flow. As Raymond fingered me, I began to stroke his penis in my hand while moving my body in time so we would touch with each thrust. Soon I was no longer content with the heavy petting and I wanted Raymond to enter, and he did. We made incredibly passionate and tender love that night. I felt like we had known each other for years. I decided we were going to be married and imagined this was our honeymoon lovemaking session.

After the loving, Raymond ran a hot bath for me, which caused steam to rise up in the bathroom. The mist from the steam enveloped us as he washed my entire body, dried me off, and rubbed me all over with baby oil. He wrapped me in a towel and carried me out of the bathroom and over to the twin bed and tucked me in.

It was just about dawn as Raymond dressed himself and prepared to leave. Before he left, he kissed me and thanked me for a wonderful night and I fell into a deep peaceful sleep—I had found my dream man.

Later that morning Khouri and Renee came to my room. When they walked in, they noticed the other bed in disarray and my panties in the corner. They were very curious to know who had been there the night before. I confessed everything and the surprise showed on their faces. Khouri looked at me. "I knew you were like us," she said. This brought me back to reality. Having crossed that line, I couldn't pride myself of never having had a "one-night stand." I felt dirty and ashamed. I slowly packed my things. I felt so confused I couldn't move. Now that I had gained the respect of my best friends, I had lost my own self-respect.

A couple of weeks went by and I was trying my best to make peace with myself and get back into the groove of things. Khouri, Renee, and I had a show to do at the Tunnel Night Club. Imagine my surprise when I walked through the door and saw Raymond.

Petrified with embarrassment, I quickly hid in the dressing room rather than face him. After an hour the bartender knocked on the door and entered with a glass of champagne and a note. I thanked the bartender and read the note:

> *Since we didn't exchange numbers, I couldn't call you. This must be fate because all I can think about is you. For some reason it was more than just sex and I feel you are someone that I need in my life as a friend if nothing else. There's no pressure so I'm giving you my number and you can get in touch with me when you're ready. Please call (212) 555-8397.*

I didn't know what to say; after the show I just left. It took me a week to finally build up the courage to call. We talked briefly and then set a lunch date for the following afternoon.

We met at the Hard Rock Café. I didn't dress too sexy because I didn't want him to think I was loose. At first it was awkward, but soon we both relaxed and spoke on all subjects from A to Z. Somehow in the five hours we spent together we reached an unspoken agreement to just be friends.

Now, many years later, Raymond and I are best friends. No, we're more like family. To this day neither one of us brings up our night of passion even though we call each other to talk at least once a week. What could have been an emotionally damaging experience was instead the unlikeliest doorway to a wonderful blessing.

Events happen in our lives and often we automatically label them as "bad." When we beat up on ourselves, we keep ourselves from discovering the beauty and gifts that God intends for us. What could have scarred me has instead led to a positive influence in my life. From that one-night stand I found a friend and a surrogate brother for life; I gained another caring, supportive member of my family.

Tamara "Taj" Johnson is one of the sexy soulful singers of the multiplatinum R & B group *SWV, Sisters With Voices.* In addition, Taj has done several cameo appearances on some of today's most popular television sitcoms and is represented by the Ford Modeling Agency.

39

I Am Just Trying to Live Holy

Pamela Shine

I never thought that at forty I would still be a virgin. Like most single women I wonder if I will ever find the right man. I am not necessarily looking for a shining knight, but a man with compassion, sensitivity, discipline, who is an achiever and has a need for a deeper meaning in life. Not a perfect man, just a man who would be perfect for me.

I began modeling at the age of fifteen. I have worked as an on-air personality for a Christian radio program as well as a flight attendant. I did my share of traveling and had high hopes of meeting a wonderful man, getting married and having children. I was sold on the dream of two souls joining together to become one. While attending college at age eighteen, I was enrolled in a psychology class. One of the assignments was to fill out a Life Chart detailing where you expected to be in the next week, month, year, five years, ten years and twenty years. In my chart I wrote that I wanted to be a good Christian—in about twenty years from that time. I figured I was still young and had plenty of time to settle down and dedicate my life to the Lord.

I was up late scanning the radio dial (it was approximately 1:30 AM in the morning) and I came across a song that was a favorite of mine. And I stopped to listen. At the end of the song, to my surprise, I discovered that this was a Christian radio station. A minister came on and spoke so eloquently about Jesus. The minister emphasized that the breadth of life, that the life expectancy, is typically 77 years, and that the decisions you make today will affect you for an eternity.

Just as you may have "witnessed" an altar call in church after a service, at the conclusion of the song the minister performed a radio version of one. I phoned into the radio station and prayed with the minister. I recited what is called a sinner's prayer. I didn't grow up going to church but, because of the love I felt I had for the Lord, I found myself making spiritual decisions that I thought I would be making much later in life. After the prayer I realized it was not a question of if I ever would get saved. The question was when. I began to spend time in prayer. I fasted and I read the Bible in solitude. I began to find out how God wanted me to live.

I made a pledge to myself that I would take on a life of temperance, which means refraining from the use of profanity, drugs, lying or being deceitful. I also read in the scriptures that sexual intercourse is a gift only to be shared through the bonds of marriage, so I added a pledge of chastity to refrain from premarital sex.

As I grew up to become a young woman, practicing the things that I believed in, it really surprised me how much everyone was caught up in sex. Chastity, as explained in the *Oxford Dictionary,* is the abstention from extramarital or from all sexual intercourse. I would refer to the dictionary because while dating, several men could not understand why I would not engage in sexual intercourse with them.

My cousin by marriage was a professional basketball player so because of him, and being a well-known model in Chicago, I socialized with athletes such as basketball players. There was a natural attraction because I am six feet tall. After dating several of them over a period of time I heard that I'd developed a reputation as the girl who "wouldn't give up any." One well-known NBA player said to me, "Well Pamela, you will just have to find a man who is going to be patient." He gave me good eye contact as he patted me on the waist and continued, "Most men are not patient."

I have met several men who have tried to manipulate me into having sex. There have been offers of cars, houses, money and engagement rings. One guy asked, "Suppose we get married and you are frigid?" Others have speculated that I would not enjoy sex. My reply has always been that I have no doubt that it is an enjoyable experience, after all God meant for it to be that way. He could have made us any other way, but instead made us sexual beings. He rejoices in our sexuality, but only to be expressed in the bonds of marriage. Sex is a gift that God gave to people for the closeness and bonding of two individuals within the confines of marriage alone.

The scripture goes on to teach that we should not be ashamed of those feelings if they occur. But if they do occur they should be equally yoked. *Yoked* means equally balanced, so the translation would be in the company of a fellow believer. In 1 Corinthians 7:9 it says that, "if we cannot contain ourselves, it is better to marry than to burn with desire."

By my standing on godly principles, men have been discouraged. I allow the men in my life to be their own persons; not judging them but simply explaining to them where I was in my own life. It has been my hope that my spirituality would encourage and inspire the spirituality in them. I am an affectionate person, however, if they were uncomfortable with the fact that the warmth I would express would not end up where they would have liked, then I would simply withhold affection. It is very sad to me that most men I have been interested in romantically only wanted to express affection sexually.

I let them know that I am saved but not dead; I did not make it this far without using wisdom, I never played doctor and postman. The notion "Let me see yours and you can see mine," was off limits and I never saw a man naked. As Christians we are the lights of the world and the salt of the earth. Jesus said, "If you love me you would keep my commandments." I wanted to consider God's happiness even above my own. After all, I built my life around things that would be eternal.

A spiritual decision is a personal one and in your heart you must decide what you believe. My relationship with God has taught me that he is a holy God and we are called to be a holy people. I never thought my life of chastity would be the reason that I would lose out on marriage. My last date was three years ago. Today I am an unmarried, dateless virgin.

The hardest thing that occurred in my life happened two years ago: I had to bury my parents alone. They died about seven months apart. Ironically, none of the men that I was interested in romantically wanted to comfort me. Instead they sought the opportunity to try to get me when I was down. Two totally different guys made similar statements. Basically they said that if they came over, they would want to have sex with me. I couldn't believe it.

I have always been attracted to tall African-American, well-groomed men. Maybe it is time to look at the other colors in the crayon box or men from other cultures where their countries' traditions dictate that there are other things prized from a mate than the willingness to have sex before marriage. I don't consider myself to be the bravest; I am not trying to nail myself on the cross. I am not trying to be righteous. I am just simply trying to live holy.

Pamela Shine is a bereavement counselor and a former on-air personality for a Christian radio program as well as a model.

40

He Had to Go

Lorraine Barrett

To say there is a thin line between love and hate is such an understatement. Where does the line between loving someone end and loving yourself begin?

We had become close friends, passionate lovers, verbal sparring partners always threatening to end things but being forced back together by an unseen magnetic force. I had been in and out of relationships before but never had someone been able to get me so *angry* and *hungry* at the same time. There was a point in our lovemaking when I remember just looking down at him and thinking, "This is just so beautiful. I love this man and our lovemaking is so sweet."

So although what he was up to was a surprise, the fact that he was up to something was nothing new to me. He called me at work to tell me he'd just gotten back from vacation with a few friends and that he missed me. I informed him that I'd found out about his little tryst and was hurt and didn't want to be bothered. Like a fool, I let him convince me to meet him over coffee after work. We met and, of course, one look at his muscled, tanned, and toned body softened me up like an ice cream in the sun. And although I was still mad, hurt, and disappointed at him, I didn't tell him he could come over later, but I didn't exactly say "No" either. Because I listened to the loud craving of my body, that night, once again, I let him convince me to come over.

In the middle of our lovemaking, I just kept thinking over and over: Did he kiss her like he kissed me? Can she make you moan the way I do? and I just had to make him stop. I was beginning to cross that line. I had to stop. I asked him to get off me and said a couple of other hurtful things to him as well and it only served to anger him. Anger him to the point of him holding me down and using our source of love as a source of pain.

The next thing I knew he was penetrating me and I was lying still telling myself that I am anywhere else but here. The whole thing lasted all of five minutes but seemed like five eternities. I couldn't believe that my friend could do this to me. I couldn't believe that my friend was capable of doing this to anyone. When it was all over, I wanted him to leave my bed, leave my house, leave my being, and he wouldn't leave. He said he was tired.

I began to call him all kinds of names, and with each and every name I called him, he returned one equally nasty. However, sitting there in the bed, wet and exposed, allowed each and every insult to infect my inner being. And I was taken back ten years to a place when I was just a skinny, dark-skinned girl who meant nothing to anyone and needed love so badly that I'd do anything to have it. I was transported to a place where I cared about any man more than I cared about myself. Where I'd give my last dime and steal my mother's last dollar just for male affection and I knew I just couldn't go there again. I couldn't love someone so much that I didn't love myself and that very moment he had to go. . . .

He had to go for all the times I'd been beaten in the past. He had to go for all the times I'd given my last and received nothing in return. He had to go for all my sister friends who've experienced pain and called me and I told them to "make him leave." He had to go because if he didn't leave my house that night, he might have left the world that night.

Lorraine Barrett is a legal secretary and the co-owner of Miramar, an events coordination group which specializes in events planning geared to the urban professional in New York City.

Your Soul's Sustenance

Know ye not that ye are the temple of God, and that the
Spirit of God dwelleth in you?
—I Corinthians 3:16–17

Before you sleep with another guy . . . stop and think: Am I just here for the moment, or is this guy worth it? Step away for a moment or ask him to wait until you are ready. If he does not stick around, oh well, he wasn't worth it anyway! Instead, pursue platonic relationships with men. There are so many women who have never had a long-lasting platonic relationship with a man. Be clear with him. Don't lead him on, and give no indication that there will be a sexual relationship. Candace enjoys her platonic relationship with her friend Al. "We have known each other since we were nine years old and the things we learn from each other are absolutely wonderful." You actually learn more and meet a lot more men in a platonic relationship. Men reveal some of the craziest things in confidence. Think about it—often they have no one to talk to. Use the knowledge for whenever you meet your Mr. Right. One thing we have learned is a man appreciates someone he can talk to instead of talk at.

Although the path to healing can be a long one, we are going to seek ways in which our pleasurable sides will bloom. Orgasm is always a big sexual issue. If you found a way to have one regularly without any hang-ups, congratulations. For the rest of us, it has been a nightmare or an unfulfilling experience. Why does it seem that our partners get all the pleasure and we get the short end of the stick? (No pun intended.) Could it be that maybe we have sex for all the wrong reasons? Taking control of your own sexual experience will not label you a slut, but it will give you the necessary power of pleasure and your partner will enjoy it.

If you want to keep the love steaming in your relationship, remember love is based on mental stimulation. Eat breakfast in bed, give your partner an erotic massage, pop in an erotic video, play dress up, and exchange roles. Even phone sex in an unpredictable situation can be arousing. Most of all, do this only if he is worth it.

Your Personal Book of Revelations

- Is there a history of sexual, mental, or physical abuse in your past?
- Describe those experiences.
- Describe your relationship with your sexual partners.
- Do you feel that you measure up sexually?
- Does your partner compare you to other sexual partners?
- Do you masturbate frequently?
- Have you ever participated in a one-night stand?
- Have you ever had an orgasm, and if yes, how frequently?
- Are you easily distracted when having sex?
- Do you believe that your partner may be cheating on you?
- What are your sexual fantasies?

IX

Brothers, Husbands, Fathers, and Sons

*To understand how any society functions you must under-
stand the relationship between the men and the women.*
—Angela Davis

Do you ever hear yourself saying or thinking: "I don't need a man! I can do just fine on my own." Do you ever find yourself wondering: "Are there actually any brothers out there who are worth dealing with in the first place? They can't all be trifling, can they?"

If these kinds of thoughts go through your head, you're not alone. If we're honest with ourselves, they go through most of our heads at some point or the other.

This section is not just about "men" but about male *energy* in our lives. No matter what we may say, the truth is that every woman needs some male energy in her life; just as men need female energy. Male energy is part of us. We have to honor that complementary part of ourselves. That male energy can come from husbands, fathers, sons, or friends, and it is a part of what keeps us alive. It is also a part of what keeps us protected. Yes, they put us through the full 360 degrees of emotion, from high highs to low lows, but if it weren't for the first man in your life, your father, you wouldn't be here *at all.*

Kings with No Nations

Black Men. These two words conjure up thousands of thoughts, words, and images. The perceptions run the gamut of negative imagery: America's worst nightmare, sexual infidels, deadbeat dads, robbers, liars, rapists, niggas on the corner, niggas in the pool hall, niggas drinking forty ounces of malt liquor, pimps, hustlers and players, drug dealing, car stealing, money making, and heart breaking, just to name a few.

But black men were also the founders of civilization. They built the pyramids, and led many an army to victory throughout the course of history. The United States economy was built on the backs of their forced labor. And their ideas have led to refrigeration as we know it, the mass production of shoes, the creation of blood plasma, and countless other contributions.

Despite all of this, the black man's world is a very lonely one: one where he turns on the news and sees himself in handcuffs. He watches a movie and has to see himself on a huge screen always depicted as a greasy, buffoon bumbling through life. On the street, he can't look at his brother for fear that he'll start an altercation with him because his brother is just as suspicious as he is. He listens to a hip-hop jam and hears himself poetically depicting the destruction and murder of everything and everyone around him, having all kinds of sex like it's nothing, and as long as he's got his money, nothing else matters. And when he asks why, he's told that's just the way it is.

The black man lives in a world that is not counting on him to win, and for that matter, doesn't *want* him to win. For him to win would mean he would disprove many of the principles of ignorance that this society has built itself on. Knowing this, he has to constantly be on guard—another brother or the police may be just around the corner itching for him to make a mistake so he can come at him. He also lives on guard from his sisters, who are many times hypervigilant to his "wackness." Whether it's there or not, they're poised and ready to strike at him with the full blast of their scorn.

Many times, too many times, black men discover that they are kings with no nations and give up on themselves. They then actually become these previously mentioned media concoctions that have been specifically designed to enslave his mind (with the hopes of imprisoning his body soon after).

We love to love black men because there is no other loving done the way they do it. And in the same breath we love to hate them for everything they do wrong, as if they are supposed to live in accordance to some standard of humanity that we do not even set for ourselves. But where would we be without him? He's our grandfather, our father, our uncle, our brother, and our nephew. Who can honestly say they can do without the overwhelming joy when Daddy comes home from work and picks you up high in the air, hugging you tightly, because he loves you so much? Or the calm that comes when you tell your boyfriend how bad your day was, and he holds your hand tightly, looks lovingly into your eyes, and tells you everything's going to be all right? Or the electricity that runs down your spine when you're at the altar, standing across from your groom and he proudly tells you that he will love you until the end of time, through the good and bad, no matter how, and no matter what?

The black man is the hopes and dreams made flesh of every mother who gives birth to him. He has his faults, but over time he has been by our side contributing to our strength, our personhood, and our lives overall. He is a part of our *beginning* because without him we would not have been born. He is a part of our *present* in the form of friends, neighbors, coworkers, and boyfriends. He will need to be a part of our *future* as our husbands and the fathers of our children and our children's children. Despite what we may say because of our personal circumstances, or misfortunes, we need black men like we need life itself if we expect to move forward, surviving and flourishing proudly.

Dependence versus Interdependence

One thing that exists for both black men and women alike is the confusion over the terms "dependence" and "interdependence." *Dependence* is the absolute reliance on someone or something other than yourself; while *interdependence* is a mutual reliance between more than one person or group. In this day and age, being dependent has been turned into such a taboo that all forms of it have been discarded for the almighty and most times, self-destructive, independence.

People need one another, and in particular black men and women need each other. This chapter is devoted to our need to come together in order to grow. Everything is an opportunity to share when we work together toward something greater than ourselves. We can come together about anything—from ideas being shared between coworkers to a husband and wife truly working to love each other. In a world that is growing increasingly strong in its systemic injustices, it is necessary that we, as sisters, tap into the power of agreement that we have available to us through our brothers, husbands, and sons. This isn't something that we should "consider," or "get around to" when the time is right. It is something that we must do right now!

41

Daddy Duke

LaJoyce Brookshire

My daddy Duke is a master at pulling disappearing acts. I remember my seventh birthday specifically, it was one of those times he had been gone a while. I had been filled with wondering if he would make it back from "his trip" to shower me with gifts on this auspicious occasion of turning seven. The party was in full swing with pin the tail on the donkey, apple bobbing, and musical chairs when my gorgeous daddy showed up dressed to the nines just like he was some celebrity guest, bestowing on me two pairs of jade earrings.

To this day he always causes a commotion wherever he goes. He has that "it," you know, *je ne sais quoi*. Duke is outright irresistible; his problem . . . he knows so. Maybe it's his tall, lean, football player frame of six feet two; his creamy cocoa complexion; his dazzling, pearly white teeth; or his impeccable speech. Whichever, as long as I have known him, he has used all of the above as part of his hustle to become a legend in his own mind.

His legendary status was fueled when Duke was a policeman (the only steady job I have ever known him to have), and there was a book written about the escapades of him and his partner Hutch. The book later became the television series *Starsky & Hutch*. Forget about it, after that he was untouchable!

My mommie probably did not see the deception at first, but after two kids, a stint of disappearances, and refusing to get a real job after being fired from Chicago's Finest, she was beginning to see clearly. Then, one day when I was in second grade, Duke went to the store to get a pack of cigarettes and never came back. The next thing I knew over that summer, Mommie had packed us up from our apartment and moved us into a *house . . . without* Duke but *with* the blessings of his mother, my grannie, and his sister, my auntie.

On Christmas Eve of 1973, I had a fever and my brother and I were watching *How the Grinch Stole Christmas* when Duke showed up at our new house. My brother and I exchanged glances. We didn't want fireworks on Christmas Eve. Under the tree were tons of gifts—none from Santa Claus, none from Duke. All of the gifts were labeled from "Mommie," "Grannie," or "Auntie."

We had gotten used to the fact that he wasn't going to be around, basically because he had not been. You see, Mommie was mother, father, adjudicator, and God's angel all rolled into one. My brother and I looked at Duke not being there as his loss. Thanks to a little help from Grannie and Auntie to keep us in dance, music, and judo classes, they, too, looked at Duke as the one who was missing out.

Sure he called every now and again with a barrage of empty promises about how he was going to make millions, but precise information as to his whereabouts, or what he was doing, we never knew. Just before my eighth grade trip, I found out he was in Washington, D.C. Naturally, I had made arrangements with Duke to see him. After one solid week of promises to be taken to dinner and to where he was living in D.C., he did not show up until our bus was about to depart. And what a scene he caused, looking good in full cowboy regalia, stopping the bus and flirting with my teachers, to get a few moments of my time.

I didn't know whether to be pissed or happy about his last-minute arrival. My teachers were, as most are, captivated by his speech and command of the language. None of that meant a "hoot" to me. Whenever he came around, I was convinced that his sole purpose for "showing up" was to send me running for a dictionary so that I could look up the words he frequently used like "loquacious" and "debacle." He never realized that after one of his grand entrances and exits, I was the one left to answer the questions about what he did for a living. What was I going to say? "My daddy is working on becoming the first millionaire in our family," even though by now the *most brilliant one* should have already been. I was always, and still am, unable to answer these questions.

Duke, with all of his incessant need to be center stage, bullied his way into walking me down the aisle for my Debutante Ball. I had planned to have his brother, my Unkie Johnnie, walk me down that center aisle. Unkie Johnnie was my tennis coach, swimming partner, bowling team mate, and mutual chess fanatic. So I was *too* through when Duke wanted to get decked out in a tux, just so he could be seen as part of one of the most momentous occasions of my life. I had already forgiven his "no-show" in advance, because Duke had proven constantly that he had his own set of rules for the game of life. Given his track record, I had Unkie Johnnie on standby.

The East Coast is where he seems to have settled down, but only generally speaking; no place specific. When I moved to New York City, naturally he found me. I had been sharing with him my woes of needing a car in spite of New York's generous transportation system, when he told me of a car he had heard was available through his church for members only at just $400! Wow, a deal I could not pass up. I FedExed the money and waited in vain for over a month for him to bring me the car from D.C. as he had promised.

It turned out, unfortunately, this was not the first time Duke had made off with a family member's car. When my auntie died, Grannie decided that she would continue making Auntie's car payments, so that friends and family could drive her around when she needed it. In the midst of his mother's grief, Duke seized the opportunity and drove the car clean across the country from Chicago to the East Coast. After Duke was gone in Auntie's car for a week, my grannie, a far less patient woman than I, reported the car stolen. So after Duke had not shown up with my $400 investment, I was saddened to follow suit just like my grannie and phone the police.

I spent Christmas 1989 with my Aunt Anita in Long Island. They had surprised me with Duke. Cool, I thought. What could possibly be wrong with spreading a little Christmas cheer with my daddy? After all, we had not spent a holiday together since I was six years old. What a time we had. My aunties, cousins, Duke, and I were having a good time sipping champagne, eating sumptuous desserts, and telling stories. You see, we come from a long line of storytellers. That day he gave me a bit of advice that I have found to be most valuable: "Stop trying to be logical with illogical people."

Then it happened. Duke began bragging about how and when he first left Chicago. How he had come to New York City and started working in the entertainment business. Mmmm, I thought, so that's where you were and that's what you were doing. He bragged and bragged about how he had taken Kool & The Gang to their first gig and was a roadie with Roberta Flack. Also about how the women he had met were giving him thousands of dollars to buy custom-made shoes and suits so he could go out to fancy places with them. Somewhere in the middle of his reminiscing, laughing, and slapping high fives with my male cousins, I lost my mind. I rained on him a series of bleeping expletives and words that for once I was hoping would send him running for a dictionary.

How dare he laugh at being given thousands of dollars for custom suits when he never bothered to send home a hundred bucks for the two kids he had left behind to help be raised by his mother's sister and brother? How dare he laugh at the stories of when he was having the time of his life with money we never saw—and other women? How dare he be so cavalier about his carefree, responsibility-less escapades with me sitting in the same room—when I was living proof he had plenty of responsibilities?

Stopping cold in the midst of my tirade, I realized that while Duke had tried to warn me of those "other" illogical people, all along he was one of them! I put to work the very advice he had given me less than two hours before. There was only one way I could sum it up: My daddy had chosen the life of a fool. The only consolation I had in coming to such reality was knowing that God indeed takes care of fools.

Duke turned sixty years old on April 30, 1998, and it was the first time I ever had a working phone number for him so that I could wish him a happy birthday. I was on my book tour in Los Angeles and I called him from my hotel room. He said he wanted to make an appointment with me at my home so that he could discuss his latest get-rich-quick scheme with me. "How 'bout that," I thought sarcastically, "I am finally worthy enough to be let in on some of his 'secrets of success.'" It was very clear that by now, at age sixty, he was never going to change. I hung up the phone and got on my knees right there in the Los Angeles Marriott. I left Duke at the altar. I planted there a grain of my faith, hoping someday, in this lifetime, to see his growth.

LaJoyce Brookshire is the best-selling author of *Soul Food*. This former publicity director for Arista Records has started her own publicity agency for entertainment and media.

42

A Choice

Chrisena Coleman

One moment I was living out all my fantasies on a postcard-perfect vacation in the Bahamas, just like a character in a steamy romance novel. The next thing I knew, I was in a bathroom stall at the Helmsley Hotel in New York during my lunch break, taking a pregnancy test. I was there because I worked next door with some of the nosiest people in the world—*New York Daily News* reporters—and we earn our living digging up dirt. The newsroom bathroom was definitely not the place for a pregnancy test.

Deep down inside, I knew I was pregnant, but I didn't, couldn't, accept that reality. At least not after the first five tests. I needed to believe that this one, the sixth test, would be negative. But it was the plus sign—again!

That was five years ago. At the time, I was afraid to become a single mom. I was afraid of living out all the stereotypical notions White America ascribes for sistahs like me. Even though my son, Jordan, and I became two more statistics—another African-American family with an absentee father. My mom wasn't a single mom and neither was her mother. In fact, my parents are celebrating their thirty-nineth wedding anniversary this year—perfect role models. And I had planned to be just like them.

When I told my parents I was pregnant, neither reacted immediately, though they longed to be grandparents. They simply reassured me that they would be in my corner, no matter what decision I made.

My boyfriend was, without a shadow of a doubt, against the idea of my having his baby, even though he had been the one to toss the condoms aside when I pulled them out in the Bahamas. I was surprised by his response because he had everything to offer a child—one of New York City's Finest—ambitious, loving, and intelligent.

At first, I didn't know whether or not I should go ahead with the pregnancy, but I decided to put it in God's hands. I knew enough about life to realize that people often say what they will or will not do, but ultimately God will work things out. I refused to have an abortion. I figured that if it was meant for me to become a mother, it would happen. My boyfriend, whom I adored, tried countless times to talk me out of it. If he could have dragged me to the abortion clinic, he would have, despite my kicking and crying. He quickly became my ex-boyfriend. I went through my pregnancy without him—it was my father and mother who accompanied me to every doctor's appointment. I was embarrassed that I was with them but happy that someone cared enough about me to hold my hand.

It was emotionally draining. Not only had I lost my boyfriend, but I had also lost my best friend. He was the man I'd shared all my dreams with. He knew all my secrets and fears and insecurities and made me feel good about myself despite them. I had been in love once before him, but it took years for me to experience that kind of love and I didn't want to lose him. I made a few desperate attempts to plead my case, but he wasn't budging. He was sure he wouldn't play a role in our son's life and even more convinced that our relationship was over.

I worked covering stories for the *New York Daily News* up until my eighth month of pregnancy. During that time, I ran into him countless times. Each time he saw me, he would act as if I was not there, mere strangers who passed on the street. One day, while up at Sylvia's Restaurant to cover a press conference and celebration to mark the release of Mike Tyson from jail, we ran into each other. My stomach was big, my feet swollen, and I was tired. He walked right by me without even acknowledging my presence. I wanted to cry, but my pride wouldn't allow me. Instead, I asked God for strength. I needed strength to get through the day and my pregnancy. I needed strength to be a good mother and to allow my heart time to heal. I needed strength to forgive him for not wanting to be a father to our child. I also needed strength to continue to love myself and to be able to fall in love and accept love into my life again, if it came. We went our separate ways that day, but I walked away feeling good about the decision I'd made. I walked away feeling good about myself and the days to come. I walked away knowing that God would not leave me at the threshold of pain. I walked away that day believing that love would find me again, one day.

My pregnancy had its share of emotional ups and downs. With a few weeks left in my pregnancy, Jordan's dad called. He had second thoughts and wanted to be part of his son's life. We came together on August 28, 1995, for the birth of Jordan Christopher Coleman, but we never rekindled our relationship. To his credit, Jordan's dad has risen to every occasion. I spent the first three years of motherhood concentrating only on Jordan— for seven months I temporarily traded in my pen, tape recorder, and reporter's notepad for midnight feedings, projectile vomiting, and Huggies diapers. By the time I'd bathed Jordan, fed him, read to him, did laundry, cleaned the house, and cooked dinner, it was time for bed. But Jordan's life inspired me to really strive for great things. His birth was the inspiration for my first book, *Mama Knows Best*. My parents kept their end of the deal too. They have been my angels, joyfully stepping in for me whenever necessary and never complaining about my late hours at work, out-of-town assignments, book signings, or speaking engagements.

For three years, I was either doing something with Jordan or working. Each day after I finished up at the *Daily News*, I spent countless hours in front of my home computer writing free-lance stories, proposals, and working on my novel. I was consumed with working and providing a decent life for Jordan. In that time, I realized that I could raise a child alone. I realized that success was indeed a journey and not a destination. I realized that I was much stronger than I'd ever expected. Sure, there were times that I felt insecure and wondered if I had done the right thing, but those feelings always went away. As I got to know Jordan, I also got to know myself, well.

Then one day, my cousin set me up on a blind date. Our initial meeting was over the telephone. After hours of phone time, we decided to actually meet. I had no expectations and neither did he, except to have a new friend. He was five years my senior and divorced with a teenage son from a previous relationship. He was tall, dark, and handsome. He was intelligent and funny and family-oriented. Our first date was to the movies and our second date was to church. He was a real gentleman. I don't think either of us was looking for the other at the time we met, but it all just clicked. We did become friends, but I knew I wanted more. I had not been in a relationship for three years and I hadn't had any real male energy in my life. I knew he was someone special, but I was still reluctant to give him my heart.

Our friendship continued and blossomed into the most fulfilling relationship I have ever experienced. It was as if God had sent my Prince Charming (yes, I am a hopeless romantic). There were times when I thought I did not have what it takes to share myself with another man. There were times when I didn't believe I deserved a good man and other times when I feared I had already experienced the greatest loves of my life, but I was wrong. When I look at him playing with Jordan or having a conversation with my parents or pitching in when I am at the end of my rope or on deadline, I smile in knowing that there are still some wonderful black men out there. I am glad to know there are black men out there who were raised the old-fashioned way. I am glad to know that there are black men out there who believe black women deserve to be loved and treated like royalty, despite our mood swings, spoiled ways, and strong opinions. And just as he encourages me to follow my dreams, I do the same for him. Together, we bring out the very best in each other. He returns my affection as generously and unselfishly as I give it to him. I am not sure where it will go or how our story will play out, but he has given me the love, support, and friendship I needed to have a more balanced life. The greatest thing of all is that he not only loves me, he loves Jordan, and my parents, too!

Chrisena Coleman is an award-winning journalist for the *New York Daily News* and is the author of *Mama Knows Best* as well as *Just Between Girlfriends*. She is currently working on her first novel.

43

Daddy's Little Woman

Karyn Bryant

When I was a kid, I didn't understand why my dad was so vehement about saying he was a black man. The hazel-eyed, fair-skinned man of the house didn't look like the black men I'd seen on TV (and I'd mostly seen them on TV because there were no others in town). I didn't understand why he didn't just pretend he was like everyone else. I was smart enough to know that being black meant hardship, and I wondered why anyone would invite that on to himself. But as I grew older, I came to appreciate my dad's strength of character and I also began to see it reflected in my own way of thinking. While we often have differing opinions concerning race, politics, and life in general, I am very happy to have been reared with his influences, and believe very strongly that much of my success can be attributed to the fact that I learned determination at a young age.

My father grew up in a time when racism was much more blatant than the sometimes-subtle tones it appears in today. It's a tough history to forget, which explains why a little negativity can occasionally shadow his thoughts. He's very positive when it comes to my abilities and my preparations for taking on the world, but at the same time he knows how hard it can be for a black person to get ahead. I am without a doubt my father's daughter, but that's not to say that I have always agreed with the tenets of his philosophy. Nevertheless, with age and understanding come curiosity and dissent. And since I do represent a new generation, my thoughts inevitably reveal more hopefulness about the human conscience, more naiveté, and the spirited notion that past injustices just might stay in the past. I have more hope that times are changing. Yet at the ripe old age of twenty-nine I think the only thing I know for certain is that being black in America is still hard. Add to that the female element, and you've got an even tougher situation.

Toughness. Well, that's something I definitely need in the television business, and something I learned to project early in life. When I was four years old, my family moved to the preppy town of Westford, Massachusetts, and we were the only black family. And before I go any further, I should clarify the whole black family thing. My father is the son of an interracial couple from Lynchburg, Virginia. My mother is not an American black woman—she's a very proud Jamaican citizen to this day still. As you may know, many Jamaicans do not ally themselves with black Americans; and even though the skin color may be the same, their thoughts and opinions can have very different shades. I've got one older brother and together we made up what the rest of the town saw as *the* black family. The only other black kids in town were two adopted boys, one of whom I, of course, had to partner with at least once at each school dance. But I'm getting ahead of myself. Suffice it to say, between the black man and the Jamaican woman, I got some mixed messages about what my skin color would or wouldn't preclude me from doing or being.

Growing up poor meant my dad had a lot of firsthand information about prejudice. I, too, had a lot of firsthand experience with it in the world of the middle class. Things weren't too bad when I was really young—kids can certainly be mean, but I don't remember things being overly miserable. I had friends, and being different hadn't really gotten in the way of things that I may have wanted to do. (I still think my Brownie Scout leader was out to get me, but I never really liked her much anyway!) But with junior high and high school come boys, harassment, and a growing awareness of my station in the social strata. On boys, I had next to none; on "harrassment," I had massive amounts; and on my "social status," I had conflicting messages. For all the things I wanted but didn't get, Dad often cited the fact that I was black, and that was why (a) boys didn't like me and wouldn't ask me out: (b) I would walk into the lunchroom to find exaggerated drawings of African "spear chuckers" with my name underneath: and (c) I may find myself accepted on certain levels, but not fully embraced, i.e. a token. So again I would think, "Why does he want to be black?" Especially since I surmised he was right. I was sad he was right. I was angry that I was different.

Well, eventually my dad's actions and opinions were elucidated to me. He's a self-made man who owns a successful business, put his two children through private colleges, has two Mercedes-Benzes, and is still with the woman he married thirty-seven years ago. Any man would be proud of these accomplishments. But to have prospered in such a fashion as a black man, I came to understand, meant even more. So as far as his protestations about skin color are concerned, perhaps it wasn't a question of him wanting to be black. Maybe it was more like not wanting to be ashamed of being black. Every day we are bombarded with images of black people doing wrong: shooting someone at the movies, having their eighth child on welfare, messing up a great career with drugs and basically "setting the race back." So to see my dad achieving and prospering and living well has been, and will certainly always be, an inspiration to me.

If you believe in horoscopes, then the fact that my dad and I are both Capricorns might tie this whole thing together nicely. We make good leaders because of our resolution. My father is the head of his company, and he is fully expected to speak his mind. I, however, am not in charge of Hollywood yet, and as a result, my conviction may at times lead to harsh sentences. In a number of meetings with the landed gentry (aka the middle ages, white male network suits), I've made the mistake of speaking my mind when I was supposed to speak theirs. I have discerned their palpable displeasure upon hearing well-formed and supported arguments coming from me—a young black woman! How dare I! I've imagined their inner dialogues: They think I'm one more insolent upstart who doesn't understand respect. They think I must talk this way to my ignorant mom and estranged dad. They think I'm just some clueless cue-card-reading, ego-tripping TV bimbo. But when they go back and check the résumé, the words "double major" and "Brown University" drive them nuts. And even though the other things that constitute who I am may not be on the résumé, you can bet that they begrudgingly come to learn the facts. I represent a different kind of black person from the ones they've come to know and subjugate. And though it's not an easy role, it's one I've grown into, and one that I try to expand and perfect every day.

It is frustrating to be faced with clichés and stereotypes, to go to an audition knowing the casting agent expects you to "act more black." Other black actress friends and I lament the lack of roles and jobs for us. It is hard losing out to less-talented but more-fair-skinned women. But what do you do when in your heart you recognize your calling? History advances and perceptions shift because some people have the fortitude to push the envelope and force a change. Just because Hollywood still likes to foster the negative images that they do doesn't mean I'll stop trying to alter that predisposition. I'll never know what the first thing that crosses someone's mind is when I attend a meeting or when he or she sees me on the air. But I know that "Hi, I'm Karyn and I'm black" is not the first thing I say or even try to project. I cannot escape my skin color, so the black thing is obvious. What I try to project is confidence, brainpower, and being real. And when I get the job, and when people like me, maybe then they will reassess their own feelings about what a black person is like. Maybe their prejudices will fall away. Maybe they'll pass those new ideas on.

Even though some things have changed since my dad's youth and more doors are open to blacks, I doubt that I will ever lose the feeling that my victories were harder won than those of the white women next to me. I do feel the bonds of sisterhood to some degree with all women, but I get so tired of fighting for things that every now and then I wonder if life would be easier as a blond.

As far as adolescence is concerned, I have no doubt that life would have gone more smoothly. I might have been teased in my youth for something I could change instead of the permanence of pigmentation. I might have gotten a date before college; which would undoubtedly have made me a happier person. I have never defined myself by the men I date, but we all know how much more traumatic life seems for the hopelessly single teens. Perhaps I would be further along in my career because I fit the mold of the TV host more as a white woman. There aren't too many Oprahs, but there sure are a lot of Diane Sawyer types. Life might have been more predictable and therefore more navigable.

The only problem with this theory is that life is not predictable, no matter who you are. Anyway I've seen some of the people from high school who seemed to have it all back then, and to this day what they had then is still all they have. They peaked a long time ago. Besides, blonde is just an outward appearance; I'd still have to contend with the same person on the inside. And I feel so much stronger and so much more focused and so much more driven making my way with the curly dark hair and caramel skin I was given. I wear like a badge the chip my dad planted firmly on my shoulder.

Let's get back to the man thing for a minute, though! Yes, I have a chip, and I know men can be easily intimidated, but I have always been a big fan of the male race. I love guys, and in fact, most of my friends are men. While I do wonder what my folks will think of each new boyfriend (although there haven't been very many of them), I actually wonder more about what his parents will think. I know that some people still aren't comfortable with interracial couples, but I personally have an equal opportunity dating policy. My family has a history of mixed marriages, and the diverse social situations of my hometown, prep school, Brown, and New York City have taught me that judging a book by its cover is a sure-fire way to miss out on some of the most interesting biographies out there. Yes, my Jamaican mom worries about the prospects of "good hair," but my folks know that who and what excites me can be radically different from what excites them. They trust that I am strong enough to choose well, or at least to learn from those expected letdowns. I may never find a man that my mom thinks deserves me, or that my dad won't investigate with that "I used to be your age and I know what I wanted to do" look, but that won't stop me from bringing the next guy home. And even though that shadow of doubt from years past reappears from time to time, and I wonder if being black has kept someone from asking me out, I understand that I'm better off without them. Men will always be a touchy subject due to those frequent early hardships, but thankfully some memories fade.

It is ironic, though, that in all this talk about being black, and how my dad has taught me things, and how prejudice has affected my life, there is the implication that I am prejudiced, too, since I speak in terms of me or us versus them. I think if we're all honest, we can admit that we are not without fault. So as much as I may ask someone to change how they think, I, too, have had to change some of my own thoughts. I know that every white man is not the grown-up version of the boy who teased me and made me miserable when I was younger. Everyone above me at the workplace is not out to keep me down.

Every day society can teach tolerance to someone new. Maybe I shouldn't worry so much about being black. After all, it's a pretty safe bet that I'll be this way forever. I thank my dad for teaching me to be strong and proud, and for showing me that even though it may be harder, I can be whatever and whoever I want. I hope the children I might one day have don't worry about all this as much as I do. I wish that throughout his life, my dad didn't have to worry so much either.

Karyn Bryant is a former MTV VJ, host of FX and TNT's *Rough Cut*. She is currently working on her acting career.

44

My Once-Dented Heart

J. V. McLean-Ricketts

Dedicated to my late husband, Angus W. Ricketts,
and to my mother, Mrs. Daisy McLean, who taught me
the true meaning of kindness and forgiveness.

It was Christmas Eve in Jamaica, West Indies, very early in the morning. It was raining heavily with loud thunder and lightning. I was about eight years old when I knew my life was never going to be the same again.

Our closest neighbor, my mother's first cousin, Miss Dora, was crying hysterically as she approached our house. My mother took her in, tried to comfort her, and gave her warm clothing. I overheard her apologizing to my mother for having an affair with my father. Although at the time I had not understood what an affair meant, I sensed that something was wrong, that my father had done something wrong. It could not be true. My father, a morally correct man, was always my hero. He sometimes advised the residents of the village in which we lived. And I knew that my father would not do anything deliberately to hurt my mother.

I instantly became confused, angry, and mostly disappointed in hearing this story. I believed my cousin was making it up to hurt my mother. My mother became ill shortly after I was born—fragile almost, making even the simplest tasks seem insurmountable, even taking care of herself and the rest of the family. I had come to know this because I overheard family discussions. For a long time I felt guilty, believing that my mother's illness was my fault. Back then listening to my cousin's confession that the reason for my father's indiscretion was because of my mother's fragile health, my guilt intensified. I remembered seeing and hearing my mother crying many times. The faraway look of disappointment and shame in her eyes was a memory that stayed with me for a long time.

Of course, my mother leaving our father would have been even more disgraceful than his indiscretions. Regardless of everything, it was her duty to stand by her man. My mother is a proud woman, so talking about this with another woman was not in her vocabulary. I became her little shrink instead. She talked to herself sometimes in my presence, and it would seem that she somehow expected to receive an answer from me in a way of comfort.

Even though my father was forgiven, my mother once told me that the disgrace, hurt, and shame that she experienced would always stay with her. Apparently this sordid affair had been going on for years right under my mother's nose. Of course she was the last one to have found out. It was some time after that Miss Dora became ill. Oddly enough, it was my mother who assisted in taking care of her and her smaller children.

Our household functioned quite normally as if none of this had taken place. My father throughout all those years was quite attentive to us. He was kind and loving with a great sense of humor. Only I did not know that we were nothing but another pretentious family. Never did I think that this situation would later determine certain choices we all made. It was almost like a code of silence—expected and understood that we would not discuss this problem among ourselves. Having lived in a small village where everyone seemed to know about each other's lives, once in a while my father's little indiscretion would be the hot topic for barnyard discussion.

I cried many silent tears. I was often confused and even resented my father sometimes for hurting us. Yet, I loved him dearly. Meanwhile, my three older brothers seemed to show nothing but love and respect for our father all the time. Little did I know how my father's behavior affected each of them. My oldest brother, Rudolph, was married very early, at age twenty-one. While he has been an excellent father and provider to my niece, Kerrine, and my nephew, Troy, he was a fervent womanizer. He placed the blame on being married too early. Of course, it was obvious he chose the path that our father once traveled.

My brother, Kingsley, would have liked staying married, but the indiscretion was regrettably revisited in his own household by his wife. While he maintained a close, positive relationship with our father, he told him that he was not pleased with him—the affair with cousin Dora had been too close to home.

Meanwhile, my youngest brother, Winston, who was married and since divorced for some time now, is shying away from making any commitments. Having had the closest relationship with our father among the boys, discussing this indiscretion would have proven to be disloyal to our father.

Years later I found myself traveling down the same rugged road myself. I migrated to the United States and was forced to seek employment when resources for my college fund fell through. I worked as a housekeeper, babysitter, and cook with different families, mostly sleeping in. It was during this period that I realized that not just black families but white families experience similar and sometimes worse problems in their households.

At first, I found it strange that my employer's entire family was seeking professional help. Once or sometimes twice a month I had to schedule appointments for the children to go to their psychiatrist. I became encouraged by the fact that this family was trying to seek help for themselves while their children were small. It prompted me to seek my own healing. I started writing to my father asking questions and he opened up to me about what happened between him and my mother. He explained his loneliness and his need for adult companionship, which my mother was not able to give. He did not offer this as an excuse, only as an explanation. I shared my feelings of guilt about my mother's illness. He told me it was never my fault. We continued to communicate.

My once-a-year visit to Jamaica used to be our therapy session. Gradually I began to realize that my father was only human—not the God, the hero, I made him out to be, but simply a man who had fallen from the pedestal upon which I had placed him. I started to let go of my guilt. Some of my pain and resentment began to ebb away slowly. My healing process began, at least I thought so.

It was in 1985. My son, Ryan, was born and it was the proudest day of my life. When Ryan's father decided that fatherhood was going to be too much for him to handle, I was left to raise my son alone. All the old insecurities and uncertainties resurfaced. Having a stable family I believed was impossible. In my heart I believed my father's indiscretion was my downfall. I built a wall around my heart. Taking care of my son was my entire joy and focus. Outside relationships were not part of my existence.

My son was four years old when we relocated. It was there I met Gus, my next-door neighbor. He and Ryan became fast friends. However, he was a bit aloof at first, and cautious about making friends with me. Gus was responsible for making me realize that there were people around us who had gone through worse situations and have moved on. Oprah Winfrey was a typical example, he would say. "If Jesus forgave His crucifiers, then it's about time you do the same and purge your system once and for all," he would tell me.

Gus became my mentor, professor, and mostly a trusted friend. Our friendship grew over a five-and-a-half-year period. Eventually, we became lovers and were married within one month. I was very happy. This new and wonderful feeling lasted only a couple of months.

My new husband's extended family began to creep into our marriage. He had assumed responsibility for his two grandchildren. My husband told me that he had a job to do in protecting them. He thought that by giving them his entire support they would not suffer from lack of a positive male role model, as his son, their father, was not in a position to be active in their lives. This was a pattern that he wanted discontinued. On top of that, I became pregnant and was placed on bed rest. I later miscarried and never had an outlet for my feelings. Seeking professional help as a family was a big no, no. Like me, my son blamed himself every time he saw me crying or whenever my husband would leave us because his daughter-in-law needed him for the girls. My son believed, as I believed about my father, that my husband was his hero. Like my mother, I pretended that everything was fine.

Of course, I was not fooling anyone. I went through the same anguish as my mother did. Ultimately, Gus's other household's dependency on him somehow got out of control. To the point where he realized that our marriage was regrettably sacrificed, and even more so his health.

It was some time later that my husband became very sick. He asked me to forgive him for his mean-spirited ways. He told me how much he appreciated my patience and kindness to him. He became softer and kinder to us. I helped him every step of the way. We began to pray together.

He wanted to make it all up to us. But it was too late. After a short illness, my husband died in 1998. To intensify the hurt and loss even more so, he died on Ryan's birthday. We had rekindled our love and had just begun to care and share everything. It finally felt good to start mending our broken hearts.

Understandably, I was disappointed, angry, and hurt when my husband died. My sister-in-law, Lynn, and my husband's childhood friend, Headley, prayed with me daily for a long time to help me through a deep depression. I made friends with Paul in the office and later Karen, Enza, and Eileen became part of my "personal help group." Sister Williams, Brother and Sister James, Dawn, Janice, Miss Daphne, and my cousin, Peggy, became my at-home "personal help group." Little Ashley and Kimberly, were a source of great joy for me during those dreary days. These people encouraged me to pray for guidance throughout this rough period. I also found out that it was all right to talk about what happened in my family without feeling ashamed or even blaming myself. As for my son, our love and close relationship helped him to cope. He was also getting his therapy from his first-grade teacher, Mrs. Williams, and her family, who to this day remains friends with us. Major credits to my brothers, especially Winston, and my son, Ryan, who were instrumental in holding my hands and praying with me all the time.

I was able to overcome most of my anguish by constantly praying and talking about it with my good friends. I also eliminated all bad thoughts and replaced them with good, loving thoughts of my husband. Thus I wrote:

Good-bye, My Husband, I Love You

My darling Gus, you look so blue
I prayed to God to have mercy upon you
So that we can have a second chance
Only it seems God has other plans.

You tried to stay alert, to open at least one eye
The look I saw told me you were saying good-bye
Happy birthday, I said, it's the second of March
Don't worry, you will live to be an old patriarch.

Our Father which art in Heaven, I prayed
Lord, help my husband make it throughout today
My darling, blink your eye if you understand
As Jesus will take care of you better than anyone can.

If we have to say good-bye
I will manage to cope if you die
With God's angels around me
I will be protected under the umbrella of God's holy tree.

Ah life! What is life, I asked
Life on this earth is not ensured
My love for you is assured
Go in peace with God without a task.

I dreamt your retirement party was planned
Only it seems a retirement to Jesus' hand.

My experience allowed me to identify with other people going through similar situations in their relationships. I have helped numerous people, quite privately, and have been asked how did I know that there was a problem. We cannot fool anyone, only ourselves. My parents over the years showed care and affection toward each other. Somehow, my mother to this day shows signs of sadness in her gentle eyes. My father and I developed a warm, loving father-daughter relationship by the time he died in 1996. My brother, Rudolph, over the years had faced his demons and is getting re-married. He is very positive and the happiest I have seen him with his new wife to-be and their four-year-old daughter, Jodi-Ann. Kingsley is living a stable family life for some time now. Meanwhile, Winston is dating steadily. Our relationship as siblings has grown stronger over the years with close supportive and positive communications. My mother and I share the warmest and closest relationship, always. Ryan and his father have been on the road toward building a closer and more communicative father-son relationship since 1997.

I have no regrets, as my experience has paved a road for me which I can now say has made me a stronger, more vibrant person, and I can impart this to others. Especially to my niece, Kerrine, who is now experiencing the same doubts and insecurities in her first relationship as I did. She is receptive and is making positive changes and has promised not to pass this negative pattern on to the next generation. To also realize that things are not always as difficult if we approach them with care and openness. My strong faith and belief in God with help from my son, close relatives, and good friends keeps me grounded.

J. V. McLean-Ricketts was born in St. Elizabeth, Jamaica, West Indies, and presently lives in Brooklyn, NY, with her son, Ryan. She enjoys sharing her cooking and baking; she attended New York University.

45

Daddy's Voice . . .

Lonai Mosley

And through his pain comes my wisdom and growth . . .

I was eighteen when Daddy died under a cloud of suspicion, and now almost twenty years later, I still vividly recall the chain of events leading to the incident.

My parents met in 1955. They were both seventeen and lived in different worlds. Daddy was an aspiring recording artist and part-time hospital orderly, and Mom worked in the hospital addressograph office. Focused on her own critically ill mother, Mom would spend all of her breaks and free time there. Mom's sadness and vulnerability tugged at his heart, while her exotic Mediterranean presence captured his soul. He knew one day they would be together.

My mom's old-school traditional roots included a protective father, descendant of Italian immigrant peanut farmers who worked hard to maintain the family boardinghouse business while being a caregiver to his ill wife. The youngest of seven, my mother was blessed with two adoring parents who showered her with love and a modest, but comfortable home life although they struggled with illness, middle age, and a rapidly changing America.

Daddy had a far more worldly and problematic childhood. At first my father's mother and her nine siblings lived comfortably on her family's large Virginia tobacco plantation. They never wanted for anything due to my great-grandfather's entrepreneurial spirit for farming, insurance sales, and the dry-cleaning business. However, when he died at thirty-four from a brain aneurysm, my great-grandmother sent several of her children, including my grandmother to a local boarding school.

My grandmother never expressed exactly why at fourteen she ran away to her aunt's home in Philadelphia, but she did tell us about having to con-

stantly fight off men's sexual advances. She was pursued for her Native/
African-American mixed beauty, high cheekbones, molasses cookie complexion, and voluptuous six-foot tall frame. One summer day while she
cared for her young cousins, their father threatened to put her out into the
street if she didn't "please" him. When she refused, he raped her and convinced her aunt that she was trouble. My grandmother left town with a local
truck driver she had met named Jack Mosley.

Jack Mosley was from Connecticut, and they settled twenty minutes
from his home town in New Haven. It wasn't long before she learned the
truth about Jack. Not only was he a womanizer, a poor provider and an incredibly abusive alcoholic, but he also tormented his own children, my father, and Aunti whenever he came home from the road. Aunti told us about
their childhood and how at times my grandmother would hide them all
under the bed overnight while they waited for their father to sleep off his
drunken state.

Gram's spirit was broken; she felt hopelessly trapped and withdrew from
her family. As children, they lived in constant fear of their father's physical
abuse and molestation. Aunti became severely emotionally disturbed, and
Daddy prone to fits of rage, hostility and a mischievous demeanor that only
creating music could sooth.

Daddy fine tuned his vocal instrument in the 1950's Doo Wop harmo-
nizing street corner fashion, performed around town, and used his pennies
and contest prize money to help feed Grandma and Aunti who struggled to
make ends meet as domestics for affluent whites. Daddy would marvel at
the lifestyles of these people and would dream about "arriving," and being
rich and famous. He would tell his "baby sis" that one day when he was old
enough and physically able, he would no longer let Jack get away with the
abuse. That day finally came during one of Jack Mosley's drunken rages. My
father had just turned fourteen and reached six feet in height when Jack
physically attacked my grandmother for not having prepared the food he
wanted. When Daddy and Aunti pleaded with Jack to not hurt their mother
any more, he called Daddy a black snake for interfering in his affairs. In a
moment of temporary insanity, Daddy picked up a kitchen chair and swung
with all his might. An eery quiet filled the room as Jack staggered backward
with blood gushing from his crown.

Daddy nearly killed his father that day and with my grandmother's help,
fled from home to join the United States Army. Several months later, Daddy
called home to say he was almost courtmartialed for smoking weed, and my
grandmother, along with the help of her influential employer, accomplished
author Thornton Wilder, implored Daddy's commanding officer to release
him because he falsified documents revealing his true age. Daddy received
an honorable discharge and returned from the New Mexico military base

focusing his energy and talents on music. He taught himself flute, guitar, piano, and formed a singing group with several friends from the neighborhood. The group's smooth, tight harmonies and clean cut, "pretty boy" looks caught the attention of a local studio manager who recorded them in a church basement and, the Scarlets were born. Later they became The Five Satins or The Satins due to their trademark satiny voices.

Daddy seemed to be on his way. His career heated up as The Satins began touring around the New York tri-state area, and although the money the group earned at times was only $300 a week, which even by 1950's standards didn't go very far between five members, musicians, road manager and band manager, he was thrilled to be doing what he loved and for the accolades that came with it. As performance schedules and the road became more demanding, tensions rose within the group and when "In The Still of The Night," a song Daddy co-wrote, catapulted The Satins to super star recognition, Daddy confronted the group's lead about financial issues and writer's credits. Feeling unfairly compensated, Daddy grew bitter and their relationship became increasingly strained.

Mom finally accepted an invitation from Daddy to see The Satins perform at a Bridgeport, Connecticut, arena. Neither had ever dated outside of their races, but magic superseded racial concerns for both. She succumbed to his magnetic appeal, striking brown skin, six-foot-four muscular physique, quick wit, and smooth trademark tenor voice, and he to her confident, feisty, fun-loving personality and, of course, radiant beauty. From that moment they were inseparable and fell passionately in love. They broke all the rules, several hearts, and endured the disapproval of both their families, friends, and threats from jealous and jilted ex lovers.

My sister, Laura, a love child, was born in 1957, not long after my maternal grandmother passed away from a staph infection after surgery. "Making it" was Daddy's first priority, so my mother coped with loneliness, grief over her mother, financial strain, and with no where else to turn she entered a halfway house where state agency representatives made her believe that her biracial child would be better off adopted by an older and more financially secure interracial family. While Mom suffered and tried to regroup from the pain of loss, Daddy continued to bask in the limelight. In an attempt to build the family foundation he never had, Daddy proposed to Mom. As they made wedding plans and unsuccessfully attempted to recover their first born, Mom's family plotted against the union, going as far as to lock her in a closet on her wedding day.

My parents eloped to New York City where for three years they struggled. Mom supported Daddy's dreams to maintain his crumbling celebrity lifestyle as their life together became unstable, filled with constant financial sacrifice, countless drug-filled parties, other women, loneliness, and racism. Mom would have to secure apartments when they were evicted and have Daddy move in at night because no one wanted to rent to an interracial couple. She worked menial jobs in order to pay their bills and endured the endless racist comments frequently accompanied by physical confrontations whenever they walked down the street holding hands. When Daddy began to vent his frustrations in physical abuse toward her, she decided she had enough and headed back to her family, who welcomed her with open arms.

Late one spring evening during an attempted reconciliation, Mom, Dad and a mutual friend were heading home from a party when it began to rain. The roads were slick and although Dad was a good driver, his Jag sped out of control while they rounded a bend in the road. The car hit a telephone pole and Mom's ankle was crushed before she was ejected through the convertible roof. Their girlfriend virtually destroyed her pretty face on the concrete, and Daddy walked away with little more than a few scratches. When Mom regained consciousness in the hospital emergency room, she asked if her unborn baby had survived, and much to the doctor's surprise they heard my tiny heartbeat.

I grew up in New Haven, seventy-five miles from New York City, in the 1960's which had its advantages. A progressive mini city, which included rich multi-ethnic/multi-cultural exposure as well as easy access to New York City, shows premiered in our city before they made it to Broadway, and it was a Mecca for live music. Our house was always filled with various creative types. The proximity to Yale University and a major Black Panther Party movement afforded me exposure to an academic environment and the Civil Rights Movement. My biracial ethnicity thrived with a variety of ethnically diverse friends from similar backgrounds. Mom did her best to expose me to both worlds, encouraging equal time with my maternal grandfather, paternal grandmother, and the numerous aunts and cousins who helped me develop a reasonably strong sense of identity, self-esteem, and family.

Occasionally my biracial background, light brown skin, and long, black curly hair was cause for defense, but I always managed to keep confrontation to a minimum. One incident occurred when I was eight years old and playing in a park near my grandfather's house. His neighborhood was fairly ethnically mixed, and I had various friends I would see when I was there on weekends. I was alone this particular spring day when several dark-brown skinned African-American girls I didn't know approached me and said that I needed a haircut. As they called me zebra, Oreo and half-breed, one of the girls held my arms, while another pulled hard at my braid and the third went to get scissors. I fought as if my life depended on it and freed myself from their grip just as my grandfather entered the park. Gramps was my hero and a loving surrogate male-role model who taught me to draw, play drums, speak Italian, and protected me.

Even though Daddy would try to keep in touch from the road by writing, telephone, and sporadic late night visits, I longed for his presence yet felt his love. My parents finally divorced after several years of separation. Mom did her best to fill our home with love and the basic necessities while sending me to private school and never letting me want for anything. She continues to be my rock and best friend. The 1960's also continued the threat of Vietnam and was a daily nationwide concern. Some of the group members were drafted into the army and another group using The Satin's name continued performing in their place. Daddy landed gigs with Lionel Hampton and The Righteous Brothers, but they were short lived and he became increasingly frustrated and emotionally disturbed as his career spiraled downward. I often convinced myself that he was "on the road," when I knew he was actually in prison, most likely for drugs. I missed our family life and although Mom did all she could for me, there were times when I needed advise that only a father could give. I longed for my father's input on things like homework, my first date, and understanding the male psyche. However, we did share a creative talent and love of the arts. Mom supported and encouraged me to stay focused and in school as I dreamed about show business, sold lemonade in front of our house, organized neighborhood plays, and charged the parents of the children involved fifty cents admission to attend. Our home seemed peaceful during those times, and when Daddy was in town, I would proudly perform for him and he would direct me. Mom and her high-school sweetheart reunited for a brief time and seemed happy. He was a father figure to me and was very good to us. However, the romance suffered when they both committed infidelities and argued constantly.

I became depressed and Mom took me to clinical psychologists who always diagnosed my symptoms as normal divorced-child syndrome. My depression peaked when I was twelve and I swallowed a bottle of pills I found in Mom's medicine cabinet. When we started to make regular visits to the doctor, I learned to "play the game," cooperate and "behave" as much as possible in an attempt to avoid sharing my innermost thoughts or feelings. Up until that time Mom had been sheltering me from most of the disturbing memories she internalized, while choosing to focus on the good ones. Over the years I heard disturbing stories about my dad's behavior from relatives and strangers. I learned about my sister and half-brother being born three months apart, which wore away at my reality. I swallowed my pain and zoomed through everything I did in an attempt to learn a lot in a little bit of time and to forget. I had difficulty concentrating in school and was bored with the curriculum, wanting only to create like my dad. When the teachers suggested I be tested for special ed, I proveed them wrong by graduating from high school at fifteen. In the meantime, Mom went to work full time, often arriving home after 9:30 P.M., and I rebelled by making the "wrong" friends and experimenting with marijuana and drinking. She tried to keep me involved in after-school art programs and summer day camp, but I became increasingly distracted and moody. I rarely saw my father as he was usually in New York City attempting to revive his career.

Mom knew she had to "do something" and moved us to a small suburban town, which caused even more inner conflict for me because of the limited access to activities, racial segregation in the neighborhood school system, and Mom's personal life choices. I was exposed to a lot during that time by observing my neighbor's lifestyles that included drugs, prostitution, and homosexuality. I seriously struggled to hear Daddy's voice within me. I felt misplaced and searched for an outlet and moved in with a man seven years my senior, who was into fast money, women, cars, and reminded Mom way too much of Daddy. I was an impulsive fifteen-year-old and was impressed by our luxurious lifestyle, but when he became abusive, I knew I had to move on and did. He continued to harass me as I attempted to work full time, go to school, and hold onto my dreams. Stress began to wear on me, and I plotted my escape to pursue my entertainment industry dream in New York City.

I can never forget that day. My intuition told me something was not quite right. Anxiety gnawed at my stomach during school. An increasing sense of queasiness, apprehension, and curiosity gripped me as I climbed the stairs to our apartment. My mother's eyes confirmed the worst as they reflected concern for me and empathy for the man she had once loved and feared. I steadied myself in the seemingly surreal moment as my mother gently mouthed the words, "Your Aunti called and your father is dead." I was numb, barely able to speak, except to ask how it happened. She was somber then angry. "He was shot in the back by an off-duty FBI agent during a supposed attempted robbery, those bastards!"

My knees weakened as shock replaced anxiety. Drained, I hazily made my way into my room and lay across my bed, choked up, and unable to cry, my immediate surroundings faded into snapshots of my childhood unfolding in my mind: *Handsome, talented Daddy and me at his band rehearsal when I was three, me on Daddy's shoulders on a sunny Sunday afternoon, laughing as I got an ice-cream brain freeze from eating too fast at five, Daddy and me in his convertible, Daddy singing "a capella" on my tape recorder, and then suddenly a flicker and a tormented Daddy scaring and stalking Mommy after the divorce, needle tracks on Daddy's arms, Daddy kicking in Grandma's bathroom door to beat his girlfriend and then a flash, flicker, flicker and ironically, "In The Still of The Night," Daddy's hit song, finally lulling me to sleep.*

My father's death began a longing within me to fill an emotional void that would last for several years, with attempts to heal and understand the reasoning behind how the erosion of a brilliant life could end in Potter's field. My body shut down, and I experienced an internal hemorrhage due to stress, and abuse. As I recovered, my life turned around. I dealt with abandonment issues, pain, and loss. I discovered spirituality and experienced visions. I listened with my soul and began hearing Daddy's voice. I realized how the delicate combination of my parents' attributes, survival skills, strengths and weaknesses contributed to the person I was becoming. Daddy's classic recordings suddenly evoked intense feelings of closeness in a relationship that was short lived but powerful in its innate purpose to capture, continue, and redefine his legacy on the next level.

I pursued my own dreams and at times wondered what it must have been like for him to at one time have tasted the fruits of success, make musical history, master self-taught artistry, become an award-winning hair stylist, computer programmer, licensed airplane pilot, who spoke several languages fluently at a time when dark-brown skinned men could barely eat in a midtown Manhattan restaurant, let alone marry outside their race. During those times, I reflected on whether it was the pressures of success, deals gone bad, childhood abuse, racism, or lack of faith in the Creator that finally broke this man, driving him to despair, crime, vagrancy, and a self-fulfilling prophecy of death at the age of forty-two. I thought about my vivid recollection of discovering needle tracks on his arms as a child and how his words telling me not to do drugs detoured me from prolonged drug use.

While my precious childhood memories include limited material treasures, such as the three-foot doll, pair of black patent leather shoes, goldtone watch, Cassius Clay autograph, personal photos, and classic recordings, I am reminded that the material belongings I do have magnify the existence of Daddy's voice on this planet. I know and accept that Daddy did love me the only way he could and that it is up to me to avoid his negative patterns and continue his legacy in a positive light as I continue to strive and make a contribution to this planet for myself, my family, and generations to come. And so I dream, work, fight and at times struggle through the arduous process of self discovery, while holding on to each life lesson as if it were a precious gem. All the while trusting that the wings of ancestral angels watching over me represents Daddy's voice ringing softly in my ears, and I forge my own niche in this temporary zone we call life.

Lonai Mosley is a writer, voice-over artist and co-owner of Event Works Plus where she develops, produces, and markets film, radio, and special events projects including The Harlem Children's Museum and a novel/ screenplay based on Daddy's voice.

46

Spiritual Being

Jane S. Bell

Then Jesus said, Father, forgive them, for they
know not what they do.
—Luke 23:34

I will not waste this precious gift of spiritual massaging on the details of my painful wounds. What happened to me still happens today. The only way for me to make sense of the abuse cycle is to know that healers do not live forever. Others must learn the lessons in order to teach others that follow and so on and so on. Those at the stages of raw pain need to tell their stories. My story is to help them know that the worst part is over. They have lived through it and now the sacred path to healing can truly begin in order that they may become teachers as I was taught. The trauma I lived did not happen for me to ask why me; it happened for me to learn and understand unconditional love. Love that is deep within my soul. Love that went beyond my selfish pain and blame to spiritual oneness with God's kind of forgiveness. There is no textbook, religion, priest, nun, or minister who could teach me how to forgive the way my unwavering faith in God has taught me to forgive. I had to live those storm-filled traumas to experience the rainbow-filled joys that have become my soul.

How strange it was to realize that I was not the only one in the world who had experienced a violation of innocence by the age of five. As I listened to this familiar stranger tell her story, I knew I could learn something from her inner strength and heroic self-analysis. She was my guardian angel sent by God to tell me of her horrors so that I might begin my journey of healing. This woman, with multicolored Mohawk hair and mountains of handmade jewelry that jingled when she walked, told me she was just like me. With the voice of an angel, a heart as big as the sky, and a veggie burger named after her, she comforted me into a place where I could learn to be a child at twenty-six years old and take responsibility for my own rebirth. I call her T.

I was your typical nerd trying to find my way in a world surrounded by cool fads and glamour girls. I wanted to be like them. All I really wanted was to be liked. T was a stranger. I swallowed my fear and asked her to help me because she had talked about her path to healing and her road to recovery. She agreed to help me, even when I couldn't help myself. There were times when the pain was so sharp and raw that all I could do was curl up in a fetal ball and cry. T would hold me and not judge me. I did enough judging of myself; I didn't need any help. Reaching out to my family was not an option. It hurt them too much. There was nothing they could do to stop the pain. And I couldn't stand the pain in their voices. The hardest part was that I felt some of them were the source of the pain. The true source was the lack of acceptance, understanding, and forgiveness. God granted me the cleansing of my soul. The dark forest which filled the pit of my stomach was as close to my soul as I knew until T the teacher arrived and showed me the sacred path.

This journey began spiritually, with a vision of me at my childhood home in my old room packing up some things. There was a little girl sitting on the bed with her head down, crying. I picked up the bag I had just packed, took the little girl by the hand, and started walking out the door. As I was going down the stairs, I turned to help the little girl and I saw my own face as a child. T told me it was a wonderful opportunity for growth, and the meaning of that vision was that I was ready to take my inner child by the hand and protect her. I never could have anticipated the value of that wonderful opportunity for growth.

At four years old, I was molested by the fifteen-year-old son of a friend of the family. I didn't remember this until I began the processing of clearing out the forest to make room for the garden which now grows around my soul. For many years I could not understand why I felt so uncomfortable when I saw an older male child with a younger female child. This mystery was solved when the memory bubble burst and I felt like I was going to throw up my insides. The sickness of pushed-away pains is still not as horrible as the incidents while they occur. This is why God creates memory blocks and allows them to come through only when we are strong enough, with enough support to help us see the benefit.

During the summer of my fifteenth birthday, I was beaten every night by my mother's live-in boyfriend for his sadistic pleasure. On Sundays he would beat Mom. The same man attempted to rape me. Luckily I was studying martial arts and had just learned a technique for attack. When he did not get what he wanted, he convinced me that my mother wanted him to check to see if I was a virgin. He put a hole in the bathroom door so he could watch us. He often stood at my door at night staring at me, once attempting to unbutton my pajamas. This nightmare ended on a cold night in November when the premier of *The Incredible Hulk* was on television. This man was supposed to stay away from our home. He called several times that night asking for Mom. She told us to tell him she was not home. After several calls from him, we could hear the anger raging in his voice. We noticed he began walking around our house. We lived on the corner and he would have to jump the five-foot fence in the back during his circling. I remember we were running from window to window peeking out to see if he had left. The top of his bush was our guide to his every step. It was as if he was planning his attack and creating his monster, our Hulk, so no one could stop him, not even his own conscience. The back door crashed to the floor and we all screamed. I tried to get my little sisters out of the house but they would not go. One was ten years old; the other was five. I was the oldest and was supposed to protect them. He was coming for me. He did not know my mom was home. As he ran toward me and my sisters, who were hiding behind me, Mom said, "What do you want?" He came to a surprised stop, turned, and jumped toward her with his hands stretched out toward her neck. Mom screamed, "I got your gun you better go." Hearing Mom choking in the background, we heard him say, "You better kill me, bitch, cuz I'm comin to kill you." Two pops like a firecracker and he fell to the floor. Again, I tried to get my sisters out of the house but they would not leave. I ran for help and the police took Mom away without any underwear or pants in the cold, snowy winter dark.

I used to have nightmares of him standing at the foot of my bed. One night I was granted a vision of him at a party which I interpreted as a celebration of my freedom. I walked up to him and said, "I understand you did what you did because you are a sick man and I forgive you." When I awoke, I felt as if my soul was flying around the room dancing and singing as it had never done before. That is God's kind of forgiveness.

I don't remember exactly when I began to believe my mother hated me, but it was something I felt. T always said, "Your feelings are valid not fact." Every time she hit me, cussed me, called me names, and told me I was a good-for-nothing, lying, sneaky child who could never amount to anything, I felt the pain of a knife stabbing my soul. No one's opinion of me mattered as much as my mother's. I spent my life trying to please her with my actions, accomplishments, boyfriends, and girlfriends. Everything and anything I thought she would approve of, I did not do, but I would seek her approval anyway. When Mom and I began healing our relationship, she told me that she said those things because she knew I would do the opposite of whatever she told me to do or be. Mom realized I was lost and needed a special kind of guidance. Very confusing but I became a stronger and more determined achiever because of her. Today, my mother and I are friends. Now I don't believe my mother ever hated me. I believe she saw herself in me and that was the target of her hatred. I realized I needed to accept her for exactly who she is and stop trying to make her into someone else. I have now become all the best that my mother is, and that is all the approval I will ever need.

My great-aunt always told me that my mom loved me, but that she just did not know how to show it. She also told me that my mother would need me one day and that day came to pass. I cannot begin to express the extraordinary strength I witnessed in my sisters for being able to handle responsibilities that completely changed the course of their lives due to bad choices on the part of our mother. I had moved away and it seemed that everyone tried to shelter me from the truths that were going on at home. Maybe because of the personal pains I had suffered and the strides I had begun to make toward healing, they were protecting me, but I honestly don't know. What I can say is that during the next three years of our lives we all experienced the same crisis in very different ways. The results? We became a spiritually stronger family of four black women bound by our loyalties to each other and our blood lines that have no color.

We are all successes. We have embraced our differences. We have united in times when most would have grown apart. We have held each other's hands through every storm and over every mountain that has separated us. We are a family spiritually being.

Jane S. Bell is a pseudonym to protect her family's identity.

Your Soul's Sustenance

Today write a letter to a man in your life. It doesn't have to be a mate or significant other; you can write to your son, brother, friend, relative, or father. It doesn't matter if he's living, dead, or no longer around. Tell him what he means to you. Forgive him for anything you feel he's done to you wrongly. Let your anger and pain go once and for all, or let your joy and gratitude for his presence in your life flow. Say the things you've wanted to say, but may have never been able to say before. It's up to you whether you ever mail the letter or not. Don't be afraid to let him know exactly how you feel.

Your Personal Book of Revelations

We all have male energy in our lives. Sometimes we take their presence for granted, hoping to replace it with a figment of our imagination. Take some time and explore your answers to the following questions:

- Describe the individual relationships you have with men in your life.
- Do you have a platonic male friend?
- Is there a steady male role model in your life?
- What types of relationships would you like to have with men in your life?
- Do you possess the same characteristics that you desire in a man in yourself?
- Are you waiting to be rescued?
- Are you thankful for the roles that men play in your life?
- When you meet a man, do you find yourself trying to change him?

- Are your conversations filled with complaints and how your day was at the office, instead of fulfilling and enlightening conversations?
- If there has been a string of bad men in your life, ask yourself if you have been projecting negative energy.
- Do you choose the wrong partners because you do not really believe that you have what it takes to be a partner in a successful relationship?

Know the men in your life and embrace their presence!

X

Sister Feel Good

*The most sacred place is not the church, the mosque or the
temple, it's the temple of the body.
That's where spirit lives.*
— Susan Taylor

Our health is one of those things we take for granted until something goes wrong. It's like the gutters on your house, or the toner cartridge in your printer. Who even thinks about those things unless there's some kind of problem? Unfortunately, this reactionary way of approaching our health is not benefiting us in the long term. All it does is allow us to dig holes for ourselves that we then happily jump into—they're called graves. Sometimes the health problems that we've created for ourselves are so severe—the holes that we've dug so deep—that it's difficult or impossible to even climb our way out. Why don't we value our bodies? Why don't we heed the old adage, "An ounce of prevention is worth a pound of cure?" Our patterns and practices are gleaned from our families. Most of us were taught to go to the doctor only if you are literally dying.

The body is a remarkably well-built and designed machine. Physical and mental stress can trigger a wide variety of diseases that lay dormant in our body. These diseases are prevalent among African-American women and include diabetes, systemic lupus, leukemia, and multiple sclerosis. Emotional stress can affect everything from our menstrual cycle to muscle tension that can lead to pain in the back, neck, and head.

When the mind is bogged down with anxiety-depression and stressful thoughts, we are inclined not to provide the necessary nutrition to our bodies. We then resort to old habits such as consuming fatty foods, smoking, and drinking. We also fail to provide the body with the necessary water and exercise needed for proper balance.

There's a commercial that plays on the radio right now that sheds some light on why we don't. It advertises a new lottery game where you can win two thousand dollars a week for life. One part of the commercial quotes a man who has *actually* won the lottery saying now that he's won, he's going to be taking care of himself: he's stopped smoking and he now wears his seat belt every time he gets in the car. This is amazing! Just because the lottery is going to pay him two thousand dollars a week for life, he now feels like *he has a reason to live!* He actually is admitting that if he hadn't won the lottery, he would never have stopped smoking or taking unnecessary risks that might shorten his life. Life alone wasn't worth stopping smoking and minimizing health risks. This is really something to think about. And the only logical conclusion that you can draw from this is that he doesn't value his body because *he didn't pay any money for it.*

Unfortunately, this is too often the case and we disregard the fact that our bodies are the very embodiment of the gift of life. We don't do the simple things that everybody agrees will make our lives better, like eating right and working out. The result is a nation that is overweight and generally in bad health, with sisters leading the tally in numerous categories.

We're no good to our children, our mates, or anyone we love if we're no good to ourselves. Stress is the single most common ailment that seizes our souls and manifests itself as diseases that can destroy our bodies. From AIDS to breast cancer to uterine fibroids, hypertension, and sickle cell anemia, when it comes to our bodies and our health, it often seems that we come up with the short end of the stick. It is true that the black community has been hit hard by health problems of every kind. And indeed, we as African-American women are hit particularly hard. But there's nothing that compares to the strength, resolve, and faith in our Creator that we can develop when we openly listen to our sisters who have stood fast, even while they looked serious disease and death squarely in the eye.

There's not always a happy ending. We wish it was, but life simply isn't a fairy tale. There may *not* be a cure for the illness, but the true spirit of healing shines through brightly and can be a great source of inspiration and peace for others when we learn how to quiet the fear in our minds and to move forward with godliness.

Come with us as we share the stories of some of the women who have inspired us to know and trust that, no matter what happens in our lives, we should let nothing steal our joy.

47

Not a Death Sentence

Maria Davis

I have two beautiful children of my own, who are doing excellent, considering the fact that I am HIV positive. Jhanna is ten and Joshua, seventeen. My two nephews are also here and I try to spend as much time as possible with them. My daughter doesn't really like to talk about my disease because she sees death. I tell her it's not necessarily a death sentence, that each new day is a special moment.

Today is a good day. My T cells are stable and my viral load is undetectable, which is great, especially since it has been as low as five.

When I first found out that I was HIV positive, I wasn't even feeling sick. I was running a fever of 104 degrees, however, and I had to be admitted into the hospital. I applied for an insurance policy for $100,000 and was required to take an HIV test. My doctor asked me if I had AIDS and I told him he must have been joking. When I was released and I arrived home, a certified letter was waiting there for me. I was devastated, to say the least. One, because I wasn't sleeping around, and two, because I never even used drugs.

I was diagnosed in 1995. I contracted the virus through heterosexual intercourse and didn't physically get sick until 1999. That was my worst year. I was hospitalized quite a bit. I had thrush, a bad yeast infection in my mouth, and a hole in my tongue that stopped me from eating. I was rapidly losing weight. I was never a heavy woman to begin with, and when the virus began eating away at the protein in my body, it ate me up pretty fast due to the stress of my work.

I don't have much muscle tone left in my legs and it's difficult for me to get up by myself and stay on my feet for long. They are swollen, from cellulitis and I also suffer with neuropathy from the medicine. I caught a nasty opportunistic disease, MAI, a microorganism in my bone marrow which is hard to treat. This has left me with a weight of approximately 100 pounds. God is good because I got better later that year with exercise, proper nutrition, and faith. I can now ride my stationary bike, stay active, and always remain thankful for each new day. I remind myself that I have many reasons to count my blessings because there are some people who have suffered more than I have and have lost their eyesight.

I believe what my doctors tell me and I cooperate. I changed my diet and used traditional and natural medicines to keep my blood clean and my organs flushed out, and when I stopped eating sugars and salt, I began to recover quicker.

When rumors first started flying around the entertainment industry, I denied them and some people were cruel, but others surprised me. It was then that I found out who my true friends were. Deirdra Tate, who is now the president of Queen Latifah's company, Flava Unit and her dad, the *Black Elegance* magazine's publisher, were extremely helpful. Brenda Edwards, Justo, Jeanine, Chrissy Murray, Charm Warren, Cynthia Horner, Angelo Ellerbee, Benny Pough at MCA, Sincere Thompson, Jeff Redd, who was a singer for so many years, Monifa, Queen Latifah, and O. J. Wedlaw all supported me through this tough time.

I was born in Cincinnati and grew up in the South Bronx with my single mother, who raised me and my four sisters, Brenda, Debbie, Denise, and Jackie. My sister Jackie McGee is best known for her duet "Make It Last" with Keith Sweat and me. I also have several half-sisters and step-brothers, Malika, Sharif, Deirdre and Rasheed, Cecil, who are all being really supportive.

When we were young, our house was always filled with people, parties, and large seafood spreads that I can still see so vividly in my mind. Mommy loved to entertain away the loneliness, and her strength always inspired me. When I was sixteen and graduated from high school, I put myself through college and longed to spread my wings. My mother was not happy about my leaving home, but I knew it was time.

I always loved Harlem and was drawn to learn more about the black entrepreneurs that lived and prospered there like Madam C. J. Walker. I, too, was determined to be something, which was a model at the time.

I used to frequent Macy's, and Reggie Wells, who is now Oprah's makeup artist, said if I really wanted to model, to bring in some pictures. My good friend, Larita Rock, who was a well-known chef in the restaurant industry, had a boyfriend who was a French photographer at the time, and he did my portfolio for me. Reggie, in turn, introduced me to Pat Evens, who had a thriving modeling agency, and she signed me on the spot.

It was hard work beating the pavement, but we carved out jobs for ourselves as black women in the fur showrooms, hair shows, and finally with Soft Sheen, Budweiser, and Newport cigarettes. That was when the fees, royalties, and recognition got really good. I was on the right track and my close friends were all successful. They included Adelyne, Imeisa, Alva Chin,

Magic, BJ, and Peggy Dillard of Turning Heads Beauty Salon here in Harlem. Models were very friendly to each other back then and would look out for each other and share job leads and industry information. Audery Smaltz always kept me working, and I did my part by being friendly and upbeat. I studied the business and maintained myself for several years.

When my children were born, I became more involved in their activities and wanted to make their days as full as possible. My priorities changed and I became bored with modeling, so my children began modeling and they became exposed to various cultures and people.

My first exposure to the music industry was through my friends, Deidra Tate and her father, Bob Tate. Like my mother, I always loved the whole concept of entertaining people and wanted to promote parties myself. I also knew there was a lot of good young talent out there that was not being heard so I decided to become a liaison between new acts and the label execs that were my friends. People often asked why I wanted to produce MAD Wednesdays (short for Maria Antoinette Davis), but I just stayed focused on my mission to be supportive of the youth—just like back in the days when party promoter Shelly Brooks and Bob Tate first gave me a chance, paid me to watch the door at their parties, pushed me, found clubs for me, and started me in my promotional career.

My mother always worked hard and encouraged me to stay true to myself. So I studied, ate, drank, and slept the business, gave out a ton of flyers, faxed the whole world about my parties, and worked two and three jobs tending bar and waiting tables at the famous Cellar Restaurant on New York's trendy Upper West Side. This was the hot spot so many artists frequented and got their big breaks there like Phyllis Hyman, whom I used to serve ribs to, Patrice Rushen, Chaka Khan, Audery Wheeler, Patti Labelle, who loved the Southern cuisine, Atlantic Star, Freddie Jackson, Vincent Henry, and my good friend, Johnny Kemp.

In the beginning my parties were empty at times and some other male promoters tried to undermine me. I just forged on like a real trooper and looked at it as if they were doing better than I was than we were all winning in the end because we are all African-American.

We had so much real talent back then and great venues like Mikell's on Columbus Avenue where groups like The SOS Band, The System, and Stax artists like Carla Thomas led the way. These artists read and wrote music, played instruments, and could really sing. They followed in the footsteps of our forefathers and mothers like Ethel Waters, Shirley Caesar, Nat King Cole, Lena Horne, Dorothy Dandridge, Sidney Poitier, Paul Roberson, and Ella Fitzgerald, who broke down barriers when they couldn't eat and perform in the same venue and had to come and go through the back door.

It took years, but after a while I would produce shows in some of New

York's hottest clubs around the city. Legendary places such as Sweetwaters, The Country Club, Esso, Terranova, Kilimanjaro and SpoDeeoDee's, and my events became a place for undiscovered talent to shine. Stars would come out to relax and dine in privacy. My partner Rudy's mom and I cooked wings and macaroni and cheese, and I did whatever I had to do to keep it fun and as safe as possible.

The record labels were supportive of me and provided new talent for my showcases. Debra Cox, Brandy, Bernie Mac, Joe Clair 112, Monica, and D'Angelo Bill Belamy were some of the acts that performed for me before they climbed the *Billboard* charts. I was a big supporter of Hip Hop, Jay Z, and Exibit and got tons of talent support from O. J. Wedlaw, Cold Chilln' Records, and Fly Ty, who provided the group Quo, which was Michael Jackson's group.

I gave people opportunities and kept it real. If you were not talented, you simply could not perform in the showcases. I always tried to treat young people with lots of respect, even if they didn't have any money, I would let them into the event hoping it would keep them from being on the street and getting into trouble.

I haven't let my disease stop me from seeing my dreams and goals to their fruition. In many ways I feel blessed now, more so than before I became ill. I am grateful for each day, and although I may *not* get up tomorrow, it *is* all about having faith. Faith has pulled me through many days that were filled with anxiety, confusion, and the feeling of being misguided.

I keep myself occupied with the hopes that I can reeducate people about this disease. I became involved with the Actor's Fund, the Gay Men's Health Crisis, where they focus on mothers and children with HIV. Through the Gay Men's Health Crisis I have met so many people who have had the virus for twenty years and haven't contracted AIDS. A few years ago I did a benefit with DJ Red Alert for Hale House, at the Puck Building in New York City, where their special soups and round-the-clock loving care cures HIV-infected babies.

This disease is affecting black women as well as other minority communities hard. Only we can take control of the reeducation of our children. You don't get AIDS from holding somebody's hand. But you do get AIDS from having unprotected sex. I know this is an overused adage, but loving yourself is one of the primary reasons that you will not allow any man to have sex with you without a condom. It is so important—to go out and get tested, because not knowing can kill you. You never know where people you trust have been.

In my short time on this earth I have seen and learned so many things. I realized that the simple things count. I have found solitude in God, friends and Reverend Wyatt Tee Walker and the Canaan Baptist Church of Christ and I have also learned that overcoming differences and not judging is half the battle won. Believe half of what you see and none of what you hear, because your enemy today might turn out to be your angel tomorrow. Most of all, it's so important to love and cherish people: your children and family, cause that's what prolongs life.

I sometimes wonder about my death. If I left this earth right now, today, I would want my tombstone to say *learn to love each other*. The best part of life is that, no matter how much anyone tries to darken a situation, the light always shines through. I would want my legacy to be "to love each other."

Maria Davis is still fighting her fight and plans to utilize her experience and use her time wisely to educate young people.

48

Member of the Club

Angela Kinney

I awakened from the nightmare screaming out in pain. I had dreamt that I'd lost both my breasts in a horrible accident that left me scarred for life. Suddenly I realized I wasn't dreaming. The pain was real and I was in the recovery room of a hospital in the aftermath of a bilateral mastectomy. I tried vainly to focus on my surroundings as I slipped in and out of consciousness, holding on tightly to my youngest sister's hand. Thank God she was there! Also at my bedside was my boyfriend, so steadfast despite all the trauma he'd endured with me. He'd been through this once with his ex-wife and knew what to expect. My roommate was there, looking disoriented and exhausted after waiting eight hours through my surgery. The general surgeon had been late, extending what would have been a four-hour surgery into an eight-hour wait. Relief soon came in the form of a nurse with a bedpan who gave me an injection that rendered me blissfully numb to the pain.

I got the news that I was a "member of the club" on July 16, 1998. The week prior had been filled with appointments to see my general practitioner and the surgeon. The G.P. delivered the news that my mammogram taken a week earlier had been irregular, showing "microcalcifications highly suspicious for malignancy." I was urged to go immediately to see a surgeon for a breast biopsy. One look at the surgeon's face after he tried vainly to aspirate the two-inch lump in my breast with a needle confirmed my suspicions. I was in for big trouble and I had only myself to blame for listening to the resident doctor who had a year before naively told me, "You're under forty so it's okay for you to do your mammogram every two years." Fibrocystic disease had been a part of my life for several years since I had been diagnosed with it in 1992, so I was accustomed to having lumpy breasts, but somehow this lump felt different, harder and very painful during my monthly cycle. I vacillated between blaming the resident doctor for the fact that I had skipped my yearly mammogram and admonishing myself for waiting so long to investigate that solid lump which I'd felt for at least a year.

Life turned into one big blur following my diagnosis of breast cancer, which occurred two weeks after my mammogram. Being the impatient person I am, I forced the surgeon to tell me I had cancer over the phone instead of waiting to be told in person. He reluctantly admitted that the tumor he had excised a week prior was not benign. I stood there dumbfounded, trying to comprehend how the hell I'd managed to get myself into this situation. I felt totally at the mercy of my doctors and their power to heal me. The breast biopsy to remove the tumor was fairly painless. I was placed under light sedation that allowed me to hear during the procedure when the surgeon commented under his breath, "This does not look good." Afterward I felt lucky that I had a good relationship with my surgeon and was comfortable with him. He's an extremely competent physician who has performed many breast surgeries over a thirty-year career. Nevertheless, on a visit following my biopsy, he seemed quite agitated and a little sad when he told me he would have to do yet another surgery, this time a lumpectomy to remove more breast tissue. The path reports, which I had waited a week for, had shown that the cancer was quite extensive and that further surgery was needed. Emotionally I was a wreck and in constant fear of death.

When you have cancer, fear is your greatest enemy. You fight *it* harder than you fight the cancer. You battle against fear of what is to come, fear of death, and fear of rejection by those who know of your plight—and most of all, fear of the unknown. My surgeon, who is an advocate of breast preservation, wanted to go back into my breast and extract more tissue to remove the remainder of the cancer. I trusted his judgment and allowed him to do so.

Reading has always been my way or relaxing. I am a librarian by profession and have always enjoyed reading a good book before bedtime, at lunch, or on the subway. During my ordeal, I found myself voraciously reading everything I could about breast cancer. I read articles in medical journals, books given to me by friends, and tapped into a number of web sites on the Internet. My surgeon had dissected sixteen lymph nodes from my left arm and put me in a sling for two weeks. I had a drain hanging from my left side, which sucked up the fluids that my nodes would normally have absorbed. The pathology reports showed that I had carcinoma in situ, a type of cancer in which the malignant tumor settles in the milk ducts of the breast, but my lymph nodes were clear of tumors, which meant I had Stage I breast cancer. I rejoiced with my surgeon, hugged him, and shared tears of joy with his nursing assistant.

Shortly thereafter I saw an oncologist, who promised me the best treatment possible through breast conservation and chemotherapy. At that point I wasn't even sure I wanted to keep my breast. It was so hideous with the nipple bait severed and mutilated from surgery. My chest looked like a car that had been wrecked with its headlights pointed in different directions, one higher than the other. To compound my confusion, the surgeon had promised a different treatment than the oncologist, which consisted of radiation therapy. He assured me that he had a number of patients who had a history of long survival from using this approach. I was thoroughly confused and in a quandary as to what method of treatment to choose. Finally I did what I believe saved my life. I put my professional life on hold in order to begin the process of deciding what would ultimately determine my future existence on this earth. No more sitting at work making phone calls to doctors in between catering to my staff's needs and attending board meetings. No more crying hysterically and making everyone's life around me miserable because I felt sorry for myself. I resolved to heal myself emotionally and physically by taking a leave of absence from work and continuing to read and learn as much as possible about carcinoma in situ.

The most painful part of the emotional healing involved renewing my faith in God. My belief in God had been badly shaken by all that I had suffered through. I asked myself: How could God make a forty-year-old woman, who had always been a law-abiding citizen and a hard worker, suffer so much in such a short period of time? It was only when I prayed for salvation, and was then able to more closely examine myself, that I realized my body was merely a time bomb waiting to explode. Too busy with work, which consumed me, and an active social life, I had developed a lifestyle that included lots of alcohol, fatty foods eaten late at night, and little sleep. I began to pray for the knowledge to choose the appropriate treatment and the strength to follow through with it. God sent me that knowledge in the form of a cousin of mine, a computer specialist who discovered a web site on breast cancer at the University of Pennsylvania. The information on the site indicated that there were three types of carcinoma in situ, mine being the most aggressive. Only one treatment option was recommended for my type of breast cancer and that was mastectomy. I also received divine intervention from two other oncologists whom I visited. They, too, concurred that mastectomy would give me the best possible chance of nonrecurrence. One oncologist recommended bilateral mastectomy as a way of guaranteeing me an even better chance of being cancer-free for life.

I made my decision quickly and my relief knew no bounds. I scheduled the date for the bilateral mastectomy with immediate reconstruction. Feeling the need to see my family before I faced the inevitable, I got into my car and drove nine hours from Washington, D.C., to my home town of Cincinnati, and basked in the love, prayers, and caring that only a family can give.

Even though the pain of bilateral mastectomy was excruciating and I ultimately subjected myself to a third surgery, I feel that I made the right decision. Recovery lasted two weeks, during which I received visits from friends who have been so dear to me. My women friends were especially supportive and glad to lend a hand. You know you are loved when a friend lets go of their fear of illness and helps you to bathe your sick, smelly body or wraps your bloody, scarred chest in an ace bandage to keep the swelling in check.

Now I rejoice in every day that I wake up in the morning and see the sun rise. Nothing is taken for granted because I have witnessed how fragile life is and I know what it's like to struggle to survive. My future holds two more surgeries to complete my reconstruction, but in the meantime I've placed myself under the care of a homeopathic healer who has taught me a great deal about nutrition, namely keeping my liver and colon healthy with proper dietary habits and supplements such as milk thistle and vitamins B, C, and E. This is advice that no medical doctor bothered to give me, and I wonder why medical science does not teach physicians to discuss nutrition more often with their patients. In essence they are treating only the symptoms and not the core of the illness. I also use a progesterone cream to balance the estrogen level in my body because, as a premenopausal woman, I am still producing estrogen. Cancer grows from the presence of elevated levels of estrogen, but the growth of cancer is discouraged when progesterone and estrogen are both apparent in the body.

Every day I live brings a lessening of the fear of death, although the feeling never quite goes away. I am thankful, though, that what has remained is my desire to strive to be a kinder and gentler person by following the teachings of God, because I know that, without His Word, I would be lost.

Angela Kinney is one of the head librarians for the Library of Congress.

49

I Refuse to Lose My Womb

Marsha Bowen

In my lifetime I hope to see female medical complaints taken more seriously. Some of the most popular female complaints such as endometriosis, ovarian and breast cancer, cysts and fibroid tumors are still largely an uncurable mystery.

The one complaint which affects my life are fibroid tumors. Once they grew to a substantial size, my physician took them more seriously. Why? Because surgery when they are small is considered unnecessary.

What are fibroids? They are blood-filled muscle tissue growths in the uterine lining and walls. I nicknamed them "false babies." Causes of these growths range from heredity to stress and a woman's diet.

Why did I get them? Well, after studying my family history on both sides, I was informed that women on both sides had suffered from these critters.

At age twenty-five, the fibroids curse was diagnosed in my womb. At that moment my physician instructed me not to be alarmed, but I should monitor them.

By age twenty-seven, I was in danger of losing my womb. Excessive bleeding and painful cramps every menstrual period were taking a toll on my well-being. I felt like my womb was carrying "false embryos." My womb had extended to the size of a four-month pregnancy. The sad part of it was if I did want a child, the chances were slim due to the fibroid tumors taking up "real estate" in my womb. Doctors wanted me to have a hysterectomy.

After two medical opinions, I decided to have a myomectomy. This procedure would enable me to keep my womb, but could make childbearing a little difficult. I thank God that the surgery was a success. My doctors were stunned at the sizes of my fibroids, especially the one the size of a football. I had given them nicknames: two "softballs" and a "football." A total of twenty pounds of fibroids were removed from my body. Hospital doctors considered my surgery to be miraculous because I didn't require a blood transfusion for three hours of surgery. *Praise the Lord.*

After surgery, I had gas complications that made my hospital stay more stressful and painful; however, with the support of family and friends, I was able to get through it. Upon leaving the hospital, I was twenty-two pounds lighter and ready to start a new life.

I began dating and working out two months later. Life was improving for me day by day, month by month, until I moved and my workout routine was interrupted. This continued until the end of 1996.

Another wave of excessive bleeding and menstrual cramps started to kick in. This time the bleeding was worse than before. For example, at times it would be so embarrassing for me that I would need to visit the ladies' room frequently. If I didn't make it in time, then an accident would happen. I needed to carry an extra pair of undies just in case. I also had to always carry extra amounts of sanitary supplies wherever I went.

By 1997, my condition worsened, causing me to have extreme anemia. I felt like I was losing control of my body. I became depressed, stressed, but determined. After having three medical opinions, again I was faced with the decision to remove my womb or withstand another myomectomy. Since I had already had a myomectomy, my doctor stated that this procedure a second time would be extremely risky. My options at this point were very slim and dreadful.

One day, I woke up and said to myself, "Okay, fibroids, it's time to rumble." I was going to fight these growths till the end. I would never admit that I had a sickness; it was more of a setback to me. I didn't see fibroids as an infection that could kill. I decided to take the herbal route and I visited an herbalist. This was one of the best things I could have done. I did an herbal detox, which helped to clean out my system and balance my blood circulation. Unfortunately, the bleeding had worsened, probably because now the bloodstream was able to flow better to my uterus. The bleeding was starting to come twice a month and lasting longer than my last bout.

Again, another doctor suggested I remove my womb. I left her office in tears and again I refused to consider removal of my womb. This time I wanted and needed more answers. I began to read books about herbs, fibroids, and alternative treatments. A procedure called embolization was lightly touched on in a chapter I read in a book. This procedure was considered minor surgery. Afterward, I went directly to the Internet to gather more sources for information on this procedure. This is considered a fairly new procedure; therefore, information was limited. After reading about embolization from the Internet information I had gathered, I was able to catch a brief news report about it. This was a blessing in disguise; it just so happened that the report and procedure were conducted by the hospital where two of my doctors were affiliated.

After discussing the procedure with my doctor, I decided to give it a shot. There were a few risk factors involved, one being infertility and the other substantial pain after the procedure. I was willing to take the risk. In early 1998, I had the procedure for my fibroids and so far so good. As a result, I haven't had any cramps, my menstrual cycle has become regular, and bleeding is no longer excessive.

Over a period of a time, the results of this procedure are still unknown; however, it was well worth it, considering the mental pain and stress that the fibroids put me through. To compliment this procedure, I am also adopting a different lifestyle called the "process of elimination." This is a new way of eating that involves the following:

- Eliminating red meat, dairy products, saturated fats, hydrogenated fat, fried foods, and caffeine from my diet.
- Maintaining healthy weight and size.
- Staying stress-free: handling problems and concerns if possible, and if not, simply letting them go.
- Eliminating toxic people and toxic environments (such as smokers and chemical environments).
- Eliminating anxiety and financial worries.

I haven't mastered these; however, not one day goes by where I am not striving to remain fibroid free. I am so thankful that I refused to lose my womb.

Marsha Bowen is a retail marketing and sales director of a major record label.

50

Why Me?

Tionne "T-Boz" Watkins

I always asked the question why me? I spent a lot of years trying to find an answer. I didn't understand why I was different; why I couldn't play outside with other kids; why I was told by doctors that I couldn't dance, or how I'd have to live a different life than most. So it caused me to rebel and go against everything I was told not to do. I put myself through a lot of unnecessary pain. I did not want to accept the disease I was diagnosed with [Sickle Cell].

Then years later, I found out the doctors did not even understand the disease. That discouraged me even more! So I danced, became sick, and I would get up and dance again. One thing is for sure . . . I became very strong minded and determined! I did a lot of stupid things like going swimming in a cold pool of water, knowing I could not. I became very ill, and I realized that was one thing the doctors were right about, my body can't handle anything cold.

After going through the rebellious stage and getting tired of beating my body up and breaking it down, I decided to learn about my own body and this "so-called" disease. Getting to know myself wasn't all that bad. I looked normal, and could participate in certain activities, except for a select few. I had the ability to remain well depending on my mind frame, the way I eat, the amount of rest received, and my stress factor. Plus, I thought about all the people who were worse off than me and don't have the advantage of feeling good at all.

I can and will have days without pain; I just have a few setbacks. Then those days become blessings! I just blocked my blessings! I stopped feeling sorry for myself. This is the only life I know and I have to make the best of it! I know I am here for a reason. That is why God's grace has covered me so. There are a lot of people with the same disease that did not pull through, but every time I've had hard times, I always pulled through. So I know I'm here to make a change! I am a true and firm believer in the saying "EVERYTHING HAPPENS FOR A REASON."

Why me? Because I am strong.
Why me? Because I am in a position to help others.
Why me? I can overcome certain situations.
Why me? Because the grace of God covers me and allows me to
rise above the bad things.
Why me? Because I am here for a reason, and every day I still
learn good reasons to answer my question: Why me?

Tionne "T-Boz" Watkins is the lead singer of the internationally acclaimed group TLC. Born with sickle-cell anemia, Tionne is a survivor. She
has overcome the challenges of the disease and has reached new heights
with her music, acting, and her book, filled with poetry, insights, and thoughts.

51

The Human Touch

Linda A. Myers, M.D.

Being in the twenty-first century has a profound effect on us all. Everyone seems compelled to create his or her own "spin" on what it means to be living in the year 2000. The computer age is here, front and center, and I have just begun to get to know this side of the human potential. What has brought me to this point, to say the least, has been life altering. Thoughts and ideals once held high in regard are now repackaged and manufactured into quips, clichés, or anything at all to hold our seemingly thirty-second attention spans. But all this makes me think about something that no computer or machine can provide—the human touch.

It was December 1991. I was just beginning that part of my medical school training called an acting internship, where I would, in fact, "act" like an intern. I was placed in the Veteran's Memorial Hospital in Cincinnati, Ohio. This part of our training was quite exciting because this was our chance to shine. We were working toward the last six months of school, on the brink of graduation, and ready to put our knowledge to work. My caseload was particularly challenging because I had many patients with social issues as well as medical concerns.

On the first day, I met with the medical student/acting intern who was leaving the service. I was to take over his patient load and continue to give them the appropriate medical care. After carefully reviewing each patient, he began to tell me about one patient in particular whose family he was concerned about. They had had many disagreements over the patient's medical care and had questioned his judgment many times. This patient had a brother who was not very trusting of doctors in general. This news put me on guard. I asked myself, "How is he going to take the news that his brother has a female doctor? Or that she is black?" You see, I had already had patients call me "nigger" before.

So, finally I met this new patient. He seemed not the least bit concerned about who his new doctor was, or what her skin color was. Then I met his brother. He shook my hand and told me how he had had "trouble" with the previous acting intern. I maintained my guard and informed him that I was there for the sake of the patient and that I would do everything possible to medically help his brother. I have to admit, I saw this as a challenge—an opportunity of sorts—to prove that I could be effective regardless of any racial overtones. Despite my highest endeavors, I had to understand the reality of the fact that this was a very ill man. He was stricken with heart, lung, and kidney disease as well as diabetes, his blood vessels were in poor shape, and he didn't have much longer to live. I, however, had four weeks to optimize his condition and make him as comfortable as possible, that is, to get him home to be with family in his last days.

And I did work hard. I stayed on top of every test. I would transport him by wheelchair to the X-ray department myself. I drew his blood for laboratory tests. I had every bit of paperwork completed for home oxygen therapy and transport. Anyone who knows about paperwork should understand how tedious a process this can be. I even gained his brother's trust. Finally, I did it! The patient was going home for the holidays to live out his remaining days in peace and the comfort of his family. His discharge was two days away. I arrived early the morning of his discharge and saw my patients on prerounds. He seemed a bit distracted and asked for a cup of water, which I promptly gave him. He showed no other signs of distress and I returned to my team. During formal rounds, we approached the patient's room and the nurse called us inside. He had no pulse. He was not breathing. He had expired. The man I had just spoken to was gone. There was no code blue, for he had a "no-code" status—in other words, we were not supposed to resuscitate him. Oddly enough, I remained calm.

I believe the reason I remained calm was because I knew I had worked so hard on this patient and had done everything I could to get him medically stable enough to be discharged. On top of that, I had also done my share of helping him to remain comfortable. You see, once a patient is medically stable, my biggest concern for them is allaying their fears. I believe this is why I wanted him so much to be at home with his family. Once I came to grips with this, the challenging part came. I had to tell his brother that he had just passed away. This was the most difficult part for me. Although it was only three weeks, I had earned a trust in the patient's brother. When you are that ill, one day can seem like an entire year because you do not know if you are going to be around to see the next day. Each moment is crucial. I'll never forget how nervous I was when I had to make that phone call. I never had to tell anyone that a loved one had just died. I mean, where was *this* part of my medical training? I certainly don't remember sitting through this lecture, but even if I did, I don't think it prepared me for what I was about to do.

I took several deep breaths and dialed the number. His brother answered. When I identified myself, I got the feeling that he knew why I was calling. This didn't make it any easier. We talked for several minutes and I expressed my sympathies. Before our conversation had ended, he told me that he was impressed with his brother's care and that he appreciated that I "went the extra mile." This spoke volumes to me. To me, this is what the "human touch" is all about.

We must remember that we all possess the human touch and we must learn to rely on it more and more to maintain our connection with each other. Computers are nice, but instead of stroking those keys all day, how about a hug?

Linda A. Myers, M.D., is a doctor at Montefiore Hospital in New York City. She is currently completing a book of children's stories.

Your Soul's Sustenance

Naked came I from my mother's womb, naked shall I return
thither. The Lord giveth and the Lord taketh away.
Blessed be the name of the Lord.
—Job 1:21

The age-old adage *An ounce of prevention is worth a pound of cure* could never be more apropos than today. We can't continue to live our lives by sticking our heads in the ground to the reality that we are largely responsible for our own health or sickness. We cannot continue to live our lives carelessly and expect the doctor to be able to "fix" everything when we finally "break" ourselves. Doctors are not miracle workers, and as any good doctor will tell you, we have got to become partners in claiming the health that we are meant to have. This means adhering to a proper diet; getting plenty of exercise, fresh air, and sunlight; and finding quiet time each day to pray or meditate so that we can remove ourselves from the stress that seems to be everywhere in our lives.

Candace and I try to encourage each other to keep a health handbook. Now we encourage you to keep one also. Create a health handbook where you can log in your various doctors' visits. Write down your questions and your mental and physical health history. Know your body and don't take no for an answer. Always get a second opinion and keep track of all your correspondence with your various doctors in your book.

Your Personal Book of Revelations

Your health is your best asset. You must know how you feel to be able to tell a doctor how you feel.

- Describe your health.
- What types of foods do you eat?

- Has anyone in your family died from a stroke, cancer, high blood pressure, diabetes or suffered from a mental disease?
- Describe that experience.
- What would you like to change about your health?

Refocus your priorities to incorporate health as part of your lifestyle. Schedule time at the beginning of the day for meditation, exercise, and preparing the right meals and snacks. Pamper yourself with a massage. A massage is not a luxury but a necessity. The body is designed for the human touch; massages are excellent for the circulation of the blood, and the healing power of touch is vital to the soul.

You are your best medical advisor. Remember that.

XI

"Isms"

We are living in a world where your color matters
more than your character.
—Sister Souljah

Aunt Ruth always wanted to be a lawyer. From the earliest age that she could remember, that had been her single-minded goal. She just honestly loved the law, and nothing would keep her from her goal. In high school and college she did everything she needed to ensure that she would be able to go to law school. Not just any law school, but Harvard Law School—the best law school of all.

Even though she had the grades and all of the other prerequisites to go to Harvard, Aunt Ruth was flatly rejected. The reason being because back then Harvard Law School simply would not admit women—especially not a *black* woman. Aunt Ruth was coming face to face with sexism at a time when no one had her back. She had not only one strike against her because she was a woman, but another because she was black.

One, Two, Three Strikes You're Out . . .

As black women we often have three strikes against us before we even step up to the plate. Many of us have experienced *all* of the "isms": rac*ism*, sex*ism*, and class*ism*. There aren't many demographic groups who can say that they have experienced *all* of the isms in one lifetime! However, black women are unique in that most of us in our lifetimes *will* experience all three. Personally, we certainly have. White women can't say they'll experience all three. Black men can't say they'll experience all three. White men definitely can't say they'll experience all three—just one at the most.

We're unique in that in the time of affirmative action, black women are hired because we fit two categories. You can kill two birds with one stone. You couldn't do that with a white woman or even with a black man. So we have a unique outlook on all these things and a unique way of dealing with them. And also a unique place in corporate America. But more often than not, making our way means charting a new path, working around obstacles, and not letting anything take us away from our goals.

That's what Aunt Ruth had to do when she found out she couldn't go to Harvard. Did she give up her dreams of being a lawyer? Of course not. Not even when she found herself raising her newborn baby by herself. She decided that she would go to school where she could go and that she would excel regardless of what anybody else had to say about it. She wasn't going to let one monkey stop the show.

So that fall she began at Brooklyn College of Law. It wasn't long before her legal prowess was coming to the fore. And it wasn't long before she was practically teaching the classes that she was in because, on many occasions, she was the only student in the class who actually *understood* what in the world the teacher was saying and could translate it to the other students. When she graduated, she was the undisputed valedictorian of her class. And the consensus was that she probably would have been valedictorian anywhere she went. Aunt Ruth hadn't let the isms stop her and had no intention of starting now.

Hers was exactly the kind of resolve that is needed to counteract the racism, sexism, and classism that confronts sisters every day. It can even come from sources close to home. A black woman can experience racism from other black women. Being light-skinned in a group of dark-skinned black women or vice versa can be fuel for the intrarace fire. By giving into old slave ways of thinking, we keep ourselves from moving forward.

And, of course, there's what you get from the larger society. It can be little things like the "secret shoppers" following you around clothing stores or guards making you check your bag when everybody else in the store has theirs on their back.

Sisters face sexism every day when they see men in their industry get paid a lot more than they do for the same or less work. When it comes to classism, you need not even look outside of the black race because there are very definite class issues *within* it. That's what society has set up for us. You have poorer people who assume that you're something because you're not as poor as them. You have richer people who assume you're something because you're not as rich as them.

But the only way to get through the haze of all the isms is to know in your own mind where you are going and to ignore the interference. Aunt Ruth knew where she was going. She went on to be a successful trial lawyer in New York and eventually became the second black woman ever appointed to the Federal Bench. When she also became the first black resident of the then-exclusive City Island, New York, she provoked the ire of the residents by living in a beautiful house surrounded on two sides by the water with a pier up to the back of the house. But she ignored it. When certain small-minded whites became blinded by their classist and racist views and couldn't figure out how this "nigger bitch" could be doing better than they were and decided to try to make her life hard, again she ignored it. And when the Hon. Judge Mary Ruth Johnson Lowe issued a decision that put members of the Gambino crime family behind bars, she bravely ignored threatened attempts on her life and living with federal marshalls to protect her twenty-four hours a day—and went about her business.

It's a shame that in the early days of the 21st century we must still address so many isms. When will we grow up as a society and begin to tolerate and appreciate all people, regardless of their background? When will we learn that we all need each other and that hatred and separation only breed contempt and continue long-standing conflict? Until our society develops a racial, sexual, and class-oriented maturity, we will have to insulate ourselves from what would otherwise destroy us.

Aunt Ruth wanted to write an essay for *Souls of My Sisters*, but she passed away before she was able to do so. Even as her health deteriorated, she refused to stop trying cases and literally worked until the very end of her life. The legacy that she leaves us can teach us a lot about not listening to what life's "isms" have to say. She and countless other sisters daily are robbed of their self-esteem and self-worth—but nevertheless stand up and fight. People like Aunt Ruth refused to be denied what they felt was theirs and fought so that we can have the things that we take for granted today. If Aunt Ruth were growing up today, it is not an exaggeration to say that she might well have ended up on the Supreme Court.

This part will help us to know that it's up to us to honor the sisters who have gone before us and to keep that ball rolling so that sisters tomorrow will not have to fight the same battles that we are fighting today.

52

Don't Hate the Player, Hate the Game

Janeula M. Burt, Ph.D.

This letter was excerpted from a letter submitted to editor Jamie Foster Brown of *Sister2Sister* magazine (March 2000 issue).

Dear Jamie,

I'm sorry but I would like to challenge some of your Black male readers. I am a white female who is engaged to a Black male—good-looking, educated and loving. I just don't understand a lot of Black females' attitudes about our relationship. My man decided he wanted me because the pickings amongst Black women were slim to none. As he said they were either too fat, too loud, too mean, too argumentative, too needy, too materialistic and carrying too much excess baggage.

Before I became engaged, whenever I went out I was constantly approached by Black men, willing to wine and dine me and give me the world. If Black women are so up in arms about us being with their men, why don't they look at themselves and make some changes.

I am tired of the dirty looks I get and snide remarks when we're out in public. I would like to hear from some Black men about why we are so appealing and coveted by them. Bryant Gumble just left his wife of 26 years for one of us. Charles Barkley, Scottie Pippen, the model Tyson Beckford, Montell Williams, Quincy Jones, James Earl Jones, Harry Belafonte, Sydney Poitier, Kofi Anan, Cuba Gooding Jr., Don Cornelius, Berry Gordy, Billy Blanks, Larry Fishburne, Wesley Snipes . . . I could go on and on.

But right now I'm a little angry and that is why I wrote this so hurriedly. Don't be mad with us White women because so many of your men want us. Get your acts together and learn from us and we

may lead you to treat your men better. If I'm wrong, Black men, let me know.
 Disgusted White Girl,
 Somewhere in VA.

Like hundreds of other folks, I received the forwarded "Disgusted White Girl" email in early February. I was scanning through the message when my eyes got stuck on the sentence: "My man decided he wanted me because the pickings amongst Black women were slim to none. As he said they were either too fat, too loud, too mean, too argumentative, too needy, too materialistic and carrying too much excess baggage." I felt the blood rushing to my face and my eyes widening as I sat there at my computer frozen by her "casual" indictment.

She was talking about *me.* "*Jan,* you are too fat, too loud, too mean, too argumentative, too needy, too materialistic, and carrying too much excess baggage." But wait, ask anyone who knows me—I am none of these contradictory adjectives! Yes, like anyone, I have my own personal faults, but I am none of what this white girl is describing, and neither are any of my friends. To hear my friends describe me, I am one of the most laid-back, nonconfrontational, brutally humble people you will ever meet. How can this girl say that I am the exception and not the rule? Does she even know any black women? I went back and read every word of this email, letter by letter, searching for the signs of what I had done to cause this girl to go off on me.

After reading this email, like most people when they feel they are under attack, I immediately wanted to counterattack. I started typing the "Jerry Springer"–like response that countered and attacked all of her points. I had typed about a page and a half of "personal" experiences of things that white girls had done to me that pissed me off. It was late, so I paused, emailed my initial letter to myself at home, and began my commute home—still fuming from the words in her letter.

Somewhere between uptown D.C. and home, I started to question myself and my motives for writing this letter. Was my anger at her and her letter, or was it my anger and frustration with the interracial folks that I know (or have known) who, over the years, have overtly and covertly attacked me as a black woman? Was my anger directed toward the hateful or spiteful looks that I had gotten from interracial couples before I even realized that they were "a couple?" Was my anger directed toward Charles (my first childhood crush) and the other black men whom I would meet later in life, who would tell me that I was ugly just because I was black? Or was my anger directed toward the woman in graduate school who sincerely wanted to know how old I was when I "learned to speak" the articulate English that I spoke, as opposed to "Black English?"

By the time I got within five miles of my house, my anger subsided and I refocused my intentions and my anger toward addressing the problems that I initially had with the letter—she attacked not only me, but also *every* woman of African descent. I thought about the stereotypes she threw out that her fiancé had filled her head with and thought about the stereotypes that men like her fiancé had disclosed to me. "White girls are easy, white girls are stupid, white girls will let you walk all over them, etc., etc., etc." But then, I thought about my white girlfriends, friends that I've had since elementary school and friends that I've met recently and thought: "Wait a minute, why didn't I buy into the same stereotypes that this white girl did?"

The difference, I found, was that I had loving and meaningful relationships with white "sisters" that I value just as much as I do with my African-American sisters. That was why I didn't hate, misjudge, or feel intimidated by white women. I knew and I loved them because I know and I love them.

A while ago, I told a brother who was "in-cog-negro" with his interracial relationship that I felt that before a white girl could love a black man, she had to first love a black woman. I don't care if that woman is his mother, his sister, his cousin, or her own personal friend—she had to truly know and truly love a black woman. She needed to know and love a sister, not just on a superficial level, but on a spiritual and emotional level. Loving black men and black men only provides her with only part of the puzzle or part of the equation that is the black experience—which means that she only loves a part of the man. Like it or not, in our community (and in the communities of other women of color), the black woman is the purveyor and transmitter of our history, culture, and experience—we hold the keys to the past, the present, and the future of the black community. Not making an effort to get to know us (much less find meaningful relationships with us) is interpreted as disrespect for *us*—not only as African-American women, but also as people of African descent.

We all know about the "some of my best friends are black" syndrome, which we as black folks know is the ultimate insult. It's an insult because we all have "acquaintances" that talk at us or think that because they have been around us, that we are now their "friends." It was this attitude and undertone that I detected in her letter, that prompted me to let her know that "she don't know us like dat!" She felt that because she was sleeping with a "brother" that she had the privilege and the right to call us out of our name in a magazine that is written by and published by African-American women.

When I said that you have to love a black woman to love a black man, it cuts deeper than the interracial relationships that I was describing; it also applies to sisters lovin' brothers. You cannot legitimately love a black man, until you can love yourself and other black women. You cannot love a black man if you don't have loving and respectful relationships with other black women. It's not about "Oh, she's just jealous 'cause she don't have a man," or the "Women are messy, so all my friends are guys" or the "When you got a man, your girls are the first ones trying to get with your man" syndromes, because we are falling into the same traps that this insecure man's woman has set for us.

A real sister does not sleep with her friends' or any other woman's man (knowingly or otherwise), because she wants her own loving relationship, not a man who's ready to cheat on her too. Don't hate the player; hate the game.

Real sisters do not worry about bringing a sister down because she has a man and her "friend" does not. Real sisters are cheerleaders who say to her, "Get some for me!" or "Does he have any single friends?" or "Let me rub some of that good luck off on me."

Real sisters don't look at other men and try to "steal them away." Instead, they know that the minute the insecure sister or white girl turns her back, he (the insecure brother) is the one who is winking at her or trying to give her his pager number on the sly. When he gets caught is when he plays the "blame the victim" blues, "She approached me because she's jealous and wants to steal me away from you." (1229)

What annoyed me most about the letter is that she inaccurately portrayed the relationships between black and white women. We are not adversaries; we are allies. Women are nurturing; men are the ones who are competitive. I didn't want to allow this woman to perpetuate what I know her ignorance and her weak-ass fiancé were leading her to believe. I know what I like (and don't like) about white women from the relationships that I have (and have had) with them. And yes, I do have great relationships with women (black, white, and other) who are (or have been) in interracial relationships. We all face the same struggles, the same fears, and the same hopes and dreams for the future. I'm not jealous of anyone who is doing well; I'm happy for them, as they would be for me, if they love me. Unfortunately, we do not live in a colorblind society where color (or gender) does not give some people advantages and privileges over others. I had to let this uninformed woman know all these facts. As one woman called it, I unleashed the dragon:

> Dear "Disgusted White Girl":
> Unfortunately, I did not have the opportunity to read the article in Sister2Sister *magazine for which you are challenging my African-American brother's commentary. However, I do feel the need to respond to your deranged communiqué since you have chosen to assault and offend African-American women in this African-American women's magazine.*

First of all, how you feel that your fiancé's provincial experiences are genuine or representative is beyond my level of comprehension. Nor do I understand how you can base your arguments on the insinuations of an obviously acrimonious and embittered member of our community. Perhaps if I saw the world through your hegemonic eyes, I guess I, too, would feel this brazen antipathy for white women that you apparently feel for African-American women.

Like you, I could base my opinions of all white women on what I've heard about you from black men. From what I hear: White girls are sexually permissive, they will do things that African-American men won't even discuss in the presence of a true African-American woman. White girls are stupid; they have this guilt thing that makes them want to give black guys all of their money, their car, their house, and whatever worldly possessions they own just to keep these black guys around. White girls are docile; they will let black guys do or say anything to them. Like children, they never challenge and they never question. White girls will leave their family, their friends, their job, their children, or whatever, just so that they can continue to have sex with the men who possess these unusually large members that they apparently can't find among their white male counterparts. White girls are gullible; you can tell them anything and they believe it without question or investigation. White girls are easy; the only thing that a black man has to do to get a white girl in bed is buy her a drink and maybe give them a weak pickup line. Later, she will pretend that she was "so drunk that" she didn't know what she was doing. White girls are insecure and have low self-esteem; all you have to do is reassure them that they are as anorexically thin as Kate Moss and they are happy.

Like you said, "I could go on and on" but I won't, because these, like your insipid arguments, are simple stereotypes and falsehoods. Unlike you, I know that these statements are fallacious because, like many African-American sisters, I have real, eternal, and enduring relationships with white women. Some of these white women are in, or have been in, relationships with African-American men. No, I do not endorse or delight in these interracial relationships that you so narcissistically display. My disapproval, however, is not rooted in or related to your shallow perusal of African-American women.

My rejection of black male/white female relationships stems from the very tone, purpose, and disrespectful intent that your letter discloses.

Before you, or any white girl, can "love" an African-American man, you must first love an African-American woman. I am stupefied by your audacity to display your ignorance behind the cloak of an anonymous letter to a nationally recognized magazine founded by and designed for African-American women. To use an African-American adage that you probably won't understand the profundity of: You do not know us like that. Because if you did, you would have kept your witless opinions between you and your partner. Was your white hood at the cleaner's or in your parents' trailer?

The "attitude" that you so ineptly described is not about our jealousy, resentment, or envy. You are doing me a favor because "wining and dining" is not what I value in a man, but rather Love of self, Love of our people, Love of humanity, and Love of our God. If you truly loved this man, you would seek help because your man has issues that a hundred years of counseling could never fix. The attitude that you feel is from sisters who know that the black man that you are undoubtedly with (as you reconfirmed in your letter) has effortlessly convinced you that we are the enemy that is not to be trusted—while secretly wanting for us to chase him down and affirm that he is indeed a man.

Instead of asking your fiancé or challenging the opinions of African-American men, you should go straight to the source. I'd be happy to send you to the library or provide you with an enlightened discourse. Oftentimes sleeping with, dating, and/or marrying a white girl is not an affirmation of your supremacy, but rather a weak man's attempt to gain footing or power over white men. White men, not African-American women, have emasculated the African-American men that you so ignorantly flaunt.

Rather than handle his obviously exaggerated ineptitude, he associates with white girls. As a lover of African-American people, I am saddened when I see that a brother is confused or feeling disenfranchised. Unlike you, I would want for him to face his demons or to help him face his demons so that he can be the man that he is meant to be. I'm not the one that grits on you when I see you with "your man." I'm the one who is laughing inside (and sometimes outside) because I know that him being with you has nothing to do with me. Otherwise, he and others like him would pick white girls who were within or above, rather than beneath his station in life.

There is nothing that you, or anyone else like you, can teach me or any other African-American sister. If treating my man better means that I let him continue to hate himself and others that look like him, well then, you are the better woman. If being appealing to African-American men means that I should disrespect the institutions of marriage and family, well then, you and "Bryant's girl" are the better

women. If being coveted by a black man means that I have to turn my
back on my friends and family, well then, you are the better woman
for him. If it means being ignorant and disrespectful of African-
American women like your fiancé's mother and the African-American
community, well then, you are indeed the better woman.

If loving my people and myself means that I lose the endearment
of brothers like Dennis Rodman, Charles Barkley, Wesley Snipes,
Clarence Thomas, etc., well then, you definitely win! I'll take Denzel
Washington, Colin Powell, Samuel L. Jackson, Martin Luther King,
Jr., Courtney Vance, and my daddy any day! Fortunately for me, I
don't have to look to disgruntled white girls for affirmation of my al-
lure or desirability as an African-American woman—all I have to do
is look at four hundred years of history.

Ask any white man, he'll tell ya' all about it.

Fondly,

"An Auspicious African-American Woman"

After writing the letter, I realized that we would never be able to level
the playing field when ignorance and disrespect continue to rule people's
actions. The key to resolving this issue is not in snapping on who has this or
that, but rather to refocus the issue to the real issue that matters, which is
love. Love of self, love of others that share in your experiences, and then
love of others—if we could just do that, all the rest will follow. Until we as
black women *love* one another, we will continue to be dishonored and disrespected by others.

Dr. Janeula M. Burt is currently a postdoctoral research fellow at the
Center for Research on the Education of Students Placed At-Risk (CRES-
PAR)/Howard University. An undergraduate alumna of Howard University,
Dr. Burt received her Ph.D. in educational psychology and M.Ed. in higher
education administration from Auburn (AL) University.

53

Reflecting on a Life Spent Fighting for Civil Rights

Hazel Dukes

I have spent a lifetime fighting for civil rights. I've seen a lot of change, but much has stayed the same. Where is the fire in our belly for our children? The greatest fight still needs to be fought and it begins with us.

In Montgomery, Alabama, when I was growing up, I couldn't go and drink water at the fountain. The signs said WHITES ONLY. We were mistreated. Mistreated just because we were black. I know the feeling of being denied just because of the color of your skin. But the home church of my parents now sits on Rosa Parks Avenue. So, we have a history, or a system that has produced victory. And black women have endured and sacrificed to contribute their part of that history.

I come from a long history of people who have made contributions. My dad belonged to the Pullman porters. Being the only child, I always had a sense of "speak up and speak out." And so seeing my dad fighting for his rights just kind of got into my system. During that time the trains were segregated. They had to work in the white cars and dining rooms, but they were mistreated. That is how A. Philip Randolph got involved, and my dad was a part of that movement.

Growing up in Montgomery during a time where your family and community worked to create an environment where young people had a chance was important. The strong males and females grounded me in my life; they were passionate and fought for what they believed in. I come from a background of ministers on one side of the family. My religious upbringing plays a great part in my life and helps me to endure and maintain my identity. I had grandparents on both sides who played an active role in my life. It was in this nurturing environment that I flourished. It is this same village and or community environment that I think is the missing link for our children in the twenty-first century.

I know that many people have worked hard in some areas to try to bring that important environment back. A heritage, so to speak. I know I have tried. I have been working closely with a group of young men in Harlem. We are mentioning them. My sorority is working with girls and young women in the hopes of inspiring and encouraging them.

Since our communities lack community centers and parks that are safe for our children to play in, churches are now filling the void and providing recreation but in a respectful way so that our young people can continue to have an outlet for their energy.

It takes the whole village to interact—homes to schools, churches to sororities and fraternities. We all have to play a part and create the environment that we want our children surrounded by. That environment is not necessarily rap music (although I am not totally down on all of it), but it can't be the only thing we expose our children to in our culture. We have to monitor and continue to challenge the system and to challenge ourselves. We must become role models and be more positive to our children so that they do not have to suffer because of us. Freedom has a price that we must all pay. And we must remember that our biggest fight comes from within.

Other cultures face the same issues but manage to come together anyway. In the Jewish community you have the conservatives. In the Jewish community you have the liberals. But when you talk about Israel, all that is put aside and they come together. For us African-Americans, there is always division. People are always in fighting. We need to learn again how to speak in one voice. As black women, we must accept the charge to come together and lead.

We have to remember our blood connection to Africa because, as Martin Luther King said, a threat of injustice anywhere is a threat to justice everywhere. We have to remember our history, before we openly kill each other off.

When you know your history, you have to have a commitment to what you are doing. I have truly been fulfilled by the work I have done. It is very important that you are actively involved in making whatever you find important better. For example, I gave a certain young man a lifetime membership to the NAACP. I wrote letters of recommendation for him. He got an internship to Washington, D.C. He went to Italy and he speaks three languages. Now he is at a big law firm. I got a letter from him. Now will that send you on your way? You don't always receive the praise you deserve. But when you have had an impact, you need to know it in your heart and that's all that matters.

In my involvement with the NAACP I think that I have given some encouragement and hope to an organization that has provided so many opportunities to members and nonmembers. I am glad that my little part is just a ripple in a big ocean of men and women whose names will never be known. People who have given their lives to a cause greater than themselves.

I think growing up in Alabama gave me a real foundation. It was a winning combination—family, community, and people who cared. I am a person who looks at life and understands that you need to take some vitamin C: Conviction, Commitment, and Courage. If you do not have those ingredients, you won't make it in this work.

Whatever you are doing, you are going to have disappointments in this life. My parents instilled this in me early on. I can remember growing up and being told, "Life is not a bed of roses." As a child I thought that sure was silly, "What do you mean 'bed of roses'?" I sleep in a *bed*. I used to hear, "If you fall down, get up and don't wallow." But what does that mean to a child?

But if you're alive and keep on living, you will begin to understand the truth of these old adages. Of course I have kept on living. I've been blessed to live and so I have taken those isms and put them into reality in my life. That means if a misstep comes or you don't keep on the straight path, make a detour and find your way back to where you come from. Don't blame other people. Revisit yourself. You *do* live in a glass house. You shouldn't criticize your brother or your sister. If you have something that you believe is hindering your friendship or your working together, you should sit down and talk about it. I have never openly criticized another civil rights leader even though I might not agree with them. I would never let the majority paper quote me as degrading another black civil rights because all of us have the same goals with just different ways of accomplishing them.

Nevertheless, with all the contributions I have made, I do feel underappreciated as a black woman. It happens in our own community. And it is there in the majority community too. There has been a regretful tug-of-war set up between black men and women. It pains me that the black woman has made more strides than the black man. So, therefore, black woman becomes the distance between our men. This is unfortunate. And it needs to stop.

The majority community plays into that by seeing our women as more aggressive than our men. They will accept the African-American female aggressiveness but they won't accept the black male. I think that we African-American women have to be very careful not to fall into the trap. This type of thinking sets black women up to be discriminated against on both ends—from black men and the majority community.

Women should respect their men. This ideal came from my parents' environment. I never heard of the woman being out front to outdo the man. Back then it was a family working together. But this has gotten lost. We have allowed people to play us against each other, helping foster the notion that the black man is no good. The media tells you . . . our men are going to prison . . . or selling drugs . . . or not being responsible for their children. This is the kind of thing that is portrayed all the time. The stereotyping of our males.

But we do have problems. I don't think the college degrees changed us. The looseness of our culture did. There is not the bond there used to be in our community. Everybody is out for himself or herself. People don't even know their neighbors. Black folks live next door to each other and they don't even know their neighbors' names. Not to mention those folks who move out to the suburbs. We also need to remember the church. The church is a place I go to be revived, renewed, and to gain new strength to meet the challenges I face.

Today we are past marching. Today we have to get to understand economics. Education is more important than ever, and we must get our children to understand this. It's not enough to just know how to read and write. Children today can't be what our great-grandparents were. It just won't work. Everybody is not going to be an athlete. Everybody is not going to be a rap star. Therefore, you need something else. If your skills are not transferable, it leaves you in a vulnerable position.

I would like for my legacy to be that I made a difference and assisted in turning the lives of young people around.

Hazel Dukes still continues to work with the NAACP and touch the lives of young people.

54

Complex Number Three

Lorraine Robertson

First it was my height. Big Bird. Tree. Sasquash. Kids can be so cruel. These were just a few of the names I was called growing up as the tallest kid in the class. From the sixth grade until what seemed like forever, I towered at least two inches over all my other classmates, growing quickly and leaving them all in the dust to catch up—and to tease me. Eventually, in high school, they did catch up—some even past my five-foot-eleven frame—and the jokes dispelled, but the complex was too strong to fade with them. It was so strong, it wasn't until my senior year in college that I would dare put on heels more than one inch high to accent my beautiful long legs. I couldn't imagine purposely making myself any taller, I mean really!

Next it was my color. White girl. Red bone. Yellow isn't really black—it's different. It's different? The black kids called me white girl. The white kids said I was different. Why wasn't I just another kid in their class? Why did it matter that my skin was fair? Why wasn't it good enough that I was smart, that I could make it to third base every time I was up in kickball, and that I knew all the moves to the Jacksons' infamous Motown 25 performance? After all, weren't those things more important than the color of my skin? So, there came complex number two. The same complex that haunted me most of my teenage years. The one that told me I should sit on a beach in Saint Martin with nothing but baby oil on my skin, so I would get as much color as I possibly could. And color I got, only I couldn't see it because the painful sun poisoning that came with it swelled my eyes up so tight I had to stay in bed for the rest of the vacation.

But I was young then. For both of my previous complexes. A mere child. An inexperienced teenager. I got over both of them learning to love my height, stand tall and wear fiercely high heels, and to love my color, as it's only one part of my beauty—beauty that's more than skin deep. So what's my problem now? At twenty-eight years young, I'm finding my body expanding in places that used to be so tight. The same pile of pasta and stack of Oreo cookies I used to devour daily doesn't just miraculously disappear anymore. Now, they linger and make friends with various parts of my body. It seems like just yesterday I was eating a Big Mac and two large fries with no sweat—and no weight gain either! More and more I find myself staring in the mirror at my naked body that used to be so lean. Worry creates flip-flops inside my stomach as my eyes immediately zoom in on the bulge outside of it, and on the cottage-cheese-like ripples that have taken over my thighs. Sadly introducing complex number three—my weight.

I, like millions of my sisters, am obsessed with my weight. If I could only lose ten pounds. Ten—that's it. Now that ought to tell you I'm not obese. I didn't say I need to lose fifty pounds or one hundred pounds—just ten. That scares me even more. I'm consumed with something so minor and obtainable. And to make it even worse, I have no one to blame for this complex, but myself. There are no kids taunting me on the playground, laughing at me and calling me Miss Piggy. None of my family or friends suggest that I look a little hefty; in fact, it's just the opposite. My mother tells me to stop being so critical and my husband assures me I'm gorgeous just the way I am. Yes, I could blame society for flaunting bone-thin white women in magazines and on TV, but I would like to think I'm stronger than that. So, where did complex number three come from and why won't it leave me alone?

Complex number three had been stressing me out—and in turn my poor husband, too—for months until one morning, as I lay groggily in bed, barely listening to a women's talk show on TV, when I heard a compassionate, understanding voice describing exactly how I felt about my weight. I shot straight up in bed—covers flung to the floor—and desperately gave her my full attention. Then she said it. Something so simple it made me jump up and dash to the bathroom mirror just to see if it worked. The woman explained that most of the time we're harder on ourselves than we are on other people. She urged every woman watching to take a brown paper bag and put it over their head then look in the mirror at their bodies. Imagine it was someone else's. There. It's not so bad anymore. And she was right. As I stood in the mirror with a T-shirt wound around my head, stripped of my clothes and my personal prejudice against myself, I saw a beautiful curvaceous, well-figured woman. I think I stood there for a good ten minutes—looking a bit ridiculous but feeling wonderfully beautiful and sexy.

By the time I walked out of the bathroom, the show had ended, and I had no clue who that amazingly intelligent woman was. But I didn't care. I was just glad she was there when she was to help me see how silly I've been. Now that's not to say I've imagined my body going through changes. Maybe I can't devour chocolate milkshakes and cheese fries and expect them to vanish like they did when I was nineteen, but that's not the point. The point is that I was doing what others had done to me for years—making myself feel unnecessarily inadequate over something so superficial, my appearance. I was the cause of complex number three, and I had the power to make it go away.

Now when I look in the mirror, I don't need a paper bag to put over my head. I look myself right in the eye and smile at the strong beautiful woman that I am—inside and out!

Lorraine Robertson is the director of publicity for LaFace Records, Grammy Award winning producers Kenny "Babyface" Edmonds and Antonio "L.A." Reid's label based in Atlanta, GA. Her position affords her the opportunity to contribute to the success of super star artists such as TLC, Toni Braxton, Usher, Shanice, and OutKast; and to work directly with various television and print outlets including *The Tonight Show with Jay Leno, The Rosie O'Donnell Show, Soul Train, Mademoiselle, Vibe Magazine, Rolling Stone Magazine, InStyle, Essence* and the list goes on! Her debut novel, *Caught Up!,* is a relatable, humorous, heartfelt story about three friends, their relationship and the different relationships they have with men. *Caught Up!* is in production and will hit stores in 2001.

55

The Long Way Home

Gloria Gordon, Ph.D.

Home—the word that haunts many immigrants. I left my home in Trinidad and Tobago in 1958 to attend a university in Canada and later immigrated to the United States. I soon learned that to survive I must keep the memory of home close to my heart. Winnipeg, Manitoba, in 1958 was a cold, hostile place. For an overprotected woman from Trinidad and Tobago, Winnipeg was a revelation. I experienced every type of "ism" in the world. For the first time in my life I was asked questions like, "What part of Jamaica is Trinidad and Tobago? Do you live in trees? Does the color of your skin come off?" I was totally unprepared because where I came from we learned every river and every little town in Canada.

I soon became aware that if I was going to make it, I had to adopt a steady gaze and pretend not to hear the things people were saying. It is said that silence makes no mistakes. I subsequently found out that many of the questions were asked out of curiosity—especially those asked by children. Most people had never seen a black person before, and it seemed to them that the questions were innocent ones.

"Home" for me next meant a walk on Mayaro beach, a drink of coconut water, a meal of curry crab and dumpling in Tobago. But "home" was not welcoming. "Home" felt that a graduate from a Canadian University was not as well prepared as a graduate from an English University and therefore should be paid less for similar work. Attitudes and experiences on both sides resulted in my journey back to Canada. Leaving "home" was much more difficult this time, because I truly believed that I had something to offer my country and wanted to be a part of nation-building.

But nevertheless, I found exciting work with Indians and Eskimos in the Northwest Territories of Canada. This exposed me to stoicism at its best—an almost extinct people eeking out a livelihood in a most challenging environment and at the same time living life to the fullest. I met fellow Caribbeans who also worked in the Northwest Territories as doctors, nurses, and teachers. Our dilemma was always, "Why are we here? What are we doing? Why are we not at home contributing to the development of our island-nations? Did we hate ourselves so much that we preferred to be in the Arctic instead of Trinidad or Barbados or Jamaica?" We had become aliens to our own lands but the bitter truth was that we would always be outsiders in Canada too.

My decision to live in New York brought new challenges. New York in the early 1970s was exciting, full of music and art, but also full of overt racism. New York was also seeing for the first time the then baffling attitudes of African-Americans toward Caribbeans and vice versa. Despite the fact that we crossed the same Middle Passage, some of us deposited in the Caribbean, others brought to the North American mainland, despite the fact that our desperate experiences in slavery were similar if not identical, there remains, as Rosa Guy so aptly puts it, "A narrow ravine." Over the years Caribbean people have contributed and excelled in every sphere of endeavor in the United States, first as African-Americans, and more recently as Caribbeans. With the influx of immigrants from the Caribbean since 1965, it is now much more acceptable to declare that one is from the Caribbean or that one is the offspring of Caribbean parents. Yet the subtleties persist within the two communities. It manifests as blatant exclusion of Caribbean people from some media, and virtual invisibility in other quarters. The Caribbean has always been a melting pot because of its multicultural elements. There is no contradiction in being Caribbean and in being anything else. I have to admit that Caribbean people themselves are often responsible for some of the chasm that exists. Many of us arrive in America with preconceived notions of what people in the host country should or should not be doing, how other people allow opportunities to be squandered, how best to raise children without recognizing that it is because of the trials and efforts of African-Americans that we have the privileges which we take for granted.

I next returned to Trinidad and Tobago for another eight-year spell to expose my young daughter to her "Caribbeanness" and help her through high school. Single parenthood in New York had just been too difficult. I decided that the influence of the islands—the sun, the sea, the wind, and Bishop's Ainsley High School could only be a beneficial experience for her. I was older, more tolerant, and more understanding of the dynamics of the situation. I enjoyed being with my family, and was blessed with a few good friends. I knew in my heart that Trinidad was where I wanted to be and I decided to work toward that end.

My return to New York brought two most gratifying experiences. The first was the opportunity to work and live in Africa. But even with the beauty and majesty of the motherland, I was still not ultimately "at home." Through the journeys that life has taken me on, I have been able to grow—

try, fail, and grow again. I learned that New York is not home. Canada is not home, and neither is Africa or Trinidad. At the end of the day I figured out that home—my place of solace—is the peace I find within myself.

Gloria Gordon, Ph.D., is a former professor at Medgar Evers College in Brooklyn, NY. Dr. Gordon is in the process of developing a documentary on the Caribbean to educate the rest of the world on the rainbow people and to begin the elimination of isms among African-Americans.

Your Soul's Sustenance

Judge not lest ye be Judged.
—Matthew 7:1

Universal laws are meted out with an ultimate evenhandedness. Just like gravity. No one is above the law; no one is beneath the law. And there's no getting away with *anything!*

In case of isms we pull out what we call the forgiveness test. Ask yourself where forgiveness comes from. Healing may come slowly, but if you don't let go of the hurt, pain, or loss, you will live with a lifetime of regret.

Forgive someone who can't forgive you back. We've got it wrong when we think that forgiveness is about getting someone else to accept our forgiveness. Forgiving isn't for the recipient, it's for the giver, and when you forgive, a burden is lifted off of you. A weight that you've been carrying around is lessened. Jesus told His followers to give their burdens to Him because He knew that when you let something go, "Your yoke becomes easy and your burden becomes light."

The person that you forgive today might be a long-deceased parent who left when you were just a baby. It could be a man who left you in a bind. It might be a friend whose long gone or a child who has lost his way in life. It doesn't matter. The point is that you stop carrying around old unnecessary emotional baggage.

Your Personal Book of Revelations

In instances of ignorance, the best way to cope is with knowledge and understanding. Here are some questions to help you reflect on your experience with isms.

- Have you experienced any isms?
- Describe each incident.

- How did it make you feel?
- What did you do at the time?
- What have you done since then to heal?

You are always the master of your own destiny. People can't do to you what you don't let them.

XII

Why Me?

Someone was hurt before you; wronged before you; hungry before you; frightened before you; beaten before you; humiliated before you; raped before you; yet, someone survived.
—Maya Angelou

The doctors told her that her daughter, Wilma, would probably never be able to walk, much less run—or even enjoy the things that most children take for granted. "Why is this happening to me?" thought Wilma. "Why can't I just be like other children? Why can't I run and play games outside? It just isn't fair. If God loves me, why would He make it this way?"

A lot of us tend to ask, "Why me? Why is this bad thing happening to me? Why was I raped? Why was I attacked? Why do I have cancer?" When we go through a hurting experience, most of us don't expect it. Most of us, when we are put through a hurtful or tragic experience, in the darkest hour, we wonder, "Why is this thing happening to me?" But oftentimes, as bad as situations may seem, something good actually does come out of it. And that's why it's you, because you're able to be strong and deal with it. And it's all right to say why me. Because you come out on the other end knowing why it's you. You may not know it now, you may not know it when you're going through it, maybe not even a year or ten years after you've gone through it, but it will reveal itself to you, and that's why it's you.

Little Wilma didn't pay any mind to what the doctors said she would or wouldn't be able to do. She knew that she wanted to run like other children. Not just run—but run fast. In her childlike enthusiasm, she refused to be confined by the limited ways of thinking that so many of us buy into every day. We adults accept as fact when people tell us that there's something that we can or can't do. But the truth is that only God knows the limits of our potential. Wilma hadn't yet decided that she was going to be limited, and so she set about trying to learn to walk—and to run. She didn't care if she fell on her face a million times and there didn't seem to be any progress. She didn't waste time asking herself, "Why me?" because she was too busy sticking with her program. She was determined to keep with it because she knew in her heart that it was her destiny to run.

Too Much to Bear?

We've all heard the saying that God never gives us more than we can bear, but every time we actually find ourselves faced with a crisis of magnitude, deep down we begin to question whether or not this is exactly true. It just doesn't seem fair. Why should one person have to go through so much and not another? But the truth is that everyone has a cross to bear. There's no point in comparing crosses. There's no point in looking at someone else's life and asking yourself why so-and-so has it so easy and why you have it so hard. You don't actually know what is going on in that person's life. You're only looking at one small aspect of their life. The person that you look at with envy may be the last person in the world that you'd like to switch places with if you knew the weight on their heart that they're actually carrying around with them.

There have been lots of things that we've all experienced that we've said "Why me?" about. The fact that you've made it through all those times is a testament to your strength and will to survive.

For many women, the "why me's" in life revolve around being violated by disease, violence, or mental enslavement. Violence is not just a physical invasion of the body, but a savage act against the soul and can be the most difficult "why me" to answer. Surviving an act of violence can lead to pain, hurt, and disappointment. Some women are ridden with guilt, anguish, and deep-seated hate, all the while asking themselves *"Why Me?"*

The pain of mental or physical violation is a silent pain that we live with. When faced with the pain, we ask ourselves why did this have to happen to me? What did I do to deserve this? Is God punishing me? As black women when we are violated there is a tendency to keep it to ourselves. We wonder what other people will think. "Will they judge me? Will they look at me differently? Will I be accepted?" The trauma of the incident becomes compounded in our soul. Often if not treated, the wounds bleed into other parts of our lives. They manifest into skin rashes, anxiety, and panic attacks. Once kept inside, you live with the violence in your every waking moment and it dances in your dreams. The violence is in every aspect of your life, and you cower from others; you walk in the shadows hoping not to be noticed. You become silent because your soul dies one day at a time. Your life becomes stifling and your relationships with men take on a whole other dynamic. You either want to be controlled or you try to control others. It's a major race for the top and often you lose.

You don't trust because your trust has been violated. You start wearing clothes to cover up your body, whether the bruises are there or not. A violation causes a trauma in the soul that must be healed. What is surprising is that if you were not a victim of violence, some of the very same people that you love are violence-trauma victims.

Young Wilma ultimately showed us all the power of simply not buying into what the world says is your future. She heard what the doctors said but she didn't listen to it. She didn't give it an audience in her mind. Instead she figured out what *she* wanted, namely to run—and went after it with all her heart. History records Wilma Rudolph as a groundbreaking Olympic gold medalist who set track and field records of all kind. But the most important record of all is one that won't appear in the record books: It's the fact that Wilma Rudolph overcame the limited thinking that was all around her—overcame the so-called limitations of her debilitation—and rose up to become the best runner in the world.

In this section are women who are brave enough to come forward and answer the question "Why me?" They are survivors, and the tales they tell will teach us all how to learn to love life all over again.

56

Dreen's Song

Andreen Therese Barrett

It was pain that brought her to life
the kind one feels when invasions have taken place
and who can save face when lost dignity
permeates the very Soul.

Then the door opened
leading her into a world she never knew existed
a world of pain-filled tears and stolen kisses.

A world of selfishness and trickery
where no one even cared to see
the light—as it lay hidden in that Child's heart—
this is how it's written.

The virginity most women lose on their wedding night
she lost the Easter of her 12th year.

Full of fear, not knowing where to turn
the light of her Soul started to burn
Calling her to come within
No Dreen, innocence is no sin
only its theft . . . is the message that was left.

This freed her to grow and helped her to know
that she is indeed worthy of Love
and is Loved by the Love which created her.

I was twenty-six years old when I wrote this poem because it was that
age that I finally began to face myself and what I had endured over the last
thirteen years. From hardcore drug use and promiscuous sex to physically
and mentally abusive, nonnurturing relationships and, of course, becoming
a mother at eighteen.

What a whirlwind I had been in, and then one day, I finally realized I really needed to seek help so that I could sort out some of the craziness of my life. You see, as a little girl, before the drama began, I always thought I was supposed to be a princess. I thought I was very special and that maybe, just maybe, I was in the wrong household after all. "I'm supposed to be hugged and kissed and smiled at and looked upon admiringly," I would think. The things that most children take for granted, I never really received. I now realize that it was not that I wasn't loved—my mother simply did the best she knew how. During the course of those tumultuous thirteen years, whenever I was really troubled and needed healing, I would write poetry. I think I started writing when I was about seventeen. It helped me to collect my thoughts and feelings and put some things in perspective.

Actually, I was prompted to seek therapy through a spiritual reading. The person who facilitated the reading suggested that I get closure on the pain of my past. I then asked God to guide me to a therapist who would really help me. I felt at ease enough to give it a try, and my inner healing work began. Oh, I would ask God to help me all the time. And I sincerely believe that had I not been surrounded, protected, and empowered by God, I wouldn't be here now at thirty-nine embarking on the greatest adventure of my life—a newly divorced, beautiful, spirit-filled sister who is using the pain of the past as building blocks to a solidly positive future. I am also finally learning to let the child in me come forth. I realize that, after being attacked, she ran away and hid. In this writing I am working to help let her shine forth. Her doing so is a very important step to my being whole.

Pain and growth are what I feel defined my existence until very recently. I grew up with so much pain (mainly because it was all around me) that it just became second nature. My mom, a single mother, worked three jobs and had no assistance from my father or my brother's father and I always felt that, somehow, it was my fault. On top of that, I was always tall, skinny, and awkward, and everybody teased me (Green Giant, Big Bird, tree, you name it). I felt so abnormal all the time that I just wanted to crawl under a rock and hide.

The only person who did not seem to regard me with disdain was my grandmother. As I now think of it—she was really a pillar in my life and loved me in spite of all my troubled moments. Because I didn't love myself during that period, I got into a lot of trouble and would always hear things like, "You'll never amount to anything," etc., from all of my family except for Granny. She believed in me and was the Angel in my life. I can remember not knowing where to get food for my baby, and out of nowhere Granny would call me to come and get food and would share with me her meager income, so that we could eat.

I only remember fragments of my life between the time I was born and the time I was viciously attacked by my mother's third husband at twelve years old. I was a tall girl and looking a bit more mature than my friends, but it never occurred to me to be a problem until he began to covet me. The first time he raped me he said that, since I was "doing it" with the boys in the street, I *owed* him. After all, he had brought my mom and us from a low-income neighborhood to a nice little home—he had "done so much for (me) us." This was his pitiful justification for stealing my innocence. As a twelve-year-old whose sights were set on being a high-fashion model, I was no more trying to entice the neighborhood boys than I was him.

The most humiliating part of the violation was not only him tossing a few dollar bills on my dresser every time he finished, but the fact that he would always show me his gun and tell me if I said anything, he would kill *all* of us (my brother, my mother, and me). In order to ease the pain, one day I decided to kill myself by swallowing a bottle full of aspirin and other miscellaneous pills. The only thing I killed was my stomach as I wound up having diarrhea for about three days.

I remember trying to tell my grandmother what was going on but I was afraid he'd hurt her, so I simply got smart and, after about two weeks of abuse, decided to start leaving the house when he would take my mom to the train, because it was afterward that he'd do his dirty work. After therapy I came to realize that his intention all along was to abuse me. My family ultimately realized this as well when it was learned that he attempted to abuse his niece several years before he met my mom. He was a very sick individual indeed.

I knew my method of avoiding him wouldn't work forever but I had no other option until what I call "the miracle" happened. My girlfriend had come by to pick me up for school one morning and he told her I was upstairs and told her that if she'd wait, he'd go and get me. She waited and waited but he didn't find me upstairs. Then he asked her to stay home with him to help him with the housework and he'd pay her for it. Well, she ran out of the house, found me up at the candy store near our elementary school, and told me what had happened. It wasn't until his attempt to get my girlfriend that I was finally able to escape him. After she told me, we told her mom who, in turn, told my mom, and he was arrested and thrown out of the house. Hallelujah!! God, I still remember my heart racing every time I saw a blue Chevy Impala in the neighborhood. I was convinced he was coming back to get me.

Even after the incident with my stepfather, my mother never asked me if he had harmed me in any way. I was too afraid to tell her because, after he was gone, she was back to working two or three jobs and I thought it was my fault that she struggled so hard.

Even though the physical part of my nightmare was over, I struggled with feelings of worthlessness. I didn't love myself, so early on I developed a pattern of looking for love in all the wrong places. When I was very young, I began to have promiscuous sex and I had my first pregnancy and subsequent abortion at fourteen. Four more abortions were to follow. The fathers of my unborn children were always roughnecks. I thought I had to have the toughest guy in the neighborhood to validate myself and to get attention and respect. At the tender age of eighteen I was a young mother and my daughter's father was no different. After he beat me within an inch of my life, I realized that my daughter and I deserved better. My four-month-old daughter was in the stroller and I had to get her home, which was about four blocks away. As he kicked me in the head the fifth or sixth time, all I could scream was, *"God help me!"* Finally someone pulled him off me and I managed to get my baby home.

Since I did not want him or his family around me at all, I really struggled with being a single parent. I didn't love my body or myself and had no qualms about selling my body for food or to pay the rent. It wasn't a big deal to me especially since my virginity was taken for a few dollars. Sex without love wasn't even the worst of my self-destructive behavior.

The excruciatingly painful impact of my young life pushed me so far away from myself that between the ages of thirteen and twenty-five I tried every mind-altering drug I could get my hands on. My adolescence was marked by red devils, heroine, Quaaludes, angel dust, PCP, cocaine, marijuana, and of course, alcohol and cigarettes. I could not for the life of me rid myself of the feeling that I was worthless. At sixteen I dropped out of high school and went to a trade school so that I could make money to afford my habits. The skills that I learned from trade school did not benefit me until much later.

At nineteen with a baby girl and my first apartment, I went to beauty school and ended up quitting because I couldn't find adequate child care. I did work in a beauty shop for about a year and had to quit because of yet another meaningless sex/drug relationship I had developed with the owner of the shop.

No one knew the pain that I was experiencing within because on the outside I was always able to put on a happy face. I modeled for local fashion designers, produced fashion shows for up-and-coming designers, attended dance school with my daughter, and did everything else I could to feel good about who I was. All this and I still didn't know who I was.

Therapy became what led me to answer this question and begin the healing process. My sessions were the first time that I realized I wasn't worthless. That it was not my fault that my mom struggled so, that my own father didn't love me, that I sought love and nurturing in the wrong places, and that I was attacked at age twelve.

Around the age of twenty-seven I quit therapy (it became unaffordable) and began indulging in reading all the self-help books I could get my hands on. I started meeting new and more positive people and began on the path to self-discovery. At twenty-eight, as I was on the path to self-discovery, I took a ten-year detour and became entrenched in a semifulfilling marriage. Even though my ex-husband was a good man and attempted to provide me with whatever he could—it just wasn't enough. Not to mention he became very controlling and insecure as time passed.

It was only when I started school at thirty-two that I began to come back to myself. The next four years from thirty-two to thirty-six, the marriage began to unravel thread by thread. I started realizing that I did not need a man to validate my life and was not happy being defined as simply a wife and mother. I would tell myself that there is so much more to me and ask God to help me figure out what that *more* is.

Then I read in a book one day (I don't remember which book), "All my life I have been someone's daughter, wife and mother . . . now I'm ready to take care of me" or something like that. It really stayed on my mind. The more I began to affirm feelings of this sort, the weaker my marriage became and the stronger I became. I graduated from college in the spring of 1997 with a BFA in fashion design and began to build my company. In the fall of 1997 I knew I couldn't go on in a marriage that I wasn't happy with. This was the single most stressful decision of my life so far, as I also had loads of debt, was starting a business that my husband was very involved in, and was simply afraid of what it would be like to be single again. Fear kept me from acting on my desire to be free until the spring of 1998 when I realized that in order to fully grow—the marriage had to go.

Now I'm on my own and everything is okay. I've never been happier, although at times, after being with someone for ten years, I do get a little lonely. I'm holding out for the right stuff this time and am learning to love myself. When I need a physical release, I simply please myself.

I realize beyond a shadow of a doubt that I am sustained by God and creation, which is gearing me up for a fantastic future with myself and the OCS Apparel Group, my fashion business. We have our first line out and are working out all of the kinks that go along with being new and African-American in the fashion industry. I have great business partners, and life is finally getting good.

I thank God and the spirit within for bringing me this far. I couldn't have made it without that mustard seed-sized grain of faith that is growing in me every day. I'm looking forward to seeing a lot more of the world, and enjoying more and more of God's abundance—because I am loved by God and I know I deserve the very best that Life has to offer.

The Strong One

Who can you turn to when the pain you feel inside
has you to a point where you almost miss your stride

And your tearing on the pillow when you're in the deep of night
has you bending like a willow—only you witness this sight?

You're The Strong One
The tall and proud

No matter how it hits you—you dare not say it aloud
you keep it to yourself until it vanishes like a cloud.

You're The Strong One
Within you know you are.
Can't let this get you down 'cause you're your very own star
Shine on, baby, shine on and one day soon you'll see
THAT THE STRONGER YOU ARE—THE FREER YOU'LL BE!

Andreen Therese Barrett, currently a resident of Atlanta is not only a grandmother and certified kickboxing instructor, but founder of the fashion company DreenScrapes, Inc., which designs private label and couture for private clientele. Andreen is also author of *Love Themes and Other Realities,* a book of soon to be published prose.

57

A Reason to Continue

Simone Marie Meeks

What can I give to my sisters? Perhaps all I can do is to pass along what was given to me—my mother's precious admonition that "silence equals complicity." My gift then is the gift of voice.

Just before Valentine's weekend, February 1998, I went for a routine prenatal checkup. My doctor entered the room smiling, and asked, "Feeling any kicking yet?" I replied, "No." He repeated my answer with surprise. I was pregnant for the first time and didn't know what it was *supposed* to feel like.

The doctor put the stethoscope to my stomach and listened for a heartbeat. And despite seven years of seeing this doctor, and going through my only operation with him, it was the first time I had ever seen panic flash in his eyes.

He picked up another device he said was to magnify the baby's heartbeat. I heard what sounded like water gushing, but no heartbeat. He turned the device off, picked up his stethoscope, told me to get dressed, and asked my husband and me to join him in his office. When we did, he said we'd have to do some tests. "Don't panic," he said. "Call tomorrow, and we'll know more then," he continued. We told him we were going upstate and he encouraged us to keep our plans, just call him and he'd get back with us.

Somehow we managed to drive upstate. And as I cried, my husband encouraged me to believe everything would be all right. After all, I was already in my fifth month. I heard people say, "You're in the clear after the third month." Finally, I started to believe my baby was just different, but he was all right. Somehow we had an enjoyable day seeing old friends and trying our hardest to believe everything would be all right.

The next afternoon, my husband and I went to his Assembly office to begin packing some of the things he would take back to New York. You see, Gregory had just won a seat in the United States House of Representatives on February 3, 1998, and we were trying to move things so he could begin taking what he needed to take to Washington, D.C. Taking care of business like we always do. In the middle of the task we called our doctor's emergency service. It was about a half hour before he called back. When he did, Gregory had just stepped out of his office to speak to a friend. I was alone when the return call came.

"Hello," I said. "Simone?" the doctor asked. "Yes," I replied. "Where's your husband?" he asked. "He stepped out, but just tell me," I said. "Can you get him?" he asked. "No," I said, feeling I could handle the news. I was sure what was coming. "You're not going to be able to carry this baby to term," he said. "Okay," I said as I closed my eyes and the streaming waterfall ran over my face. "What happened?" I asked. "We're not sure. But you are not going to be able to carry this baby to term," he repeated. I think he asked us to come back to the city as soon as we could. And he asked that Gregory call him once we get back. I whispered, "Okay," and hung up the phone. I believe Gregory returned about two minutes later, with a huge grin on his face. Somehow I'd wiped my face and was sitting numbly. He looked at me sitting at his desk, and saying, "Oh, babe. Oh, babe." He then sat on the couch and asked that I join him. But with tears flowing freely and frozen in pain, I just couldn't move. We cried on opposite sides of the room for a while, and then he said, "Let's go." But before we left, we told one of his friends so the packing could continue and we wouldn't be stopped leaving the building.

We returned to our hotel room to pack. And Gregory asked if I needed anything. I asked him to find my former boss. I needed to tell a woman who I knew cared; someone I trusted, and who I knew would provide a hug. I knew she knew how much I wanted this baby—this expression of me and my husband.

Gregory did as I asked, and found her. We hugged each other and then she said she wouldn't let me go back to the city until a doctor in Albany had checked me. She was unaware of the test done in New York City. But once she realized that I did not just *think* I had lost the baby but *knew* that fact, she hugged me and told me how sorry she was.

I realized my husband must have been in bad shape because he would not share the news, intentionally, with anyone we did not know well. There was no other explanation. Gregory returned to the room and we prepared to leave. But before we did, we said a prayer. It felt good to hear her pray; it provided momentary consolation.

As we left the hotel, we ran into a friend of ours who'd lost his daughter only months before. I hugged him and wanted to collapse into his arms. But we were in the lobby and something in me wouldn't let me bare all the pain. After that moment, I recall crying in the car, arriving at a hotel in New Jersey and asking to be taken home to my own bed, so that I might attend church in the morning and then enter the hospital in the afternoon.

Unbelievably, the next day there was a guest preacher at my church, and I heard no message.

Going to the hospital was tough. I was in the maternity ward. I could hear babies crying, and I knew I would never hear my child's cries. I was given intravenous medication that was supposed to cause "spontaneous abortion." But it didn't happen that way. After many hours of medication, being repeatedly checked, visited by my sisters, my husband, and my mother sitting with me, I asked everyone to go home. All through the night the checking of the IV, the taking of my temperature, the prodding went on. And whatever was to happen did not.

My husband and Mom arrived early the next morning, and it all began again. During one of the examinations I began crying. My mother asked, "Is she in pain? What's wrong?" The doctor replied, "No, she's not in pain. It's just the finality of it. She knows it's almost over." I said nothing. In reality, the exam was quite painful, and I was angry that the nurses and my doctor were now referring to my baby as "the fetus." I never said anything. I just cried.

Finally, the doctor said I was ready and I was taken to the operating room. I remember awakening in the room and being told I could go home soon. But privately I felt horrible. I just wanted to curl up in the hospital bed. And I did just that, opting not to go home until the next day.

The following morning, bright and early, the doctor came in and asked, "What are you still doing here?" I had previously said I wanted to leave the hospital as soon as I could. But when the moment came, I did not want to leave the hospital bed, and the place I somehow told myself my child was. I finally left. Listening to other children crying in the background. Empty handed. It was awful.

When we came home, the phone rang with members of my family. My father, recently diagnosed with bone cancer, scolded me for asking my family not to tell him right away. And all the while flowers and plants arrived. And in the days that followed, cards and more flower arrangements arrived. I lay in bed crying. I cried for the baby I would never see. I cried because I heard people say I had run too much during my husband's campaigning, and I cried because all the flowers felt as if there had been a funeral, but I had never had the opportunity to bury my child. I had never even gotten to see my son. (I intuitively knew I was having a boy, and when I pointedly asked the doctor what my child's gender was, he confirmed the feeling.) Despite knowing my life was filled with abundant blessings, not the least of which was my husband winning an election to Congress, I could not stop the feeling that I had lost what was beyond words.

In the days that followed, I came to the realization that life had to get back to "normal." But I could not move on. My husband asked my doctor for a name of a psychiatrist. We went to see her, and in that visit Gregory described how I was blaming myself. He told her of my inability to sleep most nights, and restless sleep I had most other nights. Gregory said, "She tries to act as if she is all right, but I know she isn't." The doctor replied, "I can see it in her eyes."

Slowly things changed. I kept going to the psychiatrist, trying to talk through my feelings. And dreading my birthday, the birthday I was sure I'd share with my son. It was an extremely lonely time. I made plans to be very busy that weekend, but it was Father's Day, and there was a baby between us. I was grateful that my husband had children, but I felt cheated.

There are still days when I cry, though I sleep well again. And I've learned to look past it when some people approach me as if they are looking at a wounded pup. I remain hurt by talk of my doing my child in, and by statements like, "If you were a mother," or "Maybe someday when you are a mother." And when there are commercials about babies or when I see pregnant women on the street, I ache a bit, but I keep going on. Because I still feel cheated, I sometimes think maybe the Lord was saving my child from a harsh life.

My birthday will never, ever, be the same. Valentine's Day won't soon be the same. But I still count my blessings, even when I'm crying. And so all I can offer my sisters is to say that if you're going through something like this, there's someone out there who understands. But I will also tell you that neither I nor anyone else has ever been quite where you are. No one has ever been, or ever will be you, and that creates nuances which make your situation particularly yours. So if one day you hear of another sister going through this and hear someone telling her, "You're young, you'll have other babies," or "It's no big deal, I lost three children," just take her to the side and give her a hug. In that hug she will know that you understand. And that will make more of a difference than she will be able to say or I ever put into words. In that hug she will know your silence is free of judgment, and you understand that the sting remains in her smile. You will have given her reason to continue on.

Simone Marie L. Meeks is principal in the consulting firm of The Lipscomb Lord Group, Inc. providing public relations, event planning, and advocacy on behalf of such clients as Pfizer Women's Health, Medical Services for Women of Westchester, Brazil Sports International, and Julie and Marie's Beauty Salon. She is the former Deputy Press Secretary for the

Bronx Borough President, and the former Chief of Staff for a State Assembly Member. She remains committed to helping as many people as possible understand and positively use the political process. But her greatest joy is found in family (immediate and extended) accomplishments and being loved by the very honorable Congressman Gregory W. Meeks (D-NY) and three amazing daughters.

58

A River Of Thanks

Chatarra Hamlett

There is a time where all I do is cry.
My heart has been broken too many times.
But when I look out, reach out, I'm always careful of who or what I may touch.
Who or what may be hot, but when I look up God is right on top.
My God is there to keep me safe.
My faith is there because I'm saved by His grace.
My God is there so no weapon shall prosper.
My faith in Him will never leave me stray.
I get happy because God has done so much for me.
Can't you see He lives eternally.
When I wake up , that's my God.
When I can walk and talk,
Yes, that's my God.
All I can do is praise Him, Glorify His name and thank Him,
For Yes, that's my God.

Chatarra Hamlett is the twenty-year-old president of the Heavenly Praise Dancers of Cornerstone Baptist Church. The Heavenly Praise Dancers have enjoyed wonderful reviews in several major publications. Chatarra plans on completing her studies in speech pathology at Medgar Evers College.

59

Life and Times

Jacqueline Rowe

Why me? That question has plagued me all of my natural life. After finishing a bout with life's miseries that feels like it lasted thirty rounds, I can finally take the time out to reflect and put all of this into perspective. What does God have in store for such a noble soldier as myself? I've weathered the storm for as long as I can remember, now I patiently await my next assignment, my next fight. Well, if someone's struggles are any indications of their return or good fortune, then I got more than enough coming to me.

I've known pain on a personal level before I knew myself. Even though I was born into a loving family of seven brothers and sisters, death has always played a big part in my life. At the tender, delicate age of three I lost my older brother to a freak traffic accident in my homeland of Jamaica. An erratic driver killed my brother and till this day I believe that marked the beginning of the severance of my family unit. Shortly after that in a span of months I lost a second brother to a misdiagnosed fever. Needless to say this tragic chain of events sent my family into a tailspin. My father, who was a decorated police officer at the time, decided with my mother that our family had a better chance in the States. So when I was around five we migrated to America with the hopes of a brighter future.

I could only pray that we had left our misfortunes behind in Jamaica. I was only allowed about a year of peace in my Flatbush, Brooklyn, neighborhood before the Angel of Death returned. My youth was torn from me the day that my father succumbed to sickness. It was a loss that I'm still recovering from. My connection to my father was one that held me together personally, so when I lost my daddy I almost lost my composure. How could God take someone who was so instrumental to my existence? No one had any answers and as a result of that my relationship with my mother began to suffer. As a young girl I remember noticing how this took its toll on her. The woman who once represented strength and determination, in my eyes, was buckling under the despair caused by my father's untimely death. That had an ever-lasting emotional effect on me. I became bitter at the world and very rebellious because of my inability to correct the wrongs that God felt suitable to curse my family with.

Like most children though, I didn't realize this public display of frustration did nothing to help my mother's condition. Before I could reconsider my attitude toward life I was dealt another blow. At the age of seven I was still doing what most children my age do after school, taking in some TV, when I witnessed the live broadcast of a body being removed from a very familiar address. It took me no time to recognize the victim as my older sister. An intruder had shot her in the head in front of my niece and nephew. He also beat them in the head with a hammer, severely damaging them mentally.

Why me? Where would you go from there? Do they provide shelter for children so disillusioned with life as I was at such a young age? With nowhere to turn I turned to the street, where I searched for a replacement for my father and possibly an answer to these questions. I never did find my answers, but I did encounter the comfort of the five boroughs of New York. I became attracted to the strangest love, the kind that the streets have to offer. The kind that can consume the blackest of coal and turn out the rarest of diamonds, but as we all know not everyone survives this transformation. My transformation was hard to say the least. After becoming a permanent fixture on the corners of all five boroughs I was soon initiated into various gangs, the Cats being the most significant. My tour of New York gangs included the Tomahawks, the Puma Boys, the DooWops, the RRC's, and as I mentioned before, the Cats. My rebelliousness, which had started at home, had now taken on a new meaning. Not only was it reflected in my street life, it was affecting my academic life a great deal. Before I knew it I'd been placed in one of the 600 schools designated for problem kids. I rebelled on this front as well. Instead of imposing on fellow classmates, I channeled my discourse toward school bullies and always found myself taking up for the underdogs.

So even though I'd become the baddest of bad asses I would never lean on the weaker man. I was always an advocate for the downtrodden, displaced youth, and that's whom I fight for till this day. One of these nasty encounters with school bullies landed me in the principal's office. When they learned of my gang ties the matter was referred to Juvenile Hall. Never one to fear, my unruliness didn't rescind; it only escalated.

The courts responded by ordering me to undergo a psychological evaluation. When the ruling came back that I was a menace to society I really lost my cool. I vehemently cursed out the judge and the psychologist only to find myself on Rikers Island at the age of twelve. For the first time I must admit I felt a bit of fear because of my present surroundings. You see, I was one of the first teens to fall under a new law that permitted the state to reprimand juveniles to facilities like Riker's. I was out of place to say the least. Like most tests I've encountered in my life, I quickly overcame my fears and the rebellious side of Jacqueline. That experience turned me out and returned me to society with a new edge. I was glad to be back in the comforting arms of the streets where society alienated people like myself. Upon my return to this world I met my children's father at the age of fifteen. He was a rebel like myself and also spent most of his adolescent life in and out of institutions. Needless to say we were bonded like magnets and from this bond I became pregnant with my first child, Prince Michael. My fierce loyalty to my man carried me to every upstate institution you can think of. I did the entire tour like the trooper I was. On a personal level I was still committed to improving my current situation. During my pregnancy I enrolled in a school designed for young teen mothers. I was very thankful for the opportunity to interact with the rest of my peers and still work toward a diploma while carrying Prince. In fact after the birth, when they tried to close the school because of bureaucratic reasons I took it upon myself to spearhead a campaign that eventually kept their doors open. That's how I showed my appreciation. By this time I was on my own, holding onto an apartment with my children's father whenever he was in the free world.

Our time together was very challenging because of the heavy abuse involved. Till this day I can't honestly say if it was because of our youth combined with our responsibilities or because of personal reasons, but nevertheless the beatings took its toll on our relationship. As I prepared to leave him another chain of events sent me hurling back into his arms for comfort and support. The Angel had returned. This time he had taken the life of my youngest brother, my closest. My little brother died violently from a gunshot to the neck. Why me? Luckily I had my child's grandmother as a rock to lean on. She was like a second mother to me, definitely there when I needed her. On this day her presence was instrumental in keeping me together. We had just gotten home and she was preparing me a meal when suddenly she too was snatched from me. She died of a heart attack right there in my kitchen.

On that night with the weight of these deaths looming over me I conceived my second child, Antonio. My union with my children's father lasted for two more years until I finally decided I had enough of the abuse. Severing a relationship isn't as easy as it sounds and I'm sure any woman can attest to that. My situation wasn't any different but I was determined not to relapse. Just when I was feeling so low and thought I couldn't be knocked down any further, I got the news that finally floored me. Apparently my mother had been living with cancer for a few years and never informed anyone. Till this day I believe my youngest brother's death accelerated the disease to a point where chemotherapy was useless. In her last days she chose me as her rock to lean on, as opposed to me depending on her for that role throughout life. Regardless of all the death that I had seen in life, nobody could convince me that my mother wasn't immortal. I clearly recall the conversations we had over Sunday dinners when I would ask my mother, "Mom, you would never leave me, cause you'll never die, right?" She would answer me back by smiling, but as long as she never said no, I was convinced. Meanwhile, while I was going through the motions of caring for my mother in her final stages, God must've thought it suitable to double up on my pain. My oldest brother was overcome with a mental breakdown. So here I was, dealing with my mother's condition in Downstate Medical Hospital, and directly across the street my brother was being treated at Kings County Hospital. Suddenly my mother was overcome by a stroke. Between waiting night and day for her to return to me, and running across the street to check up on my brother, she succumbed to her sickness a few days later. My brother remains in and out of hospitals to this day, clinically diagnosed with depression. Every day that passes is a day spent with my mother, whether it is through vision, memory, or conversation. She has left a lasting impression on me for the rest of my life. I live to please my beloved Mrs. Hazel Rowe and hope one day to fulfill her dream of one of her children becoming a "shining star."

One day, overcome with the grief of losing my mother, I found myself walking forty blocks from my neighborhood to the Empire Skating Rink in Brooklyn. Outside of the Rink on this particular day there seemed to be some spectacle because of the big gathering. It didn't take long for me to muscle my way through the crowd and discover the hysteria was over none other than Mike Tyson. When I saw my lil' bro I walked straight into his arms and started weeping. Mike and I were first joined at the youthful age of twelve when we were both youngsters running with the R.R.C. Needless to say he made his escape from the streets not too long after that, leaving behind family and friends. Now here was the hometown hero, he'd returned home not only to show love but also to receive some. This was around the time that he was going through a bitter divorce from Robin Givens, also he had recently lost his loving sister, Denise. At this time he suffered his first loss ever to Buster Douglass plus the many media attacks were taking form. No sweat though, we piled into his Porsche, and I've been riding shotgun ever since. From that day on we've struggled through the fights of life not only in the ring but through the trials and tribulations of everyday living. We both shared in our losses in that I reminded him of his sister that recently had passed and he reminded me of the baby brother I had just lost. I've been there for the charges, the losses, and there when there was no one and he's done the same. His many accomplishments have driven me to a different understanding of obstacles. No one can ever doubt that we were separated at birth. Unfortunately my undivided attention was unwisely split between Mike and the new love in my life.

Someone once told me a wise man (or woman) learns from his or her mistakes. Well that wouldn't be the case for me the second time around on the love circuit. Around the time Mike had come back into my life I became heavily involved with a man from my neighborhood. This abusive union lasted for ten long, painful years complete with black eyes, busted lips, and raw verbal abuse that affected my esteem and my diet. Like I said I've always been attracted to the strangest love, first the streets, then my children's father, now this man. Whoa! Luckily I was able to escape this arrangement with my life intact.

The lessons I've learned from these relationships are the type that have propelled me to the heights of success that I enjoy today. From the love I was able to generate from Mike and my children, I finally arrived at the realization that anything that wasn't conducive to my growth and development was a hindrance.

After shedding all of my hindrances I was able to proceed and blossom into the individual that today owns and operates a fledgling entertainment company. I am now able to offer that refuge for the many underprivileged, over-talented children stuck in every ghetto and city dwelling in America. My personal pride comes from assisting the underdogs. Finally I have obtained the answer to that lingering question, Why me?

Jacqueline Rowe is currently the CEO of Iron M.I.C. Enterprises, a Brooklyn based entertainment company geared toward the vast pool of talent stuck in the inner city. As an addition to her company she is also incorporating the Iron M.I.C. Foundation, whose main focus is to extend research in mental illness and cancer. Although she has escaped the mental confines that once held her back, Jacqueline Rowe continues to live and delegate from the same Brooklyn neighborhood that she has always called home. The proud mother of two children, she also recently attended the graduation of her eldest son, a rare feat in her neighborhood but a priority in her household. The underlying theme of Jacqueline's life story is that life is never what it seems, especially when it seems gloomy. We are all masters of our own universe; in Jacqueline's instance Mike Tyson held the key. The challenge is to find your cause and unlock your future!

60

Where Is Life's Manual?

Eneida Martino-Laguerra

I am the youngest of four daughters, Angela, Sandra, Lourdes, and Eneida (me). What a bunch we were—who needed brothers to protect me? I had my sisters. Growing up with them was so much fun. We played and laughed together and you can imagine with four girls what kind of fights took place. I wouldn't trade it for the world. My parents separated when I was seven years old and we moved to Brooklyn. Growing up in Brooklyn was no different from Little Italy in Manhattan. When you are a child, nothing really matters as long as you can go outside and play. I did miss my father dearly, but being an alcoholic was not his best trait.

My father verbally abused my mother and that led to the separation. I was very close to my dad, but when it came down to the separation, I took my mother's side. My dad tried to help as much as he could. It just was not enough. My mother worked very hard to support all four of us. Growing up poor was not an option; it was a way of living. We always had food and clothes on our backs. As we got older, we got jobs and helped around the house.

I'm glad we moved again, this time to the Marcy Projects in Brooklyn. I think facing the gritty part of life at a young age makes you a poet. A part of you would like to get an affirmation that you are not the only one going through this pain. Is my life supposed to be a web of bad relationships, death, and illness? Life sometimes puts you in tough spots to see if you have what it takes to make it. It's like going back to school—the more you learn, the smarter you get. But there are obstacles you have to encounter along the way. But I always felt cheated—growing up in those days like most teenagers. I watched a lot of television and I felt like I was supposed to have a life like Joanie from *Happy Days*. It just didn't happen that way.

When I was eighteen years old, I started dating this guy. It started with one black eye, and he promised not to do it again, but he did. I never expected to be a victim of domestic violence. I guess no one does—it just happens. I was scared, but I kept my silence. I was too embarrassed to let any-one know what he was doing to me. I hid the abuse from my mother and pretended that things were fine. At the time I didn't realize it, but she knew what was going on. I tried to appear happy around her so she would not see how afraid I was. I would cry in the bathroom, so if my eyes were swollen, she would think it was because I got soap in my eyes. I wanted to protect her from my pain, because I knew that if she saw it, it would hurt her, and I would rather die a thousand times than see my mother hurt. Eventually, I got to the point where I couldn't take it anymore. I thought about killing him. I am sure other women have felt the same emotions. You start plotting; waiting for a moment when his defenses are down, or you think of ways that he could go, perhaps being run over by a truck. One day I stopped being afraid and started to fight back. I felt as if I was not only fighting for myself but for all women. Once I lost my fear of him, nothing could stop me. I was free. I'm glad for pro-choice because I would have been a hanger statistic. Looking back, I'm glad I didn't kill him because I might have ended up in jail and he wasn't worth it.

On April 30, 1990, I lost the first man I ever loved. My papi. He made me laugh, patched up my bruises, and taught me how to ride a bike. He was an amazing father and was always there for his family. His death was sudden and unexpected. There are still times when I cannot believe that he is gone. But the worst was yet to come. Almost two years later, on March 20, 1992, my mother passed away. With both my parents now gone, I felt like I was dropped into a deep black hole. Parents are only supposed to die when they are very old. My soul was hurting, and I was on the verge of insanity. I was mean, angry, and unbearable to be around. I was going out of my mind. At one point, I wanted everyone's mother to die so they could feel my pain and know what I was going through. I cried myself to sleep every night. But one evening my mother appeared in my dream and held my face in her hands. She said, "I am okay. Please do not cry for it is here that I am really alive." I cried with happiness that night and felt an incredible sense of peace, which had eluded me for a long time. I learned a lot from my mother. She was an incredible woman and an amazing philosopher. In my heart and through my soul, my parents will always be alive. I am blessed to have had the parents I did because I will take their love and support and one day share it with my future children. Cherish what you have because you only have one father and one mother. If there are any misunderstandings, you should settle them before it's too late. Make amends now or you will regret it forever.

But life wasn't through with me yet. My older sister has HIV. I always looked up to her and finding out was like being hit with a ton of bricks. If I were granted only one wish, it would be for my big sis to have another chance in life. I don't know anyone who deserves it more than her. I'm afraid how I'll feel if she dies, but I will stay strong. If that day comes, I'll tell her to let our mother know how very much I love her.

If all of my family's tragedies weren't enough to get me down, it was my best friend, Lorraine, telling me she has cancer that finally took what little hope I had left for life away. I couldn't believe it. This was the person who knew all of my innermost secrets and I knew hers. She is the one who consoled me through the abuse, through death, and now God was going to take her away too. At first I thought, what am I going to do? But I know. I'll support her, take care of her, love her, struggle for her, and help her believe that good things happen to people in their time, and I want to give her any good that's coming my way.

I have to be honest with you—there are times that I want to die, cry, live, and even laugh. There are times that I want it all to stop. Maybe I can find a cure for all this madness, but most of all I want peace. I have a million emotions inside, some wanting to burst open. Sometimes I wish that the emotions could keep quiet so that I can enjoy something simple like a good night's sleep. But I know that no one is promised tomorrow and I can accept that.

It got so bad that I was used to bad things, so that when something good came my way, I questioned it. I want to go to the highest mountain, and yell, "Why is this happening to me? Why me? Why me?" I just want things to stay the way they are—with both my sister and my best friend alive and no more chaos on its way. I don't know how much more my heart can take.

I never thought I would love again, until the day my junior high school sweetheart came back into my life. Our relationship felt like a dream, but it was all real. He gave me true love and mended my heart. At our wedding I yelled, "I do, until death do us part," and meant it. My husband is my guardian angel, my protector, and my best friend. I thank God for him every day. Now I can rule the world knowing that he'll always have my back. My husband is a gift from God. It's a wonder that he didn't get hurt when he fell from the heavens into my life. His love and strength help me to cope with whatever life has in store for me.

I know life does not have a manual, you make it up as you go,
You do your best and go with the flow.
I'll take a chance and be aware
That life can be fun, but also unfair.
My life is not over, only just beginning.
There will be struggles, but I'll still be singing.
My only words of wisdom are to hold on and pray
For tomorrow is another day.

Never give up and keep your faith
Because good things come to those who wait.
There will be times that you just wonder why?
But this is bigger than we are, for it comes from the sky.
I am the way I am today
Because of what happened to me yesterday.
So life, you better bring me more because I'm not afraid.
Guess what I'm doing with all these lemons? I'm turning them into
   lemonade.
And still working on reading life's manual.

Eneida Martino-Laguerra is a design room manager at a sportswear company and writes reflective poetry. She is wirting a screenplay, sitcom and book.

61

What Is Behind Kym's Bench

Kym Hampton

One of the hardest things I have ever had to do in my life is to believe in and love myself. I know it sounds crazy, because most people know me as Kym Hampton who played in Europe for twelve years. Or the Kym Hampton who was one of the founding members of the WNBA's New York Liberty. But life isn't always about career statistics. Don't get me wrong, I am grateful for all of the experiences that my God has chosen for me to perform. But believe me I went through my entire career wrestling with self-doubt. Sometimes I would go over every move I made on the court and convince myself that there was a better move or shot that I could have made. That in itself can be exhausting, but the same phenomena has plagued me on all levels since I was a child.

I have not met one person in my life who isn't insecure about something or another. As a little girl I was extremely shy, and I was two grades taller than most boys were in my class. When you are at that age you just want to blend in, but I couldn't. In the fourth grade I was 114 pounds, five feet four inches, and solid. One day our class was all taking our yearly physical in the gym. There were different stations set up such as weight, height, and eye stations with nurses positioned at each one. When I got to the weight station the nurse hollered out "Kym Hampton, 114 pounds." All the kids were like, "Dag, Kym weighs that much!" I was of course humiliated.

I come from Kentucky and most of the people in my family were supportive of me while I was growing up. But there was always an undertone that I always sensed that seemed to say, "If you were light skinned, that your life would be easier." A lot of my family is of light complexion. When I was born my dad was looking for me in the section of the nursery reserved for white children. My grandmother directed him to me, a caramel-colored child. He said, "Are you sure that's our baby?" I was his "baby girl," Dad never let it affect me overtly, but I always felt the undertone all around me.

From my earliest memories, he potty trained me, laid out my clothing and dressed me, not to mention attended every one of my games. Although my parents later divorced, my father even to this day plays an active role in my life and even challenges me to a game of one-on-one to see who has bragging rights.

In high school the really cute guys would go after the petite light-skinned girls. I remember overhearing them talking, "Kym has a pretty face but she is just too big."

When I was about fourteen my mom had a nervous breakdown and was diagnosed with paranoid schizophrenia. Her symptoms would vary, and she would check herself in and out of mental clinics. Our relationship became strained when her actions became paranoid. There was the time that I didn't even start my period yet and she thought I might be pregnant. It was awful; she forced me to take a pregnancy test and this happened on three occasions, at least. At fourteen years of age you are very fragile and at that point of your development you are seeking to define who you are and you are looking for stable parents. It really scared me because I needed a mom at that time in my life and she was not available to me. I felt abandoned, embarrassed, angry, hurt, and had a tremendous amount of self-doubt. To make matters worse my siblings were separated after a divorce from my stepfather. My aunt and grandmother would step in and try to provide some comfort.

To this day she refuses to sign papers or fill out any forms. Growing up with that was difficult. She has zero income and financially everything is left up to my grandmother, my aunt, and me. Sometimes she appears normal and you get this feeling that she knows what she is doing. Mom has her own house, but she chooses to stay with my grandmother the majority of the time and causes my grandmother a great deal of stress not to mention the rest of the family. You get the feeling that she is manipulating the situation. I say that because she calls me when she needs something and is always extremely specific and has very expensive taste. I am just really beginning to understand what her disease entails. I try to be patient with her, but it is hard when she refuses to get any help.

One specific time my self-doubt really affected my career was when I was trying out for the 1984 Olympic Team. Back then I had made a decision to attend Arizona State University based on what knowledge I gathered from reading pamphlets. When I was making my decision about a college career NCCA college visits were not paid for nor was women's basketball highly visible in the mainstream. Unless you had someone who was knowledgeable about the politics of basketball and picking the right schools you were lost. The weather and I chose to go to Arizona State—not because it was a great basketball school but because the campus was beautiful and warm. Later I realized that the better choice of schools would have been Tennessee or Louisiana Tech (they were pretty hot) because of the good

teams and visibility. My college coach, Juliene B. Simpson, played on the
1976 Olympic team; that was a big help because she knew what it was like
to be on that level and instilled a lot of toughness in our squad. I then realized basketball like most things is very political. The top players from highly
visible teams or schools made the team. I never stood a chance going into
the Olympic trials. In my own head I made the assumption that they would
not let me on the team anyway. At least I felt that mentally, it was, "Hey, I
wasn't going to get a shot so I didn't give 100 percent. . . ." I think I did it so
that I would not be disappointed with the outcome. That day has haunted
me ever since. I often wonder if I had given my all what the outcome would
have been.

I thought my dreams of playing basketball past the collegiate level were
gone. Then an agent approached me during my senior year at the Margaret
Wade Trophy dinner, which is the equivalent of the Heismann Trophy but
for women's basketball. The top 50 women players come together and only
one is selected. I didn't win that year but it was a win/fail situation. I met an
agent who placed players in the European leagues. So I jumped at the opportunity. For me playing basketball was simply something I loved to do. I
played a total of twelve seasons in Europe, and I really enjoyed it. I absorbed the culture, learned a couple of languages, explored, traveled, and
most of all played ball.

I first played in Spain for six straight seasons. A season is usually seven to
eight months depending on how far your team gets in the playoff. Consider
yourself lucky if you get a week off for Christmas (depending on your
coach). Then I played one year in Italy, one year in Japan, one year in
France and then back to Italy for three years finishing up my European
league career. I started as one of the top foreign players in the Spanish
league and quickly was asked to play on the championship team. I may have
become a little complacent by playing on such a good team because my last
two years I changed teams and had to play a more aggressive role, and I
began to doubt myself. I haven't been able to shake it; it still affects me to
this day. I can start and if I miss two or three shots, the doubting gets bigger
and bigger.

After that I might not look to shoot as much and have sometimes passed
up open shots. But when I am aggressive I feel completely unstoppable.
Sometimes I end up putting so much pressure on myself that it becomes a
snowball effect, and I have even asked my teammates to tell me to snap out
of it. Doubt is a crippling disease that can keep you from growing.

The start of the WNBA was a breath of fresh air. I would have a chance
to live in America and play in front of my family and friends. The WNBA is
a part of history as well as an excellent vehicle to wind down my career.

There are also a lot of other things I would like to do, and the WNBA/New York Liberty can provide those opportunities.

It's a great feeling to know that so many little girls are screaming for you and looking up to you. That is why I feel that it is my obligation to be a role model to many. Through my various experiences and talents I feel like I can reach young women who have gone through the things that I have.

My determination to succeed has caused me to sacrifice time with friends and family and brought about the isolation I suffered in Europe. The emotional lows such as losing a championship and discovering I needed to have arthroscopic surgery just as I was looking forward to a great season with the Libertys are just some of the obstacles I've had to face in my career.

The next chapter of my life is about creating the legacy that I want to leave behind. I want to touch the lives of as many little girls and people as possible. I want to be able to let them know that no matter how they look, no matter what other kids say about them, no matter what society tells them they can't do, there's absolutely nothing that can hold them back if they are willing to believe in themselves and persevere. I want to help them realize that they don't need to let insecurities create limitations in their minds. There's a little voice inside of each of us that's always talking to us—always urging us on to become the absolute best that we can be. It's high time that we all started listening to that voice.

Kym Hampton is a WNBA/New York Liberty player, who spent twelve years playing overseas and is pursuing a music, acting, and modeling career. Add motivational public speaking to her vitae, but Kym is mostly pursuing being real.

Your Soul's Sustenance

The Lord is no respecter of a person.

All these women have triumphed over tragedy and showed us how they've survived. We need to be able to recognize how faith brought them through their ordeals. We've created an exercise designed to do just that.

Climbing the Faith Tree

The faith tree is a drawing of a tree that allows you to see your own growth in faith. Draw a tree (it doesn't have to be perfect). On the branches leave blank spaces so you can fill in your trying times that faith has pulled you through.

Your Personal Book of Revelations

In addition to your faith tree, come up with a Faith Prayer, and after you say your Faith Prayer, write down what you fear and keep your Faith Prayer in mind as you write your fears down.

- Have you ever asked yourself why is this happening to me?
- Have you been a victim of some type of mental or physical abuse?
- Describe the incident.
- Have you healed?

You are never alone and you are never a victim, but always remember that God, faith and time can heal all wounds.

XIII

Better with Time

If you haven't got it, you can't show it. If you have got it, you can't hide it.
—Zora Neale Hurston

At a time when most people are picking out burial plots and revisiting wills, Saddie and Bessie were busy living life to the fullest. Anybody who would listen would get an earful from either or both of these spirited elders. Why not? They had always had something to say if someone wanted to listen and with 200+ combined years of experiences, they felt pretty entitled to make their opinions known.

When we don't revere our elders and seek out the stories and experiences that they have to impart to us, we doom ourselves to perpetually reinvent the wheel. As a matter of fact, one of the problems facing the African-American community as a whole is the fact that we have never been able to truly build on the successes of the preceding generation. In Reconstruction, in the 1870s, for example, there were more black Senators and businesses than there are today! Our collective history has not been the kind of smooth upward-sloping growth that other groups have experienced. Instead it has been one of never-ending ups and downs: Jim Crow followed Reconstruction; the collapse of black businesses followed the end of segregation; the self-absorption of the eighties and nineties and new millennium followed the Civil Rights Movement of the sixties.

Until we start to learn from our mistakes of the past, we will forever keep repeating the same patterns of self-defeating behavior both personally and collectively. A big part of this is not buying into the current American notion that basically shuns older people, but instead honoring our elders as the source of wisdom and realizing, as many a grandma has always said, "Honey, I ain't getting older, I'm just getting better." How many times have you told yourself: "If I only knew then what I know now!" The truth is we can use the experiences of our mothers and grandmothers to embrace the present and seize the future.

Why is it that most black women are afraid of getting old? A stigma is attached to growing in years. Some women believe that they will lose their good looks while others are afraid there will be no available men. Whatever you believe, you are facing the inevitable. If this is the case, why not age gracefully?

We were recently talking to a woman who "dreads turning forty." She thinks it's horrible, and that she's getting old as she sees wrinkles in her face. Candace and I are both in the thirtieth year of life and we both love it. We're embracing it. You should only get better with time. What would it mean if we got *worse* with time?

Women especially connect time with deterioration. That's because our society is so fixed on physical appearance that we believe that instead of growing in wisdom and knowledge and spirit with time, we look at ourselves as getting wrinkled and fatter. All the negative things aren't important. I would rather someone say, "Wow, look at her, she's seventy years old, look how much she knows!" than to have someone say, "Look at her, she's seventy years old and she looks like she's fifty because she's had ten plastic surgeries."

Black women age gracefully, and within that grace comes a maturity, wisdom, and knowledge that years and experience can bestow on you. Only after reaching their forties do some women really learn to love life. Some women maintain the same number of activities throughout their lives until they are in their eighties. The key to vitality in life is to keep active. *Essence* puts out an issue every year that features ten or so black women who are ranging from fifty to ninety and up, and none of them ever really looks her age. If you read their bios, it's not because they tried so hard to stay young, but because they are so much more at peace with themselves than when they were, say, twenty or thirty. There's a look of accomplishment in their eyes. There's a grace in their stature. And a peace of mind. Being able to have all those things is just a testimony to our ability to grow older and *better.*

On a recent trip a woman we met told us her secret to aging. "Mark my birthday with milestones. I am constantly reinventing myself. I think of all the things that I want to be, and I start encompassing them every day of my life. A daily plan for living and a design for life. So each birthday gives me a renewed sense of self and a spiritual shift which I look forward to every day of my life."

Not to mention as you get older, responsibilities of family and household decrease and you may be able to do things you could not do before. Walks in the parks, trips to a local casino, and bridge and card games with friends. Enjoy them all and heal the wounds so that you can make room for the wealth of life that awaits you.

What is different about Sadie and Bessie Delaney is that these sisters saw more for themselves than just talking to whoever might chance upon their doorstep. They happily participated in bringing their voices to the masses in a way that had never really been done before. Their book, with Amy Hill Hearth, *Having Our Say,* was a best-seller and received international acclaim. It influenced countless people to go realize the gems that were buried right under their own noses by talking to, interviewing, and recording their own elder family members. The impact that they had is something that would have been hard to imagine. There have been everything from TV specials to popular plays based on the Delaney sisters' lives. But by being open to new things and new opportunities, no matter how many trips they had taken around the sun, the Delaney sisters taught us all something valuable about our own potential.

In this part, wise veterans of life share stories that embody the true spirit of self and defy the concept of time. Like what we learned from the Delaney sisters, we can all learn from what they have to share with us.

62

Connecting Kinetically

Rosalyn McMillan

Love, in the sexual sense and taken as a whole, is the synthesis of desire and friendship in a relationship. After fourteen years of marriage to my second husband, J.D., whom I lovingly address as "my old man," I feel fortunate to be able to say that today the emotions between us are even stronger than ever.

In all fairness, please don't let me forget to add that he calls me his "old lady," and I love it! At age forty-five, nearly all my defenses are down. I'm beyond playing games. I'm serious. I expect the man I choose to spend the rest of my life with to be on the same wavelength. Let's dispense with the game-playing and move on to more important things. Namely, our future. Neither one of us is getting any younger.

Twenty-seven years ago, I made the naive mistake of spending more time trying to satisfy my mate sexually than I did building a bond of trust and friendship. However, the desire I feel for J.D. is more powerful because the love I feel for him is based on trust and friendship. It is enhanced further still by acknowledging our weaknesses to one another, and recognizing our united strengths.

I've been married twenty-six of the twenty-seven years I've been considered an adult—you know, working and paying taxes. Through triumphs and disappointments, I know that I'm a very strong woman. But in all fairness to my husband and myself, I feel I must acknowledge the elements out of my control that make me weak. Human. Lord knows, I want to be human. Not immune. And I also know that understanding who and what circumstances put me in a vulnerable position actually becomes a tool toward building my spiritual defenses, therefore, building my power.

J.D. is my primary weakness, as are most mates. I accept that.

J.D. is a very strong man. He's gentle. Loving. Sexy. He's my idea of the perfect man. But in the general sense. He's not a perfect individual, nor do I expect him to be. I want him to be a man who benefits from the love of a woman who strives to be as strong as he claims to be. Me. Strong. That's me. That's J.D.

I believe because of that, we connect. We challenge each other. It's primal. It's sexual. It's desire. It's love. And then again, it's more. More than either of us care to understand. Or even, at times, admit. But we know, we connect. We link together like the Eiffel Tower, like Niagara Falls, Siamese twins. It's a chain that doesn't end. We're steel. We're liquid. We're love, the strongest element of them all.

We understand each other's shortcomings. We accept them.

A few days ago, our dog, Kai, chewed through my old man's satellite cable wire. Lo and behold, my old man could not watch his beloved Western Channel. John Wayne, Gary Cooper, and Randolph Scott would not be entertaining my man in the ensuing weeks if something wasn't done soon. J.D. was pissed. He whipped Kai. But I could tell that Kai didn't understand why his master was mad at him. Kai couldn't know that I was pissed at his master for punishing him. Something had to be done.

While J.D. was away running errands, I took action.

"I need a repairman out at my home today," I said, not so calmly into the telephone receiver. "I'm willing to pay whatever it costs."

Watching the Western Channel, which runs twenty-four hours a day, is a small pleasure that my old man has been addicted to for fifteen years. Boy, am I glad it's not another woman! I surprised him by calling a satellite business and having the ripped-out wire repaired before he returned later that evening.

I couldn't wait for him to notice the repaired wire. He did, but it seemed insignificant. I was startled. My special gift that I had assumed would give him as much pleasure as I did went ignored. Instead, he prefaced his homecoming by telling me how hard he had been all night with his desire for me. My feelings were hurt. I felt that taking the time to do something small for him that I knew he enjoyed was more important than his sexual desire for me. It wasn't like this was the first time we'd made love. We were old pros at this. Almost ancient, in fact. I told him so. In doing that, I hurt him. He apologized for being so crass. That's the power of loving, and aging together. We're not ashamed to say, "Baby, I'm sorry, I wasn't thinking."

I melted. Forgave. I know he loves me. Needs me as I do him.

It's been a cycle between us, as I've learned from my friends that they experience as well. We argue. Make up. He wants to make love. I want to talk it out, work things out so that this problem doesn't come up again. We argue again over which way we're working things out. We come to a Mexican standoff. Neither one of us will budge. Again he wants to make love. I refuse. But feel weak, needy. I need him to show me that he still wants me, needs me, but not through sex.

My need for him while we're apart is almost unbearable. I don't know how much longer I can hold out. Somehow, I know I must. But as sure as there is a God above, he knows how much I can bear.

As a fragrant flower owes its brilliance to the nourishment which it draws from the earth's bosom, so do I compare my need to fuse together with my "old man." It's sublime in its expression. In both the physical and spiritual attraction between us, we are melded in a harmonious and indivisible whole. It's our own special kind of love that we understand affects both of us kinetically. A love that is worthy of the name, body and mind, heart and soul.

The great souls of all time, from Zarathustra and Jesus Christ to Voltaire and the leaders of thought today, have all been perfectly aware that love, no matter how sublime in its expression, has its root in the primitive physical instinct. That love in the primitive sense of the word is the sex instinct guided by the brain, that organ of the soul.

For sanity's sake, I know that I have to show my man that I'm strong. Not weak. But after days of not resolving our problems, I'm questioning how this argument began in the first place. Was it my fault? What did I do wrong? I began to make excuses for him. At this point my body is weak. We haven't made love in a week. I'm steadily weakening. I know he knows that I want him. Still, we haven't solved our initial problem. Should I give in? No. Because I know that my man loves a strong woman. Respects me when I'm strong. When I'm right. Knowing that he's wrong, but won't admit it.

I didn't understand the games men employ fifteen years ago. I do now. So I regroup and focus. Focus on positive things. I force myself to go to the movies. Watch comedies. Laugh. Forget about how much I need his closeness. How much I need my man. Temporarily the diversion works. I feel his eyes admiring my strength. Weakening to his relentless, endless power. We're on our way back to the way it was. The way it should be. The way it needs to be so that we both can respect each other once again.

Voltaire said it best: "Paradise is where I am," to which I might add, "Paradise is with you, my love."

Sometimes I wonder during the space of time that J.D. and I are apart if what I feel for him is as strong as I think it is. I have my doubts. But when I touch him, and he touches me, I know. It's still real. And his eyes tell me that all the emotion, all the love that I've felt and still feel, fills my heart once again. We reconnect, knowing that feelings that powerful could never diminish.

We never say that we're both checking on our power. He needs to know how strong his power is over me. I need to know how powerful my power still is over him. In a 3D kind of motion, we slowly move back toward that synergism we feel each time we reconnect. Sending a soft shiver through me, like a magic cloud challenging my imagination, the moment he touches me. Even now, I can't begin to understand how he does it.

Another part of me doesn't care to understand, or know why. I only know I need him. Now, more than ever.

Thereby, we must connect, to reestablish our power.

In the Bible, love is mentioned only a few times in the story of Rachel and Jacob. However, sex is continually mentioned throughout the text. Even in their wonderful love story in which Jacob worked many years to win his beloved Rachel, desire was more important than love in the highest sense of the term. Another example is in Solomon's Song of Songs: The beloved one's body, her eyes, her perfume, her voice, her complexion, and the taste of her are described in the minutest of detail so that all of the senses share equally in exposing her overall desire. From that passage I understood the rich sensuality that thrills the entire body and senses, and is not limited to the genital organs.

I've cried. Read my Bible as God wants me to. Still, I'm only partially comforted. Forgive me, Lord, I know that God made man a little lower than the angels. But forgive me once more in knowing that I'm still here on earth. I look forward to making that trip toward heaven one day. But not now. Today, I'm human. I'm flesh. I desire. I need. I need J.D.

No one can make me feel the way my man does. Nor do I want any man to. I only want the man I love. I don't need a young man screwing me every day, all night long. I need a man that knows my body—can love my body well in a short period of time so that we can hug, snuggle, go to sleep, wake up, kiss, snuggle, go back to sleep, and caress each other throughout the night. We do that from maturity, not sexual depravity, or a need to be some young thing that we know we're not.

J.D.

J.D. Where are you? Don't you realize how much we've grown together? Aged together. Gained weight together. Lost weight together. Understood one another. Disagreed with one another. Made unbelievable love. Felt unbelievable love toward one another without making love. I can look at him. He can look at me, and we both know, there's no one else for either of us.

I'm not worried about a twenty-two-year-old young thing taking my man. Because she'll never know him. Never know his needs, his body that seventeen years have taught me to learn. Understand. Implement my moves that no one but me can duplicate. No. A twenty-two-year-old young thing can't compete with that.

And to tell you the truth, my man knows he can't keep a twenty-two-year-old either. He might make me try to think he can. But we both know better. He wants me to know that he's still viable, exciting, sexy. That young women still appreciate him. I know that. But I also have to let him know that young men find me exciting and attractive as well.

So what do we do? We take it all in stride. Smile. Appreciate each other more. Love each other more. Because we both know if we didn't love each other, we wouldn't be together. We'd be pretending that we were both these immature people that needed other people to validate us. Make us feel that we're not getting older. Weren't out of the loop.

What's the point? Forty-five feels great to me. My old man says that age fifty-three feels equally good to him. We don't have to prove anything to anybody. All we need to do is make each other feel good. Try different methods of showing one another how much we're willing to sacrifice to show that we appreciate getting older, maturing. Enjoying mature loving that determines our intellectual possibilities and the formation of our ideals.

It's over. We reconnect. Our love is stronger than ever. I feel like God has answered all of my prayers. I can identify with paradise with a loved one as does Voltaire. But my strongest belief is in a man that I feel kinetically associated to. Someone special who also identifies with heat.

Zarathustra.

Like the fire worshiper, Zarathustra, my sacred fire burns continuously by the altar of our marriage vows, our love, and burns brighter each time we connect, kinetically.

I already knew that J.D. is and will always be my most ardent lover. What continues to astound me is that he is, most certainly, my dearest friend.

Rosalyn McMillan is the best-selling author of *Knowing, One Better* and *Blue Collar Blues* and her latest best-seller *The Flip Side of Sin*. She is currently working on her latest novel.

63

Your Silver Crown

Phyllis Maria Beech

Never! Never give up your dream! I was married at eighteen, before the baby came—you see in the early fifties "You get pregnant . . . you get married." They didn't care how bright your future could be. It was okay by me because I was in L-O-V-E! But ten years later, with three children, a house, rental property, and a good job, I could not take the *beatings* anymore! The last straw came when he not only beat me, but also told my son when he tried to stop him from hitting me that, "You saved your mother's life." He then proceeded to throw all of my clothes in the swimming pool—when I say all, I mean all . . . my dresser drawers were on the diving board! My son's stomach was bothering him and I took him to the doctor. We found out that he had an ulcer at seven years old! That was it!

My grandmother raised me, and I received spiritual and character values from this wise old woman. I had an "illustrious" childhood for middle-class blacks, which included my own radio show. I also wrote for the school newspaper and the citywide African-American newspaper. If that was not enough, I was a Girl Judge at my high school, was active in my church youth group, and had about 150 personal friends. I was even awarded a scholarship to Howard University. Getting pregnant was quite a blow to everybody and especially to my future of becoming a lawyer.

After I went to divorce court, I took my children now ages one, seven, and ten from California to Michigan, where my mother and sister lived. I figured that if I divorced their father, the children should not be affected financially from the decision I made. That included having their own room and going to private school. So I proceeded to go to the University of Michigan and Michigan State at the same time. Driving 100 miles a day because I was on a mission. I had to get my degrees, so I could take my children back to California and get a good job. I did, finishing a four-year degree program in two and a half years. The University of Michigan mailed me my degree. I didn't even wait to have it presented at graduation.

I returned to California and got a job—not making what I thought I was worth, but my grandmother always said, "It's not what you make, it's what you do with what you make." For the next few years it was my kids, my grandmother, and their father's parents and me. My two boys were heavy into their music and stopped going to Catholic school but my daughter continued. After attending the University of Southern California Graduate School, I was accepted into law school. Finally I was going to get a chance to fulfill my dream. It was the early eighties, and I was a single mother raising three children, working full-time, and going to law school at night. I'm afraid I was a victim to the supermom syndrome. But then, I was no different from the strong black women who have always juggled three or four different things at a time. I think the term is multitasked individual.

After one year, I couldn't afford to pay for my tuition and books as well as my daughter's. I felt that she had had the basics from her years of Catholic schooling, so I put her in public school. It was a disastrous choice. At the end of the first semester, I found out that she was so scared to go to class she decided not to go at all, although she left home every day for school. Finding a new school for her was an uphill battle since most private schools in California adhere to a strict policy of not registering students mid-school year. Fate was kind, and through a family friend I stumbled upon a small finishing school for girls in Compton, California, run by Sisters of the Holy Family.

The name of the school was Regina Caeli High School. During the course of the first semester there, my daughter was doing some research for a classroom writing assignment, and of course, Mommy was helping. We discovered the rich history of the Sisters of the Holy Family and their foundress, Henriette De Lille. They were founded in New Orleans in 1842. This was in 1981 and they were still flourishing. History reflected that Henriette chose not to follow the tradition and lifestyle set for Creoles at that time, but rather chose to follow her heart. I learned of the struggles that these free women of color went through at a time when African-Americans were not even considered people—but property! Contrary to the standards of the time, they taught slave children to read, cared for the elderly and sick, and were astute businesswomen, raising money and buying land and houses and building schools throughout Louisiana, Texas, British Honduras, and Kenya. Not to mention the thousands of lives they touched. The Sisters of the Holy Family taught some of the most notable African-Americans in our country.

This story had to be told. Everyone in America must know and never forget about this woman. What an inspiration! All we ever hear about is slavery, and there is nothing wrong with that. If you don't know where you have been, you can't know where you're going. The institution of slavery we must never forget. Just like we can't forget the Holocaust. But there were a lot of positive and successful things that were happening during that period in the lives of African-Americans and we also need to know that as well. The yearning to tell the story began in the pit of my stomach and continues today.

I am thankful for a wonderful daughter, Jaynesa; a successful son-in-law, Demmette Guidry, who is a senior vice president of urban music for Columbia Records–New York office; and three beautiful grandchildren. Through them and the Sisters of the Holy Family, I was able to build my self-esteem and deepen my pride in being a black woman in America.

Now the lines of fate took a twist and I had an opportunity to visit the Motherhouse (convent) of the Sisters of the Holy Family in New Orleans. What an awesome experience! I walked the grounds, which were immaculate and serene. It was during the visit that I learned that there was a strong (ten-year) movement to canonize Mother Henriette. That would make her the first African-American woman to receive sainthood. I cannot even describe the excitement that surged through my body. I came home asking myself what I could do to help the cause. Make Mother Henriette a household name, make her famous! This would be the most positive thing that I could contribute toward her journey to sainthood.

I began writing, and by Christmas 1997, I sent a treatment to Vanessa Williams, who I had already concluded was perfect to play the role of Mother Henriette. This world is based on relationships. It was through my oldest son, Kipper Jones (an award-winning songwriter and producer who wrote "Right Stuff" and "Comfort Zone"), that I was able to contact Vanessa Williams. I had always admired her enormous talent but most of all her example of what an African-American ex-single mother can accomplish regardless of the adversities.

Vanessa Williams to me represents a woman with the same drive, beauty, and inner strength and courage as Henriette De Lille. Most importantly, she was a daughter of the Catholic Church. Vanessa read it, loved it, and the rest, as they say, was history.

The Courage to Love is the story of Henriette De Lille, the foundress of the Sisters of the Holy Family. It is a movie that has been developed by Lifetime Network. The executive producers are Vanessa Williams, Emily Gerson Saines, and Ron Ziskin. I am credited as the associate producer. According to my youngest son, Matthew Jones (CEO of Matty J. Co.), this is your "first but not your last film."

My message to all women over fifty is never give up on your dream. I don't care what! It doesn't matter that the kids are grown. I know you are feeling empty, thinking that you've done your job and now there is nothing left to do but retire. Absolutely not! You've always been there for everyone else. Well, now is your time! Precisely because of all the things that you've been through, you have a story to tell and nobody can tell it like you can. Write it down. It may be slow at first, but keep it up. The words will come. Promise yourself that every morning when you get up, you'll write something.

What about labor pains or how scared you were when you started your first job or describe the feeling you had when you met Mr. Right, or better yet, what did your grandmother tell you about life and the hard times she had? Ask yourself the four W's: Who am I? What made me what I am today? When did my family move to where they are now? Where did I really come from? It is so hard to do real research on "us" because there is so little written down. We have got to stop this cycle, and sharing our wisdom and telling about families in writing are a beginning.

Many media avenues are open to black women now. If you can't find one, make your own. You raised children; went to PTA meetings and basketball or football games; were active in church, cultural organizations, and sororities; and went to school. You worked or you were a housewife—maybe even a single parent. Some of us were all at the same time. You are the original superwoman.

What do you mean you have nothing to say? What does the Bible say? It is written and you have to write it! It's your story and can't nobody tell it like you can. At 100 years old, the Delaney sisters had their say; at 50-plus I am having mine.

Phyllis Maria Beech is a film developer, producer, writer, and one of the original superwomen.

64

As I Tend My Garden

Lady Bird Strickland

As I tend my garden in my cottage-style home in a suburb of Philadelphia, I think of all that I have achieved. I have been called a Renaissance woman, but I tend to differ on that. People have told me that I have the power to heal through the arts—that lost souls find a conscience through my work. And it has been a blessing. My work has afforded me the opportunity to travel the world and meet with some of the most powerful leaders in the world.

My paintings bring joy to many and find themselves in the homes of some of the most affluent people in the country. But as I tend my garden, there's nothing I cherish more than my relationship with God. He is my shepherd and guide. Often in tumultuous times, He was the backbone I needed to get through. It was important for me to succeed because I truly believed that, in doing so, I would prove that black women have countless talents. I had to be a renegade and to do it through art.

My career began in Georgia in 1929. I painted to add color to my life and bring joy to others. In 1941 I moved to New York to help my older sister care for her children. I attended Wadleigh High School, majoring in costume design and fine arts. My art teacher was so impressed with my paintings that she entered them in the R. H. Macy's Scholastic Achievements Contest. It took my breath away when I won first prize over a thousand high school students and my paintings were bought by two Broadway producers.

I received a scholarship to Pratt Institute along with a gold and silver medal. During my tenure at Pratt I focused on vivid colors and honed my skills. During my time at Pratt things became hard so I left to earn a living. I worked feverishly for months, producing paintings that I could sell for money. I began getting write-ups in the *Daily News, Herald Tribune, New York Post,* and *Amsterdam News.*

With all of my accolades, I was still a black woman. There were so few openings in those days because there was much less acceptance of blacks as artists. I had to resort to painting neckties in a window on Broadway. But I made it work for me, and from there people from around the world were exposed to my work.

I also worked on executing the ultraviolet animated three-dimensional advertising billboards on the New Jersey Turnpike and for the New York subway station at Times Square, where my work appeared for over ten years.

Although I worked downtown, I was a constant on the scene in Harlem. Some of my work reflects a social conscience. I wanted people to see my art through another person's perception. I never forget the people whence I came. I focused paintings on the aspects of life during the periods of slavery, Harlem during the 1940s and scenes of the Civil Rights Movement. I wanted my paintings to tell a story, I refused to be pigeonholed for any reason, commercial or otherwise.

My paintings are a testimony to my spirit and my insistence on creating a way for other black artists. So as I tend to my garden on this bright sunny day, my advice is this: If you believe in what you are doing and you have a gift from God, share it because you will be building a foundation for many generations of women to come. Believe me when I tell you that, standing in this garden, it only gets better.

Lady Bird Strickland is an artist in semi-retirement and is a "seasoned" citizen living in a suburb of Philadelphia. She tends to her garden daily.

65

I Know Now

Marie B.

"Chicago, Chicago, my kind of town." That familiar Frank Sinatra tune often plays in my head as I drive along Lake Shore Drive. Being a new resident of Chicago, I am still in awe every time I pass Lake Michigan on my way home. Fortunately for me, I was able to find a wonderful two-bedroom brownstone on the north side of town. I really love my apartment despite the fact that there is no designated parking available. As I circle in the evenings, trying to locate a spot to park, I keep reminding myself of how much I love the place. My landlord is great. She lives right next door and has welcomed me to the neighborhood as if I were family.

My divorce is finally final. Sometimes I wonder if I was ever really married since the divorce ended with so much ugliness. I am single now and life looks completely different.

I met my husband many years ago while he was relocating in my hometown. Despite a warning from his mother about the "women of D.C.," he was very much on the scene trying to find his special someone, or *someones* in his case.

Our meeting was quite by accident. A friend of mine had just had a major blowout with her boyfriend and needed to get out for a while. I think she just did not want to be there when the phone rang. This was before Caller ID. She called and asked if I wanted to get out for the evening with her to check out a new club located in downtown Washington. I didn't really feel up to it, but I wasn't doing anything else, so I decided to throw on my standard "go out" black dress, jump into some bareback black shoes, put on some lipstick, and hit the road.

The radio personalities had been promoting this place for weeks, and it was being billed as the "happening place to be." When we arrived, we discovered that it was "happening" for the same people we saw everyplace else we ever went. Same old brothers lining the walls, same old sisters lining the dance floor. Linda and I just decided to take a seat at the tables and watch the sights.

We were sitting there only about twenty minutes when a gentleman came over to ask me to dance. He was actually coming to ask Linda to dance, but turned for some reason and asked me. At first glimpse, I almost said, "No," because the brother was not really my type. He did wear glasses and I was digging that. I'm not sure whether it was in my best interest or not, but in those days I seemed to be attracted to the cooler gents. This guy was quite a switch.

We hit the dance floor with vengeance, or shall I say, I did. He was not a good dancer at all. I'm not sure how many times he stepped on my toes. I think I lost track. After dancing a few songs, we decided to step outside for a little conversation. I cannot even remember what we were talking about; all I can remember is grinning so much that my cheeks were hurting. A year later we were married.

When we married, my spouse made $18,000 and drove a Chrysler Horizon. Who would have thought that he would have soared up the corporate ladder as quickly as he did? At the time of our divorce he was well into six figures. But not without a price. Our family moved five different times. Our daughter never went to the same school two years in a row during her elementary years. We had no choice because in order to get the promotion, he always had to move. Chasing the dollar can be dangerous. We made the money, but we lost our family.

At the age of twenty our daughter carries the scars of our mistakes. I own that, but my spouse never did. His feeling was that we provided the very best of everything for her, "there is no reason that she should be having problems." Definite denial on his part. The reality is that we lived our lives for ourselves, forgetting to sacrifice for her. Yes, we did provide her with the best, but at what cost? She lived in absolutely the best houses, but in all-white neighborhoods, in all-white schools, with a father who seemed to forget his race a long time ago. It seemed to me that his idea of beauty was "light bright or damn near white." Perhaps that would explain his choice in a white woman today.

Despite the obvious signs of my daughter's distress, and her struggle to fit into a white society that was not accepting of her on her terms, I still chose to follow my husband. Why I did not jump ship and save her a long time ago, I cannot answer. Perhaps it was fear. And perhaps I believed my husband was as committed to our family as I was. I thought it would all work out.

Rebellion is an interesting thing. I am not sure that my daughter understood why she was rebelling. I think the root of it all was chronic unhappiness. The only problem was, she never told us what really was going on in her head. We just had to try to piece it all together.

I have spent many years attempting to figure it all out. I've spent many years regretting my decisions of life. Unfortunately, my spouse was not one to discuss it with. He had problems of his own that he was in denial about, so how could I expect him to help me with her? He was carrying so much stuff.

Looking back, I wonder if we should have ever married? I did not have the best relationship with my father growing up, and no relationship with my only sister. I was insecure and unsure about who I was and who I wanted to be. I suffered with codependency. I thought I could save the world and I was everyone's shoulder to cry on. The problem was I made everyone else's problems my priority and forgot to make *myself* a priority. The world did not provide a safety net for me and I have fallen many times as a result of my own decisions.

As for my spouse, he suffered from chronic denial. Denial about everything related to him. He was great, however, at analyzing others.

My husband never really accepted himself. He was never comfortable with his size or his race. The problem was he lived a life of façade, trying always to convince the world that nothing bothered him and that he was comfortable with himself. He had a heart, but never really wanted the world to realize that, despite growing up in Detroit, he somehow adopted a "white is right" mentality.

My husband and his sister never got along once they reached adulthood. He never felt she was good enough or successful enough for him to be bothered. It did not seem to matter to him that she lost her kidney and had to have a transplant at a very early age, or that she was disabled from her job before the age of thirty. For some reason, he had no patience or tolerance for her. The fact that she and I were like blood sisters never really set well with him either. I cannot tell you the number of arguments and fights we had around her. I'd struggle to be there for her, and he would fight me every step of the way. There were many times that I, totally disregarding his opinion, did what I thought was right in terms of helping her. Not only her, but my in-laws as well, whom I grew to love as parents.

As in the case with most parents, my in-laws did all that they could for my sister-in-law, their daughter-in-law. She was not always the easiest person to deal with, and often caused quite an uproar wherever she went; nonetheless, through it all, to their credit, they hung in there. My husband never agreed with their approach and it manifested itself in the raising of our daughter. Everything that he saw them do in relation to his sister, he did not do with our daughter. In many ways our daughter suffered the consequences for what he felt his sister should have received from his parents.

I have been struggling with my daughter for many years now. She has been involved in almost everything imaginable, from gang affiliation to shoplifting. She has never worked to her potential, nor cared to identify exactly what her potential was. I own the fact that I parented her through fear. At every turn I was afraid of what was next. I loved her like my next breath and did whatever it took to clear the way for her every time she got into trouble. It didn't matter to me—if she was in danger or if she needed me, I did whatever it took. Even when it was destroying me physically, mentally, and financially. I suppose it is no wonder that she thinks the world owes her something.

Our family is now divorced. My children live separate from each other, as well as from me. I have landed alone in Chicago facing new challenges. When I look back over the years, I foolishly ask myself how I ever made it through. The reality is that I followed a man and his career for years, sacrificing my own life believing that he loved me. I have a daughter that I have struggled with for years and still continue to. I have a son who is now denied his family unit in its original form, and financially I am living at a third of what our income used to be. My debt is great and no money is in sight.

Having gone through this and much more, I know that the key word is "through." I have made it *through*. The road has been rough and there has not been much rest, but God has blessed me at every turn. He has blessed me in the good times and He has blessed me in the horrible times. He has blessed me with experience, knowledge, insight, and battle scars. He has been my energy. There were days when I had no more than a nickel in my pocket, but I made it. There were days when I did not know where I was going to live or what I was going to drive, but I made it.

The promise is real!! My rebirth has been better than my life before. God has surrounded me with people who have helped me every step of the way. It seemed that every time I needed something, or was stuck, there was someone already in place to lead me out. A year ago, I started a new position within a company that I have been with for over seven years. Finally I'm rebuilding with interest all that I lost. I am enjoying my relationship with my children and they are enjoying their relationship with me. We share joint custody of our son; however, our son made the decision to stay with his father the majority of the time because of his involvement with sports. It wasn't any easy decision for him and it was tough on me too. But God has blessed me to understand my son and what he needs. He and I are doing great. My daughter is living on her own and struggling daily, but these are her training times and I am strong enough now to let her go through them. In addition to all these blessings, God has given me a bonus. He has blessed me with a companion tailor-made for me. My grandmother used to say, stay away from a relationship that is unevenly yoked. Of course, I paid no attention to her and chalked her up to babble. But now I'm evenly yoked, and it feels damn good. He offers love. I trust him and he walks in truth and spirituality. He is secure enough in himself to allow me to be myself. He is smart and full of conversation. We laugh together and share together; he is my friend. We appreciate each other.

How I made it through is simple. I held on to the promise of our eternal Father every step of the way. When I got off course, there were those around me who reminded me of faith. Faith was my secret weapon.

Marie B. has relocated out of Chicago. She continues to benefit from her life lessons, paving the way for a brighter future. Her dream is to break into the speaker circuit and hopes of encouraging others.

66

The Rug Pulled Out from under Me

Jerry Lucas

It was May 1977. That morning I left my home knowing I would not be returning to my children anytime soon. As I drove myself to the courthouse, I asked myself, What was I going to do? How was I going to survive? This was, and at times still is, the story of my life. But I knew that whatever happened, until I returned to my family, I was going to survive and be better for it. There was no question about that because that's the way it's always been.

I told myself, You can do this, you've been dealt worse hands than this before and still came out on top. I grew up very poor in the projects of Newark. But I always tried to make something of myself. I went out on my own at eighteen and for a time was homeless and jobless. Now, seven years later I was driving a 1976 white custom-made Lincoln Continental with a lipstick red interior and sunroof. I thought about how far I had come. I lived in one of the nicest houses on my block—complete with an in-ground heated pool—paid for in full. I had been a poor uneducated black ghetto girl who grew up to be a successful businesswoman, and at the tender age of twenty-six I owned mink coats, cars, property, several businesses, and managed a recording group who had at least two Top Ten hits, according to *Billboard* magazine.

Ain't nothing to it but to do it, I told myself as I drove along. I didn't want to think about the shame I was feeling or that I couldn't bring myself to tell my family where I was going. Just do it, I said to myself. All of my so-called friends told me I was worrying over nothing.

They know you weren't involved, they said. But from the beginning I knew, I just had that feeling—that same feeling that I got every time something bad was going to happen. That's how I felt that morning on my drive to the courthouse to be sentenced for conspiracy to violate the narcotic laws of the state of New Jersey.

I tried not to worry too much because at the time I had the utmost respect for the justice system. I knew they couldn't prove that I was involved—because I wasn't—so there was nothing they could do to me. I didn't even know how drugs looked, had never used any, nor had I ever sold or exchanged drugs.

I found myself in criminal court in front of the Honorable Judge Ralph Fussco. He was the only judge that I had ever stood in front of in my entire life. Everyone said he was tough and gave out his sentences by the clock on the wall; if the minute hand happened to be on the half-hour, you were going to get thirty years in jail. I was sentenced to eight to ten years to be served in Clinton State Prison. I was immediately handcuffed and whisked off to serve time in a maximum-security prison with such people as Joanne Chasimar, among others.

I had been arrested and tried with over thirty other individuals, most of whom were my husband's family. This was one of the largest drug busts at the time. Everyone had been given an opportunity to plea-bargain except for me. I was told later that I was not offered a plea because I was being used as a pawn to get my husband to plead guilty or to bargain. My husband was sentenced in three different states to serve thirty-seven years concurrently.

At the time my two children were ages five and seven, and it broke my heart to leave them because I had never been separated from them. In addition, I was taking care of my brother, four sisters, and my mother. I only saw my children once during my incarceration because it was too painful to see them leave and not be able to go home with them. I rarely called because I didn't know how to tell them that I wouldn't be coming home. I tried never to lie to my children, or to anyone for that matter. I find it easier to tell the truth or say nothing at all. The humiliation and embarrassment of being incarcerated was like nothing I have ever experienced before or since. In prison, I was considered less than nothing to those who were in charge of running the institution. They told me when and how to do everything. During that time I made up my mind to learn not to be so trusting or allow myself to be used, misused, and abused ever again. I made up my mind that I would not be ashamed of my past, present, or future because of what society dictated. Come hell or high water, I was no longer going to go along with the flow if it wasn't flowing my way.

After serving two years in prison, I was released on parole. I had lost everything, including my home and my businesses. I was broke, homeless, afraid, and ashamed. But I had a newfound courage and faith that nothing but death could stop me from succeeding and that it was all in the hands of the Lord. I had to find a new direction and dissociate myself from the past. In essence, I had to recreate myself. It's taken me years to stop asking, "Why me?" But I've learned to go with the grace of God in whatever I do.

Starting over again wasn't easy. I didn't even know how to take a bus. I found jobs that at one time I would have considered beneath me, but I worked them, including stints at McDonald's, telemarketing, and customer service. Sometimes I worked two or three jobs at a time just to make ends meet. I worked twelve to eighteen hours a day, six days a week, and sometimes on Sunday.

I went to jail for my first offense; I never even had a traffic ticket. Conspiracy is what they get you on when they can't prove anything else against you, and most of what was said in court was untrue. At times I feel sad about the whole thing because, if they could do that to me, they could do it to anyone. In fact, I am fearful to speak out about it even after all these years because they could still come after me now for any reason. Sometimes I am so afraid that I can't leave my home because who knows if it could happen again.

But now, more than twenty years after my world came crashing down around me, I am the president of my own real estate firm. I've raised my children to be productive human beings, and my husband and I are still together and have rebuilt a new life for ourselves. In spite of it all, I would not have changed a thing, because without all the trials and tribulations, I would not be able to appreciate the life I have. Now I consider myself a Sophisticated Lady, which I define as someone who is able to carry or present herself in any situation without feeling as if she needs to change herself to fit in. I am the same person I was when I was in jail as I am with the executives I now deal with. I am myself no matter who I am with. Every woman can be a Sophisticated Lady, but it just takes some of us longer to realize it than others.

Jerry Lucas has decided to write a book on her experiences. Writing poetry and motivating others is her passion. She also hopes that she will be able to help others that have traveled similar paths.

Your Soul's Sustenance

We all get better with time. We need to embrace the knowledge and wisdom that comes with age instead of fearing the worst. We need to see ourselves as we see our grandmothers. Maybe you don't know your grandmother, but you can imagine her strength, poise, dignity, and grace. Picture yourself as her. Know that as your midlife right of passage, you too will receive all the blessings of age and time.

Work toward enhancing your personality every day. Opportunities sometimes only knock once. Open the door and embrace it, because procrastination can leave you stranded. Never retire, but use the time to find a newfound love, hobby, or desire. Travel and take a grandchild or a young person along because true immortality occurs only when your legacy lives within others.

Your Personal Book of Revelations

Whether you are young or old, you need to take stock in what you have experienced thus far in life. Explore your answers to these questions.

- Reflect on the greatest moments of your life.
- Describe the greatest challenges.
- Are you comfortable with who you are?
- Do you have any regrets in your life?
- What type of person would you like to become?

Time is an old friend just waiting for you to feel right at home.

XIV

Amazing Grace

I am not going to die, I'm going home like a shooting star.
—Sojourner Truth

Why don't people celebrate someone's life when they die? The answer, although difficult to accept, is "because we're selfish." A lot of times when we grieve, we're not grieving for the person, we're grieving for ourselves. We're not thinking of the good times, we're thinking of them being gone, we're thinking of the void. How will we go on? Rarely does someone grieve for the pain of that person, because the pain is over. The pain isn't there to grieve for. We grieve for ourselves because that person was such an intricate part of our lives or touched our lives in such a way that we don't know how we're going to go on without them. We're not celebrating their lives because we don't know what we're going to do with our own now.

We will all bury loved ones if we're fortunate enough to live long lives. Death is life. And instead of denying it, ignoring it, and being afraid of it, we should learn to look at death as the transition from one plane of existence to another.

We get attached to physical people in our lives—and in the process often neglect the spirit which is the true core of the person. So when the physical body is gone, we despair. We think our loved ones, our friends and family, are no longer with us. But when we truly realize that the most important part of the people we love is not their physical bodies—their arms, legs, skin, and hair—but their spirits, we will realize that the spirits of those we love are just as with us in death as they were in life.

Even when we say to ourselves that death is more of a passage of spirit from one realm to the next, preparation for this final rite of passage is painful for those of us left behind.

The essays in this, the final part, will help change that perception of death and help us to see that the spirits of our loved ones continue to live and grow inside us. These women who have experienced saying good-bye to that special someone—and have grown because of it—share their insights.

67

Young, Gifted, and Dying

Michelle L. Buckley

Breast cancer is contagious. Underwire bras cause breast cancer. Small-breasted women can't get breast cancer. Only white women get breast cancer. Only women with a family history of breast cancer will get it. Only women who smoke will get breast cancer. Only women with known risk factors get breast cancer. These are the myths of breast cancer. I know the realities of it because my best friend of fifteen years died from it at the age of thirty.

The anger, grief, pain, and disappointment of losing my best "you go, girl" friend to breast cancer is something I often battle. It's something many of us battle because the truth of the matter is that more than five thousand African-American women die of breast cancer each year. Black women are 29 percent more likely to die from breast cancer than white women because we are more frequently diagnosed with cancer in its advanced stages. By the age of forty, 1 in every 212 women get breast cancer, and the under-forty incidence is even higher for black women. *Pretty eye-opening statistics, huh?*

Maybe it was my best friend's I'm-too-young-to-have-a-life-threatening-illness mentality or her fear of hearing the words *breast* and *cancer* in the same sentence that kept her from picking up the phone to have herself checked out after discovering the lump in her breast. Perhaps she feared the "psychology of breast cancer," which dictates that a woman is considered subpar if there is something "wrong" with her physical endowments. Because whether we want to admit it or not, society's fixation with the female breast has conditioned us to believe that we're not real women if our breasts are less than "perfect"—a perfection that's determined by a paternalistic society's unrealistic and unhealthy standards and expectations.

But I cannot tell a lie. Because of this "perfect" ideal, I've abused my breasts, and unfortunately, I'm not alone. Our nation's collective breasts have been padded, lifted, powdered, pushed up, pushed out, contoured, shaped, separated, supported, minimized, and maximized. Some have even been permanently pierced, tucked, liposucked, reduced, and enlarged. Often, a woman's self-esteem is intrinsically interwoven with the cells that make up this, the world's most overexposed (and I mean that literally) mammary gland.

It has taken me a while to realize it, but I now know that my self-worth cannot be measured by my cup size. Daily, I'm reminded that my cups runneth over. The wisdom, strength, and spirit I possess and inherited from my ancestors cannot be restrained by a thin, flimsy piece of lace material. My values, ideals, and morals cannot be held up by underwire or by straps— spaghetti, camisole, crisscrossed, or otherwise. And the sooner my sister friends and brother friends—black, white, and other—realize this, the better off we'll all be.

But until then, one thing is certain . . . as a society we will continue to worship breasts and why shouldn't we? Breasts can reduce men to blubbering idiots and make them do mind-numbing, idiotic things. Breasts sell products, they sustain life and quiet babies, and they can inspire envy in the most confidant of women.

Having to live without them is a fate no woman wants to face. But since one out of every nine women will develop breast cancer during her lifetime, it's a fate many of us will have to deal with. Facing this fate with dignity, integrity, and courage, as my best friend did, is something all women should aspire to.

When my friend first learned about her cancer in her mid-twenties, we were both card-carrying members of the "I'm Young, Gifted, Black, and Ready to Conquer the World" Club. And for us, membership had its privileges. To be young, gifted, and black meant we were privileged to dream of bright tomorrows. To be young, gifted, and black meant the world was an endless oasis of opportunities and possibilities. To be young, gifted, and black meant we faced each day with a fortitude of will and an abundance of love, emotion, spirit, and imagination.

Like most African-American women our age, we were busy with careers, relationships, and self-discovery. Death and cancer were not in the realm of our possibilities. Her life, our lives, were all planned out. Ours were to be long lives that consisted of perfect jobs, perfect husbands, perfect families, nice digs, and fabulous write-home-to-mama vacations, birthdays, and anniversaries. There was no room in the picture for cancer. But as the saying goes: "Life is what happens while you're busy making other plans," and with time, the truth behind this maxim became painfully obvious.

I really don't remember how my best friend and I met; I only know that for fifteen years, she was a constant in my life. She was a beautiful, smart, warm, and compassionate person who was known for her wit, intelligence, and ability to make men fall in love with her, seemingly forever. She had the sensitive heart of a poet and the creative eye of an artist. She was the quintessential girl, a true diva. She was sophisticated, independent, and honest, and her zeal for life was contagious. She liked gardening, old school R & B, reading, writing poetry, sewing, cooking, and nurturing. She was soft-spoken, yet she didn't allow people to take advantage of her (she'd curse you in a hot second if you even tried).

She was respectful of everyone and extremely close to the elder women in her family. She was my biggest fan and I was hers, and although she never knew it, she saved my life on several occasions. She was the one person I could turn to and talk about anything with. We took in each other's pains, triumphs, and loves as easily as others breathe in the same air. She wasn't perfect, but who among us is? Like the rest of us, she had her faults, her fears, her foibles.

As far as faults, fears, and foibles go, I had my fair share upon learning of my friend's diagnosis. There is something about illness and death that discombobulates even the most stalwart of us. It can reduce the strongest of us to tears and encourage within us denial mongering and varied degrees of dementia.

Unfortunately, I suffered from all of the above. There were times when I didn't know if I was coming or going. There were times when I admit I was a sometimes friend. Sometimes I feared calling my friend, afraid that she would want to talk about her illness and I wouldn't say the "right" things. Sometimes I'd call and burst into tears and *she'd* end up comforting *me*. Sometimes I'd call and I'd have a million and one questions but she wouldn't want to talk at all about her illness, preferring instead to talk about mundane things. Preferring instead to pretend that her illness didn't exist.

I later learned that pretending an illness doesn't exist is a common defense mechanism. Many people with cancer vow to lead as normal lives as possible, and while they fight their battle with every ounce of their being, they refuse to let it consume their lives and become the very definition of who they are. My best friend once told me that, around people she didn't know, she could pretend that the cancer wasn't ravaging her insides, devouring her cells, her body, her soul, her spirit. To the outside world, she appeared to be full of life and vigor while inside she was tired, always physically tired.

There were those in the medical profession who were kind, caring, and concerned beyond belief for my friend—like the doctor who repeatedly called her and her mother at home, trying to convince them that a radical mastectomy would be a better course of treatment than the lumpectomy coupled with chemotherapy option she'd chosen.

Unfortunately, in contrast, incidents of insensitivity ran rampant (like the disease inside her body) during the course of my best friend's bout with cancer. Chief offenders included indifferent seen-it-all doctors and nurses, lousy boyfriends, concerned friends, and Bible-toting, Gospel-quoting do-gooders. Doctors and nurses topped the insensitivity list. My friend once told me about overhearing a nurse tell another nurse that there was a "breast lump in the examining room." Upon hearing this, I couldn't believe it. *Had the medical world's heart stopped beating? Stopped feeling?* To hear that my friend had been reduced to a breast lump enraged me. She also had two arms, two legs, a head, and a generous heart.

Insensitivity didn't stop with the medical profession. People said things to my friend as if their brains and tongues weren't connected through their brain stems. Friends called to *"see if she was still alive,"* some bragged about the fact that there was *"nothing in their lives that they couldn't handle,"* and others told her she was ill because *"God was trying to teach her a lesson"* for some unforgivable, nonexistent sins. Still others called to tell her they were *"thinking of her"* and *"hoped she'd get well soon"*—both overused, meaningless phrases like the ubiquitous *"2-good-2-B-4-gotten"* nonsense people who didn't know you well scribbled illegibly in the back of your junior high and high school yearbooks.

Through it all, I believe it was my friend's faith in God that helped her get through the tough times. She didn't mope around acting as if the world owed her something. "Handing it over to God" became her battle cry, her mantra, her creed. That's not to suggest that she didn't take an active role in fighting for her life. It just means God was an integral team player, and they fought the good fight together.

Never once did I hear her question God's plan or his intentions. She didn't spend a lot of time asking the question that has no real answer: "Why me?" She sensed that knowing the whys and hows would provide her with no real comfort, no real relief. *Who knows what factor or factors contributed to the dreadful disease that ultimately destroyed her body?* Most likely, she was a victim of her own hereditary gene pool, because she, her sister, and her father were all diagnosed with cancer within months of each other. But instead of allowing herself to concentrate on the hows and whys of her illness, she concentrated on fighting it and she accepted as best she could that everything happens for a reason—the good, the bad, and the deadly.

It was her faith in God and her true individuality that helped her make some of the final, toughest, most substantial decisions of her life. While some of her choices may not be "popular" choices and some of them I still don't understand—they were very personal choices that were right for her.

Throughout her illness, people recommended that she attend survivor group therapy sessions on a regular basis. In today's age of psychological self-help and self-healing, group therapy is considered the preferred modus operandi when it comes to battling societal issues and problems. She attended one meeting, heard heartbreaking stories, and vowed to never go back. She believed the meetings were nothing more than venues for people full of desperation and lacking in hope to use to outpity each other.

Another important decision that she made during this time was her decision not to undergo a badly needed bone marrow transplant. She was confident she'd beat the cancer and she wanted to have kids. If she had the transplant, she knew she wouldn't be able to have children, and for her, that just wasn't an option. Also during this time, she told her family that she didn't want to be kept alive by artificial means and she told them that she didn't want anyone but family around her when she passed. These were both wishes that her family lovingly honored. The decisions she made during this time are indicative of the kind of person she was—caring, compassionate, individualistic, and extremely private.

But not all was hapless. Her last years were not spent waiting to die. During her last years on earth, my friend went on a cruise, rekindled a relationship with an old college boyfriend, visited friends across the country, and purchased a new car. Our conversations were filled with shared passions, victories, and joys, and unfortunately, they were peppered with melancholy talk of malignant cells, death, hair loss, weight loss, alternative therapies, and medical miracles.

During my friend's ordeal, I was reminded of some valuable lessons that actually date back to my childhood. They are lessons to live by that are not just applicable if you're dying. They are not earth-shattering, world-altering lessons, yet they are important lessons all the same. These lessons were the most important legacy my friend left behind for me and others she loved.

First, I was reminded of the fact that we are indeed our brothers' keepers. The basic concept we learned as babes, the good old-fashioned Golden Rule: "Do unto others as you would have them do unto you" holds true. There were people who touched my friend's life in positive and negative ways. While my friend didn't relay to me every act of kindness or indignity that she encountered, I can only hope she experienced more of the former than the latter.

Second, I was reminded of the fact that, regardless of our age, it's easy to get lulled into a false sense of security. We must remember that nothing is promised, especially tomorrow. We have to make the most of our time here on earth today. We have to start doing, thinking, feeling, living, loving today. We have to enjoy what we have, and be it a little or a lot, we have to thank God for it today.

Third, I was reminded that it's never too late (or too early) to begin taking proper care of ourselves. We have to remember to feed the mind, body, soul, and spirit. It's important that we feed the mind with knowledge because knowledge allows us to act from a place of power. It's important that we treat our bodies like the temples they are and pay attention to what they try and tell us. It's important that we feed the soul with that which moves us and touches us deeply because in this stressful world it's imperative that we stay positive and upbeat. And last, but certainly not least, it's important that we feed the spirit with the word of God. *'Nuff said.*

Finally, and most important, I was reminded that in the scheme of things, only the three F's matter: faith, family, and friends. We can't allow ourselves to get bogged down by the small stuff because it distracts us from the bigger stuff that sooner or later touches all of our lives. By celebrating the unconditional love of God and our parents, the potential of our off-spring, the sincerity of our siblings, the devotion of friends and lovers, and the wisdom of our elders, we show appreciation for the people in our lives we love most, the people who have helped shape our worlds.

Although my friend is now long gone, my memories of our time together are sweet and will forever sustain and comfort me. During those times when I need someone to talk to, really talk to, I often find myself reaching out to my friend in Heaven. There's no doubt in my mind that she's there holding court—enchanting God and his angels. There's also no doubt in my mind that she hears me and that she knows she's dearly loved and missed.

After my friend passed, breast cancer became the proverbial monkey on my back. Every day, I felt for lumps, checked for unusual moles, and watched my weight meticulously. I had two mammograms in as many years. Given what I know now, my concerns and obsessiveness have been tempered with the fact that I know breast cancer doesn't have to be a death sentence. There are many women who have lived for decades after their original diagnosis. Early detection, aggressive participation in their own treatment, and positive thinking are just a few of the reasons why tens of thousands of women diagnosed with cancer aren't just surviving, but are thriving.

I'll always remember March 8, 1995, because it so changed my life. That was the day I lost my best friend, my sister—not my blood sister, mind you—but my soul sister. I can still see her beautiful brown face, gorgeous long hair, shining, twinkling eyes, and enchanting megawatt smile. I remember her as young and fun and zestful—her heart and home open and full of love, light, life. I dearly loved my best friend, and even now, years later, when I think of her, I often cry. Not only do I cry for what I lost, a kindred spirit, but I cry for what she experienced and found, both in life and in death.

It's important to remember that when we lose someone we love—that which we treasured, loved, and appreciated most about them stays with us always and becomes even more precious, once they are gone. I write this essay in hopes of honoring my best friend in the way that she honored me, by being an important, treasured part of my life.

Michelle Buckley, a publicist for Hallmark Cards, Inc., has just completed her first novel, *Promise of a New Day*. Michelle is also a freelance writer and a former radio and television reporter. She received her undergraduate degree in journalism from the University of Kansas.

68

When the Wind Blows

Reverend Elaine McCollins Flake

As I waited for the light to change at the corner of 133rd Street and Francis Lewis Boulevard, I realized that there was a wind blowing so strongly against my car that it felt as if some madman was trying to push me into the middle of oncoming traffic. I had to press the brake pedal with more force than usual just to ensure that I maintained control of the vehicle that sheltered my son and me from the unfriendly winds outside. This was one of the mornings that I had missed the weather report, so these forceful thrusts that had already begun to knock over garbage cans and send baseball caps flying through the air were truly a surprise to me. I looked over at twelve-year-old Hasan to see if he had worn his hat and a warm coat, afraid that he had once again underdressed. Too often, we had been caught off guard by weather conditions. Going from the basement into the garage and jumping into the car before we pressed the button to lift the garage door often kept us ignorant of outside temperature. The reality of the weather was kept at bay until we arrived at our destination. I was glad to see that today, however, he sat adorned in a hat and his big black thermal jacket.

The light changed and I eased across the street that was divided by an island of small trees and bushes. I looked to the right only to see a sight that was hidden by the wall of greenery in the middle of the street. Police cars, fire trucks, emergency vehicles lined the street. Uniformed police officers and firefighters and passersby were scattered around the area. As they disappeared from our view, Hasan and I exchanged questioning glances that proclaimed in unison: "What's going on?" Of course, neither of us could answer, but amazingly the newscaster on 1010 WINS answered it for us.

"Tree down on Francis Lewis Boulevard in Queens, as damaging winds take their toll on the city. It is feared that passengers are trapped in a car."

Instantly my heart filled with concern for those who were the victims of this fallen tree. I began to pray for them. As dark thoughts raced through my head, I was almost convinced that this news report had withheld information that I did not really want to hear. I was certain that before the day passed someone would call the church and reveal that one or all of the passengers in that car were members of the church. I drove on and prayed.

"God, don't let anyone be hurt. Don't let anyone be dead."

Almost before the prayer left my lips, I felt the force of the wind once again against my car. My fear for the victims trapped in the car was immediately overshadowed when I remembered that my husband and oldest son had left the house a few minutes before our departure. I recalled that he had mentioned that after he dropped Rasheed at school, he would drive into the city for a meeting, and then on to Washington after his meeting. I glanced at the clock and it read 7:40 A.M. They should be at the school by now. Were they safe? I dialed the number for Floyd's car phone. I really needed to hear that they were safe. I knew that this was not a good morning to fly and I wanted to express my concern for his safety. He was not likely to cancel his trip but I was worried.

Floyd answered the phone with a "Hello" that meant that he knew it was me. We talked about our vibrating cars, the fallen tree on Francis Lewis, and our concern for the people trapped in their car. Just as I predicted, when I cautioned him against flying out to Washington in the midst of the wind storm, he brushed off my concerns. He then suggested that because there were some votes that he did not want to miss, he would let the airlines determine whether or not he would travel. Oh well, so much for being the concerned wife.

Hasan and I entered the school, and without parting words, he turned the corner and ascended the stairs to his seventh grade classroom while I headed into my office. He was the only one of my four children who remained at the school where I have worked as educational director for the last fifteen years. Hasan was always resistant to any motherly affection at school, so I controlled the urge to call out, "Bye baby," as he walked away.

I walked into the office where the director, administrative assistant, and a couple of tardy teachers went through their morning routines. Our morning greetings mingled with the noise of ringing telephones, clunking time clocks and the chatter of the children. Seconds later, I saw Mrs. Depass hang up the phone and shoot me and Mrs. Morant a look that told us that we had better pay attention to the information that she was about to give us.

"That was Mrs. Capers. A tree fell on the van and they are going to be late." Her tone was casual and her face gave no indication that we should be concerned. My mental picture was one of a fallen dogwood or pine tree that was not large enough to do any real damage, but would serve as a definite obstacle.

"Where are they now?" I inquired, not yet connecting our van with the scene that I had passed just a few moments before. If Mrs. Capers had made the call, surely everything was okay.

"They are on Francis Lewis Boulevard, right at 131st Street."

"Hey, I just passed them. But I did not know it was the Capers' van. The news report said that it was a car." Then I remembered the report of trapped passengers.

"Did she say that everybody was okay?" I probed.

"She said she had some scratches and that some of the kids had scraped knees."

Before I could get my thoughts together, Mrs. Morant suggested that we go to check on them. The radio played softly as we made our unsuspecting ride to the downed van. Our casual conversation was hushed when the voice of the newscaster pierced our hearts. "At least two believed dead in an accident in Queens where the wind blows down a tree . . ." Horror drowned out the rest of his words. I stopped the car in the middle of the street and stared incredulously at the radio. *"What did he say?"* I shrieked. Mrs. Morant did not say a word. She just groaned. I had not heard sounds like that since my last trip to the labor room. I looked at her for some sign that I had heard wrong. Was he talking about our kids? Her eyes were closed and her body was rigidly shaking. This could not be happening.

My hands trembled on the steering wheel as my numbed foot dropped onto the accelerator. We rode the rest of the way without speaking, but the car was filled with sounds of agony and disbelief.

I parked the car as close as I could to the accident scene. The street was blocked off and a police officer directed traffic away from the place we needed to go. Before I could remove the key from the ignition, Mrs. Morant jumped from the car and barreled around the corner. I tried in vain to catch her. Someone recognized her, and steered her into a house on the street. An unknown hand gripped my arm. It was apparent that they were not going to allow us to see what had happened. In spite of the attempts to rush me away, I managed to see the crushed two-tone van lodged between unrecognizable objects. The front of the van was in tact, but the back was so badly mangled that it was hard to believe that it was the same vehicle. Then I saw the tree—the deadly tree sprawled from the curb to the other side of the street. And then came a voice in my ear.

"Mr. and Mrs. Capers are okay, four of the children are fine. They were in the front. But the ones in the back . . . we lost four." I muffled my scream with the sleeve of my coat. "No, God, no! Not our babies!"

My wobbly knees only half carried me up the stairs into a house that was being used as a crisis center. The room was filled with whimpers and sobs. Strange and familiar faces blended to create a collage of fear and agony. No one talked; we just exchanged looks and cried. The faces of the surviving children jarred me to remember that all was not lost and I thanked God that they were alive. This was what it felt like to have "joy in the midst of sorrow."

I walked over to the surviving children and held on to each one for just a moment. They all had cuts, scrapes, and tears, but they looked okay. Then I saw the two drivers of the van. They wore neck braces, had plenty of scratches, and were in shock, but they looked okay too. They were physically okay, but after having been so close to death, would they ever be okay again?

I heard one of the girls asking, "Where is Kristen? Where is Olivia?" They did not know yet.

A police officer identified himself to me and, with my permission, showed me the names of the four fatalities. Olivia Warren, Kia Satterfield, Kimberly Washington, and Kristen Washington. Instantly, I began to argue with God, stating all the reasons that this should not be.

"Not Olivia! Her father just died. Now Joyce will have no one.

"Not Kia! She was her mother's world!

"Both of the Washington girls. God, not *both* of them."

Of course the debate was useless. The girls were gone.

Suffering and tragic loss never make sense, especially when they involve innocent children. Christian theologians and thinkers have always sought to give explanations and rationalizations to a phenomenon that I have concluded is beyond human understanding. No matter how many discussions we have on the origin, purpose, and meaning of suffering, there will always be suffering and situations that defy theological explication. The thought of having to face distraught parents, an overwrought student body, a minister, and a pastor, was frightening. I had no answers for any of their questions. I had my own questions. How could God let this or make this happen?

Theoretically, suffering at the hand of another human being is easy to call moral evil or human sin. Human-generated suffering permits us to fulfill our deepest need to point the finger at the sinner. The rapist, the racist, the drunk driver, and the abusive spouse are the agents of suffering easily identified and judged. But when a woman or a man gets breast cancer, or a child is diagnosed with lupus, or a tree falls and crushes four children to death, there is no human to be the object of our rage.

In the days that followed the deaths of the girls, I heard ministers, politicians, and church members offer various theological explanations for this tragedy. God took the children because they were special or because God loved them best or because God needed them in heaven. Paradoxically, others declared that Satan, knowing their potential, snatched them from this life to try to stop the good that they would do. As I examined the faces of grieving parents, family members, and classmates, I was convinced that these explanations did not satisfy the need to give meaning to our loss. They certainly did not satisfy me. With all of my heart and soul, I have searched for the words that could give intellectual and spiritual insight to this tragedy. Still I have found none.

Having to hear the questions and face the grief of heartbroken parents and family members was one of the most difficult tasks of my ministry. Looking into the bewildered, grief-stricken faces of the classmates of the four girls brought me face to face with my own inability to convey and explain the mind and the ways of God. My belief in the wisdom of God was challenged by my own grief and questions as I stood in front of four little coffins. I wanted to defend God, to exonerate God from any culpability in this matter, but I do not know how to do that. Rejecting God was out of the question, because more than ever we needed God if we were to come through this with our minds at least marginally intact.

Once again, life has shown us that humanity cannot give meaning to tragedy and suffering. The world injures us and life sends us to places of despair. While none have been exempted from suffering, every day we are harshly reminded that some suffer more than others, and we know that it has little to do with sin, merit, or building character. It simply happens. We can only hope and pray that we are spared the worst that life inflicts. And when the worst happens, our only choice is to live or die.

I have now grown to fear the wind. When the wind blows, I remember and I pray. I avoid tree-lined streets and try to convince my children to stay home. But still, there are no guarantees.

Reverend Margarett Elaine McCollins Flake has distinguished herself as a preacher, teacher and effective leader in Christian Education and Evangelistic and Outreach Ministry. Dr. Flake is an itinerant Elder in the African Methodist Episcopal Church and currently serves as co-pastor of the Allen A.M.E. Church, Jamaica, New York. She is also the educational director of the Allen Christian School which she co-founded with her husband and pastor, Reverend Dr. Floyd H. Flake. She and her husband are the proud parents of four children: Aliya, Nailah, Rasheed and Hasan.

69

Good China

Melissa E. Brooks

Flowers and foliage grow in graveyards. In their simplicity, they remind us
that beauty and life can grow from death. Blooms take time, as does our
healing process—rising from the winter of the deceased to the sweetness of
a new day. For every day that I am alive, I try to remind myself of the healing power of those flowers and the wisdom their roots bear. I think about
those flowers most often when I remember the life and death of my grandmother. Her presence is so rooted in my consciousness, in my very being,
that I sometimes think I am here to carry out the things she didn't finish
doing while she was alive.

My grandmother used to serve my brother, sister, and me sandwiches off
her good dishes. My mother still does the same. When asked why waste
such nice things on the grubby little hands of three scrappy-looking, smiling
children, both always responded, "Who's more special than them? What
guest could possibly be more important and more deserving of fine china
than family?" Today, when occasionally sitting on a plastic-covered sofa in a
living room reserved for *company*, I chuckle to myself at the memory of it
all.

My grandmother made life colorful. Little, perpetually smelling of Estee
Lauder and always old since I was born, she had the loudest voice of anyone
I've ever met. She had opinions on everything and was quick to tell you to
speak up, speak clearer, stop mumbling, or look at her when you were talking if she couldn't understand your words. The age, gender, occupation, or
social importance of the person sitting before her didn't matter. She was in
charge, and often held court from her afghan-covered La-Z-Boy chair in
her living room on Upsal Street in Philadelphia. She was never alone.

To see her, about five feet two inches, maybe 120–130 pounds with
white hair, huge bifocal spectacles, velvety pale skin made smooth by layers
of wrinkles on every corner of her body, you would think she was the sweet-
est, quietest thing in the world. With her patterned housecoats or brightly
colored dresses and slow, cautious walk—traffic lights never seemed quite

long enough for her to make it across the street—you might even want to reach out and help her. But her appearance masked a sharp contrast to her inner strength and security of self. Feel sorry for her and you would quickly feel sorry for yourself as she reprimanded you for being presumptuous.

She taught me that it's okay to appreciate what others consider junk. We would sit upstairs and look through her brightly colored baubles and admire whatever crazy fashion I was into at the time, and convince ourselves that it was the rest of the world that had no taste. She taught me that just because you're old doesn't mean you're not hip, up on current events, interesting, full of life, full of stories, or full of love. My siblings and I never dreaded going to visit our grandparents, because their doting, quick wit, donuts, and candy dish made every day we were with them feel special. Plus, they loved to pick up trinkets on the road to give us as gifts—we'd chew on long rolls of button candy while clinging to crisp one-dollar bills in our sticky fingers as if we'd been given Nintendo.

She taught me that being African-American and female is good. That it is actually kind of special and something to be proud of. My parents did the same and always made sure there were tons of black history books in the house or that we were going to So-and-So's lecture on black achievements, but Grandmom made it seem even more real. I think it's because she was so unassuming in her presence and looked like she couldn't even go to the store alone, much less marry twice, help found *Jack & Jill,* and serve as an officer of a number of other African-American female and family organizations. Grandmom held true to her beliefs in making a better life for herself, her family, her friends, and the people who would come after her. She just didn't shout it very loud or demand credit. To my chagrin, I only learned of many of her accomplishments in passing, and from others after her death. You see, when you spoke to her, you were the most important thing to talk about . . . always.

My grandmother was supposed to live forever. At least that's what we all thought. The irony is that she was perpetually dying. In her later years, one of her favorite pasttimes was checking herself into the hospital. My mother said it was for "rest," a vacation for both my grandmother and my grandfather. He remained home and played golf. When Grandmom got cancer after chain smoking for the better part of fifty years, we all just assumed she'd be okay. Any African-American person will tell you that, at any given time, elderly relatives are always "taking sick" and on their deathbed. Two weeks later, you're all at dinner somewhere as if nothing happened. I confess, sometimes it is hard to take the latest health-related drama seriously.

An oxygen tank supplying air to her lungs served as one of my grandmother's last conversation pieces. My mother used to snap, "You're a fire hazard! You can't smoke with an oxygen tank next to you!" At this remark, my grandmother would look up sweetly, innocently, even slightly confused, before telling my mother to mind her business and to take care of whatever task came to mind. I had settled in New York by then and didn't see Grandmom as much, thinking she would get better. She had to, because as much as our family loved to squabble, we all needed and loved having her around.

When she died, I read a poem I'd written in the car on the way to the funeral. I'd actually slaved over a mushy, flowery iteration prior to arriving in Philly, but it seemed forced and not true to who and what she was. The one I read highlighted why she was special to all of us, from her "snaps" that could quiet even the fastest talker, her cute little face and body, her ever-present cigarette, and how she was now gossiping in heaven while ordering God to get her some juice from the kitchen.

When I have kids, I will serve them sandwiches on nice plates and I will keep striving to make my mark in the world. From my grandmother I know that it doesn't matter what stereotypes tell me I am supposed to be; I am in charge of my own destiny. I understand the power, the beauty, and the wisdom of growing older and still enjoy dinners with my remaining older relatives, who read more trashy books than the head of Fabio's fan club, gossip more than any columnist, and stay on top of current events better than most CNN analysts. I know the value of family, of extended family, and of those who will live after us, touched by our lives, even though we will never meet.

And though I miss my grandmother, I am better for having known her. For each time I pass flowers, whether they're in a graveyard or in a garden, I think of the memories their roots hold, and the wonders their petals will bring.

Melissa E. Brooks, a native of Baltimore, has lived in New York City for over ten years. She is an aspiring writer and published poet, who moonlights as an advertising executive during the day. Her specialties are poetry, short stories, business presentations, and launching brands. She recently completed a book on America's fascination with diet myths and is working on a number of other projects.

70

Tell Mommie You Love Her

Jill Merritt

Tell Mommie you love her. "I love you, Mommie." Tell Mommie you are gonna take care of me. "I'm gonna take care of Jill." Tell her that you are gonna take care of Daddy. "I'm gonna take care of Dad." Tell her that you are gonna take care of the house. "I'm gonna take care of the house." Tell Mommie it's okay, we are going to be fine. "It's okay, we are going to be fine." My mother was dying. I had gone out in the street to find my sister and bring her back to say good-bye to our mother.

This was our saying good-bye. She could not speak in those final minutes so I asked her to blink her eyes if she understood. "Mommie, do you understand?" She blinked twice for yes, and then I walked away. I stood in the kitchen with my hands on my hips just pacing. I was fourteen but you couldn't tell me I wasn't forty. Everyone was in complete chaos. It was the first time it hit my family that Mommie was going to die. Kim, my sister, was in shock, Dad had punched a hole in the hallway wall, and me? I was fine. I had already dealt with this part. But Kim, my older sister by four years had spent a lot of time hanging out and had no idea how ill our mother was.

My father worked real hard and drank real hard. I know they were both avoiding what was going on in the living room. But still I needed help. It was my mother and I in those last days. I decided I would take care of her and I did. I would go to the farmers' market and buy fresh vegetables and fruit to make her meals. Back then I thought liver was the end all and be all. So Mommie got a lot of liver and onions. I slept with her so if she moved a muscle, I knew it. I became a light sleeper; I don't recall sleeping a lot during that summer.

If she needed anything I was by her side, responding in seconds. I massaged her feet and because the chemo took her hair, I'd grease her scalp to stimulate growth. I gave her baths, and wash downs when the baths were too much. She took care of me when I was sick, and now I was taking care of her.

As I stood in the kitchen I knew Kim was still with my mother. I felt very anxious because I knew it would be soon, and before I could finish that thought I heard my sister scream. My mother's spirit had decided it was time to leave its body. I knew from the kitchen. We had a house full of people, and they all tried to hold Kim back. They threw her in her room and she came out of the other door trying to get to her mother. I remember laughing at that. I just thought let her go see her mother's body; Mommie's gone, I'm going to sit on the stoop. I left them all in the house.

I sat on the stoop reflecting. I thought about what I was going to do and *damn, she'll miss my first year of high school. Couldn't you just stay a little longer? I know you'll be with me, won't you?* I thought of the fire. That's the reason why we moved to Park Slope. We had a fire, not like having a barbecue, but like the whole damn house burned down. I remember I had just come back from running our dogs with my father. He went next door to our neighbors and I went inside. I pulled off my clothes and got right in bed with my mother. It was a Saturday night thing. She read the paper, and I read the pictures. I was all up in her arms so she had a hard time turning the pages. We heard, "Fire! Fire!"

We jumped out of bed. Kim was in the living room and we all ran into the hallway to see my grandfather standing on the second landing, which was a feat for him. He had something wrong with his legs so he never ever came upstairs, but there he was looking up at us yelling to call the fire department. We could not go downstairs because the fire was coming up from there. My sister and I ran to the window, while my mother called the 911. We tried our best but could not open the window. Now we often played on the fire escape countless times, in and out of that window, and now it would not budge. I was going, "Come on Kim, come on." I turned around and saw thick black smoke coming through the cracks in the doors. That smoke looked like it had a life of its own as it pushed through and curled up into hot black clouds. I turned back to my sister, "Get this mother-fucking window open!" The window flew open, we get out onto the fire escape and I realize I'm barefoot. I run back in and go under the bed, feeling around for my slippers. I felt them, pink and fluffy. I put them on and got back to the window, while my mother is screaming for me to get out. I have no idea what she was doing but if I knew my mom, she was getting together all the money she had hidden around the house.

When I get onto the fire escape Kim is in shock. Her hands are stuck to the iron pipes and she can't move. She was much bigger than me, and I knew I couldn't leave her so I screamed my lungs out. Someone, I think it was my uncle's brother-in-law came up the fire escape and picked me up. I kissed that man all over his face. I remember telling him, I love you, I love you, and just kissing him. When I got down to the ground, I could see my sister still there, and now my mother.

My father was in the backyard next door trying to climb over the fence. My mother and sister made it down the fire escape. I could see the flames engulfing the house as I stood in the backyard watching the house burn down against a November winter's night. I would later understand fire as a cleansing element and the Universal order in which it purifies.

That night we forgot about our dogs; they died. We forgot about Damon, my cousin. Damon was a little slow, mildy retarded we would say. He wanted to come up to see Kim that night. She said no because she was going to bed. I know she felt guilty for a long time after his death, because she didn't go right to bed. I think Kim was the only person who treated Damon like he was normal, and I knew he loved her immensely.

Damon was burned over 70 percent of his body, he was blind in one eye, and he died the next day in the hospital. Soon after, my parents bought the house in Park Slope and we made it there just in time for Christmas. Nat King Cole's Christmas album was playing and my Dad just put the finishing touches on the tree. We all stood together watching the lights on the tree as my mother and father, tears flowing down their faces, said "We made it."

Little did I know I was soon to resent the house and everything in it. As I sat on the stoop reflecting, I did not cry. In fact I didn't cry at all the night my mother died. I went back upstairs and went in the living room where her body still lay. I touched her arm. She was in a fetal position as if she were sleeping. My hand went down her arm to her waist, then her thigh, all the way down her leg to her foot.

I massaged both her feet and came back up again to her face and her head. No fear, no pain, just peace. It was just my mother and me, just like it had been that summer. The night she died I had the best sleep. I was always ashamed to say that but she was at peace. I did everything, and now I could finally go to sleep. We had two funerals, one in New York and one in Florida. After I spent the summer in Florida I was to start high school. A new cycle was to begin in my life. I started really being overly concerned about my father. He began to suffer from depression, and his drinking increased. My father mismanaged the house, mismanaged his own paycheck.

I have no real idea how we got in the mess we were in but there we were. My sister was hanging hard. So she was no help, and you know how someone might think that if you take something without asking it might be stealing? Well Kim never asked me for anything and she was damn sure taking my stuff. To this day I'm not certain if drugs were her motive, or if she just wanted to hurt me.

I think a little of both. She would steal my clothes and sell them at the Jamaican salon where I got my hair done. I found out when one of the women wanted to buy something from her that it was mine and asked me about it. Then she stole from them and didn't tell me not to go back there.

Walking back into that salon could have been suicide for me, but they knew I had no part of it and they told me what happened. I slid out of that chair, never to return. The next ten years just got worse. I cooked for my dad and tried to take care of him while going to school. I was not comfortable in the house because Kim would take anything she wanted from me.

Occasionally I'd find that she'd slice my shoes or my boots out of resentment or jealousy. Once she sliced my graduation picture across the face and put it back in the frame. When I think about that I swear I can hear the theme from *Psycho* in my head. That sight made me nervous. So eventually I kicked her out of the house, but not before we tried to kill each other. We fought so much. Everyone had pretty much left the scene. Although I was young when my mother died, none of her friends came around. No one on either side of the family reached out to me. My dad had checked out, my sister and brothers were doing their own thing and so I felt completely alone and I hated God. I would scream and yell at the ceiling in my room. Once I beat my pillow in the dark, banging my head on the mattress, crying and screaming at God, "Aren't I Your child? How could You do this to me? You took my mother and left me here with this alcoholic and this thieving nut. Is this what You want for me? I am tormented, and You just leave me here, and You don't let anyone comfort me. You must hate me and I hate You." Then I'd yell at my mother, "You knew you were sick and you didn't make yourself better. You could have ate better, you could have beat this and now I'm alone. I can't believe you did this to me. Why did you have to leave me? You just left me and I'm here by myself!" So, clearly I have some abandonment issues. The anger and resentment just grew stronger and stronger. I went on to college and got involved in a relationship where my anger would play out fully in several fits of rage when I thought I was going to lose my boyfriend.

After my first year in college, during the summer I had an ovarian cyst that ruptured. I was bleeding internally. The blood flowed into my stomach and I slowly, calmly, started to go into shock. The nurse in the emergency room looked at my tongue and screamed, "She's going into shock, she's going into shock." I hung over the side of the wheelchair looking at white nurse shoes running along side of me. I could see several pairs of feet. I remember thinking, *so this is what shock is, feels like you wanna sleep.* My body was not moving but my mind was alive with observations. They cut my T-shirt, I thought, *did you really have to do that? It's not a heart attack, damn!* Before I knew it, and I know people use that term loosely, but really when I had an awareness of myself again I was in a hospital gown with an oxygen mask on my face. I thought, *where are my pink stretch pants?* It was 1986. I had the worst experiences of my life within those first few days of my illness. Everyone had to give a vaginal exam, which was incredibly painful. They would always hit the spot where the cyst had ruptured and send me writhing in pain. Eventually they sent the hospital social worker to see me, Mr. Rodriquez.

I asked him, "Are you a psychologist?" Yes, he told me. "Well I'm in pain, between my legs not between my ears." As we talked I would have crying bouts he called psychosomatic reactions. I was so worried about my father who was waiting outside, I asked him to go check on my dad. I told him I had to get better because my dad had lost his wife and could not loose me, too. As I talked with Mr. Rodriquez the nurse asked me if I was okay. I kept going in and out of my crying bouts. I told her, "Yes, I'm just having a psychosomatic reaction."

Two days after my emergency surgery I was still in the hospital. That night I had a visitation from my mother. It was the second and last time she was to visit me. I awoke to see my mother only from the waist up over my bed. I immediately rise up to try and hug her and she said, "Don't touch me." Not like before when we hugged each other. She hugged me so tight I fell on the floor; I woke up in my dad's room.

That first time we talked, she said she missed me and wanted to know why I didn't talk to her anymore. I told her I was busy, and I was about to go to Syracuse University. She asked when can I come, and I told her not now. Our spirits were talking, my soul was visiting hers, and I imagine we both were having a hard time adjusting and needed to touch each other. But this time she was grounded. She was serious. And so she just stared at me, no words. I didn't speak either. I just felt warm as we looked at each other, and I knew I would be okay. I am a survivor. She had come to let me know that. As soon as those thoughts entered my head, I awoke but not like I was asleep; my awareness just shifted. Some people know what I mean and others will find out. I stayed in the hospital four more days and then was sent home. I tried to eat very healthy, so of course it was liver and onions every day.

As things got worse I also noticed that things got better. At this point I had taken over the house and was paying the bills, getting repairs done, and basically just being the landlord. It was a big load for me and I hated it. But somehow I began to see beautiful people come into my life who were like angels. I had friends who would make me laugh and their mothers embraced me as if I were their own. I began to thank God for them. I started seeing a man who told me that my experiences with my mother's illness and subsequent death were to prepare me for something later in life.

Jeff was a huge inspiration to me in my spiritual growth. He became my teacher, my mentor, and I thanked God for such a friend. Although I had grown up Baptist, I had strayed from the church and did not know much of the Bible so my prayers were filled with simple giving thanks. My angry conversations with God became quiet meditations. I began to fast and read books about the healing powers of food. My first fast awakened me spiritually and I have not been the same since. It was intuitively that I understood there was a connection between food and my spirit. I was able to become focused and clear when eating well. I also began to keep a journal and read books about spirituality. Everyone seemed to be on this journey. People would seek me out for advice, and I always seemed to say the right thing. The more I prayed, the more I understood that a higher power was guiding me to say those right things. I began to understand that I was not on my own. I became a seeker of truth, constantly trying to understand.

In my understanding, one thing I got was that I was to be thankful, no matter what. I understood that in spite of myself, I was still blessed. Yes I was angry at God from time to time but I was still blessed and therefore I must always acknowledge that I am not on my own but blessed and guided by a higher power who uses me, as this power used my mother on this earth to fulfill a purpose within God's plan. I knew this when hundreds of people of every background had come to my mother's funeral to pay their respects. Today I know my mother's spirit is at peace or busy doing what they do in the spirit world. A conversation with my girlfriend's mother confirmed this when she told me how my mother once bragged to her about me—that I was a little lady who cooked breakfast and cleaned the house. She went on to tell her all the food dishes I could make at the age of ten. I just thought, *she knew, my mother knew when I was ten years old she had instilled in me all I needed to survive in the world without her.* I cried gentle tears in that realization and I knew, no I felt that Mommie was truly at peace.

Jill Merritt, wardrobe supervisor and costume designer, will be living her life's purpose as a Certified Nutritional Wellness Counselor & Image Consultant.

71

For CC

June Joseph

Do you know what it feels like to hold someone's hand as they slip off this mortal coil? To hear the last breath leave their bodies? To watch the rising and recession of the chest as life begins to cease? Facing the death of others made me confront my own eventual demise. Or is demise too cold a word? My ceasing to exist. My passing. I'd never given much thought to dying. In my childlike state, death was strictly for the movies. Actors die dramatic deaths, only to appear another day in another movie to die yet another death. Never gave much thought to the umpteenth pet goldfish that succumbed due to my lack of care. Or the little ants I callously crushed with my fingers. No Karmic guilt to weigh on my little shoulders.

I first acknowledged the finality of death when my great-grandmother, a God-fearing woman of fine stock, died before my twelfth birthday. As my mother gently relayed the news, I experienced abject guilt. Some months prior to her passing, Granny asked me to aid her with something and I hadn't completed the task properly. Gently, she had asked me again for help. I stamped my foot and whined, fat tears welling up in my eyes. I'll never forget the look on her long-suffering face. Crestfallen because she hated to see me, her beloved great-granddaughter, cry.

"It's okay. This is fine. This will do. Don't cry. It's okay," she murmured.

She loved me deeply, forgave me completely, and still I'm consumed with guilt. I didn't cry for her for over a month after her death. Then one night, I realized she wasn't there. Not there to shape my eyebrows after she braided my hair. Not there to fling her protective arms around me when my mother scolds me. Or there to feed me juicy oranges and tell me I'm beautiful, smart, and a child of God. And for the first time in my naive state, I know grief. I feel loss. I acknowledged finality. And it is ominous. I try to imagine her in heaven, smiling down at me. Granny as my guardian angel in a white robe with huge dove wings and not a cold cadaver in a dark mahogany box. Some nights I have this vivid recurring dream where she comes for me. Obscured by a half-closed door, she calls to me from the kitchen, imploring me to come and be with her. She misses me terribly. Invisible hands push me in her direction. Screaming, I struggle free and run away. No matter how far I run, I always end up in the same spot, her plaintive voice calling me to join her.

In my youthful imagination, death is a dark place, where you are conscious. Aware. But all around is dark, no sound. Oppressive. I want to scream, cry, beg for someone to save me, but no one comes because I am dead. And so my irrational fear follows me through to adulthood. Lodged deep in my subconscious.

New York City, 1993. My surrogate big sister, Anne. Cerebral. Smart. Beautiful. Gone. It's sudden. Unexpected. My fear of dying, long suppressed, erupts, rocking me to my core. Again, I'm forced to face my mortality. She was young. I am young. What if I'm next? I'm not ready. I haven't made my peace with God. My family. My life. It's not my time. I am scared. The nightmares return. I try to picture Anne in a good place. I see darkness. I search for enlightenment, the alleviation of my fear of the inevitable. I delve into my Christian beliefs. Buddhism. Hinduism. Science. What happens to us after we depart this life? Why doesn't anything reassure me?

CC eyes me with that "Who's that other black girl?" stare. We're introduced by a mutual friend. We look each other up and down, appraising every feature. We eye each other's waists. Our curves: mine ample, CC's lack of. Rivals, maybe. The first meeting, guarded, but polite.

"Don't worry," says our mutual friend. "CC's always a little shady to start with . . ."

CC cuts a dashing figure. Diaphanous hair, fluid mannerisms. Supermodel walk. Prefixing sentences with a "Lady," and punctuating them with a resounding "Genius!" CC knows lots about fashion. I know squat. This Nubian beauty can even pluck a mean eyebrow. For a boy, CC is the fiercest girl I know.

We find common ground. He lived in Europe for a little while. He knows the score about being black in England. We reminisce about English chocolate and the etiquette of tea making. We laugh like drains at the very thought of pasty, low-class English "slappers" (tarts) wearing their $12 white stilettos with the scuff marks painted over with correction fluid. CC collapses in a quivering heap of giggles, tears streaming down his round, pretty face with the breathtakingly long eyelashes. Like my knowing big sister, he fusses over my thick rug of hair as we sip PG Tips–brand tea. "Lady, you need to do something with that hair!"

I later learn he's sick. HIV since 1990. Contracted it from a philandering lover, he says. He's too busy living life to be bitter. But sometimes he's profoundly sad. Every so often, he disappears for weeks on end. His friends worry that he's terribly sick and needs help, but we know he wants us to leave well enough alone. I've heard he's been at death's door before. Several times, but he's a fighter.

It's 1995. One balmy night in early autumn, Greenwich Avenue, NYC, this slender figure approaches me, cinched waist, shiny ponytail swishing like a metronome keeping perfect time with his model-girl gait. His eyes are bigger or is it because he's thinner? Much thinner. We hug. Then retire to a window table at Big Cup on 8th Avenue with two big mugs of steaming hot English Breakfast. He tells me he's been very sick. That he's been going up to Bellevue Hospital for nutrient shots and regular checkups.

He's full-blown. We don't mention death. Right now, it's not an option. He'll bounce back. He always does. I tell him I'll go to the hospital with him for company. Maybe I can meet a fine young doctor. We giggle conspiratorially.

It's almost the close of winter, I finally meet him for a hospital appointment. He disappeared for a while. Now I see CC, I barely recognize him. He's emaciated. No longer the fierce supermodel with the lustrous hair. Still regal and proud, but frail. He swallows several Dilaudid pills and I watch his pained expression melt into heady contentment as the painkiller's effects kick in.

"I feel the relief creeping up my toes, feet, and legs," he offers dreamily.

We hang out for several hours, sometimes talking, sometimes silent. We go our separate ways. The next scheduled appointment and things are terribly wrong. The doctors say his case is critical and admit him into the AIDS ward. He's disoriented, spacey. I sit with him as he lies in bed, telling him how much I love him. I leave the hospital late into the night. He'll bounce back. Death is not an option.

CC has two lives: the uptown and the downtown. Sean lives downtown, but he's tagged "uptown." Erudite, corporate, solid as a rock. I'm definitely "downtown." Club girl, in the arts, soft, but streetwise. Worlds collide. CC is our chameleon-like link. We watch over CC in shifts. A few friends join us as we keep vigil. It's been about a week, he's rail-thin, not eating, but he'll bounce back.

Ironically, these days I don't think of death. I'm stuck in a surreal state, where I've become oddly oblivious to it, despite the changing name plates on the patients' rooms. Despite the empty beds where a sick young man once lay languishing . . . (dying?) CC'll bounce back. I'm sure of it . . . I think.

The nurses move him from his bed to the gurney, so we can take him to Radiology. He calls out for me. He grabs my arm so tight. He winces in pain. His legs riddled with Karposi's sarcoma. He feels safe.

Beaming like a father, whose child just made straight A's, Sean proudly informs me that CC drank almost a whole McDonald's milkshake. I run to my ailing friend, kiss him, tell him I love him and that I'm so proud. Then I quietly sob in the hallway. And finally, I realize death is inevitable. He's not bouncing back like he's supposed to. I feel profound loss and he's still here. Sean and I comfort each other. The AIDS patients that are mobile comfort me. My darling CC is dying and he comforts me.

My suppressed fears begin to resurface. I fear for CC. My stoic religious faith is tested. Dear God, I'm scared. Give us all the strength to face this. The fears, they come back and they're irrational. Nonsensical. What will he see when he goes? What will he feel? What if he can't breathe? I'm scared for him. I'm scared for me. I'm a coward and I'm weak. I cry for his life as it slowly ebbs, for the lives of the patients, who face death every hour. I cry for my own mortality and my cowardly attitude. No more weakness. CC needs me. CC needs Sean. Put your fears aside. Get a spine, girl! Sean and I are proxies. It's official. We sign the forms, so we now carry out his wishes. CC doesn't want to go just yet, but he's getting sicker and sicker. He spends more time in a "fugue" state. I watch him sleep, eyes half-closed, and I sob. Please stay a little longer, it can't be your time yet. Please fight. CC has trouble breathing. He needs to be interbated. We ask him if this is his wish. He is conscious enough to nod a weak yes.

CC is in the ICU and he's angry. I touch his hand to comfort him and he snatches it away from me. He wants so desperately to go. It's time. He's a proud, beautiful, black being imprisoned in a decaying, cancer-riddled cocoon with tainted blood. He seeks freedom, pure liberation. He wants out.

Sean and I discuss who should ask CC the big question. We decide I should. We pray that God gives me the right words. We cry and hold each other. We enter CC's room. Too many tubes, too many wires. We each take one of his skeletal hands.

"We love you. We will fight with you. We'll never leave you. Do you want to stay? Squeeze my hand once."

Nothing.

"We love you, but if you want to go, we'll be there right at the end."

Something. Weak, but something. Sean lifts his head, his eyes wide.

"Did you feel it?"

I do. But I refuse to accept it. Perhaps a mistake. How can he say yes? It's too final. I repeat myself guardedly. "My darling, we love you so much. We'll never leave you. Do you want to stay and fight this thing, because we can beat it? Squeeze my hand."

Nothing.

"Do you want to go?"

He musters all his strength and squeezes our hands so hard, there's no mistaking it. It's an emphatic, a resounding yes. Copious tears flow. It's the hardest thing we've ever had to do. And yet CC comforts us. Relief sweeps over his ravaged body. I cry for hours. My right eye gets infected and swells up. Now I face death at close range. Granny, Ann, acquaintances I barely knew. Suddenly I see the inevitability of it all, and I finally accept death because they accepted it. They had no choice, they just accepted. I, too, must combat my fears, step forward, accept. No fear.

Do you know what it feels like to hold someone's hand as they slip off this mortal coil? Yes, I know what it feels like because I am there. I hold his hand. Beth, a close friend, rubs his feet, the doctor removes the tubes and administers morphine, so CC can finally be free and comfortable. He squeezes my hand, reassuring me. He squeezes to indicate laughter, if we say something funny. He rolls his eyes in a shady "whatever" when I make a silly, girlish joke. He's happy. He's CC again. Fierce to the end. I ask him to say hi to Anne and my granny for me. "Yes," he squeezes hard. I momentarily release his hand, while I sign the "Do not resuscitate" form. The last of my proxy duties.

"I'm signing your boarding pass, Hon," I say.

I can't think of anything else. I take his hand and I watch his chest rise and recede. His breathing shallower. The heart monitor skips arbitrarily to match his erratic heartbeat. His breathing stops.

"His soul is gone . . ." says the doctor quietly.

His half-open eyes stare heavenward. We're all silent.

And suddenly I feel profound love and gratitude to my dear friend and the gift he gave me. I liken his death to a birth in reverse. CC went to the next level in the grand scheme of life and death. He faced it head on and embraced it. His passing taught me that even as you exist you can be dead if you don't live life to its fullest. He taught me that death is something to fear when faced with regret and bitterness.

The night after his death, I dream CC is in a World War II fighter plane. His hair shiny and full. He is whole again and he has a companion. Buff and comely. As the plane increases altitude, he waves good-bye to me and smiles. Thank you, CC. Thank you for opening my eyes and showing me the way. I have no more fear.

June Joseph is a British-born music journalist and club DJ who resides in New York City. She has written for numerous publications including *Billboard, I-D, Paper* and others. This is her first published essay.

Your Soul's Sustenance

Ashes to Ashes, Dust to Dust

A lot of us have experienced or will experience the death of a loved one in our lifetime. It's but for the grace of God that that person was in your life in the first place. If that person didn't touch our lives so dearly, would we be mourning for them the way we do?

Sometimes we have to get through that mourning and grieving to know that it's but for the grace of God that they were in our lives in the first place. To be able to learn from that relationship with that person, be it our mother, our grandmother, our fathers, whoever that brought us to that point where we felt such a deep and tragic loss.

The song "Amazing Grace" came from a slave master who was in a shipwreck and he was cast away at sea for so long, hanging on to a piece of driftwood or something and somehow managed to survive but a lot of people died. After that horrifying event, he had an epiphany, freed all his slaves, became an abolitionist, and wrote the song which is now an integral part of our American tradition:

Amazing Grace, how sweet the sound that saved a wretch like me,
I once was lost but now I'm found, was blind, but now I see.

It can take time. We do learn—some sooner than others—when we're fortunate enough to open ourselves to learning. At the time, it's hard for us not to separate the two—the person's life and the treasures they brought us from their death. It's only natural when the person is gone. But we also have to learn to be able to move on. List everything that you love about someone in your life who has passed away.

When my grandmother died, I didn't know what to do with all the grief I was experiencing at the time. Candace consoled me and told me that I should celebrate my grandmother's life.

We all have a choice on how we live. Some choose to live inactively by letting things happen and race to make amends. Others live protectively incorporating a renewed faith in their destiny and an appreciation for another human being and their spirit. Living inactively is when we miss some of the most magical times in our loved ones' lives. Instead we send flowers, gifts and money. Those are absolutely wonderful, but if you reviewed your schedule you would find that you missed the precious moments because of something inconsequential or work related. It can always be done another day. Be proactive with your energy and be generous with your time; instead of giving gifts provide memories. A simple dinner, bring an older relative with you on a business trip, show up at your children's sporting events and recitals. Purchase a camera and take lots of photos, remember birthdays and anniversaries, show up for events that you are invited to. Visit elderly relatives, incorporate it in your schedule to call them daily, visit the sick, write notes saying I am thinking about you. Most of all tell members of your family, extended family and friends how much you love them as often as possible. Don't assume they know because they don't. Encourage them to fulfill their dreams, tell them what you admire about them when it counts, when they are alive. Better late than never, start today. If you ever get the feeling that people aren't appreciative. Don't worry, God is.

Your Personal Book of Revelations

Death is not the end. It is merely a passing into another level of existence. Create a dedication to the loved ones who have passed away. Fill your book of revelations with photos, letters, newspaper clippings that reminds you of the joy these people have brought to your life.

Our bodies may deteriorate but our souls are timeless.

- What are your feelings about death?
- What type of life have you led?
- Are you able to go in peace now if it is your time?
- How have you lived inactively or proactively?
- How have you attempted to fulfill your destiny?
- How can you change your life to give it new meaning?
- Have you contributed to the pain and suffering of others?

Soul Sources

Here are a few resources to get you started on the road to healing. We hope you find these Web sites and organizations helpful in your journey.

DOMESTIC VIOLENCE

National Hotline 1-800-799-SAFE

www.domesticviolence.com

"You are not alone. You are not to blame. You do not deserve to be abused," says this Web site devoted to helping women deal with domestic violence. The site provides a "domestic violence survival kit" that provides everything from using courts to get orders of protection to getting help from the social service system.

www.divorcesource.com

This Web site provides valuable divorce-related resources specific to all fifty states. Included in the information provided for each state is a guide to divorce professionals in that state, an overview of divorce law in the state, articles on child custody, property distribution, and other issues. Numerous books are available for sale on scores of important topics.

Cybergrrl: Violence Resources for Women
http://www.cybergrrl.com/fs.jhtml?/views/dv/

A collection of resources, statistics, bibliographies, and violence projects for women are at this site.

EDUCATIONAL RESOURCES

United Negro College Fund
  www.uncf.org
Having supported the studies of over 300,000 African-American students, the UNCF is doing its valuable work everyday. The UNCF is widely known for its popular tag line "A Mind is a Terrible Thing to Waste." If you are a student, contact the UNCF about ways that they can assist you with your education. If you're not a student, a tax deductible contribution would be a concrete way that you can assist in the UNCF's valiant mission.

  United Negro College Fund
  8260 Willow Oaks Corporate Drive
  Fairfax, VA 22031
  1-800-331-2244

www.kaptest.com
For over 60 years, Kaplan has helped more than 3 million students pursue their educational goals. Through their Web site, you have access to their SAT and other test-prep courses, tutoring services, admissions consulting, and financial aid guidance. A service such as Kaplan is highly recommended if you are thinking about college or graduate school.

www.africana.com
This Web site focusses on African and African-American interests, in particular news, history, culture and other educational content. In part the site is based on Microsoft's Encarta African-American encyclopaedia.

ELDER CARE (& CHILD CARE)

www.careguide.net
This online "personal caregiving resource" provides directories, articles, newsletters and more about issues concerning dealing with older loved ones. There is also another channel that deals with child care concerns.

www.hospicenet.org
A site for patients and families facing life-threatening illness, it offers a great deal of assistance for patients and caregivers. It covers everything from resolving pain without medication to talking to children about death to preparing for approaching death.

HEALTH

American Cancer Society
The ACS is the foremost group in education and information on all types of cancer. The organization conducts a wide range of programs.
www.cancer.org
1-800-ACS-2345

American Heart Association
www.americanheart.org
American Heart Association, National Center
7272 Greenville Avenue
Dallas, Texas 75231
The AHA is dedicated to providing education and information on fighting heart disease and stroke. Their Web site is a valuable resource for women. The organization is affiliated with the following hotlines:
Customer Heart and Stroke Information
1-800-AHA-USA1

ECC Information
1-877-AHA-4-CPR

Stroke Information
1-888-4-STROKE

Women's Health Information
1-888-MY HEART

www.FibroidZone.com
This is the most comprehensive Web site on the subject of uterine fibroids, a condition that affects millions of women in America and impacts African-American women three to nine times more frequently than others. Click on FibroidZone's "Ask the Experts" section to ask a personal medical question of their team of doctors.

Sickle Cell Disease Foundation of California
www.scdrf.org
5110 W. Goldleaf Circle
Suite 150
Los Angeles, CA 90056
phone: 323-299-3600
fax: 323-299-3605
Toll Free (outside of Los Angeles) 1-877-288-CURE
The Sickle Cell Disease Foundation of California has committed itself to "education and life-enhancing programs and services to individuals with sickle cell disease" to broadening public awareness about sickle cell disease and to promoting medical research and education to ultimately find a cure.

Susan G. Komen Breast Cancer Foundation
www.breastcancerinfo.com
National Breast Care Helpline
1-800-I'M AWARE (1-800-462-9273)
The mission of the Komen foundation is to "eradicate breast cancer as a life-threatening disease by advancing research, education, screening and treatment." Their Web site offers a valuable array of information and support for people dealing with breast cancer. The foundation is most known for its annual "Race for the Cure."

www.unspeakable.com
According to unspeakable.com, one out of every five Americans carries a sexually transmitted disease. This site is designed to be "a frank, accurate, and unembarrassed guide to the prevention and treatment of sexually transmitted diseases. The site aims to dispel common misconceptions about STDs and to encourage people to get routinely tested for STDs.

INTERNET RESOURCES (GENERAL)

www.about.com
The African-American culture section of about.com offers expert-guided Internet resources of interest to African Americans.

www.blackplanet.com
Simply the best black online community on the Web, with hundreds of thousands of members; you'll find lively discussions on just about any subject you can imagine.

www.blackwebsites.com

Here is a somewhat comprehensive collection of links to African-American Web sites on every subject.

www.netnoir.com

Netnoir is a very popular black Web site of general interest that boasts half a million visitors every month. Its channels include news, music, virtual communities, shopping, chat rooms, personal e-mail accounts, and much more.

www.SoulsofMySisters.com

What started out as this book has become an exciting movement of sisters. SoulsofMySisters.com is a community of sisters working together toward peace and healing. By sisters we mean women of color who share a kindred spirit that gives us strength and faith. The community is like a second home for its members. It is a community where women of color can come together for an intimate sharing of information and heart-filled support. Its like sharing secrets over a cup of coffee or having a late night phone chat with one of your closest friends.

At SoulsofMySisters.com you can: get the latest information on your spiritual health and well-being, find out if you're truly in love, enter contests to win fabulous prizes like trips and spa days—and much, much more. Meet sisters like yourself who aren't afraid to tell their personal stories to aid in the healing of women of color. SoulsofMySisters.com can start a spiritual journey toward healing yourself and your sisters.

MEMBERSHIP ORGANIZATIONS

National Association for the Advancement of Colored People
www.naacp.org
NAACP, Washington Bureau
1025 Vermont Avenue, NW, Suite 1120
Washington, DC 20005
phone: 202-638-2269

Founded by W.E.B. DuBois, Ida B. Wells, and others, today the NAACP boasts over 2,200 branches in all fifty states and internationally. The NAACP sponsors scores of educational and political programs from voter registration initiatives to college counseling, placement, and scholarships.

National Council of Negro Women
633 Pennsylvania Avenue, NW
Washington, DC 20004
phone: 202-737-0120
fax: 202-737-0476
Founded by the legendary educator, Mary McLeod Bethune and now headed by Dorothy Height, the NCNW is focussed on the concerns of African-American women. The NCNW is composed of 33 affiliated constituency organizations and 250 chartered sections.

National Organization for Women
www.now.org
P.O. Box 96824
Washington, DC 20090-6824
phone: 202-628-8669
fax: 202-785-8576
NOW's activism is apparent in the full range of issues of interest to women, from reproductive issues to racial and ethnic diversity.

National Urban League
www.nul.org
120 Wall Street
New York, New York 10005
phone: 212-558-5300
fax: 212-558-5332
e-mail: info@nul.org
Founded in 1910, the National Urban League is the premier social service and civil rights organization in America. The League is a nonprofit, community-based organization headquartered in New York City, with 115 affiliates in 34 states and the District of Columbia.

MONEY RESOURCES

www.blackenterprise.com
Black Enterprise magazine's Web page serves as a good financial homepage. It offers such information and market tools as stock quotes, tickers, and financial news. It also offers general news of importance to African Americans.

Debtors' Anonymous
www.debtorsanonymous.org
The focus of Debtors' Anonymous is to help people "recover from compul-

sive debting." The only membership requirement is that you want to stop incurring unsecured debt. There are no dues and DA is not affiliated with any sect, denomination, or political viewpoint.

POLITICAL ORGANIZATIONS

Congressional Black Caucus Foundation, Inc.
www.cbcfonline.org
1004 Pennsylvania Avenue, SE
Washington, DC 20003
phone: 1-800-784-2577 or 202-675-6730
fax: 202-547-3806
Established in 1976, the CBCF is a non-profit research and educational institute that seeks to assist African-American political leaders of today and prepare those of tomorrow.

PROFESSIONAL ORGANIZATIONS

Black Women in Publishing
www.bwip.org
P.O. Box 6275
FDR Station
New York, NY 10150
phone: 212-772-5951
Black Women in Publishing (BWIP) is a trade organization that is "dedicated to increasing the presence, and supporting the efforts of African Heritage women and men in the publishing industry." Through meetings and publications, BWIP seeks to facilitate education about publishing, provide career opportunities, and recognize those who have achieved positions in the publishing field.

National Association of Black Journalists
www.nabj.org
8701A Adelphi Road
Adelphi, MD 20783-1716
phone: 301-445-7100
fax: 301-445-7101
The National Association of Black Journalists (NABJ) is an organization of "journalists, students, and media-related professionals that provides quality programs and services to benefit black journalists worldwide." Foremost among the goals of the NABJ is increasing the numbers of blacks in the

media, especially in management positions. The NABJ also sponsors numerous informational and educational programs.

Sororities

Alpha Kappa Alpha Sorority, Inc.
www.aka1908.com
5656 South Stony Island Avenue
Chicago, IL 60637
phone: 773-684-1282
fax: 773-288-8251

Delta Sigma Theta Sorority, Inc.
www.dst1913.org
1707 New Hampshire Avenue, NW
Washington, DC 20009
phone: 202-986-2400
fax: 202-986-2513

Sigma Gamma Rho Sorority, Inc.
www.sgr1922.org
8800 South Stony Island Avenue
Chicago, IL 60617
phone: 773-873-9000
fax: 773-731-9642

Zeta Phi Beta Sorority, Inc.
www.zpb1920.org
1734 New Hampshire Avenue, NW
Washington, DC 20009
phone: 202-387-3103
fax: 202-232-4593

Soul Books

Here are a hundred and one books that some of our contributors have authored and others have suggested as books that inspired them along their spiritual journeys. We have provided the publisher and date of publication to aid in your effort to find these books. We hope they inspire you along your journey as well.

About My Sister's Business: The Black Woman's Road Map to Successful Entrepreneurship by Fran Harris with an introduction by Terrie Williams. Fireside, 1996

Acts of Faith: Daily Meditations for People of Color by Iyanla Vanzant. Fireside, 1993

Africa Cookbook: Tastes of the Continent, The by Jessica B. Harris. Simon & Schuster, 1998

Ain't I Woman: Black Women and Feminism by bell hooks. South End Press, 1981

All About Love: New Visions by bell hooks. William Morrow, 2000

All God's Children Need Traveling Shoes by Maya Angelou. Random House, 1997

Assata: An Autobiography by Assata Shakur. Lawrence Hill Books, 1988

Behind the Scenes by Elizabeth Keckley. MasterBuy AudioBooks, 1996

Biology of Success, The by Robert Arnot. Little Brown, 2000

Black Books Galore! Guide to Great African-American Children's Books by Donna Rand, Toni Parker, and Sheila Foster. John Wiley & Sons, 1998

Black Unicorn, The: Poems by Audre Lorde. W. W. Norton, 1995

Black Woman's Guide to Financial Independence, The: Smart Ways to Take Charge of Your Money, Build Wealth, and Achieve Financial Security by Cheryl D. Broussard. Penguin USA, 1996

Bluelight Corner, The: Black Women Writing on Passion, Sex, and Romantic Love Edited by Rosemarie Robotham. Three Rivers Press, 1999

Bluest Eye, The by Toni Morrison. Plume, 1994

Blush by Courtni Wright. Pinnacle Books, 1997

Body and Soul: The Black Women's Guide to Physical Health and Emotional Well-Being by Linda Villarosa. Harperperennial Library, 1994

Breaking Ice: An Anthology of Contemporary African-American Fiction by Terry McMillan. Penguin USA, 1990 (paperback)

Breath, Eyes, Memory by Edwidge Danticat. Random House, 1998

By the Light of My Father's Smile by Alice Walker. Random House, 1998

Caucasia by Danzy Senna. Riverhead, 1998

Celestine Prophecy, The: An Adventure by James Redfield. Warner Books, 1997

Collected Poems of Langston Hughes, The by Langston Hughes. Vintage Books, 1995

Color Purple, The by Alice Walker. Pocket Books, 1996

Colored Woman in a White World (African-American Women Writers, 1910-1940) by Mary Church Terrell. G. K. Hall, 1996

Contending Forces : A Romance Illustrative of Negro Life North and South (The Schomburg Library of Nineteenth-Century Black Women Writers) by Pauline E. Hopkins, Introduction by Richard Yarbrough. Oxford University Press, 1991

Conversations With God: An Uncommon Dialogue (Book 1) by Neale Donald Walsch (Introduction). Putnam Pub Group, 1996

Course in Miracles, A: Combined Volume by the Foundation for Inner Peace. Viking Press, 1996

Denmark Vessey: The Buried History of America's Largest Slave Rebellion and the Man Who Led It by David Robertson. Knopf, 1999

Disappearing Acts by Terry McMillan. Pocket Books, 1995

Ditchdigger's Daughters, The: A Black Family's Astonishing Success Story by Yvonne S. Thornton and Jo Coudert. Plume, 1996

Does Your Mama Know? An Anthology of Black Lesbian Coming Out Stories Edited by Lisa C. Moore. RedBone Press, 1997

Don't Block the Blessings: Revelations of a Lifetime by Patti LaBelle with Laura B. Randolph. Boulevard, 1998

Fibroid Book, The: A Guide to Treating the Most Common Cause of Hysterectomies by Francis Hutchins, Jr., M.D. The Fibroid Center, 1999

48 Laws of Power, The by Joost Elffers and Robert Greene. Viking Press, 1998

From Fear to Faith by Merlin R. Carothers. Thomas Nelson, 1997

Get a Financial Life: Personal Finance in Your Twenties and Thirties (Revised and Expanded) by Beth Kobliner. Fireside, 2000

God in Her Midst: Preaching Healing to Hurting Women by Elaine McCollins Flake. Empowerment Ministries, 2000

Greatest Salesman in the World, The by Og Mandino. Bantam Books, 1983

Harriet Tubman: Conductor on the Underground Railroad by Ann Petry. HarperTrophy, 1996

Having Our Say: The Delaney Sisters' First 100 Years by Elizabeth Delaney and Sarah Louise Delaney with Amy Hill Hearth. Delta, 1997

Hello, He Lied: And Other Truths from the Hollywood Trenches by Lynda Rosen Obst. Broadway Books, 1997

Her by Cherry Muhanji. Aunt Lute Books, 1990

Homegirls and Handgrenades: Poems by Sonia Sanchez. Thunder's Mouth Press, 1997

How to Write a Book Proposal by Michael Larsen. Writer's Digest Books, 1997

I Know Why the Caged Bird Sings by Maya Angelou. Random House, 1996

I, Tina: My Life Story by Tina Turner and Kurt Loder. Avon, 1993

In Another Place, Not Here by Dionne Brand. Grove Press, 2000

In the Spirit: The Inspirational Writings of Susan L. Taylor by Susan L. Taylor. HarperCollins, 1994

Incidents in the Life of a Slave Girl by Harriet A. Jacobs. Signet, 2000

Iron Pots and Wooden Spoons: Africa's Gift to New World Cooking by Jessica B. Harris. Fireside, 1999

Just Between Girlfriends: African-American Women Celebrate Friendship by Chrisena Coleman. Simon & Schuster, 1998

Kindred (Black Women Writers Series) by Octavia E. Butler. Beacon Press, 1988

Knight in Shining Armor: Discovering Your Lifelong Love by P.B. Wilson. Harvest House Publishing, 1995

Knowing by Rosalyn McMillan. Warner Books, 1997

LaBelle Cuisine: Recipes to Sing About by Patti LaBelle and Laura B. Randolph. Broadway Books, 1999

Lest We Forget: The Passage from Africa to Slavery and Emancipation: A Three-Dimensional Interactive Book with Photographs and Documents from the Black Holocaust Exhibit by Velma Maia Thomas. Crown Pub, 1997

Life Strategies: Doing What Works, Doing What Matters by Phil McGraw. Hyperion, 2000

List Your Self: Listmaking As the Way to Self-Discovery by Ilene Segalove and Paul Bob Velick. Andrews McMeel Publishing, 1996

Listening for God: A Minister's Journey Through Silence and Doubt by Renita Weems. Simon & Schuster, 1999

Look of Love, The by Monica Jackson. Bet Books, 1999

Mighty Like A River: The Black Church and Social Reform by Andrew Billingsley. Oxford University Press, 1999

Millionaire Next Door, The: The Surprising Secrets of America's Wealthy by Thomas J. Stanley and William D. Danko. Pocket Books, 1998

Mind of My Mind by Octavia E. Butler. Warner Books, 1994

9 Steps to Financial Freedom, The by Suze Orman. Crown, 1997

No Hiding Place: A Tamara Hayle Mystery by Valerie Wilson Wesley. Twilight, 1998

No Mountain High Enough: Secrets of Successful African-American Women by Dorothy Ehrhart-Morrison with a Foreword by Myrlie Evers-Williams. Conari Press, 1997

Open Your Mind to Prosperity by Catherine Ponder. Devorss, 1984

Personal Touch, The: What You Really Need to Succeed in Today's Fast-Paced Business World by Terrie Williams, with an Introduction by Bill Cosby. Warner Books, 1996

Possessing the Secret of Joy by Alice Walker. Pocket Books, 1993

Princessa, The: Machiavelli for Women by Harriet Rubin. Dell, 1998

Raisin in the Sun, A by Lorraine Hansbury. Plume, 1992

Sally Hemings by Barbara Chase-Riboud. Griffin, 2000

Seat of the Soul, The by Gary Zukav. Fireside, 1990

Sensual Celibacy: The Sexy Woman's Guide to Using Abstinence for Recharging Your Spirit, Discovering Your Passions, Achieving Greater Intimacy in Your Next Relationship by Donna Marie Williams. Fireside, 1999

Seven Spiritual Laws of Success, The: A Practical Guide to the Fulfillment of Your Dreams by Deepak Chopra. Amber-Allen, 1995

Siddhartha by Herman Hesse. Bantam, 1982

Sister Ceo: The Black Woman's Guide to Starting Your Own Business by Cheryl D. Broussard. Penguin USA, 1998

Sisters of the Yam: Black Women and Self-Recovery by bell hooks. South End Press, 1993

Some Soul To Keep by J. California Cooper. St. Martins, 1998

Song of Solomon by Toni Morrison. Plume, 1987

Spiritual Crisis: Surviving Trauma to the Soul by J. Lebron McBride. Haworth, 1998

Talking Dollars and Making Sense: A Wealth-Building Guide for African-Americans by Brooke M. Stephens. McGraw-Hill, 1996

Their Eyes Were Watching God by Zora Neale Hurston with an Afterword by Henry Louis, Jr. Gates. HarperCollins, 1999

Things Fall Apart by Chinua Achebe. Anchor Books/Doubleday, 1994

Thoughts by Tionne Watkins. Harper Entertainment, 1999

Through the Ivory Gate: A Novel by Rita Dove. Vintage Books, 1993

To Be Young, Gifted and Black by Lorraine Hansberry. New American Library, 1987

Too Heavy a Load: Black Women in Defense of Themselves: 1894-1994 by Deborah Gray White. W. W. Norton, 2000

Up From Slavery by Booker T. Washington. Oxford University Press, 1995

Value in the Valley, The: A Black Woman's Guide Through Life's Dilemmas by Iyanla Vanzant. Fireside, 1996

Volunteer Slavery: My Authentic Negro Experience by Jill Nelson. Penguin USA, 1994

Web of Deception by Lajoyce Brookshire. Retnuh Relations, 1998

Wedding, The by Dorothy West. Anchor Books/Doubleday, 1996

What Brothers Think, What Sistahs Know: The Real Deal on Love and Relationships by Denene Millner and Nick Chiles. Quill, 1999

When Chickenheads Come Home to Roost: A Hop-Hop Feminist Breaks It Down by Joan Morgan. Touchstone Books, 2000

Woman's Worth, A by Marianne Williamson. Ballantine Books, 1994

Women of Brewster Place, The by Gloria Naylor. Penguin USA, 1983

Women, Race and Class by Angela Y. Davis. Random House, 1983

You Can Heal Your Life/101 by Louise L. Hay with an Afterword by Dave Braun. Hay House, 1987

You Can't Keep a Good Woman Down by Alice Walker. Harcourt Brace, 1982

Zachary's Wings by Rosemarie Robotham. Touchstone Books, 1999